*The Quanah Route*

QUANAH
JUNCTION

# The Quanah Route

## A History of the Quanah, Acme & Pacific Railway

*by*

DON L. HOFSOMMER

TEXAS A&M UNIVERSITY PRESS
COLLEGE STATION

Copyright © 1991 by Don L. Hofsommer

*Manufactured in the United States of America*
*All rights reserved*
FIRST EDITION

The paper used in this book meets the minimum
requirements of the American National Standard for
Permanence of Paper for Printed Library Materials,
Z39.48-1984. Binding materials have been chosen for
durability.

Frontispiece by Bruce Blalock

**Library of Congress Cataloging-in-Publication Data**

Hofsommer, Donovan L.
    The Quanah route : a history of the Quanah, Acme & Pacific Railway
/ by Don L. Hofsommer.
        p.   cm.
    Includes bibliographical references.
    ISBN 0-89096-437-8 (alk. paper)
    1.   Quanah, Acme, and Pacific Railway Company.   2.  Railroads—
Texas.   I. Title.
TF25.Q53H64   1991
385'.09764—dc20                                          90-35219
                                                         CIP

*For the men and women of the QA&P*

# Contents

# Illustrations and Maps

# Tables

# Preface

DURING the spring of 1975, I stopped at the general offices of the Quanah, Acme & Pacific Railway in Quanah, Texas. I was greated immediately by Reverend, the "Heinz-57" dog that some years before had followed the agent to work and then had taken proprietary interest in the building. Reverend looked me over with care and then wagged his tail in acceptance. It was an auspicious welcome. No less warm in their reception were Raymond Johnson, the agent, and Charlene Crisp, the company's treasurer, auditor, and assistant secretary.

The purpose of my visit, I explained to Crisp, was to determine whether the QA&P had a record base adequate to support a book-length study and, if so, whether the company would allow me access. I had recently finished work on two other railroad studies that were pledged to publication and now I was looking for a new project. There were plenty of records, Crisp assured me. They represented all departments—executive, law, operations, sales, advertising, claims, and engineering—and they were under her care in the large walk-in vault just down the hall and in the freight house directly behind the office building. She would check with James Sowell, the QA&P's vice-president and general counsel, and with officers of the St. Louis–San Francisco Railway, the Quanah Route's parent. The collective response was not long in coming: I would have unrestricted access.

Current and former employees seemed flattered that their company would be the subject of a book, but others seemed mystified why anyone should invest effort in a somewhat obscure road doing business in a thinly populated part of the world. "I am surprised someone is interested in having the history published of this railroad," wrote Charles H. Sommer, Jr., president of Monsanto Chemicals and son of a former president of the QA&P, "but I am sure there is a very good reason." There were, in fact, several reasons. One was the very size of the QA&P. It was a small but significant operation stretching over only four counties of northwestern Texas. Yet compared to a giant like the Southern

Pacific, the Quanah Route offered a more manageable historical model—one small enough to allow probing and poking into every nook and cranny. Second, the history of any railroad is, by its very nature, more than simply the record of a business enterprise; it is also a reflection of the service area. This would be, in part, a broad survey of the road's territory, especially for the years of development. Third, the richness of company records offered me a unique opportunity to design an in-depth historical study that would represent a case study of an American short line during the era preceding deregulation of the railroad industry under the Staggers Act and the megamergers of the 1980s. This, then, is a history of the Quanah, Acme & Pacific Railway Company.

No project of this nature can succeed without the active and enthusiastic help of dozens of persons who share themselves and their resources in any number of ways. My undertaking, happy to say, was richly blessed in this regard. Among members of the QA&P family, Raymond Johnson, George Adams, J. D. Grimes, C. H. King, R. L. Choat, Dee Smith, C. W. Sparkman, W. C. Clawson, L. L. Tidmore, F. L. Pearce, B. E. Hines, Myrna Powell, Leo A. Elliott, Robert Medlen, C. R. Sherwood, Elton B. Marsalis, and B. H. Stone shared both recollections and insights. Francis M. Gunter suffered endless questions, Robin Morris took me on a Hi-rail tour of the line, and James W. Sowell arranged for a train trip and opened many doors for me. At the Frisco, Martin M. Pomphrey's good humor never failed, even in the face of a withering bombardment of requests. The same open spirit of support came from C. C. Roberts, A. F. Niemeier, and Glenn Martin.

Others aided in making available a wide range of illustrative material. Photographs came from Preston George, Mrs. Paul Brown, E. B. Marsalis, Eddie Guffee, B. H. Stone, I. M. George, Harold W. Ferguson, Francis Gunter, Everett L. DeGolyer, Jr., Harold K. Vollrath, A. E. Brown, Fred M. Springer, and Louis Saillard. (Illustrations in this book not specifically credited derive from collections of the Quanah, Acme & Pacific Railway.) John L. Hodson provided original cartography, and Bruce Blalock provided delightful drawings of locomotives 1613 and 1626.

Edward N. Kasparik opened archives at the Railroad Commission of Texas; Helen M. Rowland did yeoman work among materials at the Association of American Railroads in Washington; Robert A. Strong and Polly Lackey graciously responded to numerous requests for library assistance; Deborah Janezich, Toni Brown, and Jana McCledon transformed my nearly illegible handwriting into beautiful typed drafts; and Martin Pomphrey, Charlene Crisp, Andy Niemeier, Charley Roberts, H. Roger Grant, and Keith L. Bryant read portions of the manuscript and offered many helpful suggestions.

Most of all, I am indebted to Charlene Crisp, who went well beyond the call of duty in rooting out obscure materials, in offering useful leads, and in providing contacts beyond the Quanah office.

Finally, I am grateful to my wife and family, who

Charlene Crisp

understand and appreciate my curiosity with matters of steel rails and flanged wheels. To all of the above, and to any others I might have accidentally overlooked, I am greatly indebted. For errors of fact and infelicities of style that remain, I alone am responsible.

# Abbreviations

| | | | |
|---|---|---|---|
| Alco | American Locomotive Company | Katy | Missouri-Kansas-Texas Railroad |
| ARR&N | Acme, Red River & Northern Railway | KCM&O | Kansas City, Mexico & Orient Railway |
| AT&SF | Atchison, Topeka & Santa Fe Railway | LCL | Less-than-carload |
| | | The Orient | Kansas City, Mexico & Orient Railway |
| AV&L | Ardmore, Vernon & Lubbock Railway | Panhandle Road | Texas Panhandle & Gulf Railroad |
| Burlington | Chicago, Burlington & Quincy Railroad | PHP | Packing House Products |
| CRI&P | Chicago, Rock Island & Pacific Railway | PHW | Per hundred weight |
| | | QA&P | Quanah, Acme & Pacific Railway |
| Denver Road | Fort Worth & Denver City Railway or Fort Worth & Denver Railway | Quanah Route | Quanah, Acme & Pacific Railway |
| | | QSD&R | Quanah, Seymour, Dublin & Rockport Railway |
| EMD | Electro-Motive Division of General Motors | RMS | Railway Mail Service |
| Frisco | St. Louis & San Francisco Railroad or St. Louis–San Francisco Railway | Rock Island | Chicago, Rock Island & Pacific Railway |
| | | RPO | Railway Post Office |
| | | Santa Fe | Atchison, Topeka & Santa Fe Railway |
| FW&D | Fort Worth & Denver Railway | SL&SF | St. Louis & San Francisco Railroad |
| FW&DC | Fort Worth & Denver City Railway | SL-SF | St. Louis–San Francisco Railway |
| GT&W | Gulf, Texas & Western Railroad | T&P | Texas & Pacific Railway |
| ICC | Interstate Commerce Commission | TP&G | Texas Panhandle & Gulf Railroad |

*The Quanah Route*

## CHAPTER I

## Little More Than a Plant Facility

Recognition of said line by the Commission is
hereby again emphatically and finally refused.—
Railroad Commission of Texas to the Acme, Red
River & Northern Railway, 1908

DURING the mid-nineteenth century there was very
little interest—except on the part of a few aborigi-
nes—in the area now known as western North
Texas. One assessment of it was particularly blunt:
"That country is not settled, and probably never
will be to any great extent." It was hardly a new
opinion. A disappointed Francisco Vasquez Coronado had reported following his famous excursion
into the North American interior in the early 1540s
that the areas he visited, and those peripheral to
them, were mostly uninhabited deserts. Spanish
cartographers were convinced by Coronado's report; the midsection of the continent was labeled
accordingly. Later explorers, including several officers of the United States Army, concurred in Coronado's estimation. The report of Maj. Stephen H.
Long after his study of the region in 1819–20 rein-
forced the judgments of still others who had concluded that the area was, in fact, the American Desert. A surveyor for a railroad project in the 1850s
went further: he said that the desert would remain
forever an uninhabited wasteland.[1]

Others later discovered, however, that the country was not so barren. Transcontinental railroads
eventually pierced the desert with their twin strands
of iron; the cars then brought buffalo hunters; and
finally, the demise of buffalo brought the demise of
Indians. The way was then cleared for farmers, who
increasingly followed the rails and discovered ways
to use the desert for agricultural purposes. Correspondingly, the concept of the American desert
gave way to a much more acceptable and euphoni-
ous designation—the Great Plains.

Nevertheless, that area of western North Texas
with which this study is concerned—particularly
the part that became Hardeman County—long remained in ill repute. Hardeman County was created by the Texas legislature on February 21, 1858,
from land that formerly made up Fannin County.

The official census, however, recorded no population until 1880, when fifty persons—transient cow-
boys and cattlemen—were listed as residents. The
county was organized for purposes of government
in 1884, but even then it was considered one of the
most inhospitable regions of the state—unsuited,
some said, for farming, although at least adequate
for raising stock.[2]

Western North Texas is, by geographic definition, an extension of the Great Plains, bounded on
the east by the Texas black belt, on the west by
the Caprock escarpment, on the north by the Red
River, and on the south by Colorado River. Beyond the Caprock escarpment to the west is the
Llano Estacado—the Great Staked Plains or the
Texas High Plains. Hardeman County is located on
the eastern border of the Llano Estacado. The surface of the county is broken; portions of its land
are clearly unfit for agriculture. Much of the native
water is, at least before processing, disagreeable to
taste because it contains a large proportion of salt
and has the brackish flavor that is peculiar to all
streams that issue from gypsum regions. The soils
vary from reddish clay, which predominates, to
the sandy soils found along the floodplain of local
streams. Native grasses thrive on these soils, as do
small trees and shrubs, cacti, and sagebrush. The
county's elevation is about 1,500 feet; its average
growing season is 234 days; its mean annual tem-
perature is 61.5 degrees; and its average annual rainfall is 26 inches.[3]

Immediately to the northwest of the area that became Hardeman County is the Texas Panhandle, a
region which one early observer considered "as in-
accessible as Alaska," at least until the coming of the
railroad. What happened then—its transformation
from an unpopulated, barren wilderness to a productive, pulsating country—was, in the words of
Carl Coke Rister, "one of the most astonishing de-

velopments of American history in the nineteenth century." Rister might well have said the same for the part of North Texas along the Red River from the Cross Timbers area to the Panhandle. The coming of the railroad had a similar effect there.[4]

The sparse population of North Texas and the Panhandle had long yearned for rail service. But the same sparse population militated against early construction—potential traffic was simply inadequate. Construction of any railroad into those regions would have been delayed even longer except for the happy fact that any logically oriented Gulf-to-Rockies route would have to pass through them. And that is exactly what happened. The Fort Worth & Denver City Railway Company (FW&DC or Denver Road) was granted a charter by the state of Texas on May 26, 1873. It was conceived as an interregional project, to link the cities of its corporate namesake. Events, however, conspired against the early completion of this task, and it was not until November 27, 1881, that grading first began near Fort Worth. Tracks reached Wichita Falls in September of the next year.[5]

Grenville M. Dodge, who had gained fame in the Civil War and in the building of the Union Pacific, was closely linked with the FW&DC and was the moving force behind the firm that held the Denver Road's construction contracts. Moreover, Dodge had procured land for townsites along the new railroad. He and his son-in-law R. E. Montgomery subsequently formed the Texas Townsite Company to hold and then dispose of these properties.[6]

Rather than pushing on immediately from Wichita Falls, management of the FW&DC instead chose first to consolidate its gains and then to put the modest railroad on a healthy financial basis. There were other reasons why the Denver Road continued its end-of-track at Wichita Falls. There had been a distressing absence of construction activity on the northern end of the line, and the Texas company thought it wise to refrain from further expansion until its Colorado counterpart, the Denver & New Orleans, showed good faith. FW&DC managers reasoned, moreover, that the road could control the lucrative livestock traffic then emanating from the Texas Panhandle without immediately extending the line beyond Wichita Falls. Finally, they believed that Wichita Falls would naturally drain the surrounding area—Seymour, Vernon, and even Fort Sill—and thus gather "to itself a considerable and growing trade which had previously found its way to market via Fort Dodge, Kansas, the long

established shipping point" on the Atchison, Topeka & Santa Fe Railroad.[7]

Wichita Falls thus remained the Denver Road's end-of-track for over two years. Then, on February 3, 1885, grading began anew; within a few months the road advanced thirty-seven miles to Harrold. The railroad entered Vernon on October 16, 1886, and construction crews pressed forward to Quanah on February 1, 1887. Concomitantly, the FW&DC's Colorado counterpart was energized and, while the Texas company built its line on to the northwest, the Colorado firm pressed its crews toward the southeast. Finally, on March 14, 1888, the last spike was driven on the long-hoped-for Gulf-to-Rockies route. Denver and Fort Worth were linked by rails at last.[8]

A few lucky persons in Hardeman County had received privileged information, likely from Dodge or Montgomery, regarding the final location of the railroad. Consequently, when FW&DC rails reached Quanah, it already had some of the amenities of a railhead town—a saloon, a store, a post office, and even a cemetery. Quanah experienced a predictable boom, especially during the brief period it was the FW&DC's end-of-track. Many early businessmen of Quanah started their enterprises and remained for an extended time in tents because of the scarcity of permanent structures; the supply of construction materials was inadequate to Quanah's growth. This volume of commerce was reflected in the Denver Road's local balance sheet. Revenue credited to that station for October 1888 was $6,142.75; for October 1889, it climbed to $24,051.46. In 1890, Quanah received another boost when the county seat was moved there from nearby Margaret. In the same season Quanah boasted a population of fifteen hundred. All of it moved one journalist to predict that Quanah and its trade area were headed "toward the *Ultima Thule* of commercial and financial success."[9]

The cattle industry was partly responsible for Quanah's dramatic growth. When the railroad arrived in 1887, Quanah became the cattle-shipping center for the surrounding area. Many ranchers from adjacent counties drove their cattle to be shipped to distant markets, and others from counties far to the south in Texas moved their cattle by rail to Quanah from whence they began their northward trail drives. This was especially true during the short period that Quanah remained the Denver Road's end-of-track. Ranching spread over much of Hardeman County, its development marked by two stages: first, free water and free grass, then land enclosure and elaborate improvements.[10]

Nevertheless, nesters had been fencing the land and causing a decline in ranching even before the arrival of the steamcars. Wheat was being sowed in small amounts before 1890, but this type of agriculture was greatly expanded during the boom of 1891 when immense stretches of raw land were plowed up and seeded. Cotton was introduced to the area after wheat prices fell with the Panic of 1893; in 1899, 1,335 bales were ginned in the county. That total climbed to 3,848 bales for the following year. The day of the open range cattle industry had passed, but ranches still flourished within barbed-wire enclosures, although they were both fewer in number and smaller in size.[11]

The most important industrial development in Hardeman County during this period was the exploitation of its gypsum deposits. These deposits had long been known to exist, but they were not developed commercially until a Kansan, James Sickler, took an interest during 1890. In the following year Sickler formed Lone Star Plaster Company at Salina, Kansas, and then negotiated a royalty agreement with the owners of gypsum-bearing lands near Quanah. A few years later the Lone Star Company was sold to the Acme Cement Plaster Company, which called its newly acquired plant site in Texas Acme. Meanwhile, Sickler and others had formed the Salina Cement Plaster Company for the purpose of building and operating a competing plant at Agatite, a short distance beyond Acme. The Salina mill, however, would soon be sold to the American Cement Plaster Company and eventually to the Beaver Board Company, a Chicago firm.[12]

Enter Samuel L. Lazarus—a man described in one account as "a New Yorker by birth, Louisianian by education, and a Texan by accident." Sam Lazarus was born in Syracuse, New York, on February 4, 1855, the son of Henry L. and Annie L. Lazarus. He ran away to New Orleans at the age of thirteen and gained employment there with Wallace & Company, a wholesale dry-goods firm. In 1869, he accepted a new position in Ladonia, Texas, and then went on to still another in Sherman, where he stayed for some time. After a short stint in Whitesboro, where he was in business on his own, he was forced into the land and cattle business.[13]

During the Panic of 1873, his employer in Sherman, Schneider Brothers, sent him to the plains region west of the Cross Timbers to collect on accounts that had fallen into arrears. Lazarus allowed some of these debtors to settle by paying in cattle.

When apprised of this deal, Schneider Brothers balked. Lazarus thereupon paid the debts himself, took charge of the animals, and in 1877 became a Texas cattleman. But cattle must have land to graze on. Lazarus began to satisfy that need in 1882 and 1883, when he acquired extensive lands in West Texas. Records of the General Land Office of Texas show that he was the original grantee and the patentee of eighty-five tracts of land purchased by scrip in Dickens and King counties. In December 1883, Lazarus sold 25,000 acres of this land, 3,750 head of his cattle, and numerous leases on grasslands to the newly formed Pitchfork Land and Cattle Company. For this he received $125,000—most of which was in capital stock of the new company. It was at about this time that Lazarus also served as president of the American Livestock Association, a marketing agency in Kansas City.[14]

Lazarus continued to expand his economic horizons. By 1893, he was a part owner in the Schneider Dry Goods Company at Sherman. During the mid-1890s he also served as receiver in bankruptcy for the famous Diamond Trails Ranch in the Texas Panhandle. He was likewise involved in a townsite scheme in Hall County, where he owned considerable land. He appears to have had similar holdings in Childress and Collingsworth counties.[15]

One source contends that Lazarus first appeared in Hardeman County "in the 90s" and that he built "a dugout for living quarters" along Groesbeck Creek northwest of Quanah. This source also maintains that Lazarus was immediately impressed with the abundance of gypsum in the area and soon began shipping it in raw form to eastern processing plants. Lazarus acquired control of the Acme Plaster Company between 1893 and 1898 and became president of the firm in March 1898.[16]

In and about its plant the Acme company owned railroad trackage that was used to move cars to and from the FW&DC as well as to move raw gypsum from nearby dirt beds. The Acme company owned a small saddle-tank locomotive and a few cars to haul this dirt. There is no record indicating that the Agatite plant owned any trackage or equipment; its transportation needs were met by the Acme Tap Railway, a puppet of the FW&DC.[17]

No formal townsite was established at Acme; the community developed naturally to provide for the needs of employees who labored in the nearby plaster manufacturing plants. A post office was established there on January 17, 1898, and in the same year Acme claimed a hotel with two dining rooms, a school, two depots, the mills, and a company store.

Elementary motive power supplied the needs of Acme Plaster before the turn of the century.

The population numbered some eighty families.

By 1902, Lazarus was discontent with the service and the restricted marketing outlets afforded by the Denver Road. As a consequence, he ordered formation of the Acme, Red River & Northern Railway Company (ARR&N), which was to construct a line of road from Acme "in a northerly direction to the Red River . . . about 8 miles." The road was capitalized at $25,000. Ten men, eight from various Texas communities and two from Chicago, served as incorporators; Lazarus's name was strangely absent.[18]

The state of Texas authorized a charter for the ARR&N on July 12, 1902. A final location was made, and grading commenced. Some months later, Lazarus told John Summerfield, a stockholder and an ARR&N official, that the "original intention was for this road to build to a connection with the Rock Island [Chicago, Rock Island & Pacific Railway] at Mangum, Oklahoma." These plans were eventually shelved when, "after investigating the cost of the Bridge across the Red River, the ARR&N concluded that she did not quite have enough money." Lazarus then looked to a connection with the Oklahoma City & Western Railway (a satellite of the St. Louis & San Francisco Railroad), which was building southwestward from Oklahoma City. The ARR&N could provide the "Texas connection" and thereby facilitate a new route by which Hardeman County gypsum products might go to market. Even that plan soon received considerable modification.[19]

On March 17, 1903, the ARR&N board of directors met at Acme to consider an amendment to its articles of incorporation. The board ultimately decided that the goals of the ARR&N could best be met by building its road along two routes from Acme—"in a northerly direction to the Red River . . . eight miles . . . and in a southeasterly direction to Quanah . . . about six miles . . . making the entire length of . . . railroad fourteen miles." The

board also announced its intention immediately to "build and equip the railway into Quanah." Corporate strategy was now beginning to gel. Lazarus had made an agreement with the St. Louis & San Francisco (SL&SF or Frisco) to divert the planned Texas landfall of the SL&SF's Oklahoma City & Western at the Red River. Now it became the goal of the ARR&N to build its main line from Acme to Quanah, gaining there an interchange with the SL&SF's puppet. The other proposal, to build from Acme directly to the Red River, would be held in abeyance, the board decided, but would be put forward in the future to serve any new plant facility north of Acme or to secure another connection in Oklahoma if that proved desirable.[20]

On June 15, 1903, ARR&N stockholders finally got around to writing the corporate by-laws. These were quickly ratified, and the newly established aboard proceeded to elect M. Marx of Galveston as president and John Summerfield of Dallas as secretary. Lazarus, at this point, owned only four and one half shares of stock, although he was trustee for another thirty.[21]

Officials of the ARR&N spent much of their energy in 1903 attempting to get the road recognized as a bona fide common carrier. John Summerfield handled many of these requests before the Railroad Commission of Texas. Lazarus admonished him to have his "papers all up in railroad style. Get up with a good front whatever you do, because they look to see lots of papers; the Commission likes papers."[22]

Lazarus also advised Summerfield that significant changes had been made in projected operations of the road. The first of these involved lease of the 1.74-mile Acme Tap Railway by the ARR&N for $1,000 per year. Use of that line allowed the ARR&N to serve the American Cement Plaster Company's plant at Agatite. It is not clear who built or originally owned the Acme Tap. One account states that "its construction involved a quarrel between the two rival cement companies." In any event, since 1899 it had been operated by the FW&DC to serve the mill at Agatite. The second change was even more significant. As soon as management of the FW&DC heard that the ARR&N planned to build a line parallel to its own between Acme and Quanah, it announced stern objection. Lazarus and D. B. Keeler, vice-president of the FW&DC, then worked out a trackage agreement by which the ARR&N was allowed to use the FW&DC's line between Acme and Quanah at the rate of fifty cents per train mile. Pursuant to the same agreement, the FW&DC leased to the ARR&N all of its trackage—sidings, yard tracks,

The ARR&N, created by Sam Lazarus in 1902, issued stock certificates such as this one.

and a wye—at Acme. The two companies further agreed that for $100 per month FW&DC station forces at both Acme and Quanah would do all necessary billing and clerical work for the ARR&N. As a result of these agreements, the ARR&N would serve both mills exclusively, handling all traffic to and from them via interchange with the FW&DC at Acme and Quanah and with the Oklahoma City & Texas (a Frisco subsidiary) at Quanah. Accordingly, the ARR&N issued "Time Table No. 1, In Effect 12:01 A.M. July 10, 1903." The road offered daily-except-Sunday mixed train service over "all of its lines," which, in reality, were owned by others except for a short stretch of track reaching from the Acme plant to the dirt beds. The ARR&N now was in business as an "inter-city" railroad.[23]

The Railroad Commission of Texas, however, was not disposed to recognize the ARR&N as a common carrier and denied the company's request for such designation on September 3, 1903. The Texas regulatory body, it seemed, was particularly suspicious of short lines; many of the commission-

ers viewed them, Summerfield noted, as a "private highway" and not "as a public carrier in the sense of a railway built for that purpose." The commission likewise took exception to the idea of parallel lines, even to the extent of the ARR&N operating trains under lease over the FW&DC between Acme and Quanah. It did not specifically forbid the practice, though, and the ARR&N decided, as suggested by Summerfield, "to do as we are now doing and keep quiet." There the matter rested for the present. The ARR&N, which really was little more than a plant facility, continued to serve the mills and haul cars to and from them over the FW&DC's track between Acme and Quanah.[24]

Meanwhile, service to Quanah had been initiated by the Frisco. Its line from Oklahoma City, built by Johnson Brothers & Faught, a Texas firm, was completed to Quanah late in December 1902 or early in January 1903. In February, an excursion was operated from Quanah to Olustee, Oklahoma, twenty-eight miles, in connection with the townsite opening and lot sale there. This trip was probably operated by the contractor since the Frisco did not officially open the line until March 29. Railroad managements often arranged with contractors to operate pioneer trains such as this. The Oklahoma City & Texas Railroad, the company that technically had built and owned the line from the Red River to Quanah, passed to the St. Louis, San Francisco & Texas Railway (a captive company belonging to the St. Louis & San Francisco Railroad, the parent of all of these) when all Frisco properties in Texas were consolidated under one corporate canopy later in 1903.[25]

That Lazarus should be working closely with the Frisco is not surprising. His close association with the road derived from two sources—his continuing business interests at Sherman, Texas, and the appointment of B. F. Yoakum as the Frisco's general manager in 1897. Yoakum quickly reoriented the company's goals toward Texas. One of his first projects was to push south from Indian Territory across the Red River to Denison, Sherman, and Fort Worth. To do this, Yoakum gained trackage rights over existing lines and then formed subsidiaries to build the rest. One of these was the St. Louis, San Francisco & Texas Railway (the same company mentioned above) which built its own line from the Red River to Denison and then secured trackage rights over the Houston & Texas Central to Sherman. Another was the Red River, Texas & Southern, a company developed to bridge the gap between Sherman and Fort Worth. Lazarus was elected president of this road in 1901. He and others, including his friend C. B. Dorchester, a banker at Sherman, had actively encouraged the establishment of these lines and had worked very closely with Yoakum in his campaigns to expand the Frisco's domain. All of this was part of an even larger pattern, for these were the years when the Frisco and the Rock Island were operated as a single powerful and expanding system.[26]

Sam Lazarus was becoming well known as a railroader in his own right. In 1896, he had served as receiver for the Texas, Louisiana & Eastern Railroad, and in time he would be associated with construction of the Brownsville Railroad between Brownsville and Houston, Michigan's Grand Rapids Terminal Belt Railway, and the Houston Belt & Terminal. Eventually he would be president of the Red River, Texas & Southern, the Galveston Terminal, the Houston Belt, and the Quanah, Acme & Pacific. He would also invest heavily in the SL&SF and serve on its board of directors for many years. Indeed, the Lazarus offices—including those of the

Acme Cement Plaster Company—were housed in the Frisco Building at St. Louis.[27]

Meanwhile, the ARR&N was prospering; dividends were paid every year from 1903. Revenues were not large, but neither were expenses. The fiscal year ending June 30, 1907, provides an example. Earnings totaled $53,219; expenses amounted to $26,233. Of the remaining monies, $24,950 was distributed as dividends—not bad for a 9.18-mile pike with only two locomotives and a handful of cars.[28]

In 1908, the ARR&N again attempted to be certified as a common carrier by the Railroad Commission of Texas. In support of this request, Lazarus pointed out that the ARR&N had paid ad valorem and intangible taxes amounting to $2,334.70 for 1907; that its affairs were administered in a "purely railroad character"; that it was having great difficulty with demurrage claims because it did not have common carrier status from the Texas regulatory commission; and that the company was recognized by the Interstate Commerce Commission. These arguments had no effect. The Railroad Commission of Texas responded: "Recognition of said line by the Commission is hereby again emphatically and finally refused." President Marx noted the obvious—the commission had declined the request "most positively."[29]

The ARR&N simply was not, as the commission seemed to think, a private highway. After all, it served two competing cement plaster mills—offering unbiased service to each. The ARR&N was, however, without question, essentially an industrial facility.

The road's operation and function can best be understood by examining its operation for a specific period of time; the month of November 1908 is representative. Inbound cars for the Acme mill contained ammonia, hair, paper bags, flour, tubes, and wood plus dozens of less-than-carload (LCL) shipments (the latter items presumably for the company store). Carload items received by the Salina mill included plaster, paper bags, coal, and multitudinous LCL items. Total loadings were 123 cars from the Acme plant and 103 cars from the Salina plant. The Acme plant loaded up to 15 cars daily; Salina up to 10. These were generally consigned to dealers in nearby states, especially Missouri, although some cars went to the southeastern states and others to locations as far away as California and New Jersey.[30]

This traffic moved in old-fashioned boxcars of 30,000-pound capacity, later-model 66,000-pound capacity cars, or the newest 100,000-pound cars.

Divisions accruing to the ARR&N were three cents per hundredweight (PHW) on cement or plaster moving beyond the St. Louis, Memphis, or New Orleans gateways, or two and one-half cents PHW for delivery in St. Louis. During November 1908, the ARR&N received divisions—depending on car weights and destinations—of from $9 to $25 per car. The ARR&N also earned $208.50 during that month through switching services rendered on behalf of the FW&DC. A total of 139 loaded cars were delivered to the ARR&N at Acme; of these, 57 were taken to Salina and the rest were switched to the Acme mill. These contained cement, oil, lime, and coal for Salina, and corn, oats, rock, and water (shipped from Clarendon) for Acme. Finally, additional revenue was earned by transporting dirt from the nearby beds to the mills.[31]

The ARR&N handled a total of 374 cars during the month. All of these were delivered to or received from the two cement plaster companies or contained material billed to the railroad itself. Traffic in LCL reflected a similar pattern. All such shipments save four were billed to or from the mills.[32]

The operations for November 1908 were, as usual, profitable. The income account was as follows:

| | |
|---|---:|
| Passenger service | 22.55 |
| Freight (inbound) | 271.35 |
| Freight (outbound) | 3,296.75 |
| Switching | 508.50 |
| Other | 179.11 |
| TOTAL | 4,268.26 |

Expenses totaled $2,457.57; the largest items were fuel, rental of joint facilities, car per diem, and salaries for general officers. Net earnings for the month thus totaled $1,820.69.[33]

By the end of 1908, the ARR&N owned rolling stock valued at $28,913.14. Included were two locomotives, one combination-coach, ten 10,000-pound-capacity dump cars, eleven 60,000-pound-capacity boxcars, six 8,000-gallon-capacity oil tank cars, and five steel gondolas. Since the ARR&N had no shop facilities, repairs were done on a contract basis by the Gulf, Colorado & Santa Fe Railway and the SL&SF.[34]

The Railroad Commission of Texas had long viewed the ARR&N with a jaundiced eye. The commission saw it as, at worst, a private highway and, at best, an industrial railroad. Moreover, it perceived the road as being operated for the benefit of a controlling interest—the Acme Cement Plaster Company, of which Sam Lazarus was the president. The commission thus saw chances of conflict of

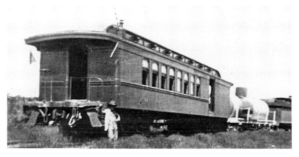

The Acme, Red River & Northern passed in favor of the QA&P when Lazarus determined to concentrate on the country southwest of Acme.

interest because Lazarus had no financial interest in the American Cement Plaster Company, which owned and operated the competing facility at nearby Salina. By 1907 the Acme firm admittedly had become an imposing rival. In addition to the plant at Acme, Texas, it owned other mills at Cement, Oklahoma Territory; Marlow, Indian Territory; Laramie, Wyoming; Grand Rapids, Michigan; and Acme, New Mexico. Yet if the ARR&N discriminated against the Salina facility there is no record of it.[35]

Shortly before Christmas 1908, the directorate of the ARR&N admitted what it long had known: the way to gain favor from the Railroad Commission of Texas was to become something more than a plant facility. And the way to do that was to expand its service area. Early in 1907 the board had looked into the possibility of building north to Hollis, Oklahoma Territory, but had concluded that it would not make "said extension at present" because of the depressed money market. Now, however, the economy was recovering and expansion seemed less dangerous. Consequently, a special meeting of the stockholders was called for January 21, 1909. There were several items for consideration, "to-wit; to determine if the charter of said corporation shall be amended so as to change its corporate name to Quanah, Acme & Pacific Railway; to increase its capital stock and number of shares; to authorize an extension of its line of railway from its present terminus, through Hardeman, Cottle and other counties in Texas in a general western direction; to select the location of its general offices."[36]

Sam Lazarus was the force behind these plans. He knew the country to the south and west of Quanah and Acme and believed it was "ready to open." Furthermore, construction of this new line would forever dispel the notion that the railroad operated only to benefit controlling interests. Finally, Lazarus had been buying ARR&N stock and now had stock control of the company; his will would be done. Small wonder, then, that the board concurred in his recommendations. Change came quickly. The ARR&N died to be resurrected as the Quanah, Acme & Pacific (QA&P or Quanah Route); the general offices were moved from Acme to Quanah; the entire operation took on a new character; and Sam Lazarus was unanimously elected president of the "new" railroad.[37]

The Railroad Commission of Texas recognized the Quanah, Acme & Pacific as a common carrier on March 21, 1909. Thus passed the Acme, Red River & Northern. It had not been abandoned, nor had it become a branch of a trunk carrier. Instead it became the antecedent of still another independent short-line railroad. In its brief existence the ARR&N had performed well as a plant facility and had paid handsome dividends to its owners. What more could have been asked?[38]

## CHAPTER 2

## On to Paducah

That whole country was drought-plagued in 1909, even cotton gins were hauling water, and we had to import every drop of that precious liquid for camp and engine use from Childress. We paid $10 per car, plus freight.—J. L. Allhands to R. Wright Armstrong, December 17, 1956

THERE had long been a clamor in and around Quanah to secure rail service in addition to that supplied by the Fort Worth & Denver City Railway. For instance, Col. Morgan Jones, an energetic and astute Texas railroader, had urged the FW&DC in 1898 to build north from either Vernon or Quanah across the Red River—provided, of course, that Congress would open the Kiowa-Comanche reserve there. The FW&DC did not move in this direction and thus lost the trade area to the SL&SF, which eventually built its line from northeast to southwest during the early part of the twentieth century. Yet two railroads—three, counting the plug ARR&N—were not adequate to quench the railroad thirst of many Quanah boosters.[1]

Among these boosters was Harry Koch, editor and publisher of the *Quanah Tribune-Chief.* Koch had worked diligently to bring the Frisco to Quanah, and a few years later he was laboring just as intently to bring about completion of what local people styled the Quanah & Gulf Railway. This informal designation gave way to the more specific Quanah, Seymour, Rockport & Gulf Railway and finally to the Quanah, Seymour, Dublin & Rockport Railway (QSD&R). That company was designed to build and operate a road from the Red River in Hardeman County to the Gulf of Mexico via Quanah, Seymour, Austin, Dublin, and Rockport—about 480 miles. Because its route would split the state from north to south, the QSD&R became known as the "Middle Buster." Boosters originally envisioned the southern terminus at Aransas Pass, across from Corpus Christi; those plans were later modified to make Rockport, about ten miles up the coast from Aransas Pass, the southern entrepôt.[2]

Boosters of the Middle Buster argued that its completion would reduce the cost of lumber to consumers in North Texas while at the same time lowering the tariff on cotton and other commodities moving south. Moreover, completion afforded by the QSD&R would, according to editor Koch, "make Quanah the most important railroad center in northwest Texas and a metropolitan city of the first rank." By mid-1910, a total of $19,000 in the road's stock had been subscribed in Quanah, and company agents were seeking bonus money payable when the line reached a junction with the Kansas City, Mexico & Orient Railway in the vicinity of Medicine Mound.[3]

A charter was filed in the early spring of 1910, and the company's by-laws were adopted on April 14 of that year. The road was capitalized at $500,000; its headquarters would be in Austin. A route was surveyed, the right-of-way located, and considerable grading done. Ground was first broken on June 12, 1911.

Financing was elusive, but a contract was negotiated in Great Britain shortly before the outbreak of World War I. That conflict, however, resulted in cancellation of the agreement. In the end, only a few portions of the QSD&R were actually used, and then by still another ill-fated road. The Quanah-to-Gulf dream perished accordingly.[4]

Sam Lazarus recognized that the Middle Buster could be a meaningful connection for the Frisco as well as an outlet for traffic originating on the ARR&N. But construction of the Middle Buster would not solve the ARR&N's general problems. It simply had to expand its own trade territory. At the same time, Lazarus worried that another aspirant would appear to block potential avenues for expansion. There were always rumors, such as the ones about the mysterious Mexican Northwestern

Railway and the equally phantom Quanah & South-western Railway.

Fortunately for Lazarus, there were plenty of railroad boosters in Quanah and elsewhere who would assist him in making the ARR&N more than a plant facility. In Quanah, Lazarus could always count on boosters such as Harry Koch. These persons cared rather little about where another railroad derived from or ran to; they merely hoped that its headquarters would be located in Quanah. Many of those who labored on behalf of the Middle Buster—including Harry Koch, Frank Brazil, and A. M. Lewis—also worked to raise money for Lazarus's Quanah, Acme & Pacific. An early drive for contributions in Quanah raised $40,000; a total of 224 individuals and businesses participated. Koch himself contributed $500. Others included Quanah Cotton Oil, $1,500; D. E. Decker, $1,200; Quanah National Bank, $1,000; and D. D. Swearingen, $25. Most of the contributions ranged from $10 to $25.[5]

Lazarus's support in Quanah reflected an area-wide desire to acquire or expand rail service. Not surprisingly, Lazarus was besieged by individuals and even delegations who hoped to escalate property values or growth in importance of their respective communities by convincing him to locate the Quanah, Acme & Pacific along a route that would serve parochial interests. Indeed, investors from as far away as Ohio wrote to Lazarus asking him for private information as to the ultimate location of the road; they wished to purchase tracts along its route and profit from sale as the area was opened. Regional speculators were interested, too. One J. C. Lofton of Garza County had considerable land which he hoped would appreciate in value should the QA&P build into that county. Lofton pointed out that he had worked with C. W. Post and was sure that the cereal magnate would offer Lazarus a bonus of $100,000 plus free right-of-way. Post had already given $50,000 plus right-of-way to secure the Atchison, Topeka & Santa Fe Railway's Coleman Cut-off for Garza County. Lofton implied that a hasty decision was necessary; the Texas Central, he said, was also wooing Post. Others saw different opportunities. J. S. Edwards, a banker, asked Lazarus for permission to handle townsite projects along any route chosen for the QA&P.[6]

Citizen groups and railroad committees from several communities offered a variety of enticements. Petersburg, Texas, would grant a cash bonus of $10 to 15,000 and a "reasonable" right-of-way. Crosbyton, Texas, offered a bonus of $100,000. A representative from Floydada, Texas, told Lazarus that his community "would be very glad to have you submit us a proposition as to what you will require of us in order to secure said railroad." Businessmen from Plainview, Texas, wanted the QA&P and offered cash enticements. The secretary of the Roswell, New Mexico, Commercial Club stated that Roswell was "ready and willing to give a substantial bonus." The editor of the *El Paso Herald* urged Lazarus to consider that city. Commercial representatives from Farwell-Texico, Texas, wanted the QA&P and promised a reasonable subsidy plus free right-of-way. Abernathy and Olton, Texas, both wanted the road. So did Lake Arthur and Hagerman, New Mexico. The QA&P's general attorney, D. E. Decker, frequently spoke for Lazarus in answering these requests. Decker said that when Lazarus decided on the route "it will be largely selected for distance as well as low grade." That was not entirely true; Lazarus was also interested in extracting the maximum bonus.[7]

Interest at Quanah remained keen. By 1909, its population stood at five thousand, and community leaders anticipated continued growth. It boasted four hotels, two newspapers, three cotton gins, a local telephone exchange, three banks, five lumberyards, a total of sixty business houses, and three cement plaster mills employing six hundred men at nearby Acme.[8]

As a progressive community of energetic and optimistic people, Quanah would do all that was necessary to assist the QA&P in any expansion effort. But there was a quid pro quo. On October 27, 1908, J. B. Goodlett and J. E. Ledbetter, trustees for the Quanah Citizens Committee, had entered into a contract with the ARR&N that called for at least a forty-mile extension of the ARR&N (soon to become the QA&P) in a southwesterly direction into Cottle County. It also called for the railroad to provide in Quanah a passenger station, a general office building, a freight depot, a roundhouse, and tracks connecting with both the FW&DC and the Frisco. Furthermore, the agreement required that the railroad maintain its general offices, roundhouse, and depot "in the town of Quanah forever." For its part, the committee promised that it would acquire rights-of-way in Quanah; land for depots, terminals, and shops; a hundred-foot right-of-way from Acme to the western boundary of Hardeman County; and give the railroad a bonus of $40,000 when it ran the first train to a station in Cottle County— at least forty miles. Amendments later stipulated that construction costs for the depots, general office building, and roundhouse aggregate $20,000 and demanded that all these be completed by the fall of 1911. Another alteration affirmed that the first train to Cottle County had to be "at least ten freight and one passenger cars."[9]

Lazarus was agreeable. The fledgling ARR&N, he understood, had to become more than a plant facility, was in good financial condition, and had been a profitable operation. Dividends ranging from 50 to 100 percent had been paid annually from 1903 through 1909. At the same time the national economy seemed on the upswing. Moreover, Lazarus was familiar with the country southwest of Quanah and confident of its potential. He knew the cattle culture there would never support an extensive settlement, but he also perceived that a change in the economic base from ranching to farming would result in significant population growth. Such a shift, however, was predicated on the successful remediation of problems of transportation, fencing, and water supply. The first of these could be solved by the construction of the ARR&N's successor, the Quanah, Acme & Pacific Railway; the second by the availability of inexpensive barbed wire; and the third by the windmill, the development of machinery and methodology adequate to extensive agriculture, and, ultimately, by irrigation. Lazarus knew that Hardeman County had already undergone the transformation from ranching to farming, and now produced cotton, alfalfa, wheat, corn, and oats.[10]

Lazarus was in the mold of other Texas railroad builders such as Col. Morgan Jones, Frank Kell, and J. A. Kemp. All of them knew it was foolish to build lines far ahead of the frontier, yet all had an uncanny ability to anticipate when the construction of a rail line would, in fact, open a frontier. Lazarus was convinced that the time was ripe for expansion into the country southwest of Quanah.

What Lazarus had in mind for the short term—a line of at least forty miles into Cottle County—was clear enough. Yet he also had a long-term objective for the QA&P—El Paso. Extension of the road to that place would open a huge untapped area and generate a heavy volume of local traffic. At the same time, it would forge a logical transcontinental connection and, if undertaken in relationship with the St. Louis & San Francisco, would appease that company's historic interest in the Golden State. These were the years, of course, when the Frisco and the Rock Island were under the skilled and energetic leadership of B. F. Yoakum, an expansionist if ever there was one.

Nevertheless, Lazarus kept a close eye on the immediate project. A survey team was in the field during December 1908. Two months later, D. E. Decker reported that "after getting five miles away from the [Pease] river they are getting a beautiful profile and above all . . . long tangents." The location of the line had progressed as far as Shortie Creek under the direction of Chief Engineer Charles E. Ensminger.[11]

The railroad's board of directors was aware of its obligation to push the road to some location at least forty miles southwest of Acme and began to consider the prospect of driving on a few more miles to Paducah, the seat of Cottle County. A twenty-two-member citizens committee quickly bound itself to an agreement calling for a $60,000 bonus, free right-of-way in Cottle County, and forty acres of land in Paducah to be presented as inducement. Lazarus and his board were agreeable, and contracts were signed on March 24, 1909. Nevertheless, there were those, such as the editor of the *Paducah Post*, who demurred. "Throughout the West it had actually gotten to the point that a person thinks a town is slow and not progressive," complained the newspaperman, "if it does not 'ante up' a few hundred [dollars] when the wish to put an ox-cart in the city for hauling tin cans." Unfortunately, his view anticipated strained relations between the QA&P and Paducah over the coming years.[12]

Meanwhile, the railroad announced that it intended to construct its own line from Quanah to Acme, "a distance of six miles," and also from Acme in a northerly direction to the Red River, "a distance of about eight miles." Nothing ever came of the latter project, but a two-hundred-foot right-of-way was secured on the south side to the FW&DC between Quanah and Acme. Subsequently, however, the FW&DC made the local road a very reasonable proposition for continued trackage rights between the two points; the Denver Road agreed to a fee of fifty cents per train mile with a minimum charge of $3,000 per annum. Thus, at least for the present, the QA&P was spared the need to spend money for the construction of its own line there.[13]

There was much activity in and around Quanah. On August 16, 1909, Ensminger reported that the QA&P's trackage in Quanah was complete and that he was now ready to receive materials for the freight depot and general office building. "Send the concrete mixer over by our first train," he told a subordinate at Acme. Before that could be done, however, a connection between the FW&DC's main line and the QA&P had to be built. On September

It was a gala day for Quanah when the QA&P occupied its new office building.

24, the FW&DC gave the QA&P permission to construct such trackage from the west edge of Quanah to the QA&P's new line along South Street. Under that contract the Denver Road was allowed to use QA&P tracks to switch industries such as the cotton compress; the QA&P, in turn, gained the right to use the FW&DC's stockyards. At the same time, the QA&P built a connection with the Frisco on the east edge of town.[14]

A gala day for Quanah and for the QA&P was January 5, 1910, when the railroad occupied its new office building on Mercer Street. Designed by C. H. Page & Brothers of Austin, Texas, this striking edifice was built in the Mission Style and featured frame and stucco construction with a smart red Ludowici Seville Spanish tile roof. The lower floor served as a passenger station with a general waiting room, women's waiting room, "colored" waiting room, baggage facilities, ticket office, and rotunda. The upper floor afforded offices for the accounting and operating departments, offices for the auditor and general manager, a drafting room, an engineer's room, and, of course, a pleasantly appointed space for the board of directors. It was a building in which both the company and the community could take pride; Lazarus observed, pointedly, that it had cost a whopping $22,519. Adjacent, to the northwest, was the company's less handsome but equally new and functional 43,680-cubic-foot concrete freight house. Just to the south on Mercer Street was the Quanah, "a $20,000 hotel," which offered both convenience and comfort for QA&P patrons. Also strategically located were offices of the Wells Fargo Express Company, midway be-

The company's roundhouse and shops were located a few blocks west of the office building in Quanah. *C. C. Roberts collection*

tween stations of the QA&P and FW&DC to the northeast.[15]

The QA&P's new office building and freight house were lighted by electricity generated by the railroad's own facilities located at the roundhouse a few blocks west. That structure had seven stalls and was of brick construction. The shop facility contained a lathe, drill press, flue welder, headlight turbocharger, anvil, vertical steam engine, and the usual shafting, hangers, and pulleys. Nearby stood a car repair shed, a water facility, and a frame coaling dock with air hoist and buckets.[16]

Before these facilities were built and before construction began beyond Acme, Lazarus had been forced to flesh out the corporate structure and to arrange for necessary financing. The road was capitalized at $70,000; 700 shares of stock were issued at $100 each. In 1909, Lazarus held or controlled in trust 556.6 shares. A total of twenty-six others held from one-half to thirty-two and one-half shares each. Among them was M. Marx, the former president of the ARR&N, who, for a short time, held ten shares. The initial board of directors was composed of Sam Lazarus, C. H. Sommer, and R. D. Yoakum from St. Louis; George Henderson, New York City; C. B. Dorchester, Sherman, Texas; Charles E. Ensminger, D. D. Swearingen, and T. K. Hawkins, Quanah, Texas; and Samuel Burke Burnett, Fort Worth, Texas. Not surprisingly, Sam Lazarus was the road's president, Charles Sommer was elected first vice-president, and Ensminger was appointed second vice-president (and given multitudinous other offices as well).[17]

Additional funding for construction would come from the sale of $920,000 in first mortgage, 6 per-

cent, thirty-year gold bonds. As soon as these were authorized, the QA&P entered into a contract with the Pacific Construction Company, a dummy organization in which Lazarus and the other QA&P stockholders were involved. Under an agreement dated March 9, 1909, the construction company accepted, at par, $800,000 in the railroad's bonds; no cash value was attached to this consideration, which was given for the construction of the line. The Pacific firm assumed the responsibility of realizing, whether at a profit or a loss, whatever the securities might command. The construction company, however, was also to receive all aids, gifts, grants, or donations (except right-of-way) given to the railroad in aid of construction. This eventually aggregated $100,000 to $150,000. For its part, the Pacific firm was obliged to construct the line into Cottle County as well as all sidings, yards, and requisite buildings and facilities.[18]

The contract with Pacific Construction was of the usual type but contained a few additional items of interest. For instance, it stipulated that the "contractor shall not permit the sale, or distribution, or use of any ardent spirits or fermented liquors to be brought on, to or near the line" of the railroad. Additionally, the instrument mandated that any person deemed "intemperate, riotous, disorderly or otherwise troublesome" be discharged by the contractor. Lazarus would have none of the "hell on wheels" atmosphere that had characterized earlier construction projects elsewhere.[19]

As soon as the contract was awarded to the Pacific company, it sublet the work to P. M. Johnston, Son & Allhands, a Texas firm, which, in turn, recruited subcontractors. The work was divided into residencies, each with an assigned engineer. Mules were used in all phases of the building—pulling plows, slips, fresnoes, and wheelers. Many of the laborers were local men who sought work during slack times; others were drifters who followed railroad work all over the country.[20]

The route from Acme to Paducah closely followed an old wagon road that had been used by freighters for several years. Land for right-of-way was acquired by deed, warranty deed, contract, right-of-way deed, quitclaim, and release; it was necessary to employ condemnations in only four cases.[21]

On April 3, 1909, Ensminger advised one of his resident engineers that he would "arrange for track laying to start immediately." There was great exhilaration at the start. Yet there was much planning and worrying for the chief engineer. Lazarus told him: "Whatever you do, don't get excited and let things worry you too much. Have a system and maintain it, so that you will always know where you are, and when we consult, you can give me reliable data." It proved to be good advice; work went smoothly. Efforts were aided by the easy terrain, which was flat to gently rolling. By July, Ensminger's biggest problem was keeping adequate supplies at the front: "Indications are that the tracklayers are going at it in earnest, and unless ties come somewhat faster than they have, work will be delayed." To expedite transportation of materials to the front the railroad leased one locomotive and assigned one of its crews to Pacific Construction for work train service.[22]

By August 13, track had been laid ten miles from Acme to the first new station, Lazare, astraddle the Hardeman-Cottle county line near the fabled one-hundredth meridian. Three days later A. R. Gasway was installed as agent there at a salary of $15 per month. The agent was a partner in the nearby Beard & Gasway Store, which also served as a temporary freight depot for the QA&P. Gasway was told that "a box car will soon be sent for use as a depot."[23]

The townsite of Lazare was established and promoted by W. J. Hoetzel, manager of the Lazare Development Company. The relationship between this firm and the QA&P, if any, is unknown. The community, however, received its name from Lazare Baker, grandson of Sam Lazarus. Its design was impressive and, at its apex, Lazare boasted two churches, a post office, cotton gin, barbershop, telephone exchange, hardware store, café, drugstore, lumberyard, newspaper—the *Lazare Herald*—gro-

cery store, general store, blacksmith shop, and, of course, in time, the QA&P depot. That structure was a 24 x 27 x 16-foot combination frame station. The railroad also built a stock pen, cotton loading platform, and passing track. A writer for the *Quanah Tribune-Chief* predicted that Lazare was "destined to become a good-sized town within a year or two, and being situated in . . . one of the best farm sections in Texas, its future is assured."[24]

Shortly beyond Lazare the engineers' stakes took the QA&P right-of-way into rough country contiguous to the Pease River. A passing track was built on either side of that stream at approximately the pinnacle of grades in each direction. The one on the east was designated Sommer and the one on the west Baker. Pagoda passenger shelters with cinder platforms were built at each location in anticipation of business there.[25]

The second important townsite on the new line was located 24.4 miles from Acme at a place called Swearingen, named for D. D. Swearingen, a resident of Quanah, a QA&P director, and joint owner of the White-Swearingen Live Stock Company. G. S. White, Swearingen's partner, wrote to Lazarus late in August 1909, advising him that they were "selling the land around Swearingen right along and will soon have a lot of farmers there and you will have a nice lot of freight from that point. We would like to ship calves and fat stuff from there this fall if you get your pens up in time."[26]

A certain mystery surrounds Swearingen's origin. QA&P records suggest that the White-Swearingen firm set aside 320 acres of land for the Swearingen townsite and then placed about 1,000 acres of adjoining land on the market. Another source says that the community was founded in 1908 on land sold by Swearingen to George W. Hare, "who owned the entirety of the townsite." It is possible that Hare was an agent of the Quanah Route Townsite Company. In any event, Lazarus clearly owned much if not all of the townsite land.[27]

Swearingen grew rapidly. In 1910 it featured a two-story hotel, a bank, a lumberyard, a drugstore, a livery stable, a hardware store, a cotton gin, two grocery stores, and several residences. School was held initially in the Presbyterian church, but later a red brick school building was constructed. Along the railroad's three-hundred-foot right-of-way, the QA&P constructed a frame depot, a cotton platform, stock pens, a section foreman's house, a toolhouse, and a water station with pumphouse.[28]

Regular triweekly train schedules had been instituted as early as mid-August between Quanah and

Lazare. When that service began, Charles Sommer had told the road's superintendent to "see that special effort is made to keep our coach as clean as possible, also that drinking water is provided at all times. As special compartments have been provided for the negroes, you should see that they keep these quarters. No freight of any kind should be carried in the baggage compartment of this coach." This service was supplemented by a daily-except-Sunday round-trip between Acme and Quanah. The construction company's pioneer trains began service to Swearingen with the arrival of rails there in the fall of 1909; the QA&P began its own operation to that point early in December and established regular tri-weekly trains effective December 24.[29]

Paducah had long craved rail service, and that craving grew as the QA&P inched closer. In October, a Paducah banker urged that the railroad company send "a box car for an office here at once, or as soon as steel reaches here." He noted that cotton for shipment was already on hand and impatiently inquired as to the "exact time you can handle freight in and out of this place." In the same month a number of Cottle County citizens trekked to the road's end-of-tracks to board a special train for the Dallas Fair. But a labor shortage combined with unsatisfactory weather to delay completion of the road into Paducah. Steel finally reached there on December 9, and the next day pioneer trains began hauling emergency shipments of "coal, flour, and groceries in such quantities to meet immediate requirements" under tariffs which had taken effect on December 1. The total volume of traffic generated on the new line was impressive. On December 15 alone the QA&P had in the yards at Quanah thirty cars of lumber, canned goods, and various other commodities billed to Swearingen and Paducah.[30]

The first passenger train to Paducah was a special on December 14. When it arrived, business houses closed, school was dismissed, the brass band showed up, and, according to one account, "the crew was given a royal, musical reception." For local residents, however, the real music came from the locomotive's whistle; it represented the arrival of the steamcar civilization in the seat of Cottle County, Texas. For one unfortunate woman, though, it was a mixed blessing. The locomotive startled her horse, which ran away with the buggy; the wild ride ended when she was thrown out, breaking her leg.[31]

Business was good from the start. In short order a seedhouse, icehouse, oilhouse, and set of oil tanks were built along industry tracks. The railroad's own facilities included a frame passenger depot, frame freight station, cotton platform, and large stock pens. The passenger station was officially opened on January 1, 1910, and daily round-trip service was initiated on that date under a schedule calling for departure from Quanah at 8:30 A.M., arrival in Paducah at 11:00 A.M., departure at 12:30 P.M., and arrival in Quanah at 3:05 P.M.[32]

The quality of railroad built and operated by the QA&P was a matter of dispute. One of Lazarus's subordinates reported that the "entire line is in first class shape," and another official promised the Railroad Commission of Texas that an inspection would prove "it to be the best piece of new track construction ever attempted in the state of Texas." Local observers were not as sanguine. A reporter for the *Paducah Post* said he would not "hold it up as the best line in the state" but thought making "the first twenty miles [from Paducah] in fifty-six minutes with one stop" made the Quanah Route "a credit to this country." Service was uncertain. At least once a train was severely delayed by Johnson grass, which had grown tall next to the track and had blown down over the rail, making a slick goo that denied traction as the weeds were crushed by the locomotive's wheels.[33]

Nevertheless, the railroad had an immediate and dramatic effect on the area it served. In the past, the head of each family traditionally had taken a wagon to Quanah two or three times yearly to shop. The availability of railroad service made these trips unnecessary. Ranchers were among those most affected. Now they could avoid lengthy drives by shipping or receiving their cattle at pens along the QA&P. Swearingen, for example, serviced the needs of the 7L, OX, McAdams, and Brothers ranches. Between six and eight thousand head of cattle were shipped at Swearingen each year, and a large number of animals were unloaded annually. Now, too, cattlemen could receive shipments of cottonseed cake at local stations.[34]

Ranchers benefited in still another way. The QA&P penetrated a relatively undeveloped area that was devoted primarily to the raising of livestock. Many ranchers soon perceived that there was more immediate profit in selling their land than in raising cattle. Quick sales were made to eager and aspiring farmers, with the promise of economical transportation services. Consequently, several area ranges were transformed into productive farms.[35]

The railroad brought still more changes. The inception of Swearingen and the resulting celebrations held there are illustrative. Swearingen's two-

The QA&P's passenger station at Paducah was officially opened for business on January 1, 1910.

day picnics or "cowboy reunions" drew crowds of up to three thousand people; festivities included a parade, rodeo, and ball games. The QA&P ran special excursions for these events at reduced rates. The entire affair reflected Swearingen's rough-hewn character. Citizens included well-known bootleggers and gamblers; fights were commonplace. A relaxed and extralegal code of conduct was established by the local justice of the peace and the constable that was typical of the informal interpretation of the law in many western communities. The code included the following rules:

Poker—Allowed only in the livery stable
Drunks—Somebody had to carry them home
Ladies—If one came to town, drunks had to get off the streets
Breaking School House Windows—Don't
Hoboes—Not prosecuted [36]

Paducah boomed with the coming of the rails. The town grew as if by magic. Builders and tradesmen of all stripes hurried to the community to ply their skills and make a dollar. Shacks gave way to houses; an electric generating plant was built; ladder sidewalks were replaced by concrete; telephones were installed; and "modern methods of living" were introduced. When the QA&P arrived, membership in the First Methodist Church—established in 1892—grew by leaps and bounds. Soon a new church building was required. It represented an area-wide phenomenon. A significant population increase in both Hardeman and Cottle counties resulted. It was much as Mark Twain wrote in *Roughing It*: "Behold, civilization is established forever in the land." [37]

CHAPTER 3

# A Game of Cat-and-Mouse

In that era before good roads, automobiles, busses, trucks, and airplanes, railroad trains linked villages to the outside world—to the life of the cities, distant factories, and markets. In that day, when you either went by train or stayed home, people packed into coaches until there was no room to sit.—J. L. Allhands, *Railroads to the Rio*

EVEN before the Quanah, Acme & Pacific reached Paducah, Sam Lazarus was looking again to the southwest. Reports reaching his St. Louis office were encouraging. "I can see a great future for our line if extended, as it will open a country equally as good as that surrounding Paducah," wrote Charles Ensminger. Yet there were disturbing reports, too. A rumor had begun to circulate which suggested that the Atchison, Topeka & Santa Fe Railway (AT&SF or Santa Fe) would move to capture this same potential trade area, and it was well known that the Fort Worth & Denver City Railway had run surveys southwestward to the Plains from both Quanah and Vernon. A decision as to whether the QA&P should expand was required—and soon.[1]

Delegations representing several communities had met with the QA&P stockholders on April 9, 1910, in hope of persuading them to extend the line from Paducah to the border of New Mexico Territory. Among these delegations was one representing the area immediately west of Paducah in Motley County. Residents of that area had made propositions to other aspirants in 1886 and again in 1906. Now they pinned their hopes on the Quanah Road. Perhaps they knew, too, that Ensminger, A. F. Sommer, and D. E. Decker had recently spent several weeks in the field examining the area between Paducah and El Paso.[2]

That news was widely circulated, and it resulted in a great amount of gossip and speculation—especially on the West Texas Plains, which had been bypassed by the great railroad boom of the late nineteenth century. Several communities put up in-

tensive campaigns to woo the QA&P. Plainview and Lubbock were especially active.

Those same communities sought other railroads as well. In particular, they watched the activities of the Santa Fe and hoped it would choose to project a line their way. Santa Fe's strategy was well known by this time. As early as 1888 AT&SF management had advised company stockholders that "the history of Western railroad construction for the past quarter of a century has demonstrated that successful results can only be obtained by occupying territory promptly." But Santa Fe management had not followed this policy in West Texas. The reasons were simple. Company officers felt no compulsion to move quickly because there was little to attract a railroad there before the turn of the century, and there were no immediate pretenders of consequence.[3]

By 1906–07, however, there were several justifications for expansion—not the least of which was the very real threat of competition. The Santa Fe was ready to move. A line from Canyon to Plainview was swiftly completed, and then the road announced plans for construction of a twenty-seven-mile branch southeastward from Plainview to Floydada. The citizens of Plainview were ecstatic.[4]

In Lubbock, forty-six miles south of Plainview, there was only a feeling of watchful expectation. "The activity of the Santa Fe in invading this virgin region where railroad transportation facilities are so badly needed," wrote the editor of the *Lubbock Avalanche*, "is causing other systems of railway to become aroused to the fact that they must do extensive railroad building on their own account in order

The Santa Fe moved southward from Canyon with a line from Plainview and then completed a branch from Plainview to Floydada. Here the construction train is near Lockney, about midway between Plainview and Floydada. *Standifer Collection, Llano Estacado Museum*

to protect their territory and traffic interests." It was true. The busiest years for the early railroad movement on the South Plains of Texas were 1909–13. During that brief period, about twenty-five promotional schemes were put forward with varying degrees of success, and more than two-thirds of all lines on the South Plains were constructed.[5]

Lubbock provides an example. In May 1909, citizens of that village anticipated the arrival of a Santa Fe extension from Plainview and the construction of another Santa Fe line from Lubbock to Lamesa via Slaton. In addition, they joyously looked forward to completion of the Santa Fe's Texico-Coleman cutoff. With all of these lines, Lubbock would be crisscrossed by the AT&SF. Yet there was more. Competition would be afforded by one or more of several aspirants that Lubbock citizens felt certain would build into the area. Among contending roads and their real or imagined plans were the following:

Chicago, Rock Island & Pacific—Graham, Texas, to Roswell, New Mexico Territory, via the South Plains

Fort Worth, Mineral Wells & Western—Fort Worth, Texas, to Roswell, New Mexico Territory, via the South Plains

Quanah, Acme & Pacific—Paducah, Texas, to El Paso, Texas, via the South Plains and New Mexico Territory

Roscoe, Snyder & Pacific—Fluvanna, Texas, to Amarillo, Texas, or to Roswell, New Mexico Territory

Stamford & Northwestern—Aspermont, Texas, to Dickens, Texas

Texas Central—Rotan, Texas, to Gail, Texas, or across the South Plains to Roswell, New Mexico Territory[6]

Press reports also mentioned the Texas North & South, the West Texas & Northern, and the Altus, Roswell & El Paso—the latter the most important to the QA&P. This company undertook impressive grading west of Altus, Oklahoma, and between Memphis, Texas, and Lubbock. Its promoters then ran into financial difficulty, and it was rumored that the projected road and passed to the Frisco or to the Missouri, Kansas & Texas Railway. Only a small portion of the Altus, Oklahoma & El Paso's route was ever tied and railed. Had it been completed, it would have shortened the mileage between Oklahoma City and El Paso by over two hundred miles, become an important part of a new transcontinental traffic pattern, and short-circuited the QA&P's long-range goals.[7]

Lazarus studied all this activity with intensity, but he would not be goaded into a hasty and possibly disastrous decision. He also studied the QA&P's traffic statistics and account books. Tonnage from the plaster mills at Acme led all other commodities in 1910. Others, in order, were lumber, crude petroleum, railway material, coal, sand and gravel, and merchandise. Traffic from the mills also led in revenue, followed by merchandise, lumber, railway material, crude oil, cotton, livestock, coal, household goods, and grain. Lazarus was pleased. Although the line to Paducah had only recently been completed so that an accurate forecast of traffic and profit from local business was impossible, Lazarus felt comfortable in its prospects. For April 1910, the QA&P turned an operating net of $8,331.60 on revenues of $14,987.38; from July 1, 1909, to May 1, 1910, it earned an operating net of $134,710.52. For the fiscal year ending June 30, 1911, the road had a gross income of $177,152.31, up by $12,721.98 over 1910. Dividends were 25 percent in July 1912 and 10 percent in November of that year.[8]

Would Lazarus press on? In February 1910 the *Lubbock Avalanche* reported that a projected line of the QA&P was expected to run through the counties of Cottle, Motley, Dickens, Frosby, Floyd, Hale, Lamb, Lubbock, Hockley, Cochran, Bailey, Lynn, Terry, and Yoakum and then into New Mexico Territory. In fact, Lazarus may have leaked that story. In any event, he ordered letters sent to QA&P stockholders asking them to authorize an extension of the road through these counties and to raise the capitalization of the company to $500,000 at a meeting scheduled for April 19. After a full discussion at that meeting, however, it was decided that "it was not advisable to undertake an extension at the present time . . . and the resolution was withdrawn." Lazarus had changed his mind; extant records do not suggest why.[9]

A year later, in April 1911, Lazarus authorized preliminary surveys between Paducah and the eastern edge of the Caprock escarpment. One area editor waxed expansive about this news: "The corps was instructed to find a way of getting up the Caprock in Motley County thence on to Roswell and El Paso and also in the direction of Los Angeles." The surveyors, of course, had no such broad powers. Lazarus, however, stated that the El Paso extension would go forward, "money matters having been arranged satisfactorily, if no hitch occurs." The editor of the *Lubbock Avalanche* was predictably euphoric. "In the face of present developments," he said, "the early construction of the QA&P to Lubbock and Roswell is a foregone conclusion. As a matter of fact the extensions have been positively decided upon and work will be under way before September of this year." Events conspired otherwise. In September, Charles Ensminger reported to the board of directors on engineering lines he had run from Paducah, and "after a consideration thereof, it was ordered that the work be discontinued and the matter of selection of route be deferred until the extension could be financed." Possibly the

depressed economy dampened the board's enthusiasm. Nevertheless, ten months later the board authorized amendments to the company's articles of incorporation that increased the capital stock to $100,000 and allowed the company to extend its line "across and through the Counties of Cottle and Motley, to a point in the Western boundary line of Motley County, and the Eastern boundary of Floyd County." Lazarus had not suspended his hopes for a line to El Paso; he simply chose to move cautiously.[10]

Lazarus ordered an "exhaustive examination of the country west of Paducah" to the escarpment of the Caprock. This resulted in several preliminary surveys. The first extended from Paducah southwestward to Spur, the terminus of the Stamford & Northwestern Railroad. Ensminger told Lazarus that this projected line of 54.33 miles would cross the Croton Breaks some four miles southeast of Dickens City; both men were optimistic about it. Lazarus inquired about potential townsites; he wanted three, each of 1,280 acres and "far enough apart so that the towns could grow." Ensminger suggested two locations, one at the headquarters of the Swenson Ranch and one four miles east of Dickens City. Said Ensminger: "If we were to build a town at that point, the county seat would be moved there." He had met with the Swenson people and believed that they would "bear a great deal of the expense of the heavy construction, in addition to any bonus which may be asked of them." Moreover, the Swensons realized that if the QA&P were built to Spur, it would mean "a division at that point, and a wonderful growth to their town." Ensminger pointed out that a line to Spur would mean bypassing Roswell but that it would facilitate a more direct line to El Paso.[11]

Meanwhile, forces in Dickens County mobilized support for the QA&P venture. They offered land estimated in value at $102,000 plus right-of-way and depot grounds. A representative from Dickens City put it bluntly: "What we want is a railroad and we are willing to do anything that a town of our size and financial strength can do to get one." A company representative responded by saying that Lazarus was "of the opinion that a good line can be secured passing through Dickens and on to the west, staying below the Caprock until crossing the Double Mountain Fork of the Brazos. This would yield a route through the best part of Texas, and would be almost a direct line to El Paso." Lazarus, he affirmed, was looking for "the shortest and best route."[12]

There was another option. News of the QA&P surveys had aroused great enthusiasm in Crosbyton, about twenty-seven miles northwest of Spur and above the escarpment. Julian M. Bassett, manager of the CB Live Stock Company at Crosbyton, wrote Lazarus: "Our company has taken out a charter to build a railroad from Spur toward Crosbyton to Lubbock, with a branch going from Crosbyton to Plainview, and has put itself in a position to complete these roads. "We are not desirous of going permanently into the railroad business, but prefer to offer inducements to lines building through this country, rather than to open competition to them." Lazarus understood that if this proposal was accepted the QA&P could pick up a fine bonus, secure a line into Lubbock, and, at the same time, retain the integrity of his early dreams for reaching Roswell and El Paso. He ordered Ensminger to make a preliminary survey to see if a line could be run from a point four miles south of Dickens in a northwesterly direction into and then through Blanco Canyon before reaching the Caprock east of Crosbyton. Ensminger found, though, that to maintain a 1 percent maximum grade would require a horseshoe of eight miles. Such a line, Ensminger concluded, had "nothing to recommend it over others except that it offered a better bonus potential." Lazarus shelved the proposition. Bassett, however, followed through with much of his plan. On April 10, 1911, the Crosbyton–South Plains Railroad placed in service a thirty-eight-mile line between Lubbock and Crosbyton. It would pass to the AT&SF on August 1, 1915.[13]

Lazarus's attention turned to more northerly options. Ensminger already had turned in reports on several prospective routes from Paducah to the west through Motley County. There is no doubt that these surveys were designed to yield the usual information regarding topographical conditions and engineering difficulties. But they were also authorized with the idea of eliciting enthusiastic solicitations from all communities along the widest possible path beyond Paducah. The case of Matador—an established village and seat of Motley County, nearly straight west from Paducah—provides an example. Citizens of Matador hoped to woo the QA&P to a route that would serve their community; they understood that the QA&P would demand a quid pro quo; and they also understood that if they did not respond with adequate generosity they would not attract the railroad. D. E. Decker had suggested to Lazarus that several surveys be run because "this will disturb Matador people more than anything

else." Decker was right. Charles Sommer reported to Lazarus that "the Spur line has been effective at Matador. The people there are nervous about it and have sent word that they don't want to lose our line and stand ready to offer $100,000 any time you demand it." Nevertheless, Lazarus was unwilling to commit the QA&P to any route until he had studied all the surveys in relation to potential bonuses.[14]

Lazarus pored over maps and other data supplied by Ensminger. The first of the various routes through Motley County was the so-called Matador line. It passed one-half mile south of Matador near the headquarters of the Matador Land & Cattle Company. It presented great obstacles in getting away from the Tongue River and demanded five miles of exceedingly expensive curvature, bridge work, and even a tunnel west of Matador. Ensminger reported that "this is the only practical line by which Matador can be reached and is probably as short a line as can be found from Paducah to the High Plains. The advantage of this line over all others is, of course, touching as it does, the county seat and the Matador headquarters, a much larger cash bonus can be raised besides other valuable considerations obtained." Another major survey was labeled as the White Flat line. It passed eight miles north of Matador via White Flat following the North Pease River for its ascent to the Caprock. "This line can be constructed cheaper than any other. . . . This is the only practical line to Floydada, and the country adjacent to the line contains more improved farms than all the balance of Motley County," said Ensminger. It was, however, the longest of the several surveys.[15]

Ensminger knew that Floydada was one of the many communities bidding for the QA&P, and that is why he mentioned it. Yet he was, of course, primarily concerned with engineering questions and thus it is not surprising that he looked beyond Floydada when he recommended crossing Blanco Canyon seven miles southwest of that community on a route that would take the QA&P to Lubbock.[16]

D. E. Decker held responsibility for soliciting aid and for that end met with the Railroad Committee of the Floydada Commercial Club. Results were mixed. Decker later told Lazarus that, in his judgment, the Floydada boosters could raise no more than $15–20,000 plus land for the right-of-way and terminals because a local man named Massie owned or controlled most of the land and was "wrapped up in the Santa Fe, and thinks we are trespassers in his country." Decker, however, had found a Mr. Harp, who would pay $100,000 if the

QA&P would acquire four sections of land north of Floydada, about midway between Floydada and Lockney, direct the line to that location, and build a depot and freight terminal there. Decker urged Lazarus to authorize a survey if for no other reason than to cause Massie to become more plastic. Lazarus knew of another reason; Plainview, seventeen miles to the northwest beyond Lockney, had offered a $100,000 bonus if the QA&P would build to that community. Lazarus took Decker's advice. He ordered a ruse, telling Ensminger to "finish up in Motley and rush to the Plains."[17]

Lazarus wanted to keep all contenders off guard, although by this time he had quietly rejected the Spur, White Flat, and Matador surveys. He was considering only those that lay between the Matador and Spur surveys. "For your private and personal information," he wrote to an associate, "it now looks as if it will be an impossible thing to go to Matador owing to the grade getting out of town to the Plains. I have had this line run and have not as yet decided but it looks very dubious at the present time." Nevertheless, he told Ensminger: "Don't let the matter become public, but in order to keep the wires warm you run the line we spoke of south of Matador just like we were going to build it, and also the one through Matador like we were going to build that." Lazarus wanted to procure a line with the easiest grades while at the same time wresting the largest bonuses. But he was also playing a game of cat-and-mouse with the Matador Land & Cattle Company, a firm based in Dundee, Scotland.[18]

By 1910 officials of the Matador firm were committed to the disposal of certain of that company's lands in Texas. They had held preliminary discussions with several railroad promoters who were boosting their particular schemes to open the country. As might be expected, Matador officials were unwilling to grant subsidies without having some voice in the selection of a route through the firm's lands. Early in 1910, Murdo MacKenzie, manager of Matador's interests in the United States, urged Lazarus to locate the QA&P directly through the village of Matador because he believed that another carrier would then build its line across the firm's southern pastures. Lazarus had no desire to share the trade territory. Lengthy negotiations ensued with each side realizing that it had something to offer but also that the other side had something it needed. MacKenzie felt that the best grade to the High Plains lay through Matador property, and Lazarus felt that the QA&P offered the cattle company both a means of shipping and of disposing of its property.[19]

Each side tilted for advantage. On January 31, 1910, Lazarus sent a cable to MacKenzie in which he advised that three surveys had been run through Matador lands. He pushed for a decision regarding support. "Don't want to crowd you but am going to close shortly for extension. If you advise that your company will authorize reasonable donation will defer for two weeks." Nine days later, Lazarus received word that the Matador board would support the QA&P although the details would have to be worked out. On April 1, Lazarus sent copies of survey maps and an enumeration of each route's relative advantages to MacKenzie. In the cover letter, Lazarus pointed out that "the line to the extreme north, White Flat, has the best country so far as settlement and earning power are concerned," whereas the Matador line, if built, would go south of town and "practically through the Matador ranch headquarters." Lazarus acknowledged that a delegation from the village of Matador had offered a bonus. Perhaps that is why he was "a little partial to the town." Nevertheless, the Matador line would involve heavier construction costs, and Lazarus hoped to find "a line that won't take all the money in the world to go through the Matador range." Lazarus recommended "the line to the south" as the "most practical," but, with tongue in cheek, he told MacKenzie: "You know about which way would suit you better."[20]

MacKenzie had only two choices—a line through the town of Matador or the one Lazarus favored several miles to the south. He met with Lazarus and QA&P engineers at Quanah and then at Matador. In the end, MacKenzie was convinced that the more southerly route and not the Matador line was preferable. His board went along with his recommendation, but residents of Matador felt betrayed. They complained that if the railroad bypassed their community it would be the fault of the Matador Land & Cattle Company. MacKenzie suggested that the local citizenry put up money to defray the difference in expense of construction between the two lines. Lazarus, however, was not interested.[21]

Lazarus originally had requested a bonus of one dollar per acre on land belonging to the Matador firm which lay within three miles of the proposed line. This would have amounted to $640 a section, or $3,840 per mile. Lazarus also requested the usual right-of-way and water privileges. The Matador board agreed in principle, but it was not until September 11, 1911, that contracts were signed between the QA&P and the Matador company.[22]

These contracts were signed in Chicago by Lazarus and Alexander Mackay of the cattle company. The first contained five crucial elements: the railroad was to have its financing arranged for by January 15, 1912; construction was to begin by July 1, 1912; the road was to be completed through the Matador country by September 1, 1913; the railroad would receive from the Matador firm one dollar per acre on lands lying within three miles on each side of the right-of-way; and the Matador Land & Cattle Company would donate requisite land for right-of-way, stations, and sidings. The second agreement was important for two reasons. It set forth, at least by implication, the chosen route for the railroad—about eight miles south of Matador through the southern portion of Motley County, reaching the Plains via Wolf Creek Point, following closely a wagon trail used by buffalo hunters during the 1880s. Moreover, it proposed the formation of a townsite development company. The Matador Company agreed to convey 640 acres at three locations along the QA&P survey in Motley County. Stock in the townsite company was to be held equally by cattle company and railroad interests. Lazarus later proposed, and Matador officials agreed, that an agricultural development company be established for the purpose of disposing of sixty thousand acres in the southwestern portion of the Matador range.[23]

Lazarus was not able to meet the deadlines. He asked the Matador company for an extension and for more concessions. Most were granted, but when both sides wrangled over the total number of acres upon which the bonus would be drawn it appeared that the entire project would collapse. In June 1912, Lazarus asked for a flat $85,000 in bonus money plus donation of the right-of-way. The company agreed and pledged to pay the bonus thirty days after the institution of freight and passenger service over the first forty miles of new trackage west of Paducah.[24]

Lazarus and the other promoters and boosters of the QA&P venture could, it seemed, finally breathe easier. The onward march of the road to El Paso appeared assured. Yet Lazarus had experienced considerable difficulty in locating adequate funding for just the present small project, perhaps because of the depressed economy between the summer of 1910 and the winter of 1912. Lazarus's troubles led to much speculation. For some time a rumor had circulated in Quanah that the QA&P was actually controlled by the Fort Worth & Denver City Railway. It was not true. Then, early in 1910, the *Quanah Tribune-Chief* carried a story taken from the *St. Louis Republic* claiming that the QA&P had been taken over by the St. Louis & San Francisco Railroad, that the QA&P would be extended to El Paso in 1911, and that the SL&SF would extend its own line south of Quanah at the same time. These rumors were not true, but they were a harbinger.[25]

Lazarus's financial maneuverings are extremely hard to trace. Sketchy evidence shows that between August and October 1911, the SL&SF entered into negotiations with W. A. Baker & Associates for the acquisition of $70,000 in the QA&P's par value capital stock (the entire issue) and for $985,000 in the road's par value first mortgage bonds. Frisco records suggest that QA&P stock was thusly transferred; QA&P records contradict this. The bonds apparently had passed from the QA&P to the Pacific Construction Company, to W. A. Baker & Associates, to the SL&SF, and finally to W. M. Soloman & Company. They had gone at par to the Pacific firm, at 75 percent to the Baker company, and at 95 percent to the SL&SF. Baker was president of the Pacific Construction Company, the firm that had held the contract on the QA&P's extension from Acme to Paducah.[26]

The entire matter was extremely complex, but on October 24, 1911, a new agreement was made to clarify all issues. It contained the following provisions: the SL&SF agreed to pay the first mortgage of 6 percent bonds of the QA&P on or before July 15, 1921, at 105 plus interest; as long as any of those bonds remained outstanding, the SL&SF agreed to pay the interest on them as they matured; the Frisco pledged to maintain the property in proper operating condition; and the Frisco agreed to pay the QA&P's operating expenses and taxes. On the surface it appeared that the Frisco had assumed total control of the QA&P. It was not so. Confusion remained, and the question of ownership and control would trouble relations between the two railroads for several years.[27]

Lazarus tried to explain the situation. On November 9, 1911, through the *Quanah Tribune-Chief* of that date, he announced that he had sold the bonds of the QA&P and some of its stock to the SL&SF. He stated that he still retained an interest in the road, declared that he would remain its president, and promised that there would be no alteration in the organization and operation of the line. Traffic relations with the Frisco would become closer, and the SL&SF would soon begin using the QA&P's station and terminal facilities at Quanah. Finally, Lazarus underscored the fact that the Quanah Route was still under independent management.[28]

The new arrangement offered advantages for both railroads. For the Frisco, the expansionist policies of B. F. Yoakum and the Rock Island–SL&SF axis could be furthered by control of the QA&P. For the QA&P, guarantee of its bonds by the Frisco would advance their sale and facilitate construction beyond Paducah. This cozy arrangement would benefit all parties until the collapse of the Yoakum empire and the resulting Frisco receivership in 1913 caused great confusion.

On July 9, 1912, QA&P directors, having successfully negotiated with G. H. Walker & Company of St. Louis for funds to support construction of forty miles of track, determined to issue "about one million dollars" in the road's first mortgage 6 percent coupon bonds—discounted by the Walker Company by $50 each. These bonds were to be issued at the rate of $24,000 per mile; Walker & Company agreed to pay out proceeds gradually between August 15, 1912, and February 14, 1913. On August 15, 1912, the board decided to issue another $30,000 in QA&P stock to help finance the line extension and construction facilities. By the time the extension was completed, QA&P's capitalization would stand at $100,000 and the road would issue bonds at par value in the amount of $1,858,679,78.[29]

During the late summer of 1912, the QA&P entered into a contract with the Southwestern Construction Company for construction of the forty-mile extension west of Paducah. There had been five contestants for the work. Their bids ranged from $280,521.40 to $337,320.70. Southwestern Construction had not been one of the bidders, yet it received the contract and was guaranteed $23,000 per mile or $920,000. The reason for this strange decision might have been that the firm's president was John Summerfield, who had been secretary and director of the old Acme, Red River & Northern. Whether there was any relationship between the Southwestern Construction Company and Lazarus is unknown. Under provisions of this agreement, the contractor could draw up to 90 percent of the value of the work performed; the remaining 10 percent was to be given over after final acceptance of the work by the railroad's chief engineer. The QA&P authorized the construction company to use the new tracks for transporting water and agreed to furnish that water on a gratis basis. The Southwestern Construction Company would be dissolved in 1918 after all contractual obligations had been satisfied.[30]

Chief engineer John Knox marshaled his materials at Paducah for the push west. *Mrs. Paul Brown collection*

The elevation westward from Paducah increases rapidly; at Paducah it is 1,886 feet, at MacBain, the end of the extension, it is 2,891 feet. Work on this new section of road would be difficult, in part because the terrain was hilly and because it was necessary to cross the valleys of the Tongue (South Pease) River and Dutchman Creek. For the first few miles west of Paducah, the road would traverse lands that were ripe for agricultural development, but beyond that for several miles the land might best be identified as cattle country. Only near the end of the extension, at Roaring Springs, would the land be more suitable for tillage.

Construction began in October 1912. On October 29, John A. Knox, who had replaced Ensminger as chief engineer, told C. H. Sommer that 195 teams were working on the grade. By late November over 350 teams were employed, moving 350,000 cubic yards of dirt. Tracklaying began on December 26; surfacing and bridge work commenced early in 1913.[31]

The extension was subdivided into districts, which were assigned to subcontractors who hired their own laborers. On the line just west of Paducah a large number of blacks were recruited. They were fine workers, but when they learned that they could earn higher wages gathering crops, most of them abandoned the railroad project. Many subcontractors hired itinerant workers along with local men who were temporarily in need of work. A writer for the *Quanah Tribune-Chief* found itinerants particularly captivating and selected one of them as his model. He was, said the journalist, "squareshouldered and wiry, without surplus flesh around the waist, with a half-amused, half contemptuous grin for tenderfeet . . . . One could only imagine this grizzled veteran to feel at home in a wilderness, which he and his fellows had to tame, that the rest of us might travel it in chair cars and Pullmans.

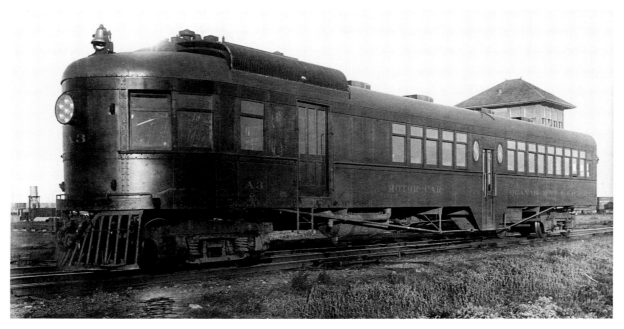

Charles Sommer insisted that service begin on the ten-mile section west of Paducah to "qualify us for bond registration." This was accomplished by employing the road's new motor car, the A-3. *C. C. Roberts collection*

He was a relic of the golden age in railroad construction, an age that has almost slipped away."[32]

The railroad's plan had been to accept the entire forty-mile extension in one block and not to operate trains over it until then. Charles Sommer, however, told Knox to open the line for a few miles early in May. Knox objected that this would "greatly inconvenience" the contractors. Sommer explained that it was necessary to operate at least part of the line to "qualify us for bond registration." Consequently, service over the first ten miles began on a Monday-Wednesday-Friday basis effective May 15, 1913.[33]

Tracklayers hurried on. In June they reached Mac-Bain Switch, as the Matador people called it. On the railroad it was simply MacBain, milepost 82.9, 3.8 miles west of Roaring Springs. It was named for John MacBain, a Scot, who had succeeded Mac-Kenzie as manager of the Matador Land & Cattle Company. The QA&P had expected to make the MacBain extension operational before June 15, but it was not until four days later that it was able to send a special train carrying prospective settlers from Quanah to Roaring Springs. Regular service was initiated the following day although the line was not officially opened until July 1. Two weeks later Knox reported that the trackwork was generally complete but that some of it was not fully tied or spiked. Nor was the bridging finished or was the fencing and telephone pole line complete. At Roaring Springs the wye and sidings were in, work on the stock pens had begun, and the foundation had been poured and the floor joists were in place at the depot site. The bridge work was not finished until August, and surfacing continued into September.[34]

The new line featured light grading; ballast of earth, cinders, and gravel; no steel bridges; sixty-five-pound rail (60 percent new open hearth, 40 percent relay); water facilities at the crossing of the Tongue River and at Roaring Springs; and, strange to say, hog pens at MacBain.[35]

The QA&P had received considerable assistance in support of the MacBain extension. That which came from the Matador Land & Cattle Company will be treated later in detail. Suffice it to say here that the railroad received construction bonuses from the Matador firm and from E. P. and S. A. Swenson totaling $98,135. It also received 1,312 acres of land in aid from various citizens committees, individuals, and companies. Land for right-of-way was obtained mostly by deed with only one condemnation suit required. This support spoke volumes regarding the desire of area people for a railroad.[36]

Lazarus was justifiably proud. His little plant facility had become a full-fledged common carrier railroad. Yet he was not satisfied. His face always was turned to the southwest. He still had his eye on El Paso.

## CHAPTER 4

## The Sheeny Short Line

The long talked of, logically expected, prophetically profitable extension of the Quanah, Acme & Pacific Railway now appears to be on the eve of materialization.—*Lubbock Avalanche*, March 12, 1912

SAM Lazarus was not alone in his desire to see expansion of the QA&P's operations. The prospect of a new line to El Paso intrigued that community and virtually all others through a broad corridor reaching from MacBain to the Rio Grande River.

Lubbock was especially enthusiastic. The editor of one of its newspapers, a strong booster of railroads, had long labored to generate support for the QA&P. "The point that the *Avalanche* desires mostly to call to the attention of the people," he had written in 1909, "is the importance of inducing this road to come to Lubbock." A few months later the editor was convinced that the Quanah Road would build to his community. "The extension of the QA&P to the Texas–New Mexico boundary will work radical changes in the Plains country. Merchandise, instead of going all around the northern part of Texas and down on the Santa Fe, will come through Quanah in car lots and train loads and will move without intervention of wagon freighters directly to the destination." The Lubbock newspaperman and his constituency remained optimistic even when the QA&P made meager progress.[1]

During the spring of 1911, numerous area newspapers reported that the road was making its sixth survey west of MacBain. At the same time, Lazarus gave assurances that "the route it pursues from the Caprock will not be so much a question of topography as of policy." This was because of physical conditions beyond the escarpment. Ensminger had told Lazarus that "the Plains, once reached, a continuation in southwesterly direction of over one hundred miles at but little more than the cost of ties and rails is assured." This was good news indeed. The QA&P already had spent $22,074.84 on surveys just for the Paducah-MacBain extension.[2]

The *Lubbock Avalanche* asserted in its issue of March 14, 1912, that "the long talked of, logically

expected, prophetically profitable extension of the Quanah, Acme & Pacific Railway now appears to be on the eve of materialization." Six months later it announced that bonds had been sold to send the road to Lubbock and that the new line would reach that place via Floydada or Lockney during the next summer or fall. Apparently the road's boosters in Lubbock confused the company's decision to build and pay for the new line from Paducah to MacBain with a larger scheme that was perfected in their own minds, which had been encouraged by Lazarus.[3]

Indeed, QA&P surveyors were hard at work in 1913. Their initial problem was to find a practicable ascent up the Caprock—and one that was compatible with Lazarus's plans for the location of the line across the South Plains to El Paso. By midyear they offered him five options from MacBain: to Crosbyton, twenty-four miles; to Lubbock, sixty-five miles; to Abernathy, sixty-one miles; to Hale Center, sixty miles; and to Floydada, twenty-eight and a half miles. The surveyors hastened to label the Crosbyton survey as "impractical account excessive mileage and heavy construction cost in crossing Blanco Canyon." They pointed out, however, that all the others would afford "short line mileage across the West Texas Plains" as well as connections with the AT&SF. Beyond these immediate goals (which were colored in large measure by both potential construction costs and potential community support) Lazarus was concerned about possible competition on through traffic moving between St. Louis and El Paso over the Frisco and an expanded QA&P. He clearly anticipated direct competition with the Gould roads (Texas & Pacific, St. Louis, Iron Mountain & Southern, and others) and with the Rock Island and the El Paso & Southwestern over their Golden State Route, and he expected indirect competition from the AT&SF. (The

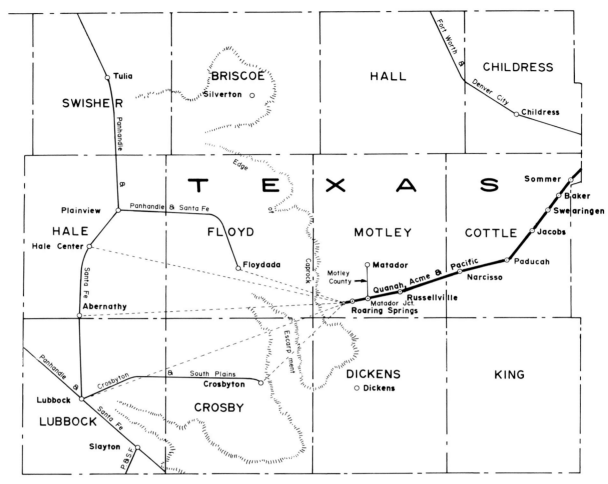

Survey options to Floydada, Hale Center, Abernathy, Lubbock, and Crosbyton from MacBain.

Santa Fe did have a line into El Paso but had no direct connection with St. Louis).[4]

Lazarus appears to have settled on two general surveys for the El Paso extension. The first of these was from MacBain on nearly an airline path through Abernathy to a crossing of the AT&SF's Texico line between Lubbock and Littlefield, passing above Mescalero Ridge through Roswell, and then to the southwest between the Guadalupe Mountains and the Sacrament Mountains—in the fashion of an "S"—and entering El Paso from the northeast. The other was from MacBain to Cochran County and south through Mescalero Ridge and Carlsbad, then skirting the Guadalupe Mountains on a line that was nearly parallel with the Texas–New Mexico border into El Paso.[5]

Several communities continued to pledge sizable donations to encourage construction by the QA&P to serve them. Roswell, New Mexico, promised a bonus contract of $250,000 and right-of-way between the Texas–New Mexico border and that community. Citizens of Plainview, Texas, already had subscribed $100,000 to provide for a right-of-way from Floyd County to Plainview. They also agreed to provide terminal facilities and a cash bonus if the road were completed by September 1915. Decker met with Lazarus and Charles Sommer in St. Louis early in January 1914. Upon his return to Quanah, he announced that a contract would be let by March to extend the road to Plainview. He predicted that the QA&P soon thereafter would be extended to Roswell.[6]

Decker was overly optimistic; the QA&P's plans for expansion soon were shelved, and they remained moribund for a decade. The reasons are not clear, although the tight money situation between the winter of 1913 and the summer of 1915 no doubt contributed. The *Quanah Tribune-Chief* of April 20,

1914, reported that plans for expansion west of MacBain had been canceled because "rumors of war" had discouraged New York investors from supporting ventures so close to Mexico. There were still other rumors. One that circulated for years was that the money to build the road to El Paso had been arranged for but that the person or persons who had been expected to invest perished with the sinking of the *Titanic*. Another involved F. S. Pearson, an English millionaire, who had extensive holdings in West Texas and New Mexico. According to a 1912 newspaper account, Pearson became interested in the QA&P "and new faith was inspired." It may have been true. But Pearson was a victim of the *Lusitania* disaster in 1915. Several years later the company explained that "during World War I the government cancelled the steel contract for the rail that was to be used for the extension" and that "the World War and events immediately following prevented this undertaking." In any event, while Lazarus continued to look to the southwest—and the QA&P continued to advertise its intentions to expand to El Paso—the Quanah Route's end-of-tracks remained at a forlorn outpost at the base of the Caprock escarpment.[7]

Meanwhile, Yoakum's Frisco–Rock Island empire became unhinged in 1913, the result of overexpansion. The St. Louis & San Francisco Railroad went into receivership on May 27, 1913, and would emerge in 1916 as the St. Louis–San Francisco Railway (SL-SF or Frisco). One of the casualties of its demise, for the present at least, was the close corporate relationship between the Frisco and the Rock Island.[8]

The reorganization did nothing to clarify the confusing stock control record of the QA&P and Frisco's involvement in it. *Poor's Manual* for 1914 simply asserted that "the St. Louis and San Francisco Railroad Company owns an interest in the stock" of the QA&P. Three years later, in 1917, *Railway Age* reported that a correspondent in Quanah, Texas, had advised that "the QA&P is to be taken over by the St. Louis and San Francisco." A year later, *Poor's Manual* claimed that the SL-SF controlled the Quanah Route "through ownership of a majority of the capital stock. Prior to reorganization, the SL&SF owned an interest in the stock, but since reorganization, the SL-SF has acquired a majority of the stock." The ICC, however, asserted that the QA&P was "controlled by the St. Louis San Francisco Railway through ownership of its entire capital stock." The QA&P's annual response to the ICC as late as 1922 would be the same: "The

Interstate Commerce Commission advises us . . . that the SL&SF Railroad Company had control through the ownership of a majority of the capital stock on June 30, 1915 but records of this company reflect no such control nor does SL&SF Railroad Company exercise control." To be sure, Sam Lazarus owned a sizable block of QA&P stock as late as the mid-1920s.[9]

The situation for bondholders was much less cluttered. Under the SL&SF's reorganization plan, holders of QA&P $1,000 6 percent bonds were offered SL-SF $1,250 4 percent prior lien bonds plus $15,000 in cash. Most were so exchanged.[10]

Although Lazarus was frustrated in his attempts to expand the QA&P's operations beyond MacBain, the road grew modestly in aggregate length. During 1914, receivers of the Frisco and the QA&P management entered into a indefinite lease agreement regarding the 8.68-mile trackage between Quanah and the Red River station. Subsequent to August 1, the Quanah Route, as a matter of economy, assumed operations between these two points, "accruing all of the revenue heretofore apportioned to the St. Louis, San Francisco & Texas Railway"— the Frisco subsidiary that, at least technically, had operated the line previously. For its part the QA&P agreed to bear the mileage proportion of operating expenses in connection with joint train service; pay an annual fee of 4 percent on the valuation of the property; and pay for all insurance premiums, betterments, additions, and taxes. This agreement gave the QA&P use of the Frisco's Quanah yard facilities and access to industries there. But the Frisco's terminal facilities in Quanah—including its impressive passenger station—became redundant immediately. An earlier agreement between the QA&P and the FW&DC had provided that Frisco trains could use QA&P tracks to get to and from the Quanah Route's freight and passenger depots. Now Frisco trains would terminate there and its rolling stock would be serviced by the QA&P.[11]

The city of Quanah took pride in the QA&P, and its citizens appreciated what the company had done for their community. Its population had doubled and its property values had gone up by 50 percent within two years after the road's extension to the southwest. Furthermore, Quanah's business volume had doubled when Paducah's trade was tapped on completion of the road to that point. Much of this trade had been lost by Childress, and the editor of the *Childress Index* responded in an ill-humored way by labeling the agent of change, the QA&P, "the Sheeny Short Line." It mattered little

Buildings sprouted like weeds in Roaring Springs during 1913 and 1914.

to Quanah residents. They were proud to have a railroad headquartered in their community. One Quanah businessman summed it up this way: "The QA&P is going to do great things for Quanah, in fact, it is doing great things now." He and other business leaders understood that the railroad had, among other things, become an employer of a considerable importance.[12]

Quanah was not the only community that benefited from the railroad. Paducah also prospered. All other towns along the QA&P were new and owed their existence to the railroad. Beyond Paducah new townsites included Narcisso, Russellville, and Roaring Springs.

Land in the amount of 640 acres had been given by E. P. and S. A. Swenson to Sam Lazarus, who promptly conveyed it to the newly formed Narcisso Townsite Company. This firm then issued $5,000 in stock—representing the value of its land—which was disbursed in equal portions to the Southwest Construction Company (in reality, to Lazarus with C. H. Sommer acting as trustee) and to the QA&P. The purpose of the new company was to develop a townsite about ten miles west of Paducah. It was platted with five streets and five avenues and with generous-sized commercial and residential lots. In anticipation of its business there, the railroad built an industry track, a ten-pen stock facility, a large cotton platform, a frame combination depot, a section foreman's residence, and a toolhouse.[13]

Area residents once suggested that this first station west of Paducah be called Niggerville after the blacks who had built that section of the road. Lazarus was unimpressed with this suggestion and selected the name Narcisso. The town, regretfully for its boosters, did not develop. No town lots were sold and most of the land was sold in acreage tracts.

The usual sales agreement was made through vendors' lien notes payable in equal annual installments with maturities of four to ten years. Each note was issued at the rate of 8 percent per annum and secured by first deeds of trust. Purchasers agreed to place improvements on each tract to the value of $1,000, to cultivate the ground, and to fence it. If town lots could not be sold, at least agricultural traffic could be generated for the railroad.[14]

Another townsite was established sixteen miles west of Narcisso. Called Russellville, it boasted the same railroad facilities that had been constructed at Narcisso. Yet it was even less successful. It appears that a post office was established there, perhaps in 1916, but it lasted only a short while. The Russellville townsite was never settled and no capital stock was issued by the townsite company. As late as 1927, C. H. Sommer would propose "that we block out this land the same as we did at Narcisso, and sell it as acreage, in the hopes of getting a small settlement there." Nothing came of it.[15]

The most important townsite development along the QA&P was Roaring Springs, eighty-one miles from Quanah. The Roaring Springs Townsite Company was formed in December 1912 for the purpose of disposing of town lots after the arrival of the railroad. It was capitalized at $50,000. Underlying support was 697.3 acres of land donated by the Matador Land & Cattle Company; it was valued, for purposes of capital stock issue, at $30,000. The remaining stock subscriptions—$10,000 each—were paid into the townsite company's treasury by the cattle company and by Lazarus. The stock, five hundred shares at a par value of $100 each, was then divided equally between the Matador company and the QA&P; the latter was then equally split between the railroad and Lazarus.[16]

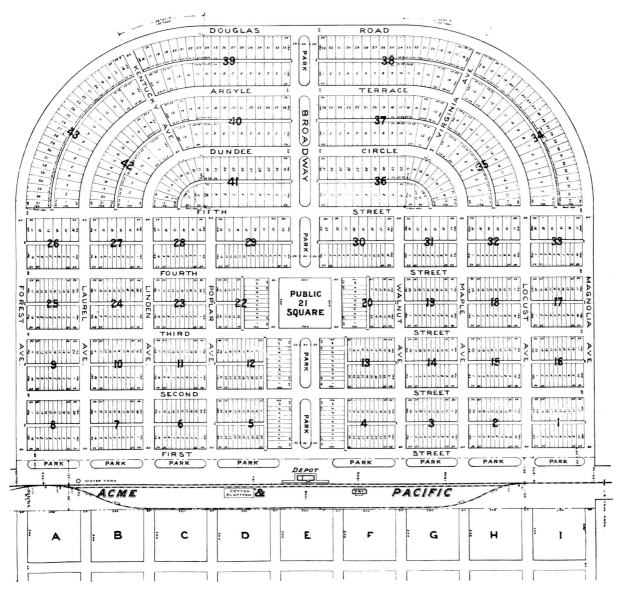

The townsite company bragged that the new community of Roaring Springs was "well laid out." It was no idle boast.

The Roaring Springs Townsite Company advertised extensively and solicited participants for a private sale on June 19, 1913. The company stressed that special trains over the QA&P would be operated on that date, and acreage property and town lots would be for sale. Easy terms were promised. It was a grand success; the company sold property valued at $24,000 within five weeks. Shortly thereafter an observer reported the erection of fifty buildings, including a bank, a church, a lumberyard, and a cotton gin. The company itself had built a hotel as well as a warehouse, store building, and even a

waterworks system. Water rates were reasonable. Monthly charges amounted to $1.00 for residences, $1.50 for businesses. and $2.00 for the hotel.[17]

The townsite company asserted that the new community was "well laid out." The design was that of a horseshoe with the railroad and its facilities—a handsome brick passenger station and a more mundane but certainly utilitarian frame freight depot—lacing the open end. In addition to the main track, the company built three other tracks, a wye, a large cotton platform, stock pens, a section foreman's house, a toolhouse, a water station with tank and pumphouse, and a frame coaling dock. Several industries quickly sprang up along the right-of-way.[18]

The Roaring Springs Townsite Company was also partially responsible for administering a joint agreement between the Matador Land & Cattle Company and the railway which provided for the opening of certain Matador lands to farm development. Under the agreement, dated October 31, 1913, the cattle company set aside sixty thousand acres of land in Dickens, Motley, and Cottle counties, which were to be allotted in installments of twenty thousand acres each. These would then be sold in smaller parcels. Title to the lands so allotted was to remain with the Matador firm until their sale and then deeds were to be made directly to individual purchasers. The QA&P, however, was to be responsible for the sales campaign and to absorb all related costs. Out of proceeds resulting from the sale of these sixty thousand acres the Matador firm was to be paid $10 per acre, or $600,000, as a preferential payment before the cattle company and the railway divided any net surplus. The contract further stipulated that the QA&P should not sell any land for less than $10 per acre; that the railway should demand a down payment of at least 20 percent in cash with the remainder due in annual payments not to exceed ten years; that the balance on notes draw 8 percent interest; that mineral rights were retained by the Matador company; and that purchasers must fence their land. Specifically excluded from sale was a spring of water known locally as Roaring Springs; it was retained by the Matador firm for the time being.[19]

After sale of the first twenty thousand acres, the QA&P would be free to call for another twenty thousand and then the final twenty thousand acres. A final accounting was due on October 31, 1923. In the thirty months following the initiation of rail service to Roaring Springs a mere 693 acres were sold to homeseekers and farmers. This disappointing record changed drastically during World War I, however, and by 1923 all of the land would be disposed of.[20]

The Matador Land & Cattle Company had driven a hard bargain. Yet both parties profited. The railroad enhanced the value of Matador land by making it appealing to farmers, and agriculture and the promise of settlement suggested a regular and growing volume of local traffic for the railroad. Beyond that there were profits from the Roaring Springs Townsite Company and its auxiliary land development organization.

The QA&P hired an immigration agent and enthusiastically advertised the good life in Motley County.

Residents of Matador, the village some eight miles north of Roaring Springs, did not take kindly to any of this. They were sorely disappointed when the QA&P failed to build its line through their community, realizing that without a railroad Matador would suffer and possibly even die. Lazarus and the other railroad officials were aware of Matador's problems but felt that the laws of economics would provide the solution—residents of Matador would be forced to move to the new townsite of Roaring Springs and the county seat would be moved to the new townsite. Such a pattern had been repeated often in the West. The QA&P had been Matador's best bet, and it had failed the town; there was virtually no possibility that another road could be attracted. Yet there was one hope. Matador's life depended on it. The village's citizens would form their own railroad company.

Some concerned citizens of Matador petitioned the Matador Land & Cattle Company early in 1913 to aid in the building of a railroad southward from their village to the QA&P. An official of the cattle company caustically responded that such a scheme was "purely the work of Socialists in that part of the country," but in the end a grant of $10,000 was made toward the project. "Apart from the value to the company of this additional means of transportation," explained the same Matador official, "we felt justified in making the payment as an evidence of our willingness to help the townspeople of Matador in a scheme upon which they had set their hearts and toward which they had subscribed very liberally." The cattle company must have been of two minds. On one hand, a railroad to guarantee the survival of Matador would hardly aid the affairs of the Roaring Springs Townsite Company in which the Matador firm had an interest; but on the other, such a rail line would help in the sale of rangelands to farmers.[21]

Matador residents had enthusiastically burdened themselves with a voluntary subscription. Nearly a hundred of their number had promised to generate a minimum of $65,000; money from the Matador Land & Cattle Company gave them a total of $75,000. On May 6, 1913, sixty-eight subscribers met to create the Motley County Railway Company. In short order, they elected A. B. Echols, the project's real sparkplug, and eight others—I. E. Martin, J. D. Morris, A. C. Traweek, J. C. Burleson, R. P. Moore, J. E. Russell, J. N. Gaines, and T. E. Leckie—as directors. These men, in turn, elected company officials: A. B. Echols, president; I. E. Martin, vice-president, J. D. Morris, second vice-president, J. N. Gaines, superintendent; J. D. Burleson, secretary; R. P. Moore, treasurer; and T. T. Bauldin, general attorney. The road was capitalized at $100,000, and Matador was designated as its headquarters. The venture was characterized by confusion. The company's goals were not clear. At one time, its incorporators argued for a 125-mile line from Spur to Memphis via Matador. On another occasion they stated a desire to build the road "from some point on Quanah, Acme & Pacific Railway in Motley County to Matador and Whiteflat and probably to other points not yet determined." And the firm's articles of incorporation stated that the goal was a line to connect the QA&P near Roaring Springs with the Fort Worth & Denver City at Memphis. Even the name of the firm was open to question; many early records referred to it as the Matador & Northern Railway.[22]

Shareholders quickly determined that modest goals were all they could afford. Consequently, they entered into a contract with Frank Fennen for the grading of a road between Matador and a junction with the QA&P south of town. The grade was built from a location, smartly labeled Matador Junction, about three and one-half miles east of Roaring Springs, to the eastern edge of Matador—a mere eight miles. Grading was light; one locomotive engineer later referred to it as a "roller coaster line."[23]

There was suspicion, even bad blood, between the two carriers and their officials from the beginning, no doubt because the QA&P had not built its line through Matador and because the citizens of that town believed that Lazarus and the railroad had attempted to starve Matador out of existence. It was true that QA&P officials believed that Matador traffic would flow to and from its line whether or not rails served the village directly. After all, the QA&P offered the nearest and most accessible transportation outlet. If Matador succeeded in constructing its own connecting line, however, the QA&P would be forced to divide revenue.

During the summer of 1913, emissaries from the two companies met to discuss a variety of questions, one of which was the construction of a connecting track at Matador Junction. There was disagreement. QA&P representatives argued that their road should own the new trackage although the Motley County road should pay for it. Motley County representatives, not as sophisticated in their knowledge of railroad tradition, failed to understand he QA&P's position and maintained that if they paid "for the connection they ought to own it." It was a minor point, and yet nothing was more basic for the small road than a junction with a larger one. D. E. Decker, the QA&P's general attorney, told Charles Sommer that he did not "believe that they [the Motley County Railway] will ever lay track on their line. They are fussing among themselves now." Nevertheless, he suggested a compromise that would divert their energies "and probably keep them fighting and not bother us." Sommer agreed: "I have never taken this matter seriously, believing that the track will never be constructed. It is for that reason we have demanded a cash deposit in advance of construction of the proposed connection."[24]

By November 20, however, Decker advised Sommer that the Motley County folks were "ready to begin laying their track and that a contract for such work had been let." On the same day another contract was made between the two roads whereby the QA&P agreed to afford the Motley County Railway a connection at Matador Junction. Under this agreement the latter company paid for all construction and maintenance but the QA&P retained "control." Meanwhile, an official of the Motley County company approached the QA&P with a request for trackage rights and use of Quanah's facilities at Roaring Springs; Sommer agreed in principle to allow this access at a monthly rate of $100.[25]

Decker still had little faith in the Motley County venture. He admitted that under Texas law the QA&P had been compelled to grant the new line a connection, and he had no qualms about doing so if only to demonstrate "right intentions." He was much less pleased about the possibility of allowing the Motley County Railway use of the QA&P tracks from Matador Junction and facilities at Roaring Springs. Indeed, he did not believe the Motley County company could pay its bills. "At the present time I doubt it is the desire of the Motley County Company to make any kind of contract with us that costs them anything." Another issue made him angrier. The new firm had urged that the QA&P build additional facilities at Matador Junction. "To sum up," fumed Decker, "they would agree that it is a duty we owe them to build and maintain yards, depot and agency there for their use." The promoters of the Motley County road were, in Decker's view, dangerous country bumpkins. "The fact is I find in the minds of those immediately connected with that road a great deal of ignorance with regard to what is right, and this is mixed with a great deal of hate." It led the QA&P's general attorney to "suggest that we arrange for the connection which they can compel us to afford them and then have as little to do with them as possible."[26]

Bad blood did not disappear. Decker referred to attitudes in Motley County as "the peculiar conditions that exist in that community," but presidents of the two companies did attempt to patch up differences through a series of letters. "I am writing you this letter," Lazarus told Motley County's President A. B. Echols, "with all of the best feeling and want you and your neighbors to understand that the QA&P wants to help everyone that it possibly can in Motley County." After all, said Lazarus, "We are in a thinly settled country and we have uphill work of our own and one touch of nature makes us all akin." Echols responded in kind: "I feel that our interests are common and that we should all work together in harmony, and I believe when we all understand each other this will be the result."[27]

Sometime late in 1913 or early in 1914 operations on the new road were commenced. Its line featured fifty-pound and sixty-five-pound Bessemer relay rail and was built on sandy soil through gently rolling plains. Facilities and equipment were modest in the extreme. The company's most impressive structure was its frame combination station at Matador. Other structures there included a cotton platform, toolhouse, windmill (10 feet in diameter on a 30-foot tower), water tank, coal dock, engine house, and stock pens. At Matador Junction, the Motley County Railway and the QA&P jointly owned a frame combination depot fronted by a cinder platform. The road's motive power took the form of number 103, an eighty-two-ton 4-6-0 that Baldwin had outshopped in 1894. The rolling stock roster consisted of three 60,000-capacity wooden boxcars and a fifty-foot wooden "Jim Crow" combine.[28]

The Motley County Railway was in operation. But its affairs went badly. Decker's fears were realized when the Motley County firm was unable to pay its bills. On February 24, 1914, the QA&P's general manager reported to Sommer that he "had been handling this matter personally with these people for the past two or three weeks, and I find they have no money to pay." Consequently, he had refused to deliver inbound cars until the debts were satisfied. By the end of the year several contracts would be drawn to work out these and other difficulties. One, in which the QA&P demanded a bond from Motley County road with seven of its stockholders acting as sureties, proved particularly bitter for the smaller company. Another spelled out revenue divisions on traffic handled jointly— 75 percent for the QA&P and 25 percent for the Motley. A per diem rate of forty-five cents on cars in possession of the Motley County road was also provided for.[29]

The new railroad eventually developed a modest freight and passenger volume. The Matador Land & Cattle Company, for instance, used the little road for the movement of its cattle and also to receive feed. Numerous other local shippers used the company for additional carload lots. Less-than-carload business was good. Much of it was consigned to local merchants in Matador, but a significant portion was destined for Quitaque, Flomot, and other communities to the north and northwest of Matador. This freight, of course, moved by wagon beyond the railhead. The volume of business taxed the talents and patience of the agent and his single helper at Matador.

In addition to their usual railroad duties, these two men were responsible for handling the large volume of express traffic generated on behalf of the Wells Fargo Company. They were pleased that the Motley County Railway did not have a contract with Western Union, and thus they were not burdened with telegraph traffic. Nevertheless, their other duties were so numerous and the pay was so low that the company had a constant labor turnover there and in all other departments as well. The road was thus a haven for boomers—transient railroaders. Informality was the rule. For instance, Motley County engine crews were also responsible for the maintenance of the road's motive power.[30]

The volume of traffic grew during 1916 and 1917. For example, from July 1916 through March 1917, a total of 925 cars were interchanged, an average of 115.6 per month.[31]

Exchanging cars at Matador Junction was a persistent problem, which came to a head in 1917. Because the connecting track at the junction held just twelve cars, and because in peak loading seasons the Motley County was required to take empties and loads back to Motley where they could be switched, the little road asked the QA&P to construct additional trackage. The QA&P's position, enunciated by Charles Sommer, was that the Motley County was attempting to force the construction of another track, which, in effect, would complete a wye at Matador Junction. This, then, would be used— free, Sommer groused—by the Motley County to turn its locomotives.[32]

Finally, an agreement was forged that allowed the Motley County Railway to use QA&P tracks be-

tween Matador Junction and Roaring Springs as well as QA&P's yard, wye, stock pens, and station forces at Roaring Springs. The Motley County was also given permission to use locomotive water free of charge at Roaring Springs and to purchase tank car loads of water at very low rates for locomotive use at Matador. For all this Motley County paid just one dollar a month. Moreover, the new agreement provided for the interchange of cars at both Matador Junction and Roaring Springs so no new construction was necessary at the junction. It seemed a equitable and advantageous agreement for both parties. The new plan took effect on October 1, 1917.[33]

By 1918, stock control of the Motley County Railway was spread among ninety shareholders with most holding between one and five shares each. A. B. Echols, the president, held the most—ninety shares. Other large shareholders were R. P. Moore, sixty-one and a half shares, and Carrie McKenzie, fifty-five shares. By 1918 the road had cumulative assets of $118,422.26. Between January 1 and August 31, 1918, its income totaled $22,682.99, but after deducting operating expenses and divisions it had a net loss of $572.79. This financial situation was, regretfully for the Motley County road, typical. The future looked uncertain at best.[34]

## CHAPTER 5

## No-Nonsense Service

> What a relief when we could go on long trips by train. Our clothes were carefully folded and packed in the valise or grip. The baby's clothes were packed in the satchel. If we had more than these would hold, we put them in a pasteboard box and tied it with a stout string. There was always a shoe box or two filled with biscuits, fried chicken, ham, pickles and cake except a corner which held the collapsible aluminum drinking cup. Sometimes we carried a pillow across our arm, but usually we rented a pillow. The poor and middle class never thought of taking a Pullman or eating in a diner. It was extravagant enough to buy coffee from the train Butch.—Blanche Scott Rutherford, *One Corner of Heaven*

SAM Lazarus and the tiny officer corps of the Quanah, Acme & Pacific had more to do than contemplate strategy and long-term objectives. There were trains to run, schedules to keep, repairs to be made, and equipment to be acquired and maintained. All of it was routine business in running a railroad.

The motive power roster of the QA&P was spare. The Quanah Route had inherited elderly number 7, a 4-4-0, and the equally antiquated number 11, from the Acme, Red River & Northern. Extant records do not divulge the disposition of these old mills. Mystery also surrounds number 17, a 4-6-0 built by Baldwin in 1889 and acquired by the QA&P from the Southern Iron & Equipment Company in 1912; it was still on the property in 1918. The QA&P's first new locomotive was number 23, a 4-6-0 delivered by Baldwin in June 1909. During the summer of that same year number 7 served as a switch engine, number 11 was in the FW&DC shops at Childress for repair, number 17 was leased to the contractor building the line to Paducah, and the new locomotive was assigned to road work.[1]

As the QA&P expanded and its business increased, the company was forced to acquire more motive power. In May 1910, numbers 25 and 27, both 4-6-0s but slightly larger than number 23, arrived from Baldwin's Eddystone plant. These were joined by an 0-6-0, number 31, in March 1912 and

Number 7, the 4-4-0 that the QA&P inherited from the ARR&N

by number 101, a 2-8-0, in August 1915. By late 1913, both 7 and 11 had disappeared from the roster and by 1921 so had 17. The remaining locomotives, acquired new and originally fired with coal, were converted to oil after World War I.[2]

Extension of the line and the resulting growth of traffic also put stress on the company's tiny car fleet. Yet the QA&P's management tried to get along with

Number 23, the QA&P's first new locomotive

the equipment acquired earlier from the ARR&N and by using cars owned by foreign roads upon which it paid the usual per diem charges. Then, on May 11, 1915, the firm's board of directors authorized acquisition of twenty-five new forty-ton boxcars. The roster, nevertheless, remained modest. In 1918, the inventory included thirty-eight boxcars, five gondolas, seven flatcars, and three cabooses.[3]

Much the same was true of passenger equipment. The only piece owned by the ARR&N had been a combination coach, labeled A-1. Late in 1909 the QA&P was pleased to add a smart new seventy-foot vestibuled coach—the A-2. Charles Sommer proudly advised the mechanical department that it would be equipped with "two bracket lamps and twenty-four cuspidors."[4]

The revenue that the QA&P management had expected from its passenger, mail, and express business did not materialize. Consequently, like other carriers, it sought to minimize expenses in offering such service by looking to motive power other than steam. On the Quanah Route this resulted in acquisition of a two-hundred-horsepower, eight-cylinder, center-entrance, gas-electric motor car. Designated A-3, it was built by General Electric Company and delivered to the QA&P during the fall of 1912. It cost $24,850. The manufacturer claimed that ninety-one persons (at three to a seat) could be accommodated in the twenty-eight-foot passenger compartment. If steam-powered trains had resulted in excess capacity, the gas-electric car apparently offered too little. In 1915, the railroad se-

cured a thirty-six-foot wooden combination car to complement the A-1 and A-2.[5]

The only piece of exotic equipment that ever graced the QA&P roster was a business car—the 6666. It was owned by S. Burke Burnett, an important Texas cattleman and member of the Quanah Route's board of directors, and was named for his famous Four Sixes Ranch. Burnett leased it to the railroad in 1917 for an annual fee of $630. The sixty-eight-foot 6666 boasted a steel underframe, composite body, and wood plating, and it rode on six-wheel trucks. Sam Lazarus used this ornate carriage for his periodic visits to Quanah and for the elaborate parties he staged for shippers and cronies in the time-honored style of railroad managers. The car was stored briefly during World War I but soon thereafter, when Burnett died, it was purchased from the estate for $11,120.66. It was eventually steel-plated, fitted with new electric lighting equipment, and converted to steam heat.[6]

The passenger train service operated by the QA&P in the early years might be anticipated by the no-nonsense nature of the equipment inventory. Early in 1910 the road offered a daily passenger turn between Quanah and Paducah as well as a daily-except-Sunday mixed train turn between Acme and Quanah. This pattern soon changed, but only modestly, to make the Quanah-Paducah train a mixed. Full passenger service was reestablished in 1913 and was rendered, except in special instances, by the A-3, which made a daily trip in each direction between Quanah and Roaring Springs, leaving

Additional new power arrived in the form of locomotives 25, 27, 31, and 101. *C. C. Roberts collection*

early in the morning as train 51, turning at Roaring Springs about noon, and arriving back in Quanah as train 52 between 4:00 and 5:00 P.M. This pattern persisted from late 1913 until the end of World War I. During these years, the QA&P advertised connections for Fort Worth via the FW&DC and for Oklahoma City via the Frisco—both at Quanah—and for Floydada, Matador, and Dickens via

"Auto Line"—at Roaring Springs. Business was modest. The total number of passengers carried in 1910 was 15,273; in 1916 it rose to 70,148.[7]

The SL&SF, meanwhile, had begun operation of two daily passenger trains over its line from St. Louis to Quanah. One of these sets offered no more than local service but the other, the *Meteor*, featured "Reclining Chair and Day Coach" equipment on a

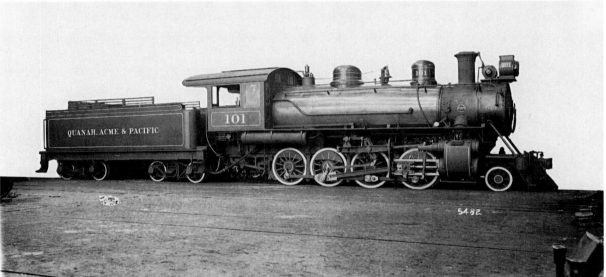

faster schedule. These trains, of course, used what had become QA&P trackage between Red River and Quanah, and it was up to the Quanah Route to advertise the service locally. President Lazarus was understandably proud when the QA&P and the SL&SF were able to procure through Pullman service between Quanah and St. Louis effective December 6, 1915. Local support, however, was slack.

Only thirty-four patrons boarded at Quanah during December, and only three of them purchased passage all the way to St. Louis. The total revenue amounted to $75, obviously inadequate to sustain the operation. Lazarus admitted defeat, and the car was removed early in 1916.[8]

QA&P passenger service remained distinctly local in character—with one exception. The road's

In 1914, the A-3 provided daily passenger service between Quanah and Roaring Springs. *B. H. Stone collection*

passenger trains in 1913 and 1914 carried a "News Agent," who, under contract with the railroad, agreed to purvey "magazines, books, newspapers, periodicals, fruit, candies, cigars, and such other goods and wares as are usually handled by Agents on trains." For this right the "news butch" paid the railroad $20 per month. Such cosmopolitan service, however, could not last; it ended before World War I.[9]

Not elegant but certainly utilitarian were the express and mail services offered as a part of QA&P passenger operations. Effective February 7, 1910, the railroad began to haul the federal mails at an annual rate of $1,667.67. No sorting was done en route; closed pouches were handled to and from Quanah, Acme, Lazare, and Paducah. The Post Office Department authorized an extension of this closed pouch service to Roaring Springs on October 1, 1913. A contract was similarly made on February 20, 1910, between the railroad and the United States Express Company. This agreement was in force until July 1, 1914, when Wells Fargo & Company assumed the rights to express business on the Quanah Route.[10]

Passenger revenues for the QA&P were never as important as revenues derived from freight traffic, yet for the patrons of its service area passenger trains were easily as important as freight. In December 1909, John B. Tannahill, a young foreman on the 7L Ranch, brought his new bride and her Adam-Schaaf piano to Swearingen aboard the cars of the QA&P. Farther west, at Narcisso, the schoolteacher flagged the train every Friday afternoon and rode it to Paducah, returning in the same fashion on Sunday. Not only did trains provide passenger service, they were also devices of communica-

# PULLMAN CAR SERVICE
## QUANAH, OKLAHOMA CITY and ST. LOUIS

TO THE PUBLIC:

Quanah, Tex., Dec. 5, 1915.

This Company now operates under trackage arrangements that part of the Frisco of Texas Lines extending from Red River, Texas, to Quanah, Texas, and arrangements have been made, effective December 6th, for the inauguration of through Pullman car service between Quanah and St. Louis, via Oklahoma City, without change, on the following schedule:

Leave Quanah—3:20 a. m.
   (Sleeping car ready for occupancy each night at 10 o'clock.
Arrive Oklahoma City—12:15 p. m.
Arrive St. Louis—8:15 a. m.
Return Schedule as follows:
Leave St. Louis—2:15 p. m.
Arrive Oklahoma City—7:40 a. m.
Leave Oklahoma City—9:00 a. m.
Arrive Quanah—5:40 p. m.
   Passengers using sleeping car may retire at Quanah any time after 10 o'clock p. m.
Charges for berth fares are as follows:
Quanah to Oklahoma City—$2.00
Quanah to St. Louis—$4.50
St. Louis to Oklahoma City—$3.25.
St. Louis to Quanah—$4.50

This service offers a short and comfortable route to all points East, including St. Louis, Kansas City, Chicago and New York, and we will appreciate your giving this route a trial when you next plan a trip East.

The saving in distance via this route as compared via Fort Worth is approximately 200 miles.

Let us suggest in routing your freight the next time that you designate Frisco Lines care Q. A. & P. via Quanah, and we promise you prompt and satisfactory service via this short route.

ROBT. CRAY,
General Manager.

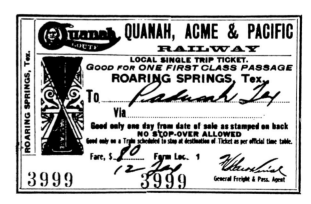

tion. They brought the mail—letters, packages, and newspapers. The *Fort Worth Star-Telegram*, for instance, became immensely popular along the line after its next-day delivery was assured by the institution of passenger service.[11]

Excursions were still another facet of the road's passenger service. The earliest of these were sponsored by the company in 1910 to afford Quanah residents a chance to see the newly constructed line. Lazarus, too, provided his own style of excursions. He told an old friend in 1910 that he was "going to run a special train and nobody but men that have been in the country at least twenty-five years can ride. They can ride at my expense, have a little blowout and come back." Old-timers later recalled the Lazarus excursions with a deep sense of mischievous satisfaction.[12]

The road similarly promoted excursions in conjunction with traveling circuses, such as the one that played in Quanah in 1914, and on behalf of the famous Dallas Fair. In 1913, the QA&P ran a special train from Roaring Springs to Quanah and then turned over the cars to the FW&DC for forwarding to the Dallas extravaganza. Fares were reasonable: round-trip from Roaring Springs, $7.50; from Paducah, $6.00; and from Swearingen, $5.50. Special sleeping cars were provided for those who wanted to go first class.[13]

The cars were also used for less auspicious purposes. In 1912, S. Burke Burnett rode the train to Paducah and to a bizarre incident there that resulted in the murder of one Farley Sayers and Burnett's trial for it. He was acquitted, much to the joy of his many friends in the area, and returned to his Fort Worth home aboard the same cars.[14]

Violence touched the railroad in the form of war. During 1917 and 1918 several local men went off to fight the Kaiser by way of the QA&P. There was the usual hoopla at departure time, but there was also somber reflection on the part of some such as Douglas Meador, a newspaperman. "When I think of war," Meador wrote, "I think of a mother screaming. A shabby railway coach and awkward youths, of various heights lined up to face the bitterest hour. There was no splendor in the martial music that could drain away the terror of that departure."[15]

Although extension of QA&P operations to Mac-Bain changed the road's freight traffic mix, it was still heavily dependent on the good fortunes of the cement plaster plants at Acme. In 1909, this traffic accounted for 87,860 tons or 87.5 percent of the total volume. As late as 1916 the Acme plants contributed 83,526 tons and 37.6 percent of traffic volume. This freight usually moved on a regular basis; June was a typical month. Between 1913 and 1917, inclusive, and annual average of 287 cars left the Acme facilities during that month. The overall pattern was gradually altered, however. By 1918, farm products—wheat and cotton in particular—yielded

26.3 percent of the Quanah Route's freight business, and livestock contributed another 10 percent. Total tons carried jumped from 169,204 in 1910 to 210,477 in 1916.[16]

Freight train miles rose in similar fashion. After the QA&P began offering separate passenger train service in 1913, mixed train miles dropped and freight train miles soared. It was, in a sense, a verbal sleight of hand since all QA&P freight trains carried passengers. Yet with the A-3 performing routine passenger duties, freight train passengers were handled only in the caboose. Between 1913 and World War I service was unchanged—one daily-except-Sunday freight in each direction between Quanah and Roaring Springs and one daily-except-Sunday turn between Quanah and Acme. Extras, except for livestock traffic, were rare.[17]

An interesting if strangely complex aspect of the QA&P's history in this period surrounds the nature and operation of the Acme Tap Railroad. In later years the FW&DC would declare that in 1899 it had constructed this line as a spur from its main line at Acme to the newly built facilities of the Salina Plaster Company, about one and one-half miles to the north. This was not true. In fact, the Denver Road had been willing to build its own spur to the Salina plant, but such a line had to pass through lands owned by the rival Acme Cement Plaster Company, which refused to sell or lease a right-of-way to the FW&DC. The Denver Road did not wish to offend the Acme Company, and matters were at a standstill until January 7, 1899, when the Salina Plaster Company received a charter for and then built the Acme Tap Railway. It hesitated not at all to employ rights of condemnation; the spur was quickly in service under operation of the FW&DC.[18]

Soon thereafter, the Acme Cement Plaster Company, the firm in which Sam Lazarus had such an important stake, looked for expanded transportation opportunities and found them in the form of the Acme, Red River & Northern Railway. That new concern, in many ways a corporate puppet of the Acme Plaster firm, was assigned the normal internal duties at the Acme mill. Moreover, the ARR&N soon gained trackage rights over the FW&DC between Acme and Quanah, where a connection was made with the newly constructed line of the Frisco. All of this was at the expense of the Denver Road, which previously had performed these services. The upshot was that costs for serving the Acme and Salina mills were increased for the FW&DC, which, with the consent of the Salina company, leased the Acme Tap to the ARR&N for a ten-year period beginning in 1903. The ARR&N and its successor, the QA&P, was obliged to pay $1,000 per annum in return.[19]

This arrangement worked well until late in 1913, when the ten-year lease on the Acme Tap came up for renewal. Dissension followed. The Salina firm had passed by this time to the American Cement Plaster Company, which was bypassed in the renegotiation process. Moreover, American objected to the QA&P's desire to designate the old Salina plant site as Clay-Bank; in the past all billing, whether from the Acme plant or the Salina mill, had been from Acme. The assumption at American was that the Acme billing designation would assist it, the lesser-known firm, in competition with Acme Plaster. There were still other problems. A price war was raging in the plaster industry, and American's management believed that Acme gained an advantage—as a consequence of the close association through Lazarus between the QA&P and Acme Plaster—regarding the names of customers that appeared as routine waybill information on traffic moving from the American plant. In an attempt to defuse the issue, the QA&P suggested, and the Texas Railroad Commission concurred, that the American plant location be labeled Agatite—the trade name used by American—instead of Clay-Bank. The Quanah Route also promised the American plant "on call" switching to be performed by an engine and crew stationed at Acme. The quality of service, however, was not at issue. The American firm simply did not want its traffic billed by the QA&P.[20]

The Fort Worth & Denver City Railway was caught in the middle. It did not wish to alienate the Acme Plaster Company and risk the loss of traffic from that source. Neither did it wish to perform expensive local switching at Agatite. Nevertheless, the FW&DC felt compelled to ask for a termination of the Acme Tap lease arrangement and did so on December 10, 1913. Lazarus contended that his objective had "been to try and give the two plants the best service for as low cost as possible." It mattered little. The American company had every right to pressure the Denver Road, and the FW&DC had every right under the contract to ask for its cancellation. On February 1, 1914, the QA&P surrendered its rights to operation of the Acme Tap and service to the American mill. One day earlier the Acme Tap had leased in perpetuity its entire property to the FW&DC. This contention cost the QA&P goodwill and, more important, a sizable chunk of traffic that had previously moved from the American mill to Quanah and interchange with the FW&DC or the Frisco. Little would be heard about the Acme Tap for fifteen years; then it would be involved in still another problem for the QA&P.[21]

These transactions reflected generally unsettled conditions. The Quanah Route paid dividends in 1912 and 1913, but neither revenues nor earnings increased as rapidly as Lazarus had hoped. In 1910, the road had revenues of $164,430 and a profit of $42,146. By 1916, the QA&P had revenues of $232,007 but earned only $377. Passenger income during those years increased by over 400 percent, but freight revenues climbed by only 65 percent. Expenses, meanwhile, more than doubled. What did the future hold for the QA&P? Lazarus could not predict.[22]

## CHAPTER 6

# The United States Railroad Administration and After

> They have made much sport of our privately owned
> railroad the Motley County Railway and it has not
> been much to behold or admire, but all must admit
> that it was and has been the salvation of Matador
> and the public spirit shown and sacrifices made by
> those who have kept it going should be a source of
> gratitude on the part of our people for time ever-
> lasting.—*Matador News*, undated, 1925

ON December 28, 1917, the government assumed operation of most of the nation's railroads, including the Quanah, Acme & Pacific. The country had been involved in World War I since April; during the intervening months a glut of traffic had rendered the carriers nearly incapable of facilitating military as well as normal transportation. President Woodrow Wilson thus determined that the railroads had to come under common direction.[1]

Congress subsequently passed and President Wilson signed into law the Railroad Control Act, which provided that the government would make annual compensation to the carriers on the basis of average net operating income for the three years ending June 30, 1917. It also promised adequate maintenance of property during the time of government operation. Final control rested in Washington under the rule of William G. McAdoo, who was appointed director general of the railroads. Regional federal directors oversaw general operations and local federal managers handled on-the-job responsibilities. J. S. Pyeatt was assigned to the QA&P.[2]

The United States Railroad Administration imposed tight controls. Routing and distribution of freight was one of its prime concerns. Government managers implemented plans for the joint use of terminals, repair shops, and other railroad facilities. It is unclear how these controls affected the Quanah Route; there are few records from that period. It is clear, however, that cooperation between the QA&P and the FW&DC became closer. The local road may have used the Denver's station facilities, and it probably sent some of its repair work to the FW&DC's shops at Childress.

The results of government control were mixed. It was successful in managing operations but not from a financial standpoint. Nevertheless, even after the armistice, Wilson pledged to resolve the "railroad problem." William McAdoo advocated a five-year continuation of federal control, but a proposal emanating from railroad labor (the Plumb Plan) urged the government to purchase and operate the nation's rail lines. Congress accepted neither idea. Instead, it passed the Esch-Cummins or Transportation Act of 1920, which returned the railroads to private management but at the same time greatly strengthened the Interstate Commerce Commission. And it directed the ICC to investigate the possibility of consolidating the country's railroads into a few large systems. During 1922 and 1923 the regulatory agency held hearings, and in 1929 it recommended creation of twenty-one major systems. Ironically, the QA&P was included in the Rock Island–Frisco System, where, in a sense, it had been during the Yoakum years. Nothing came of these recommendations; one can only ponder what might have been. The QA&P was returned to its owners on October 7, 1921.[3]

Reaction to government operation and financial settlement was nearly uniform among railroad managers, who believed that the government should not have become involved, that it had abused and undermaintained physical properties during its administration, and that it was parsimonious in the financial settlements it made with the carriers. Railroad management saw other problems stemming from government control, including the twin legacies of "inadequate rates" and "unnecessarily high wages." The government had granted a few tariff increases during its period of control, but it had allowed wages to rise much faster. In 1920 workers had been granted a 22 percent increase in wages, but the carriers were not allowed to raise their rates accordingly. Moreover, traffic decreased immensely during the postwar slump. The stage was set for strife; it was not long in coming.[4]

The carriers, again in the hands of their owners, initiated immediate cuts. During 1921 employment was trimmed by 15 percent and wages by about 12 percent. Management pointed out that railroad wages in 1920 had been fully one-third higher than those in manufacturing.[5]

The circumstance of the QA&P was a microcosm of the larger scene. Between 1918 and 1920, hourly wages for locomotive engineers and conductors in freight service went from 56 cents to 91 cents and 54 1/2 cents to 80 1/2 cents, respectively. But the major question on the Quanah Route, as in the industry generally, was rates of pay for mechanical department employees. As early as December 14, 1920, Charles Sommer had asserted that these wages were "entirely out of reason," and he recommended reversion to rates in effect before the 1920 increases. Two days later he urged a one-third cut in shop forces. The matter was urgent, said Sommer; revenues were inadequate to meet expenses. Moreover, the cost of living had gone down in recent months, and it did "not appear any longer necessary to maintain the high rate of pay." Finally, Sommer "wished to weed out those who will not work" and get "$1.00 worth of work for a $1.00 worth of pay." Cuts followed. Effective January 10, 1921, mechanical forces were reduced from thirty-one to nineteen, and those who remained saw their wages reduced by up to 30 percent a few months later. In October the nation's carriers announced their intention to make even further reductions in wages for all employees—10 percent for the operating crafts and down to the "going wages paid for similar work in other industries in the same communities" for all others. The shopmen responded by striking on July 1, 1922. Their fellows at Quanah followed.[6]

Before the strike, Charles Sommer had viewed the issue with considerable detachment: "No one deplores more than I do the necessity of retrenchment, or cutting down our rates of pay—but the other side of it involves the provision of sufficient money to keep the men employed and meet our taxes and interest, something that you cannot do with excuses. Interest and taxes require real money, and we have an obligation to perform in trying to

meet these payments by economizing and carefully supervising the operation of the property." But the strike upset Sommer's sense of balance. Always a paternalist, Sommer felt that QA&P employees had been duped or given "bad advice" by labor leaders. He argued that the men had gone on strike against the government and not against the railroads. Yet he was confronted with the reality that shopmen in Quanah *were* on strike against the QA&P. He ordered his brother A. F. Sommer, the road's senior operating officer, to importune them to return to their jobs but, failing that, to hire scabs. Former employees, if rehired at all, were to forfeit their seniority and "again start at the bottom."[7]

Meanwhile, the railroad operated on an abbreviated schedule as best it could. Bitterness was everywhere. Not all employees were sympathetic with the strikers, even though all employees had been subject to reduced wages, and the Quanah newspaper reflected the prevailing antiunion sentiments of that time and place. Tension was heightened when strikers attempted to intimidate certain of their peers and violence against company property was threatened. The local sheriff wired the Texas governor late in July asking for twenty-five men to guard the railroad's pumping station and roundhouse. At the same time, the company sought what it referred to as a compromise; in reality it was a "take-it-or-leave-it" offer. When the general walkout ended in September, *Railway Age,* the trade publication, stated baldly: "The shop employees' strike has been a victory for the railways." QA&P management was now free to negotiate with the shopmen and did so on an independent basis rather than as a part of industrywide standards, procedures, and agreements. The Quanah Route imposed its new wage scale—essentially the same one it had offered in July. Charles Sommers was adamant: "We have not made a settlement with our men; *they have made a settlement with us.*"[8]

𝔐otley 𝔠ounty 𝔯ailway 𝔠ompany

## 1925                                    No. 213

PASS --Mr. A.S. Dolan, car

      & employees

ACCOUNT Traffic Manager--C.A.& S.

UNTIL DECEMBER 31ST UNLESS OTHERWISE ORDERED
AND SUBJECT TO CONDITIONS ON BACK

VICE PRESIDENT

Meanwhile, the Motley County Railway continued to limp along, offering its tiny service area a daily-except-Sunday turn which left Matador at 11:30 A.M., met the westbound QA&P train from Quanah at Matador Junction, and returned to its point of origin at 1:00 P.M.—if all went well. Business demanded additional service only during the usual fall rush. Perhaps the 1920s would bring a greater volume. As 1919 ended, Charles Sommer said to the Motley County's general manager: "I hope conditions on your line are picking up, and that the coming year will be the most prosperous one you ever had."[9]

It was a misplaced hope. So, too, was any thought that relations between the two lines would improve. A crisis was at hand by 1921. The Motley County Railway complained to the Railroad Commission of Texas that it was not receiving just or adequate divisions on intrastate traffic. Charles Sommer was both embarrassed and deeply angered by the complaint. He told the QA&P's general attorney: "We have tried in every conceivable way to satisfy them of our sincere intentions to deal honestly with them, but I am unable to determine whether it is ignorance or stubbornness that" is the root of "this eternal wrangling." "Unfortunately," Sommer continued, "they [the Motley County Railway] have had no one in their employ who had had sufficient knowledge of railroading to conduct their business properly, and it has been up to us to always make their records and try to explain something about which they know very little." This view was confirmed by G. E. Hamilton, an attorney in the employ of the QA&P at Matador: "The entire board of directors are fully occupied with their own affairs and give little attention to the railroad; he [Motley's general manager] is the whole thing, and whatever he tells them, they think it is the *sine qua non*." Sommer was not forgiving. "It behooves the Motley County Railway not to harass or annoy

their connections by the employment of someone wholly ignorant or incapable of handling their business." The immediate problem passed when the regulatory agency ruled that division on intrastate rates would be maintained—25 percent for the Motley County road.[10]

More serious problems lay ahead. During the summer of 1924, the Motley County Railway was suspended from membership in the American Railway Association because of its "failure to meet per diem obligations." The QA&P, Motley's only connection, quickly moved to terminate the interchange of cars at Matador Junction. The smaller line's very existence was threatened. Sommer told Motley's president, A. B. Echols, that the QA&P would not "assume the responsibility of foreign equipment and maintain our obligations to return this foreign equipment to either one of our connections without some form of protection, either your membership in the American Railway Association or an indemnity bond." This crisis passed when the Motley County Railway settled its accounts and was readmitted to the American Railway Association.[11]

A brief period of guarded confidence followed. One Motley County official told Charles Sommer that he had done much to solicit new business in the area northwest of Matador. Surely, he felt, "we [the Motley County Railway] will secure considerable business there that we have never before received." Moreover, he believed that his road and the QA&P might arrange for a "package car out of Quanah" to serve "the grocery dealers in Matador," who currently secured "practically all of their goods from Floydada by truck." It was fleeting optimism and did not reflect long-standing realities. Directors of the local road felt, rightly or wrongly, that the larger company wanted to put their operation out of business. Not surprisingly, they interpreted any problems in the normal routine as "premeditated and done to annoy and irritate them." Charles Sommer correctly perceived that this attitude dated from the QA&P's decision to build its line south of Matador through the new townsite of Roaring Springs. Sommer also rightly understood that many of the small road's problems were created by its own board of directors, each member of which held different notions about the management and operation of the line. Consequently, the hired manager was, as A. F. Sommer put it, "in hot water at all times." One man who went through Motley's "revolving door for managers" confirmed this view. He categorized one of the directors, who also served nominally as an official of the company, as "an ignorant, pigheaded, old farmer—unfitted in any way to handle a railroad property." His caustic assessment was probably accurate.[12]

The inevitable happened soon enough. On July 7, 1925, Claude Warren, sheriff of Motley County, mounted the steps of the courthouse in Matador and proceeded to sell the assets of the bankrupt Motley County Railway. Included in the sale were its entire line, right-of-way, rolling stock, and miscellaneous properties. There was only one serious bidder—the QA&P. Indeed, as early as April 9, Motley's board had agreed to sell all assets to the Quanah Route, provided that the purchaser would pledge to continue operations to Matador and to undertake immediately a program of upgrading the line. The purchase price, $23,000, represented Motley's "present indebtedness."[13]

The transaction looked simple, but in reality it was quite complex. Several problems prevented the immediate integration of the old Motley company into the QA&P. The Interstate Commerce Commission, for instance, required its own approval of all such sales. Yet before this permission could be granted, the Texas Railroad Commission had to give its blessing, which was impossible without a special act of the Texas legislature because the consolidation of one Texas railroad with competing lines or "foreign" companies was specifically forbidden by the state's constitution. All would be accomplished in time; meanwhile, G. E. Hamilton acted as trustee. Operations under his direction were much as they had been previously.[14]

Early in 1926, Charles Sommer urged that the QA&P "incorporate the old Motley County line as the Matador Northern Railroad." That plan was soon scrapped, however, and a move for simple consolidation was begun. The fortieth legislature of Texas ratified sale of the Motley property to the QA&P on January 22, 1927; the QA&P board and the trustee concurred one month later; and, the ICC gave its permission on April 13. The Motley County Railway passed to history when, on July 1, 1927, the consolidation took effect.[15]

Despite the long antipathy toward the QA&P at Matador, the impact of the consolidation was distinctly favorable for that community. G. E. Hamilton told A. F. Sommer that it was "remarkable how much building and permanent improvement is going forward recently, mainly," he thought, "on the feeling that the prospect of the QA&P coming here had given a permanent aspect to the town." This optimism was also reflected in the activity of the Matador Chamber of Commerce. It had supported consolidation because it feared "serious consequences, probably the final abandonment of this small branch" operation, if the ICC failed to rule favorably.[16]

QA&P headquarters was also a scene of optimism. Already there were trackside leases at Matador for bulk oil and gas facilities owned by the Gulf, Pierce, and Magnolia companies; seedhouses owned by the Quanah Cotton Oil Company and Childress Cotton Oil Company; a coal bin held by L. B. Archers; a feed storage warehouse used by the Matador Land & Cattle Company; and, of course, the usual stock pens and chutes. Other firms, such as the Marland Refining Company, soon sought additional leases. Furthermore, the QA&P had in the deal acquired no fewer than 307 lots in Matador, which earlier had been given to the Matador County Railway as bonuses in support of construction, but because Matador had not grown as expected, they were still on the books of the old company. Now, with the combined assurance of continued rail service to Matador and the general optimism of the time, they would surely appreciate in value and, as they were sold, bring a tidy supplemental revenue to the Quanah Route.[17]

The QA&P also acquired Motley's two decrepit locomotives—number 19, a 4-6-0 constructed by an unknown manufacturer and valued at $5,000, and number 103, another 4-6-0 outshopped by Baldwin in 1894 and valued at $4,422—as well as a combination (passenger and baggage) car, two boxcars—one of which had been shorn of its trucks and shoved off the track at Matador and the other which served as the depot at Matador Junction—and a "combination Ford truck with truck body and freight trailer" used to haul mail, express, less-than-carload freight, and passengers. The Motley County Railway had undertaken its business with this bizarre if meager roster of equipment. The same roster had sufficed for the trustee between the summer of 1925 and July 1927, when the QA&P took over.[18]

With this equipment the old management and then the trustee had overseen the movement of 22,931 tons of freight in 1925. Traffic dropped to 21,154 tons in 1926 and to only 9,060 tons in 1927. During the latter year the Ford truck ran 1,656 miles, making a trip to Matador Junction about four times per week. Carload business was spare; when offered, it was, of course, handled by a steam train. That raised a problem. When a steam train was called for, once or twice a week, it necessitated

The Motley County Railway's bizarre Ford truck ran between Matador and Matador Junction.

the use of the combination car, the condition of which was so bad that, according to A. F. Sommer, "words can't describe it." The trustee, who was also a practicing attorney, looked at the issue somewhat differently. He pointed out that the car had "no Jim Crow facilities at all." Consequently, he feared that the company would be "reported to the State Railroad Commission pretty soon" and that "rather heavy penalties could be recovered were some negro minister of a little more dignity than the ordinary to suffer humiliation and mental anguish at the hands of some outspoken band of whites who might all be riding together some day

on this coach." Charles Sommer thought the problem could be resolved by the acquisition of "a 40-foot steel car, with 10-foot space assigned for passengers" from the Brill Motor Car Company. Nothing came of the suggestion. A. F. Sommer recommended the use of a forty-foot baggage car into which could be put "a few seats, to take care of what passengers there may be." The problem was finally resolved by leasing a coach from the Frisco for use on the Matador line.[19]

Charles Sommer was pleased with the acquisition of the Motley County Railway. Early in 1927, he reported to J. M. Kurn, president of the Frisco, that when acquired, the property had been "in a deplorable, as well as unsafe condition." Subsequently, he noted, "we have renewed about 75% of the ties," rebuilt all of the bridges, erected a cotton platform at Matador, constructed an industry track at Matador as well as wyes at Matador and Matador Junction, and generally improved drainage conditions along the right-of-way. This work, he admitted, had cost $22,000, a tidy sum. Yet it had added to the value of the property, which had earlier been set by the ICC at $102,342; now it was about $125,000, "as against a purchase price of $23,000," Sommer clucked. Moreover, there had been a net income of $9,032.15 in 1926.[20]

## CHAPTER 7

# *Rumors and Skirmishes*

Actual experience for 20 years has shown the people that this section can withstand the droughts and make steady progress; capital is reaching out for investment here. Power houses have been established at Plainview and Lubbock which serves the entire country with electricty by high power lines; every little town is lighted by electricity, and the country has provided itself liberally with a water supply both in town and in the farming sections by wells and windmills, and gradually good farm houses and barns are replacing the early shacks.
—G. E. Hamilton to Sam Lazarus, October 2, 1924

EARLY in the twentieth century the Panhandle-Plains of Texas and New Mexico boasted a meager population but one that clearly understood the agricultural potential of the area. Those same hearty souls also understood that this potential would not reach fruition without adequate transportation, that is, railroad service. When they gained such service, immigration would increase, schools and churches would be built, business enterprises would spring up, transportation costs would fall, and, most important for current landowners, the value of property would appreciate. Neither was this lost on railroad managers. A great construction boom followed that combined the impulses of territorial imperialism on the part of several carriers with the equally powerful urges of commercial expansion and agricultural development by potential as well as established hamlets and villages throughout the vast expanse of the Panhandle-Plains.

The Atchison, Topeka & Santa Fe Railway had expanded its operations to fill the transporation void south of Amarillo during the first decade of the century. Initial construction took the line to Plainview, then a stub southeastward from Plainview to Floydada, and finally the road was completed from Plainview to Lubbock and Slaton. This vertical artery was connected on the north with what became the Santa Fe's main Chicago-California freight line and, in 1914, on the south with its Coleman Cutoff, a new route that linked the Texas Gulf Coast to the

main gut northwest of Lubbock on the Texas–New Mexico border.[1]

Meanwhile, dryland farming methods and the potential of irrigation lured hundreds to the Panhandle-Plains area. More and more land was placed on the market as ranches were broken up into farms. Counties served by the Santa Fe doubled their populations; those not so favored grew, though at about half that rate. Plainview and Lubbock dominated the area south of the Panhandle; neither had been listed in the census of 1900.[2]

The Panhandle-Plains area, it seemed, had come of age. One persistent problem remained, however. The region was still transportation poor. If that problem were rectified, promoters argued, unbridled prosperity would follow. "When this section is supplied with ample railroad facilities, its agricultural development will be the marvel of the age," wrote the secretary of Quanah's Chamber of Commerce. No longer was the rallying cry "give us railroads." Now it was "give us MORE railroads."[3]

The carriers, of course, were not disinterested. As the mood of the country became more and more confident, boomers, promoters, schemers, as well as legitimate and aspiring developers, clamored for expanded rail service throughout the South Plains of Texas. This spirit was reflected in plans of the Texas Panhandle & Gulf Railroad (TP&G or Panhandle Road). In one way or another, all of the area's established railroads would have to deal with

Area photographers were in great demand because they could document the region's prosperity. Here, an entire carload of chickens has been loaded on the AT&SF at Plainview to show the success of poultry production. *Milton Day Henderson Collection, Llano Estacado Museum*

the "threat" posed by the TP&G.

On July 20, 1923, a Chicagoan, Clement H. Powell, president of the Texas Panhandle & Gulf, placed before the Interstate Commerce Commission his company's application to create a new rail line between Fort Worth, Texas, and Tucumcari, New Mexico. Powell's proposal envisioned construction of trackage from Fort Worth to Perrin, 57 miles, then acquisition of or trackage right over the Gulf, Texas & Western Railroad from Perrin to Seymour, approximately 100 miles. From that place, Powell urged construction of 303 additional miles of road, on an angle to the northwest, through the established communities of Truscott, Paducah, Turkey, Quitaque, Silverton, Tulia, Nazareth, Dimmitt, and Friona (or Parmerton as an alternative), and through a generally unpopulated area of New Mexico to a connection with the Golden State Route of the Chicago, Rock Island & Pacific and El Paso & Southwestern at Tucumcari. To say that Powell stole the march on the established carriers appreciably understates the case.[4]

The QA&P immediately opposed the application. J. W. Kurn, the Frisco's president, blustered that if "any new construction is desired in that territory, it would only be necessary to extend the QA&P line to the Santa Fe at Lubbock or Floy-

dada." He affirmed "that such extension has been in contemplation for years but has been held up until the proper time to make it." Kurn, always blunt, understood the ramifications: if any other carrier occupied the region, "it would ruin the QA&P." Frisco's general solicitor quickly urged that all of the established companies "agree upon some line of action and for the preparation of the necessary evidence." Meanwhile, Lazarus ordered another hasty survey of the country between MacBain and Floydada.[5]

The ICC announced that hearings on the TP&G's proposal would be held at Fort Worth beginning November 27, 1923. Battle lines formed quickly. "Citizens of West Texas versus certain existing railroads" was the way one writer characterized the exciting contest. Another correctly observed that "the old railroad building wars cannot be waged under the new Federal Transportation Act [of 1920]; otherwise one would be in full progress in West Texas at this time." No such primitive conflict was permissible any longer, and all of the participants were unsure of themselves as they prepared for combat under new rules. The hearings were held at the capitol in Austin before all three Texas railroad commissioners. Actually, the Texas regulatory body was merely taking evidence at the request of the Interstate Commerce Commission. The record of this hearing, the two regulatory bodies agreed, would then be forwarded to Washington for a decision.[6]

There was predictable speculation as to why the established carriers had not already invaded the area. The forceful testimony of D. E. Jordan, president of the Paducah Chamber of Commerce, represented the feelings of many in the outlying areas: "I firmly believe that the Santa Fe and Fort Worth & Denver City railways are afraid to extend their lines toward one another for the reason that they are very jealous of this great territory, and if one should break the ice each would build a half dozen lines in this vast territory." He may have been right, at least in part. Railroad managers certainly were aware that overexpansion was counterproductive. There was also speculation as to why neither the Santa Fe nor the Rock Island had objected to this project; both had competing lines in the TP&G's proposed service area.[7]

If the Rock Island and Santa Fe were strangely quiet, other roads were exceedingly vocal, especially the Fort Worth & Denver City, which postured itself as the area's pioneer. It was true, of course, that the FW&DC had completed its "Gulf-to-Rockies" line back in 1888. Yet the road had done little thereafter to flesh out its greater service area with feeders. Even before the hearings at Fort Worth, the Denver Road had attempted to take the bloom from the TP&G's flower by implying that the Wichita Valley Lines, a FW&DC captive, would extend its operations "as the needs of its territory might justify or require" and that the Stamford & Northwestern Railroad, itself a captive of the Wichita Valley Lines, had long anticipated the extension of its road from Stamford to Spur into the South Plains territory. The FW&DC was trying to prove that it and its satellites were pioneers and, therefore, had prior claim to construction rights throughout the area.[8]

At the hearing, Hale Holden, president of the Chicago, Burlington & Quincy (Burlington, parent of the FW&DC), testified that the Stamford & Northwestern would be "extended into the Plains country, possibly to Plainview." Holden argued that the Panhandle Road would merely parallel his own FW&DC and, equally important, that it would also represent "an invasion of territory which under charter rights, the Stamford & Northwestern intends to serve and occupy." Holden said further that the "extension of the Spur line into the Plains territory should afford an increased volume of traf-

fic" to all of the Chicago, Burlington & Quincy's captives in Texas and thus "further strengthen each of these properties."[9]

Although each took pains to deny in public that they were in collusion, the FW&DC and the QA&P worked hand-in-glove to prevent construction of the Panhandle Road. Each was looking out for its own interests, and that required cooperation. Each was, at the same time, frantically examining surveyors' reports and considering its own construction options; they exchanged engineering profiles and other traditionally secret information.[10]

The position of the Quanah Route in the matter of the Texas Panhandle & Gulf's application was put forward by Charles Sommer. Just as emissaries of the Burlington and FW&DC had done, Sommer attempted to stake a prior claim to the South Plains for his company. After all, he pointed out, the Quanah Route, from its inception, had as its objective an airline path to El Paso, where connections with trunk lines "would forge a new and direct St. Louis–Pacific route." Why had the project not been completed? The reasons, Sommer asserted, were "financial conditions preceeding the war, the necessity during the war of bending every energy toward victory," and, more recently, the impossibility of interesting "anyone in providing funds for railroad construction work, regardless of the merit." Now, complained Sommer, the Texas, Panhandle & Gulf threatened not only to invade the QA&P's potential service area but also the Quanah Route's already established service territory. The TP&G, if built, would "deprive the Quanah Route of its thin revenue on traffic originating at Paducah." Indeed, said Sommer, "were it not for earnings derived from the tonnage of" plaster plants "at Acme, the Quanah Route would starve to death." Any loss of traffic, he implied, would be catastrophic to the QA&P. Moreover, the TP&G, in Sommer's opinion, would "find itself in no better condition, if constructed, than the Kansas City, Mexico & Orient" (KCM&O or Orient), a romantic-sounding but deficit-ridden regional carrier.[11]

The position of the Gulf, Texas & Western Railroad (GT&W) was confusing at best. Its president, Ben B. Cain, stated that if the Texas, Panhandle & Gulf did not take over his line he would extend it westward to Lubbock or Plainview, probably by way of Floydada, and eastward to Fort Worth and Dallas, accomplishing much of what the TP&G had proposed and what the FW&DC's Stamford & Northwestern contemplated. Sounding very much like others who had attempted to lay prior claims,

Cain asserted that "the Gulf, Texas & Western always planned to extend west," but that it had been prevented from doing so by "the war, financial depressions, and droughts." Cain was not categorically opposed to the TP&G's plan; he sought protective provisions whether the Panhandle Road was built or not. Beyond that, he seemed to be seeking a permanent home for his isolated little railroad.[12]

Hearings on the application of the Texas Panhandle & Gulf ended on December 6, 1923. It had been one of the most keenly contested cases heard in Texas although no citizen from the Plains country had appeared in opposition to the TP&G plan. As one writer put it, the question the ICC had to address was "not so much whether the present and prospective traffic was great enough to justify the building of additional mileage, but which of the rivals has the better claim to the opportunity." Promoters of the Panhandle Road had put forward a bold plan; several carriers had voiced objections to it, and the FW&DC, QA&P, and GT&W had contended that they had pioneered the area and thus should be allowed to drive their own lines west. Yet none had offered definitive statements or timetables for construction. Nor had any formally applied for permission to engage in construction. Officially, it was a matter of waiting for a decision from Washington; unofficially, it was a time for planning and promotion by all contestants.[13]

The West Texas railroad question generated much heat but little light during 1924. Rumors were rife. One report suggested that the FW&DC was about to build three lines: from Spur to Childress via Dickens, Matador, and Turkey with a branch to Plainview; from Childress to Wheeler; and from Claude to Panhandle. During the summer, F. E. Clarity, vice-president of the FW&DC, announced that construction of a new line by his company from Fort Worth to Plainview was "probable in the near future." A direct line of 340 miles was contemplated—178 miles of construction from Fort Worth to Stamford, use of FW&DC's Stamford & Northwestern from Stamford to Spur, and additional new construction of 76 miles from Spur to Plainview. Another representative of the FW&DC implied, however, that the Denver Road was more interested in opening the area northeast of Plainview: "My investigation of this territory has made me enthusiastic and I believe that a line into Quitaque country would be a very good thing." The FW&DC was probably engaging in the traditional business of leaking rumors hoping to stir up interest in a wide area to procure the best offer. In any

event, it was clear that the Denver Road was going to build somewhere, sometime.[14]

Officials of the QA&P were studying their maps and ledger books. The Denver Road would be extending its service area; for the QA&P the issue was a matter of expanding or expiring. There were problems, though, and time was of essence. John P. Marrs, the QA&P's general attorney, worried that "if the FW&DC does build into Plainview from Spur, it might ruin prospects for going into that vicinity." Both Sam Lazarus and Charles Sommer understood that, but they were unable to secure firm support for expansion from J. W. Kurn, president of the Frisco. Sommer, ostensibly in charge of the project, did what he could to keep options open. The survey he ordered earlier was made from MacBain to a location about four and one-half miles south of Floydada. From that point, Sommer explained, it was "possible to extend the line practically on a tangent to Lubbock, Hale Center, or Abernathy," all points on the Canyon-Lubbock line of the Santa Fe. Floydada was another option. Numerous letters had been received from leading citizens there, but no firm offer had been forthcoming. Sommer's analysis bordered on sarcasm: "We need moral support . . . but it is my experience that it is not sufficient to build a railroad." Eventually, Frisco's President Kurn asked for mileage comparisons and analysis of traffic potential on an extension to Floydada.[15]

Floydada, however, was not the QA&P's first choice in 1924. Sommer had divulged the Quanah Route's short-range as well as its long-term goals to an official of the Burlington Route late in 1923: "We have always considered that an extension westward would have as an objective a main line point on the Santa Fe, preferably Lubbock, and then on in the direction of El Paso." Aside from El Paso itself, Lubbock was Sommer's choice. Its rapid growth continued unabated. John Marrs reported that "in order to get a room, even one in a private family home, it is necessary to wire a day or two ahead since the hotels cannot begin to accommodate the people." Moreover, Lubbockites yearned for additional rail service and, as Sommer said, were "very anxious, in case we extend, to have us come there."[16]

There were also opportunities beyond Lubbock. A. E. Harp, an official of Cotton Lands Company in Dallas, told Sommer that he wanted "to build 31 miles of railroad from Lubbock [westward] toward Levelland" and asked if the QA&P would "be interested in taking this over on some reasonable basis." Sommer responded uncharacteristically with a short, sharp letter: "We find ourselves simply sitting still, and unable to move forward. It is indeed a bold man who will predict the future of the railroads, and unless they are let alone, and enabled to live, unhampered by politicians and demagogues, there is only one end awaiting them—namely, disaster." Harp was not put off by Sommer's tone of self-pity. "There's nothing to be afraid of," he asserted. "You do not look to me like a man who is afraid of anything and I'll bet you six bits that you are not a man who was ever whipped, either on the inside or the outside; but such talk as this won't build railroads." Harp was a pragmatist. He did not want to build a railroad himself, but he would "raise enough bonus." A line such as he proposed would be easily graded and could "use light steel, in fact, a streak of rust will get the bonus." Beyond that only "a very cheap train making a round trip each day with an inexpensive engine (of course it would have to have a whistle, but that's about all)" would suffice. Two QA&P attorneys, acting independently of each other, certified to Sommer that there was genuine interest and capacity to support a rail line from Lubbock to Levelland. One even suggested that "a tentative bonus of $300,000" would be "given to the first railroad built into that locality." He also advised that community leaders preferred a road other than the AT&SF because they believed the Santa Fe "would only run a spur out from Lubbock," and this would not "give them the direct connection with eastern markets" that they wanted. Sommer, strange to say, was not interested; there was no further correspondence with Harp. The sentiment for rail service in the region did not go away, however. Soon there was talk of a Lubbock & Western Railway. In the end neither the Lubbock & Western nor the QA&P built into the area. The Santa Fe built a branch in 1925 from Lubbock to Bledsoe via Levelland, forever sealing the area to other aspirants.[17]

If QA&P managers missed an opportunity west of Lubbock, it did not mean that they had given up on their traditional goal—El Paso. Nor had interests in El Paso given up on the QA&P. A representative of one group trying to entice the QA&P told the Frisco's board of directors that "the citizens of El Paso, the Pecos Valley of New Mexico, and the Plains Country of West Texas" were "very eager for a direct line or railroad, preferring an independent" road over the Santa Fe, which had a near "monopoly of the territory." In support of the QA&P, the El Paso chapter of the American Association of Engineers even made a survey and gathered data for the proposed railroad. A direct line from El Paso to New York via St. Louis (QA&P-Frisco-Pennsylvania), this group pointed out, would be approximately seventy miles shorter than similar service presently offered via Chicago (Southern Pacific–Rock Island–New York Central). El Pasoans also saw advantages accruing to them through additional gateways and competition.[18]

Why was the QA&P so lethargic in the face of clear strategic opportunities? There are only clues. The Yoakum empire, on the scrap pile for a decade, was in the process of resurrection. The chairman of the Frisco's board, Edward N. Brown, began a new raid on Rock Island stock in 1924, and the Frisco's influence over Rock Island was soon clear. Perhaps Frisco's leaders felt they had "bigger fish to fry" or perhaps they could not attract adequate capital to fund all of their expansion projects. In any event, the "green light" that the QA&P hoped for was not forthcoming.[19]

## CHAPTER 8

# Wars and Rumors of War

The several applications pending before the Interstate Commerce Commission to extend lines of railway into the northwestern portion of Texas, is the most extensive program of construction that has been offered in Texas for a great many years, and the projected lines are into territory which taken as a whole is capable of very high development and great productivity.—Railroad Commission of Texas to the Interstate Commerce Commission, February 1, 1926

IN 1925 the Fort Worth & Denver City Railway took the initiative in the matter of building new lines to serve West Texas. On April 7, the Denver Road, through its recently formed subsidiary, the Fort Worth & Denver South Plains Railway, asked the Interstate Commerce Commission for permission to build 193 miles of new line. The proposed configuration was unusual. The new route would protrude from the Denver Road's Gulf-to-Rockies line near Estelline and head in a generally southwesterly direction over the Caprock to Plainview and then northwesterly to Dimmitt. Two connected branches would bisect this line at a new village, Sterley, twenty-two miles northeast of Plainview. One of these would run north to Silverton and the other south to Lubbock. This package of lines, if built, clearly would invade territory claimed by other aspirants—the Texas Panhandle & Gulf; Quanah, Acme & Pacific; and Atchison, Topeka & Santa Fe. A bitter fight was sure to follow.[1]

The enthusiasm in Plainview and Lubbock for the Denver Road's project was understandable. But there was no enthusiasm for the project among officials of the QA&P. The alliance the two had formed against the Texas Panhandle & Gulf scheme was instantly dissolved. On May 18, the QA&P filed its objections to the Denver Road's application. They were brief, even blunt. "No sound reason exists why the public convenience and necessity requires the construction of the proposed line, or any part thereof," thundered Sam Lazarus. Granting the FW&DC's application would deprive "existing lines of their already thin revenue, to the ex-

tent of seriously affecting and public already served by existing mileage." This was, of course, the same rationale both the FW&DC and QA&P had used against the application of the Panhandle Road. Lazarus even asserted that the QA&P's current policy was one of, to use his phrase, "live and let live."[2]

The matter was further confused when the Pecos & Northern Texas Railway (a satellite of the AT&SF) filed applications to construct two branches—one from near Plainview to Silverton, about thirty miles, the other from near Plainview to Dimmitt, about forty-three miles. These were obviously rival to the Denver Road's earlier application. A royal battle was shaping up.[3]

John Marrs was not optimistic. He told Charles Sommer that he did not see how the QA&P could keep the Denver Road from winning "unless we planned to build ourselves within a reasonable time." At best, QA&P objections might "hold them back until we can become able to finance such a venture, or until the time is right for action." Nevertheless, it seemed to the QA&P's general attorney "that we have waited too long if we intend to build on the Plains."[4]

There were all sorts of rumors and speculation about the Quanah Route, its missed opportunities, and its remaining options. The *Quanah Times* for April 5, 1925, contributed its share. "The QA&P railroad and the Fort Worth & Denver . . . have gone into an agreement," reported the editor, "that will result in . . . both roads using 'Q' tracks to Quanah." The idea seemed to be that both companies would use QA&P rails west of Quanah to some undesignated point from which the Denver Road would build to Plainview and the QA&P would build on to Lubbock. If such a project were carried to fruition, Quanah would stand to become the center for this system of roads, which would, said the writer, give the South Plains "ready access to the markets of the North, East as well as Southwest." It would have the additional advantage of striking "a knock-out blow to the Santa Fe's alleged attempt to to block competing roads from building on the South Plains."[5]

Sam Lazarus was in Quanah during the first two weeks in April. Perhaps he was present to put down rumors such as these; or maybe he was there to start some of his own. "I wouldn't be surprised if the QA&P didn't reach the Plains as quickly as the rest of them [the other aspirants] and perhaps a little sooner," observed the QA&P president. This statement flew in the face of a widespread report that the QA&P was for sale. One Quanah journalist asked him directly, and Lazarus replied that "he did not know." He said, however, that "a proposition had been made to the Burlington [FW&DC] but up to the present the QA&P had not changed hands." Whether the QA&P passed to the FW&DC or not, Lazarus was confident that West Texas could support additional rail facilities. "Taken on the average," he said, "crops there make as much as they do in Central Texas." There was only one problem and that was not insuperable: "When West Texas is prosperous its people forget to save their money . . . and when the dry years come they find themselves in serious shape."[6]

Negotiations with the Burlington for the sale of the QA&P were real, if unsuccessful. On June 29, Frisco's President Kurn advised Lazarus that he had "advised the Burlington that we do not wish to dispose of the QA&P." That decision was collateral with another. One the same day, Kurn ordered "blue prints, estimates and all other necessary data for the construction of an extension to Floydada." It was tardy in the extreme, and it addressed only short-term needs, but Lazarus and Sommer finally had a green light.[7]

Vigorous activity followed. On July 2, Lazarus wired Murdo MacKenzie, asking him what support might come from the Matador Land & Cattle Company if the QA&P built west. At the same time, he dispatched an emissary to Floydada to learn whether citizens there would contribute "right-of-way and ample terminals." Lazarus then hurried back from a vacation at Lake George, New York, to take personal command of the campaign. At the

same time, Kurn directed that "all matters . . . in regard to the QA&P extension . . . be made in the name of the QA&P over Mr. Lazarus' signature." On July 13, an emergency meeting of the QA&P board of directors was called in Quanah for the purpose of authorizing application for the construction of "approximately 28 miles . . . from MacBain to Floydada." On the following day, attorneys drew up the papers, pointing out that "the proposed extension would afford a new direct line into . . . the South Plains of Texas . . . thereby giving its citizens a direct outlet . . . and quick transportation" for the agricultural production of the region.[8]

There was immediate rejoicing in Floydada. On July 14 two hundred persons attended a mass meeting that was held at the courthouse. Lazarus was present and addressed the crowd. He was characteristically short and to the point: the QA&P would begin construction "within two weeks after we get a permit" from the ICC if, he cautioned, "you take up our proposal." This short address (150 words according to one account) was greeted "by an enthusiastic outburst of applause." Col. W. M. Massie, who nominally spoke for the Floydadians, said: "It's a big job we are undertaking. . . . However, we can't afford to be anything but liberal with these railroad people, and I predict great things for Floydada if they get to build." The railroad's response came from G. E. Hamilton: "There is a tide in the affairs of men, and which taken at the flood, leads on to fortune." Floydada, in his judgment, reached the flood when, on the seventeenth, an agreement was forged whereby right-of-way and terminal lands were guaranteed by "Mr. W. M. Massie and others."[9]

The response at Quanah was equally euphoric. One writer thought the modest construction project to Floydada and a connection there with a branch of the AT&SF would create "Quanah's second transcontinental railroad." It would "put [Quanah] on the map, and lift it out of the village class." The excitement was so great that the *Quanah Tribune-Chief* and the *Quanah Times* put aside their rivalry for one day and issued a "Special Consolidated Edition for the Plainview Railway Hearing to let the businessmen of Quanah present their side." Its writers waxed expansive: "When it is considered that a far flung expanse reaching from the Pacific Coast to the Atlantic is affected and that a scope of territory from El Paso to Quanah is vitally affected, when Quanah finds its interests are identical with those of El Paso, Oklahoma City with Los Angeles, and New York with Floydada and

Roaring Springs in its advocacy of the extension of the QA&P, then Quanah becomes bold and in a loud voice asks for the extension because her claims are just and logical and fraught with a good for many." The dreams of another writer were more restricted. He yearned only for an opportunity to go all the way to "El Paso on the same railroad, perhaps in the same Pullman car."[10]

The Interstate Commerce Commission, which was still examining the earlier Texas Panhandle & Gulf application, ordered that combined hearings be held on proposals of the FW&DC and the AT&SF at Plainview beginning on July 20. The Texas Railroad Commission was asked to sit with the ICC and agreed to do so. Although the Texas regulatory body had a long-established policy of refraining from making recommendations in such cases, at least one of its commissioners, C. V. Terrell, was in favor of asserting one in this situation. John P. Marrs was concerned. He believed that all of the Texas commissioners favored the Texas Panhandle & Gulf application and would "recommend that it be given a permit." Consequently, Marrs hoped that the ICC would not request a recommendation from the Texas commission but would rely on its "own judgement, uninfluenced by popular 'sympathy.'"[11]

The entire South Plains region braced for what promised to be a heated contest. When it had earlier opposed the Texas Panhandle & Gulf's application, the FW&DC had argued that the territory did not need additional transportation facilities. Now the Denver Road contended that more services were required—its own, not those offered by the Panhandle Road or any of the other contenders. The FW&DC asserted that it had a concrete plan for financing its construction; Panhandle advocates, who were present to defend the purposes of that company, maintained that the proposed lines of the Denver Road would invade territory and carry off tonnage already claimed by the TP&G under its application 1923. Dallas, Lubbock, and Plainview sided with the Fort Worth & Denver City; Fort Worth supported the Texas Panhandle & Gulf. The Santa Fe put forward its own positions. The QA&P felt betrayed by the FW&DC, its former ally in the proceedings against the TP&G, and was opposed to all.[12]

Representatives from the Plainview community were particularly enthusiastic about the FW&DC's application. Their moods and actions paralleled those of others in the West throughout the railroad era. They had rejoiced at the coming of steamcar civilization but quickly came to feel that service by a single carrier was a monopoly of the worst kind. Their earlier efforts to attract service by the Texas Central and then the Missouri, Kansas & Texas were followed in 1909 by an attempt to lure the FW&DC. Failing in all cases, they had turned to the QA&P—which "wanted $175,000 and half of Plainview," according to one obviously irked city father—then the Gulf, Texas & Western, and even had consulted with Frank Kell, a well-known railroad builder from Wichita Falls. Now the Denver Road had finally offered what Plainview citizens perceived as a firm plan; they understandably responded with energetic support for it.[13]

Sam Lazarus put a new wrinkle to the pattern. When he took the stand to testify in opposition to the Denver and Santa Fe plans, he announced a counterproposal on behalf of the QA&P. He recalled, for the record, that El Paso was the historical objective of the Quanah Route and that it was chartered to go there. Progress toward the goal had been halting, but Lazarus pointed out that papers had been filed with the ICC just days before requesting permission to construct an extension from MacBain to Floydada and a connection there with the Santa Fe's branch to Plainview. Lazarus then reduced the gathering to astonishment. He produced a letter from the late E. P. Ripley, who had been president of the AT&SF, promising that his road would grant the Quanah Route trackage rights from Floydada to Plainview. Lazarus admitted that the current president of the Santa Fe, W. B. Storey, might have other thoughts. Nevertheless, he maintained, "we want to come to Plainview." This may have been true, or it may have been a ruse. Certainly Lazarus wanted to forestall the expansion efforts of the Santa Fe and especially those of the Denver Road. He negotiated simultaneously with representatives from Plainview and Lubbock. He did not discount the possibility of serving both communities; he was seeking the best advantage and, in the classic Lazarus mold, keeping his options open.[14]

The MacBain-to-Floydada construction, coupled with trackage rights from Floydada to Plainview, would, in connection with the FW&DC at Quanah, create a short route between the South Plains and Fort Worth. According to Lazarus, there was a corollary opportunity. The Gulf, Texas & Western, he said, could build east from Salesville to Fort Worth and west from Seymour to Paducah. With new construction and trackage rights over the Santa Fe, the QA&P, in cooperation with the GT&W,

Business on the Santa Fe at Plainview was good, and the AT&SF saw no reason to share with another carrier. *Milton Day Henderson Collection, Llano Estacado Museum*

could offer a South Plains–Fort Worth route that would be nearly forty-five miles shorter than that promoted by the Denver Road. Furthermore, it was at least possible that the Texas Panhandle & Gulf could use trackage rights over the GT&W and QA&P all the way from Fort Worth to Paducah. Such an arrangement would require further building by the Panhandle Road only from Paducah to Tucumcari and thus reduce that road's capital requirements. It would negate the need for construction as proposed by the larger established roads, the Santa Fe and the Denver. All of this "burst like a bomb in the Denver's camp," according to one report. A meeting between C. G. Burnham, executive vice-president of the Burlington Lines, and Lazarus was hastily arranged. The exact nature of the meeting is not known, but Lazarus later told a journalist that he had recently offered the QA&P "to the Denver for its proposed extension on the Plains but it was declined." Now, he said, "the road was not for sale at any price to the Denver." The reporter concluded, rightly, that the "Burlington officials missed a chance."[15]

The ICC's hearing examiner, C. E. Boles, returned to Washington and the Texas railroad commissioner returned to Austin to study conflicting claims and to get ready for the next round—a hearing on the QA&P's application. At the same time there was renewed pulling and hauling as various factions lined up to support the application of their choice. In September, the state of Texas—but not the Texas Railroad Commission—came out in favor of the FW&DC's proposals but did not categorically oppose the other applicants. According to

the state's attorney general, the natural markets for the products of West Texas were the cities of Fort Worth, Dallas, and Wichita Falls: "The development of these cities from industrial and commercial standpoints is as much to the national interests as the preservation of St. Louis, Kansas City and Chicago." It was an oblique attack on the QA&P, "an afterthought of the Frisco system," as one leading newspaper called it. Fort Worth interests appeared to gain new vitality and increased their backing for the Panhandle Road. The Hearst newspaper there, the *Fort Worth Record*, was especially enthusiastic. The lead article in its issue of August 10 and the entire front page for August 16 were devoted to extolling the virtues of the TP&G and the wonderful territory and constituency it would serve. The *Record* was positive that persons living in the potential service area of the TP&G would support it—"These Westerners are simple, straight-forward thinking people"—and equally positive that the Panhandle Road would win the ICC's blessing—"The largest possible number of towns in West Texas will be on record as asking for this road." Moreover, completion of this grand project would allow both Fort Worth and greater West Texas to reach their proper potential: "The Western Plains will some day do the dairy business of Wisconsin, fatten the hogs of Iowa, and raise the wheat of Kansas," and "Fort Worth, as the capital of this West Texas empire, will soon become the Chicago for the Southwest." It was braggadocio of exceptional quality.[16]

In an attempt to advance its cause, the QA&P's management chose to attack the FW&DC venture on the grounds of its cost. As Sam Lazarus pointed

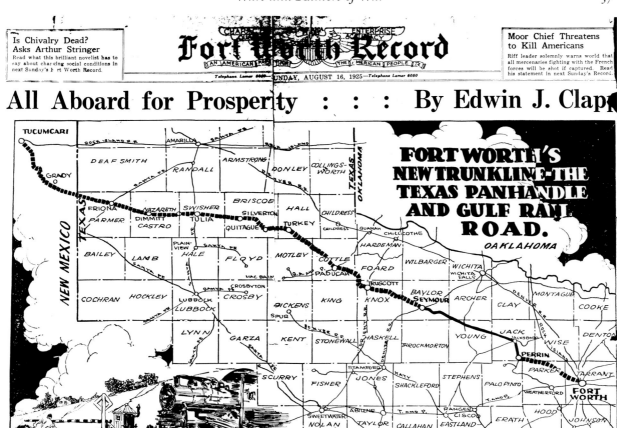

**Fort Worth Record**

SUNDAY, AUGUST 16, 1925—Telephone Lamar 6050

# All Aboard for Prosperity : : : By Edwin J. Clapp

This is the Texas Panhandle & Gulf Railroad, to be built 450 miles from Fort Worth to Tucumcari.

It will add to Fort Worth's exclusive trade territory 14,000,000 acres of the best farm land in the world.

Those 14,000,000 acres are more than the cultivated farm lands of any cotton State in the Union, except Texas.

One hundred million dollars a year is a conservative estimate of the new business that will fall to Fort Worth.

If the T. P. & G. is not an Empire Builder, what is it?

out, the Denver Road's expenditure for construction, operation, upkeep, and fixed charges and interest-bearing securities would be "practically seven times" those of the QA&P. Furthermore, under the Cummins-Esch bill, "consuming communities would be required to furnish the money, and they would do it, if business ever got the least bit slack, by having the rates raised on what little the producer" turned out. "Somebody," Lazarus groused, "has to see that the country does not become too heavily taxed by reason of high freight rates." He recalled that the QA&P had been offered to the Denver Road "at a very reasonable price." It was foolish, he was certain, for the railroads to engage in counterproductive construction warfare; potential local traffic in West Texas would not support the

Santa Fe, FW&DC, and QA&P. As a consequence, Lazarus thought the Denver Road's proposal ludicrous in the extreme. The line from Estelline up the Caprock escarpment would, he observed, necessitate a tunnel; A. F. Sommer, an engineer, considered the profile a "hum dinger." Already the Denver Road's survey had cost $200,000; "they could have built the grade to the Caprock from MacBain for that," Sommer believed. His brother Charles thought there was a simple solution. The QA&P could "accomplish with the construction of twenty-eight miles of track what they [FW&DC] hoped to do with extensive and more costly track." The QA&P could offer at least equivalent transportation, and by "utilizing" the money now invested in the Quanah Route as well as that "invested by the Santa Fe from Floydada to Plainview" a conservation of investment was possible.[17]

Preparations for the hearings went forward. A special stockholders meeting was held in Quanah on September 21 to draft the necessary amendments to the corporate charter. A few days later Lazarus asked G. E. Hamilton to drum up support for the application among area chambers of commerce. It was not a difficult task. Petitions praying for the ICC to grant the QA&P's application were received from Floydada, Matador, Cone, Roaring Springs, and Hale Center. Another, from Dickens, curiously suggested that the QA&P's recently acquired Motley County line be extended southward to that landlocked community. Roaring Springs hoped for better transportation so that it could become "a future health resort." The twelve-page *Quanah Times* for October 18, 1925, called itself "A Special Edition for the Fort Worth Railway Hearing—favoring the Extension of the QA&P to Floydada." It featured articles and advertisements boosting the QA&P's application and strongly implied its further expansion to El Paso. "Let the 'Q' Extend" was the constant theme. All seemed to be in readiness when the ICC announced that testimony on its behalf would be taken by the Texas Railroad Commission in Fort Worth on October 19.[18]

Charles Sommer expected little protest to the QA&P application. After all, he reasoned, the Denver Road had no "legitimate cause to protest," and he doubted that "the Santa Fe will fight us." He was only partially correct; both filed briefs. The FW&DC's position was that the QA&P could not "furnish a desirable outlet for products of the South Plains generally." If granting the QA&P's request did not prejudice its own application, however, the FW&DC would not protest. Counsel for the Denver Road told a QA&P attorney: "The Fort Worth and Denver City crowd felt considerable interest as well as pleasure, that the situation was thought to be one in which we could be faithful to our interests and at the same time not oppose the application of the QA&P except in an indirect and limited way." The position of the AT&SF was similar. It thought there was no need to build the line from MacBain to Floydada.[19]

The ICC now had before it applications from the TP&G, FW&DC, AT&SF, and QA&P, all filed between 1923 and 1925. The delay in reaching a decision was explained, in part, because the Panhandle Road had asked for postponements and, in part, because the several applications and contending groups had made the matter inordinately com-

plex. C. E. Boles, the ICC examiner who heard the testimony at Plainview, announced, as 1925 ended, that his report was far from finished. An attorney for the QA&P asked his friend Representative Sam Rayburn if he could determine what the regulatory agency's position might be on the Quanah Route's application. The future speaker of the House of Representatives soon advised that the ICC would refer the matter of the Texas Railroad Commission for recommendation. He was correct. The Texas agency responded on February 1 with a short statement that began by noting that the several proposals before the ICC represented "the most extensive program of construction that has been offered in Texas for a great many years" and ending with an endorsement of the Quanah Route's proposal. Some observers thought it was a moot point because rumors again circulated to the effect that the QA&P soon would be sold to the FW&DC. "There isn't one iota of truth in this report" was the explosive response of Charles Sommer.[20]

As events moved to culmination, the QA&P campaign suffered a grievous loss. Early in March 1926, Sam Lazarus went to New York City to discuss the QA&P's plans for expansion with E. N. Brown, chairman of the SL-SF board, and J. M. Kurn, the road's president. In their presence he suffered "a paroxysm of coughing" and died of a cerebral thrombosis two days later on March 6. The leadership of the Quanah Route now fell to Charles H. Sommer, the protégé and alter ego of Lazarus.[21]

Just before the death of Lazarus, the Santa Fe had further confused the issue by requesting permission "to build approximately fifteen miles of track in a generally southeasterly direction" from Floydada. Sommer was furious. He referred to the plan as "another entry for the battle royal contest" and properly observed that the proposed extension would run "out on the prairie to *Nowhere*." The application, he fumed, would "muddy the waters a little bit." An attorney for the QA&P was more detached: "It is evidently a move to checkmate us," he observed. At the request of the ICC, the Texas Railroad Commission agreed to take testimony at Lubbock but later changed the location to Floydada. Simply stated, the QA&P contended that no sound reason existed for the construction of the extension. Conversely, Sommer argued, construction of the QA&P's extension would give "Floydada and the South Plains generally a line that would serve the largest public convenience and necessity, affording a shorter, more direct line to Fort Worth, Dallas, and St. Louis than is now afforded by existing routes." Santa Fe representatives admitted that revenue from the new line would not pay for either its construction or operation. They asserted, however, that when the general benefit to the Santa Fe system was considered, the traffic would be profitable. That was labeled "the rankest kind of speculation" by counsel for the Quanah Route. Local support was nearly entirely for the QA&P and against the Santa Fe.[22]

On March 19, 1926, the long-awaited report from C. E. Boles was submitted to the Interstate Commerce Commission. The hearings had been long and complex, as reflected in the Boles report:

1. The application of the Texas Panhandle & Gulf, 303 miles, recommended.
2. The TP&G be given six months in which to secure adequate financial backing.
3. The application of the Quanah, Acme & Pacific, MacBain to Floydada, recommended.
4. The TP&G should acquire sole or joint control of the QA&P from Paducah to MacBain and then assume responsibility of extending the line from MacBain to Floydada (per item 3).
5. In the event that the TP&G succeeds in raising the requisite capital it should push branches into Plainview and Lubbock.
6. Some strong railroad system, perhaps the Missouri Pacific or the Frisco, should take over the TP&G.
7. If the TP&G fails to secure adequate financial support the FW&DC's application to build from Estelline to Plainview, Dimmitt, and Lubbock should be granted.
8. The FW&DC's application to build a line to Silverton, not recommended.
9. In the event that the TP&G fails in its quest for capital the AT&SF should be allowed entrance to Silverton but not to Dimmitt.

Boles had, in effect, recommended that the Panhandle Road be given first chance to offer general service in the prospective trade area, but with an important caveat. The TP&G had only six months to locate sufficient capital to inaugurate construction over its entire route. Failing that, it would forfeit all rights, and individual construction packages, under Boles's recommendations, would fall to the FW&DC, Santa Fe, and QA&P.[23]

These recommendations met a mixed reception. Washington observers concluded that the Santa Fe had, as one source said, "slept on its rights" to drive a new and direct connection between the Plains and Dallas–Fort Worth. Others felt that the Frisco, soon

to be wed to the Rock Island according to contemporary wisdom, was the real victor since Boles had included it as one of the major systems that might acquire the TP&G package. "The merged Frisco–Rock Island system would be in a position to upset much of the railroad calculations in the South Plains and give it a favorable status to reach the Mexican border with a new through route for foreign business," suggested a writer for the *Dallas Morning News*. On the High Plains of West Texas, there was rejoicing at Tulia and Floydada but bitter disappointment at Lubbock and Plainview. There was a celebration in Fort Worth, silence in Quanah, and an announcement from Austin that the state of Texas would not protest the recommendations. In Floydada, W. M. Massie, chairman of the Chamber of Commerce's Railway Committee, thought the Boles recommendations represented a victory for the Interstate Commerce Commission and the practical application of the law that had strengthened it in 1920.[24]

The Santa Fe, which had not chosen to intervene in the proceedings surrounding the Texas Panhandle & Gulf, changed its mind in March 1926 and asked the ICC for permission to have the various cases—except its own application to build southeastward from Floydada—consolidated. No serious objections were heard. Shortly thereafter the QA&P asked that its application be consolidated with the Santa Fe's Floydada proposal. The ICC quickly ruled that all of the cases, including the AT&SF's Floydada application, would be heard collectively. The stage was set for the final act in the lengthy drama that the ICC's Charles D. Mahaffie entitled the "South Plains Cases."[25]

Charles Sommer lost no time in alerting company lawyers that the Quanah Route would "make a determined effort to discredit and defeat the purpose of Examiner Boles' report." He conceded that the Panhandle Road had taken on a new vitality since release of the report, yet he continued to refer to it as nothing more than "paper road," a "promoter's dream." He did not see how the "commission in its wisdom" could "give serious thought" to its application. He would be better prepared than ever. The stakes, Sommer knew, were high: "The future of the Quanah Route will depend largely upon the decision which the Commission will hand down on these several applications," he told Frisco's President Kurn.[26]

Sommer perceived that Boles was deeply concerned about the need for competition in the potential service area. He reasoned that the QA&P's

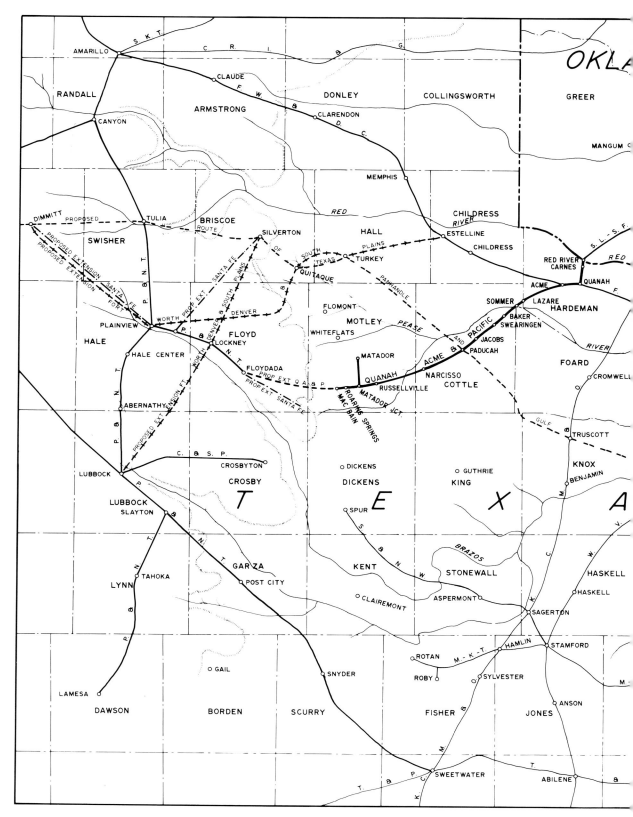

Map of the QA&P and connections. *Cartography by John L. Hodson.*

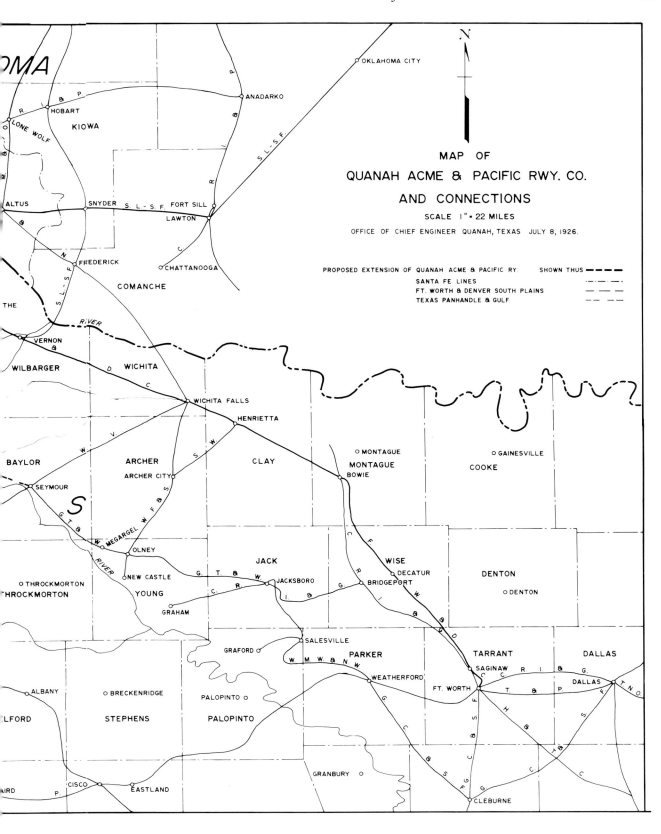

N

MAP OF

QUANAH ACME & PACIFIC RWY. CO.

AND CONNECTIONS

SCALE 1" = 22 MILES

OFFICE OF CHIEF ENGINEER QUANAH, TEXAS  JULY 8, 1926.

| PROPOSED EXTENSION OF QUANAH ACME & PACIFIC RY. | SHOWN THUS |
| FT. WORTH & DENVER SOUTH PLAINS | |
| SANTA FE LINES | |
| TEXAS PANHANDLE & GULF | |

attack on the Boles report needed to be more than just a negative response; it would also be necessary to propose alternatives. These took two forms: plans for taking the QA&P into Lubbock from Floydada and for extending the Motley County Railway northward from Matador.[27]

Shortly after the Boles report was made public, Sommer began discussions relative to a change in the QA&P's strategy. Lubbock and Lubbock County offered "by far the best opportunities" in West Texas, he told Kurn. Construction in that direction would further the road's long-stated goal of reaching El Paso, "nullify the FW&DC's claim for a necessity, and generally harmonize the entire South Plains squabble." Sommer felt that "if the Commission is of the opinion that the time is ripe" for expansion to Lubbock, the QA&P—not the Denver Road and certainly not the TP&G—should be allowed to go forward. The ICC, furthermore, should grant the QA&P exclusive rights for such construction; the country would not support two lines in the same general corridor. Lubbock, always eager to expand its importance, gave written assurance through its Chamber of Commerce and Board of City Development that it would cooperate "in every way possible" if the QA&P extended its line to that place "anytime in the reasonable future." Sentiment favored the QA&P over the Denver Road, but, of course, Lubbock already had a contract with the FW&DC and was bound to stand by it if the ICC ruled in favor of the larger road.[28]

At about this time, G. E. Hamilton reminded Sommer of potential opportunities north and northwest of Matador. Should the Denver Road's application be denied by the ICC, "the territory about Quitaque, Turkey, and Flomot would" remain devoid of rail service; "the situation," he said, "would call very loudly for the extension of the Motley County road . . . into that vicinity." Such construction would, said Hamilton, "bring a rich patronage that we do not now get." Another QA&P attorney, Cecil H. Smith, added that if the ICC gave its permission, "we would not have to be in a great hurry about building it, and if we did not build it at all, I can't see how we would ordinarily get in any trouble about it." In other words, asking for and receiving permission to extend the Motley County Railway by the QA&P might well defuse the FW&DC's bid to serve that same area. Sommer agreed. "I am somewhat apprehensive," he told Frisco's Kurn, "regarding the future of the Motley County property. If either the TP&G or the Burlington Line [FW&DC] are extended through [that section], it will deplete our tonnage at Matador by at least 50%," which "would have a disastrous effect on the Motley County line."[29]

Charles Sommer expected a hard fight but appeared confident. "I feel that the consolidation of all of these dockets is the proper procedure and will enable the Commission to pass on the merits of each proposition." He anticipated that the TP&G would "make an effort to bluff its way through" and that "a bitter contest" would "develop between the Burlington [FW&DC] and Santa Fe Lines." Indeed, he said, "the Santa Fe will leave nothing undone to keep the Burlington out of the South Plains Country." This, he thought, would be useful to the purposes of the QA&P: "Our concern is chiefly in keeping the Denver from invading this territory, and in this regard I know we will have the able assistance of the Santa Fe." President Kurn supported Sommer. There was no need, he said, for either the Fort Worth & Denver City or Santa Fe construction projects. On the other hand, thought Kurn, expansion of the QA&P was necessary to protect its interests and also to "properly serve the country and give that section the outlet they desire to St. Louis and other points." Kurn assured Sommer that he "would be glad to consider in the near future the need for further extending the line to Lubbock." That notion and any suggestion for northward penetration from Matador could not appear in written form before the final hearing in Washington, however. It was to be a surprise reserved for the oral argument.[30]

In all cases the QA&P had been reacting to the moves of others, not initiating actions of its own. Now, with a firm proposal to build on to Lubbock from Floydada—progress toward its historic goal of El Paso—and pushing a line into the untapped country above Matador, the QA&P would offer a program that would serve a burgeoning region and itself as well. The problem was, as always, whether the QA&P would be too late. Was the die already cast?

The day of reckoning finally arrived. The Texas Panhandle & Gulf, as might been expected, asked for more time to firm up its financial package or to locate a suitor from the large systems. Representatives of the Santa Fe argued that there was no need for additional rail service in the South Plains area, and FW&DC attorneys claimed that this was not true and that their company could best perform such necessary service. The QA&P, as planned, surprised everybody by committing itself to build on to Lubbock and into the territory north of Matador "if the Commission felt that public necessity existed." Sommer thought that the QA&P's position "had been well stated to the Commission and will enable it to intelligently understand the matter." He thought that the TP&G's position had been materially damaged. Time alone would tell. Meanwhile, G. E. Hamilton reported that interest was at "fever heat all over the country . . . and the Commission's decision is awaited with impatience by thousands."[31]

On November 19, 1926, Charles Sommer sent the following dispatch to J. M. Kurn, who was touring the Frisco aboard a "director's special": "The Interstate Commerce Commission has just released order authorizing Quanah Line to construct extension, MacBain to Floydada. Has also granted Fort Worth & Denver City's application, embracing lines to Plainview, Silverton via Lockney to Lubbock, Plainview to Dimmitt. He has denied without prejudice, application of the Texas Panhandle & Gulf Ry., and all of the applications of the Santa Fe Lines." The mileage represented in all applications had totaled 677, but the ICC issued permits for only 202.1 miles. Analysis of the implications would come later.[32]

Officials of the Fort Worth & Denver City were elated with the news from Washington. The road's general attorney, J. H. Barwise, called the campaign "the greatest railroad fight in the history of Texas" and pointed with pride to the fact that the Denver Road had been granted all it had requested. Frank Clarity, the Denver Road's vice-president and general manager, pledged that his company would be the region's Santa Claus for 1926 and soon made good on that promise. "Every business house in Estelline was closed for one hour" on December 21, the *Dallas Morning News* reported, "while dirt was broken for the new line." A large number of ob-

servers were on hand to witness the event, and "the Memphis Gold Medal Band furnished" appropriate music for the occasion. Company officials thought trains would begin running into Plainview about June 1, 1928. High-class service was promised.[33]

The mood in Fort Worth was mixed but among TR&G boosters distinctly grim. A representative of the Fort Worth Chamber of Commerce said he was "disappointed that the TP&G lost out." But he went on, "There is only one position for us, and that is to get as many spokes in Fort Worth's wheel as possible. The more railroads we have, the more business Fort Worth gets." He clearly understood the concept and was an advocate of classical urban economic imperialism. The *Fort Worth Star-Telegram* reflected the same sentiment; it promoted any rail penetration into the South Plains and had backed the applications of both the Panhandle Road and the FW&DC. Now at least a part of the dream had come true: "It is not only the first large scale railroad construction within the state in the last 10 years, but it is an event that holds out such possibilities for the future of the South Plains and Fort Worth that its benefits cannot be adequately pictured or determined at this time." The mood at Paducah was one of resignation. "Paducah, with a number of other towns, has fought and lost. This is the true status of the TP&G situation," editorialized the *Paducah Post.* C. H. Powell, chief promoter of the TP&G, reserved comment. Backers from Fort Worth met with Powell and his attorneys in Chicago to draft an appeal to the ICC's decision, but on December 13, 1926, the regulatory body in Washington denied the request. The Texas Panhandle & Gulf passed to the dust of history. The era of individual entrepreneurship in the railroad industry had come to an end; the established carriers had won a clear victory.[34]

## CHAPTER 9

# Decisions and Depression

Personally, I feel something should be done by
both the Rock Island and Frisco to head the Santa
Fe off in that part of Texas.—J. M. Kurn to E. N.
Brown, June 22, 1928

EVEN as officials of the QA&P labored to get construction under way west of MacBain (and they soon found that was no mean task), they were beset by a swirl of new propositions advanced by a variety of competing entities. It was necessary, they agreed, to study and take positions for or against each of them.

The first of these proposals came from an unexpected quarter. On August 16, 1926, a charter for the incorporation of the Ardmore, Vernon & Lubbock Railway (AV&L) was drawn by its promoters and was granted by the state of Oklahoma two days later. The aspirations of the new firm were implicit in its title—to link Ardmore, Oklahoma, with Lubbock via Vernon. A writer for the *Dallas Morning News* naively predicted that "little objection" was "expected because the road is planned to serve virgin territory which is rich in agricultural resources." Frisco's President Kurn told Charles Sommer in no uncertain terms, however, that it was SL-SF's "intention to oppose this construction." Sommer concurred. The reasons were clear enough. The proposed line would be in competition with the Frisco at three locations, would compete with the QA&P for its entire length as a parallel line some twenty miles to the south, and would invade the QA&P's potential trade area in and around Lubbock. Moreover, the project was initially perceived as being orchestrated by or at least on behalf of the rival AT&SF.[1]

QA&P attorney G. E. Hamilton did not believe the Santa Fe was behind that venture. Rather, he thought it was "an effort on the part of some pipe dreamer who thinks it possible some big line might think favorably of the enterprise and buy it out for a fair little piece of pocket change." Yet he did not want to take a chance of being mistaken; after all, Santa Fe lines from Ardmore to

Ringling in Oklahoma and Crosbyton to Lubbock in Texas were to be used as part of the scheme. He would draw up the necessary papers in opposition. Shortly thereafter, the AT&SF validated Hamilton's suspicions; it filed its own protests, complaining that the AV&L's potential service area was already "adequately and efficiently served by Santa Fe lines." The Fort Worth & Denver City soon joined the Frisco, QA&P, and Santa Fe in opposition.[2]

The Interstate Commerce Commission called for hearings to be held on September 6, 1927. A contest very much like that occasioned earlier by the Texas Panhandle & Gulf case seemed likely. Events then took an unexpected turn. Minutes after the hearings began, officials of the applicant asked for an indefinite postponement because they had not been able to prepare their case adequately. The regulatory agency agreed; indeed, the application was dismissed one year later. The idea would be resurrected again early in 1929, but nothing came of it. Thus died the Ardmore, Vernon and Lubbock—one of an incalculable number of America's "paper railroads."[3]

Another, nearly simultaneous, development was far more important in its short-term implications and long-range potential—the rapprochement between the Frisco and the Rock Island. In a sense it was a replay of the earlier Yoakum era. During the mid-1920s, a syndicate headed by Edward N. Brown, a New York banker and chairman of Frisco's board of directors, gained stock control of the Rock Island. According to one source, the common stock of Frisco was badly watered at that time and, to rectify the situation, Brown and his group felt that Rock Island dividends could be used to "put some money behind the Frisco." In 1927 it paid a dividend of 5 percent on a net of $12 million. At about this same time the Brown syndicate undertook to arrange a merger of the two roads; by the end of 1930, Frisco owned 183,000 shares of Rock Island. No less authority than Julius Grodinsky predicted a "union of corporate interests based upon existing interlocking directorates."[4]

Nevertheless, the Rock Island and Frisco did not merge, in part because of the Great Depression. During the years of courtship, however, the two carriers worked closely on a variety of projects. In Texas, this included efforts to acquire the Gulf, Texas & Western Railway and construction proposals designed to give the CRI&P and SL-SF a stronger base of operation in West Texas before the expected merger.

The Gulf, Texas & Western, chartered under the laws of Texas in 1902, had projected a four-hundred-mile line from a point on the Sabine River opposite Louisiana to Benjamin, and obscure location on the rolling plains of West Texas, with a connecting branch to Fort Worth. These general plans were changed later, and when construction occurred, the GT&W's ninety-eight-mile line extended from Salesville through Jacksboro and Olney to Seymour, with an additional twenty-two miles of trackage rights over the Weatherford, Mineral Wells & Northwestern Railway from Salesville to near Weatherford—all in an area northwest of Fort Worth. The road had been personally sponsored by Joseph J. Jermyn of Scranton, Pennsylvania; he still owned it when the Frisco and Rock Island announced expansion plans.[5]

The GT&W, of course, had been an active participant in the recent Texas Panhandle & Gulf escapade. For instance, it once had suggested that it be given permission to extend from Seymour to a connection with the QA&P at Paducah. Failing in that, the GT&W had attempted to make itself attractive to trunk lines, the Santa Fe in particular. The AT&SF, after all, had exhibited an interest in a new High Plains–Fort Worth "air line" that might encompass the GT&W. This idea understandably frightened Charles Sommer as well as officials of the Frisco.

Long before the Texas Panhandle & Gulf project had surfaced in 1923, Sam Lazarus and Charles Sommer had consulted with officials of the GT&W about a joint effort to link Fort Worth with Lubbock. "Such a line would," Sommer pointed out, "give the QA&P control of the South Plains traffic" as well as additional shipments billed from the Acme plaster mills. Any plan of this nature contemplated use of the Rock Island between Fort Worth and Jacksboro, but that was less of a potential prob-

lem as relations warmed between that company and the Frisco. Frisco's Kurn was slow to respond but finally, on July 11, 1927, he ordered a full investigation "as to the traffic possibilities should we acquire the Gulf, Texas & Western."[6]

Sommer rushed his recommendations to the Frisco president. He emphatically urged that the Frisco acquire the GT&W and extend it to Fort Worth via trackage rights from Jacksboro over the CRI&P and further expand it by way of a new line from Seymour to a connection with the Quanah Route at Paducah. This would both protect the QA&P and enhance Frisco's ability to compete for South Plains traffic. Sommer urged haste. He was convinced that the Santa Fe would respond to invasions of its service area by the QA&P and Fort Worth & Denver by undertaking a construction project "parallel to the QA&P, immediately south of our line, or adopt a more southerly route from Post." To be sure, President W. B. Storey of the Santa Fe had earlier pledged that his road would "furnish all rail service required by the South Plains" and had announced that the AT&SF intended to build a direct line from the South Plains to Fort Worth "just as soon as developments would justify it." In all likelihood the Santa Fe, which itself had approached the GT&W with the idea of acquiring it many years earlier, would use the Gulf Road in such a scheme. Furthermore, the Texas & Pacific Railway (T&P), a captive of the larger Missouri Pacific Railroad, was also known to be interested in the GT&W as a part of an announced plan to expand in West Texas.[7]

Early in 1928, Sommer advised Kurn that the GT&W was available for $2.5 million. The Santa Fe had already bid $2 million for the property and the T&P was expected to follow suit. This figure, of course, represented market value; the real value of the property was a special concern because the GT&W was then in receivership. Sommer concluded that the GT&W's management believed it offered "a very important link for a direct line to Fort Worth and Dallas, and are going to play their hand accordingly." Moreover, the GT&W was benefiting from increased petroleum traffic, and in a recent year had sustained a net income of over $50,000.[8]

Matters came to a head during the summer of 1928. On June 22, Frisco's President Kurn urged E. N. Brown, chairman of the Frisco and Rock Island boards of directors, "to protect that part of the country" by having the CRI&P purchase the GT&W and by authorizing the Frisco to extend its line southward from Vernon to Seymour and to construct a connecting line from Seymour to a junction with the QA&P at Paducah. "Personally," Kurn told Brown, "I feel something should be done by both the Rock Island and Frisco to head the Santa Fe off in that part of Texas." The Rock Island's president, J. E. Gorman, offered a counterproposal. The CRI&P, he advised, had for many years contemplated "the extension of its lines west from Graham, at the end of a branch leading westward through Jacksboro from the main line at Bridgeport, to the South Plains country," and now believed that the region was ready for such penetration. Gorman thought, however, that the Rock Island should not acquire the GT&W nor should the Frisco build between Seymour and Paducah. Rather, the Rock Island should build its own line from Graham to Roaring Springs "and later as it appears desirable, further extensions can be made to this line as far north as Amarillo." Gorman believed that the Frisco should go forward with construction of an extension from Vernon to a junction with the Rock Island's proposed line from Graham to Roaring Springs. Gorman argued that his plan would afford the Frisco the protection it desired and, at the same time, prevent domination of the area by the Santa Fe and FW&DC. These discussions were cordial enough and reflected growing ties between the Rock Island and Frisco. The matter was referred to a joint management team for recommendation.[9]

This team, composed of four top executives from the areas of traffic and engineering, submitted its report on October 28, 1928. The salient features were a unanimous recommendation that a new line not be built west of Graham; the GT&W be acquired immediately (by which carrier was not mentioned); new lines be constructed from Seymour to Paducah and Seymour to Vernon; and consideration be made for another new line—Paducah to a junction with the Rock Island's Memphis-Tucumcari line at Groom, Texas. The team pointed out that the GT&W could be used as an integral part of any through route to Fort Worth by way of the Rock Island connection at Jacksboro.[10]

The plan began to unfold on November 22, 1928, when the Frisco signed an agreement with Joseph J. Jermyn for purchase of the capital stock of the GT&W—subject to the approval of the ICC—for $2.3 million. Early in 1929, both the St. Louis, San Francisco & Texas (Frisco's corporate entity in Texas) and the GT&W asked for and received permission to amend their corporate charters. In the

process, Frisco revealed its intent to seek trackage rights over the Rock Island from Jacksboro to Fort Worth and to build a new line from Vernon to Seymour. The GT&W (clearly under the direction of the Rock Island–Frisco coalition) would seek to extend its operation from Seymour to Paducah. For the moment, Rock Island's role was hidden.[11]

There was general, but not universal, support for all this as Frisco and GT&W lawyers filed necessary papers with the ICC. The Cottle County Chamber of Commerce reported that Paducah was "all stirred up over the prospective purchase of the GT&W by the Frisco" and was "ready, willing, and anxious to do anything" to gain the extension from Seymour to Paducah. Fort Worth business leaders, especially grain and livestock dealers, were likewise enthusiastic. So, too, was the traffic manager of Certain–teed Products Corporation, successor to the Acme Plaster plant at Acme: "If this is done it would give us an outlet to the Southeast and make us further independent of the FW&DC." On the other hand, Ben B. Cain, counsel for the GT&W, anticipated "vigorous opposition from both the Santa Fe and the Burlington [FW&DC]." Operators of several large ranches urged that the new line from Seymour be built to serve the huge transportation-poor area south and west of Paducah instead of building to a connection with the QA&P. The Motley County Chamber of Commerce urged a similar plan modified only to extend such service northward through Matador and on to Quitaque.[12]

The year 1929 proved to be a veritable caldron for regional construction projects and proposals. Early in the year the Rock Island quietly shelved plans to seek permission for a line from Paducah to Groom and the SL-SF and GT&W did the same regarding their Seymour-Paducah proposal. At the same time rumors circulated that the Missouri-Kansas-Texas Railroad would extend its Wellington Branch (Altus, Oklahoma, to Wellington, Texas) to Amarillo and that the Fort Worth & Denver City in combination with its parent, the Chicago, Burlington & Quincy Railroad, planned a lengthy line from Childress, on the FW&DC, to Alliance, Nebraska, on the Burlington. These rumors prompted the Rock Island to consider a new proposition. On April 3, CRI&P directors approved plans for a line from Shamrock, Texas, near the border of Oklahoma and the Texas Panhandle on the CRI&P's Memphis-Tucumcari line, southward through Wellington and Quanah to a connection with Frisco's proposed Vernon-Seymour line. This route, in combination with the GT&W would facilitate Rock Island's desire for an intrastate Texas line connecting the Panhandle with Fort Worth. Such a connection would be advantageous because its Liberal (Kansas)-Amarillo line—an important new grain-gathering route—would be opened later that year.[13]

A response from the FW&DC was predictable. Early in May that company announced plans to construct a 105-mile branch from Childress, on its main line, northward to Wellington and Shamrock and thence northwestward to Pampa, all within the Texas Panhandle but roughly paralleling the prospective route of the Rock Island. "We are going to have a hard fight," predicted Vice-President H. G. Clark of the CRI&P. Sommer agreed.[14]

Quanah's business leaders quickly and enthusiastically lined up in support of the Rock Island venture. They pledged adequate right-of-way through Hardeman County and soon extracted similar pledges from the Wellington and Shamrock Chambers of Commerce for their respective counties. Much of this activity was forcefully orchestrated by Charles Sommer from his office in St. Louis.[15]

The Interstate Commerce Commission called for consolidated hearings to be held in Fort Worth beginning on July 29, 1929. There were several issues:

1. Application of the SL-SF to construct a new line from Vernon to Seymour
2. Application of the SL-SF to acquire the GT&W
3. Application of the SL-SF for trackage rights over the CRI&P from Jacksboro to Fort Worth
4. Application of the Rock Island to build a new line from Shamrock to Quanah and on to connect with Frisco's proposed Vernon-Seymour line
5. Application of the Rock Island for trackage rights over the SL-SF (should it acquire the GT&W between Seymour and Jacksboro)
6. Application of the SL-SF for trackage rights over the Rock Island from Quanah to a junction with the Frisco's proposed Vernon-Seymour line
7. Application of the FW&DC to build a new line from Childress to Pampa via Shamrock

Those issues involving the SL-SF and Rock Island were relatively simple because the two carriers seemed at that time to be headed for a merger. Regulatory investigations should have been perfunctory. But rival proposals of the FW&DC and Rock Island in the eastern Panhandle of Texas confused the issue. Several parties, including one prominent FW&DC official, suggested that a compromise over trackage rights might be reached. A Rock Island representative boldly responded: "We have

told Mr. [Frederick E.] Williamson [president of the Burlington System] definitely that we will not join with him in building a joint line between Wellington and Shamrock." There would be no compromise; a fight was assured.[16]

There was considerable news late in 1929 and early in 1930—most of it good for the Frisco, and most of it mixed for the Rock Island. In a case not directly related but which reflected the expansionist policies during the period when Brown managed the Rock Island and Frisco, the CRI&P lost to the Missouri-Kansas-Texas Railroad in a contest to secure the Beaver, Meade & Englewood Railroad, an important grain carrier in the nearby Oklahoma Panhandle. Then, in mid-December, an ICC examiner recommended approval of all applications on behalf of the Rock Island and Frisco and against the proposal of the Denver Road. The regulatory agency essentially confirmed those recommendations four months later, but serious problems remained.[17]

Nevertheless, the citizens of Quanah were jubilant over the news. "The City of Quanah now faces a future of prosperity which equals and perhaps excels that of any town in this section," bubbled the editor of the *Quanah Tribune-Chief*. The manager of the Quanah Chamber of Commerce reflected this euphoria but warned against an influx of laborers anticipating jobs building the railroad. "We already have 100 to 200 men unemployed; . . . outsiders seeking employment . . . will suffer from it." Another community leader said the ICC's decision was "a wonderful thing" but added, cautiously, "If we get a good rain this town will be booming." These observations, sad to say, showed that the combined effects of the Great Depression and an area-wide drought had arrived in Hardeman County, Texas, by the late spring of 1930.[18]

There were other important caveats. The regulatory agency had ruled that the Frisco could acquire the GT&W but at a less inflated price. The estate of J. J. Jermyn, who had died in 1928, objected, but the agreement went forward anyway; on May 15, 1930, the Gulf, Texas & Western Railway emerged from receivership and several weeks later passed into the hands of the St. Louis–San Francisco as one of its wholly owned subsidiaries. Much more important to the Rock Island–Frisco plan was the decision of the Denver Road to seek reconsideration of the ICC's decision regarding the Texas Panhandle applications and the regulatory agency's willingness to do so. The result was referred to by one observer as a "final fight."[19]

## Gulf, Texas & Western Railway Company

OFFICE OF THE PRESIDENT

———

Circular No. 1

———

Dallas, Texas, May 16, 1930.

Pursuant to orders made by the United States District Court for the Northern District of Texas, Dallas Division, W. Frank Knox, Receiver of the estate and properties of the Gulf, Texas and Western Railway Company, has delivered and transferred the property, including the railroad, heretofore in his possession, to its owner, the Gulf, Texas and Western Railway Company, effective as of midnight, May 15, 1930.

All officers, employees and agents of the Receiver will, until further orders, continue in the discharge of their respective duties as officers, employees and agents of the Railway Company.

W. FRANK KNOX,
*President.*

Arguments were heard on July 9. According to Charles Sommer, "the Denver made a dying man's plea . . . and very ably presented its argument." This time the FW&DC contended that it had no objections to construction by the Rock Island from Shamrock through Quanah. Sommer worried that both companies might be granted permits. That, in a sense, is what happened. The ICC upheld the right of the Rock Island to build according to its earlier order but ruled that the FW&DC could also build from Childress to Pampa subject to joint trackage between Shamrock and Wellington. In other words, this section of line was to be built and operated jointly with each carrier free to solicit and develop traffic for itself at stations along its length. This decision was acceptable to the FW&DC, but it was not to come to fruition. Rock Island officials asked the ICC for a rehearing, saying that joint operation would have the ruinous effect of dividing local traffic. The Rock Island was willing to allow trackage rights over its line for the Denver Road provided that the FW&DC was not allowed to handle local or competitive traffic.[20]

The prospects were grim. Sommer brooded about them. "If anything should block the pro-posed construction it would be . . . tight money. There is no getting away from the fact that we are in the midst of a serious depression aggravated by universal drought." Nothing happened during the remainder of 1930. Late in February of the next year, however, Rock Island's President Gorman asserted that the line would be built in time; its construction, he said, was simply postponed.[21]

The Rock Island ultimately lost interest in the matter. In an attempt to compromise, the FW&DC agreed to build its line with the proviso that Rock Island could, within five years, acquire one-half interest in the portion between Shamrock and Wellington. It mattered little. The Frisco–Rock Island marriage was called off, and the Rock Island was in the hands of a receiver by mid-1933. The Frisco fared no better. It had laid a very short stretch of track south of Vernon in 1930 but made no effort to finish the line to Seymour. The SL-SF, of course, did go forward with acquisition and operation of the GT&W, but that little carrier, too, fell on hard times during the Depression, would be sold to the Rock Island in 1940, and later abandoned. Of all the carriers that participated in this drama, only the FW&DC accomplished any notable construction. The Denver Road completed its Pampa extension on July 16, 1932. It may have been a Pyrrhic victory; in 1970 the line would be abandoned from Wellington to Pampa, and the remainder faced an uncertain future.[22]

As this interesting if complex chapter of western railroad history was passing to the realm of what might have been, the QA&P was involved in still another potential construction project. As early as January 1925, officials of the Motley County Railway had contemplated the extension of that little line northward from Matador to a connection with the FW&DC at Childress. Nothing had come of it, and the Motley County road had passed to the QA&P in 1927. Yet in 1926, Charles Sommer was wondering if the line might not be lengthened to Quitaque or Turkey. Little further thought was given to the matter until 1929, however. By this time the FW&DC's South Plains construction had eaten into traffic that previously had moved via Matador. To counteract this loss, Sommer recommended an extension of "some ten or fifteen miles north of Matador, to recover our lost traffic." The line, Sommer observed, should be of light construction; the cost of train service would be minimal because the mixed train currently working the line from Roaring Springs could be used.[23]

On June 25, 1929, Frisco's President Kurn gave

his blessing, and within two months the proper papers were filed with the ICC. Meanwhile, the question of the new line's eventual destination arose. A representative from Turkey hoped that it would be located near that community so that livestock and grains might move all the way from Turkey to Fort Worth over the QA&P and the new route that had been proposed by the Frisco and Rock Island from Quanah. Sommer referred to this interest as an "invitation" and was flattered by it. Yet he was unswayed. Easy construction was promised through White Flat to a point three miles short of Flomot, near the south bank of the North Pease River, and presumably far enough from the Denver Road's South Plains line to avoid a territorial skirmish with that road. Sommer did not wish to push farther into a trade area which the FW&DC could claim as its own; neither did he wish to make large expenditures to bridge the North Pease River. He was willing to terminate the line "in the middle of nowhere."[24]

There was risk in this decision. Residents of Flomot perceived QA&P's petition to build its line to a point three miles from their community as either a death threat or blackmail. Such tactics were hardly new in the West. There is no record, however, that Sommer engaged in any such duplicity. Indeed, he worried that local support would fail if the QA&P was perceived as engaging in any attempt to strangle the little community. Sommer hoped Flomot would tender an invitation and sweeten it with bonus money. He was rewarded: the hard-pressed residents of that inland area promised $10,000.[25]

Sommer, nevertheless, was having second thoughts. Just days after the Great Crash of 1929, Sommer decided that the short project was "a pretty big proposition . . . at this time." At almost the same moment, he was astonished and perplexed when the ICC, without hearings or oral arguments, granted permission for construction. He had no desire to put his "neck into a noose" so, to secure an independent and unbiased viewpoint, he hired a consultant to study the issue. This man concluded, in part, "It is usually the province of railway branches to serve territory unprofitable [to the branches] themselves but are often necessary to protect the net income of the [owning system]. Such is the case here. The incentive to build the extension is to protect QA&P's net income." In other words, the branch would not earn enough to cover its expenses, but based on system earnings it would make a contribution to net profit. Sommer was not reassured. Moreover, there were other problems. Owners of property through which the line would pass had begun to engage in what Sommer called "extortion"; he would not, he hotly announced, "pension" them by buying land at "outrageous" prices. Nor was he confident about the line's traffic potential; the state of Texas had announced construction of a parallel highway, which surely would drain business to trucks. Finally, construction costs involved in getting into and out of the valley of the North Pease—in addition to the cost of bridging the stream—seemed prohibitive. All these problems, mirrored against the deepening Depression, convinced Sommer to abandon the project. On May 7, 1930, he relayed this news to J. M. Kurn.[26]

## CHAPTER 10

## A Strong and Symbiotic Relationship

Like yourself, I believe that the building of your
extension to Floydada means a new era for us, and
we have been greatly pleased by the conclusive
tone of the letters and wires that have been coming
from you.—Homer Steen to Charles H. Sommer,
May 7, 1927

SOON after Floyd County was organized, citizens of
its seat—Floydada—boasted that it was "the queen
city of the Plains." Without a railroad, however,
that was an idle assertion. To make good on their
claim, these citizens diligently sought to attract rail
service. It should not be a problem, they reasoned,
for Floydada lay astride the "only practical railroad
route from Dallas and Fort Worth to the Panhandle." Such a contention was nonsense, of course,
because it ignored the location of the Fort Worth
& Denver City Railway, a line already in service.
But Floydada's leaders were undaunted.[1]

As early as 1890, newspapers reported activity on
the part of a Fort Worth-to-Albuquerque rail line
which presumably would touch Floydada. Nothing
came of it. Then, early in the next century, W. M.
Massie and other Floydada boosters founded the
high-sounding Llano Estacado & Gulf Railway to
connect Floydada with Hereford, a village some 120
miles northwestward on the AT&SF's line from
Amarillo to Clovis. The local firm did some grading, but the line was never completed. Its equity
was purchased by the Santa Fe in 1909, and a road
between Plainview (on the AT&SF's north-south
line from Canyon to Lubbock) was placed in service on March 15, 1910. Floydada then staged a reception that was typical of those put on by established western communities when steamcars finally
arrived to serve them. Schools were dismissed and,
according to one account, "children piled all over
the huge steam locomotive." Local citizens were
pleased when the Santa Fe later chose to upgrade
the line with eighty-five-pound (per yard) steel rail.
Yet they eventually became dissatisfied with single-
carrier service and worked hard to secure other
lines. For that reason they had early supported the

QA&P and rejoiced when the ICC gave it permission to build into Floydada.[2]

Under a contract drawn between the QA&P and
219 citizens of Floyd County, the railroad was to
receive a free right-of-way from the top of the
Caprock escarpment as well as station and terminal grounds in Floydada. The railroad was to begin construction within twenty days after receiving
permission from the regulatory agency and was to
have the "road constructed to and into the city of
Floydada within eight-and-one-half months after
work begins."[3]

The ICC decision had come down in November
1926 and had granted the QA&P permission to go
only as far as Floydada, not to Lubbock. The leader
of the railroad committee in Floydada, W. M. Massie, expressed disappointment that the QA&P was
not allowed a more expansive permit but resolved
to make the best of it: "I suppose it is up to us
now to build your road into Floydada," he told
Charles Sommer, "and for your people and the
Floydada people to make your road the best road
and Floydada the best town in this part of the West."
Sommer saw the implications of the ICC's decision and was even more disappointed, "considering
the future of our property." Traffic in and out of
Floydada plus interchange with the Santa Fe there
would be useful, but business that might have derived from Lubbock "would have balanced our
traffic in a much better way." Yet he was philosophi-
cal. Since the original application had not contemplated construction to Lubbock, the QA&P had
not filed formal application to do so before making
the oral arguments, and the QA&P attorneys had
broached the idea only at the last minute, Sommer
concluded that the ICC could not have acted on it.[4]

The QA&P's president was determined to put the best face on the situation. "First on the Plains," a phrase coined by Sam Lazarus, became Sommer's watchword—at least in public. He told his brother A. F. Sommer to begin "setting stakes for a mile so that grubbing operations" might begin west of the QA&P's end-of-tracks at MacBain. The editor of the *Floyd County Hesperian* took such efforts to mean that the QA&P would be "hauling wheat from Floydada the next summer."[5]

The editor was wrong. On January 17, 1927, Charles Sommer quietly ordered all work discontinued. He contended that the "idea of extending the line is not definitely abandoned," but his tone was ominous. Unfortunately, extant records do not explain this abrupt change of mind. Sommer's outward expressions suggested that it had to do with "business conditions at this time." It may be, however, that the fortunes of QA&P's parent, the Frisco, were not good or that the Brown combination (Frisco and Rock Island) was pushing more important projects. Before he died, Sam Lazarus had maintained that "powers that be" in the East (Brown, Kurn, and the Frisco's borad of directors) had given full blessing for the construction from MacBain to Floydada. He, too, had been wrong.[6]

Sam Lazarus had also stated, with vigor and veracity, that "we want satisfied customers." The citizens of Floydada who had supported the QA&P's application now felt that Lazarus and his successor, Charles Sommer, had engaged in duplicity and chicanery. This attitude was quickly reflected in correspondence directed to Sommer. "It does look like your company with the backing of the great Frisco System could push this little extension to early completion," complained W. M. Massie. Then he got to the heart of the issue: "As you know, Mr. Sommer, there is a contract between the QA&P and the people . . . which is plain and specific." Sommer tried to stall; Massie would have none of it.[7]

A few days later Sommer was confronted with a complaint from the Railroad Commission of Texas which asked him to "state very frankly the situation." Sommer responded, saying: "No one regrets more than I do, the apparent turn of affairs entirely beyond our control." But as he had told Massie earlier, "late in January financial obstacles developed and business conditions made it necessary to temporarily suspend work." He did not explain what he meant by "business conditions," but the word "temporarily" held out hope.[8]

Meanwhile, citizens of Floydada held a meeting on March 3, 1927, which one railroad official called "rather free, full, and hectic." The citizens appointed a delegation to visit Sommer and Frisco officials in St. Louis, and when those meetings failed to produce satisfactory results, the group determined to bring suit against the QA&P in the amount of $100,000. At the same time, President Kurn told Sommer that he might advise the Texas Railroad Commission and the Floydada citizens that "we are holding up on the extension of the Quanah Route until we complete our financing." Sommer did so and acknowledged that construction could not be completed in the allotted period of eight and one-half months; he requested an extension and promised to push the work forward as soon as the contract was let.[9]

In a few days this pledge was confirmed when Sommer announced that invitations to bid had been sent to contractors. Sixteen firms responded, and on May 6 a contract was let to the Lone Star Construction Company of San Antonio for $100,000. The QA&P agreed to provide work train equipment at $25 per day for locomotives and low per diem rates for cars. It also promised to provide water from Roaring Springs at twenty-five cents per thousand gallons. Work began on June 15, 1927.[10]

The program went forward as promised. Orders were placed by A. F. Sommer's office in Quanah for ties at seventy cents each, f.o.b. point of origin in East Texas. These and the other necessary items were marshaled at the MacBain materials yard and dispatched "to the front" as required. By the middle of summer, work was being conducted along three sections by fifty-three men who were in charge of a combination of traditional and modern machines and motive power. In early fall Sommer predicted that all grading would be completed by December 1 and that laying rail would commence by December 15.[11]

Sommer was overly optimistic. The first eight miles of construction, in the rough and broken country on the approaches to and through the Caprock escarpment, were particularly troublesome. Subsoil conditions required the use of graders, followed by power shovels, delaying the excavation process. In the early fall of 1927, the work force was greatly depleted when workers fled to the nearby cotton fields to harvest the annual crop. These delays forced Sommer to ask the Interstate Commerce Commission for an extension of the time limit given by that agency. The request was granted with the provision that service be initiated by May 1, 1928.[12]

Work on the extension from MacBain began on June 15, 1927.

A crowd, including a uniformed band, came from Floydada and Roaring Springs to see this mechanical marvel cut its way through the Caprock escarpment.

The Santa Fe, which all along had objected to the QA&P's expansion plans, sought the closing of certain streets in Floydada, which, if successful, would prevent physical connection between the two carriers. As incentive, Santa Fe offered to build a new station facility for the community. The QA&P responded by pledging the construction of its own station, "which would represent an investment of at least $35,000." A vote of the citizens was required and, when it was held, a majority denied Santa Fe's request. The incident was not unimportant; it augured ill for relations between the large company and the smaller one.[13]

Land for right-of-way from MacBain to the top of the Caprock was donated by the Matador Land & Cattle Company; that on the Plains, from the edge of the Caprock to Floydada, was secured by the Floydada Citizens Committee. These lands were acquired without problem—with three exceptions, which required judgments—through simple deeds. One of the condemnation suits involved land at the southern edge of Floydada which the company wished to use for construction of a wye. The award for it was, in Charles Sommer's opinion, "ruinously liberal," but, he added with a shrug, "the cost comes out of their own pockets." It did not work that way, however; the QA&P paid at least $5,000 of the nearly $12,000 judgment fee. There were additional problems when the local committee was unable to raise all of the money before completion of the line. In the end, the committee raised more than $50,000 and satisfied most of the debts—but not without considerable acrimony.[14]

Tracklaying began on February 6, 1928, and was done manually. The process involved twelve men with tongs who took rails from flatcars to the awaiting ties. It was an old-fashioned, laborious, and time-consuming method which resulted in numerous delays, especially during the rainy spring of that year.[15]

During the previous fall, Charles Sommer had forecast that the QA&P would have "trains running into Floydada between February 15 and March 1," but it did not. Delay followed delay. Machines failed. Orders for materials arrived tardily and were incomplete. Some portion of the roadbed required additional ballast. And the weather was awful. The ICC granted two more extensions, to October 1, 1928.[16]

Money was a matter of great concern—to pay the contractor and, for the contractor, to profit from the work. QA&P records do not yield a complete picture of the financial arrangements necessary to carry the Floydada extension to completion, but it is clear that the road's capital stock was increased by $50,000 and that it was purchased by the Frisco for cash. The SL-SF also put up the remaining funds. But when the final settlement was made, the Lone Star Construction Company reported "a loss of a little over $16,000 on the work." Nevertheless, Lone Star's manager said, "We are not kicking and will try to make it back on some other job."[17]

QA&P officials anticipated that two new townsites would be created on the Floydada extension—one at the base of the Caprock, some eight miles west of Roaring Springs, and the other between the Caprock escarpment and Floydada. As it developed, only one—Dougherty—was created; it lay midway, between Floydada and Roaring Springs. The "original" MacBain was moved four miles west but not developed. Neither was Boothe Spur, an elevator site between Floydada and the new village of Dougherty. Of course, there were no opportunities for townsite development at Floydada.[18]

As early as November 19, 1926, Frank M. Dougherty, who owned land through which the new line would run, had contacted railroad officials about the possibility of creating a townsite there. He suggested that he would "develop this myself or sell you an interest." Charles Sommer agreed that the best location was on Dougherty land but hedged on committing the railroad to participation in the actual development of it. During the summer of 1927, Dougherty proposed three possible alternatives: he was willing to sell 640 acres at $60 per acre to a promoter who would assume all risks, to enter into a "50–50" arrangement, or to undertake the entire business himself. By early 1928, Sommer agreed that the latter option was best. "At the beginning," Sommer later reported to a stockholder, "it looked that we might have an interest in the townsite, but that was waived and the matter was turned over in its entirety to Mr. Dougherty who has full control." The community was named after William H. Dougherty, Frank Dougherty's late father and a widely known Texas businessman.[19]

The new community was platted during March 1928 under the auspices of the Dougherty Townsite Company. The *Floyd County Hesperian,* in nearby Floydada, announced the event in bold headlines: "Townsite Company Launched by Local Capital to Build Modern City." Frank Dougherty was no less expansive: "We are going to build a substantial little city, for the future as well as for the present, and expect to serve a tremendous trade territory south, north, and east of our town." As rails of the

QA&P inched closer, efforts to market town lots and nearby farm property increased. On March 22, Dougherty reported that sales were "most encouraging." Indeed, two elevators, two lumberyards, and one cotton gin already had been arranged for, and construction was going forward on a new brick store building, several other structures, and filling stations.[20]

The plat of Dougherty was very appealing. It featured twelve streets and six avenues. The main thoroughfares—Floyd Street, running north and south from the QA&P depot, and Texas Avenue—met at Austin Place, a traffic circle in the center of town. A waterworks system with five miles of main and supplied by a fifty-five-thousand-gallon tower was planned; fire plugs would offer protection. The QA&P pledged to do its part in making Dougherty attractive; the railroad anticipated an expenditure of at least $10,000 for new facilities at the townsite. It would make good on these promises. The QA&P properties at Dougherty included an impressive depot, a cotton platform, a water tank, stock pens, and various sidings.[21]

Tracklaying went forward, albeit slowly, and plans were announced for interim train service. Rails reached Dougherty in mid-March 1928 and the Floydada city limits on April 6; the wye and industrial tracks at Floydada were completed during the last week of May. Sommer announced that formal freight service would be instituted on July 1 by running "the Matador stub train through to Floydada during the night." Even before that, the QA&P had quietly accepted and delivered no fewer than fifty cars of revenue freight—mostly building materials for lumberyards at Dougherty—in addition to routine traffic for the Lone Star Construction Company. It was the same with passenger service. When one A. E. Williams—"holding FWD ticket form Skeleton #1 A36324 reading Dougherty, Texas"—arrived in Roaring Springs aboard train 51 on August 14, he was "the first passenger to be ticketed over the extension." As the agent at Roaring Springs told A. F. Sommer, "We have arranged for him to go from Roaring Springs to Dougherty on Extra 19 west about 4 P.M."[22]

Plans for regularly scheduled freight and passenger service were much on the minds of QA&P officials as well as those of the citizens of Floydada throughout the summer and early fall of 1928. Sommer hired a man to canvass the new service area for traffic but cautioned him to solicit only intrastate shipments via the AT&SF at Floydada because permission to move interstate traffic through that gateway had not been secured. At the same time, Sommer urged Frisco officials to seek joint traffic via Quanah and to adjust SL-SF service between Oklahoma City and Quanah to facilitate coordinated movements over the new lines. In Floydada there was eager anticipation; each stride toward completion of the project was reported with keen enthusiasm. "With every passing day it becomes more apparent that Floydada is to have a very considerable building boom within the next six months" because of the benefits that were sure to come with the arrival of the Quanah Route. Finally, all was in readiness; the Lone Star Construction Company advised Sommer that it would have the entire project ready for the railroad on October 1.[23]

Nothing less than the establishment of a new "flagship" passenger train—the *Plainsman*—and a first-rate celebration would suffice for the formal inauguration of service to Floydada. The Chamber of Commerce at Floydada planned the festivities, and they were tremendously successful. More than five thousand persons from the Panhandle-Plains area jammed into the small city and were joined by another seven hundred from towns along the QA&P and from as far away as Oklahoma City, who arrived aboard the first run of the *Plainsman*. Sandwiches, coffee, cookies, fruit, and pie were served to each of the passengers and to other visitors by members of the 1922 Study Club. Brief ceremonies marked the historic event. Noisy band and pep squad demonstrations preceded the formal welcome, which was extended by E. C. Nelson, chairman of the committee on right-of-way finance for the new line. After these ceremonies, delegations from various cities and towns formed in a parade with the Quanah delegation and band carrying banners and badges welcoming Floydada into the QA&P family. Entertainment was provided throughout the day, and the celebration ended only when the eastbound *Plainsman* pulled out at 6:00 P.M.[24]

Only a temporary depot was ready at Floydada when train service began; the fine edifice that had been promised would come soon, however. Sam Lazarus had pledged that the Quanah Route would erect a "brick station building, sufficiently large to also accommodate Santa Fe trains, and would attempt to interest Fred Harvey in maintaining a lunch counter" there. The AT&SF building was a shabby affair, located far from the town square, and Lazarus reasoned that a "union" station would benefit both carriers and the Floydada citizenry. He was overly optimistic about cooperation from

Seven hundred persons arrived aboard the first *Plainsman* and joined another five thousand who were already there for the festivities. *C. C. Roberts collection*

The Floydada station was as handsome as Lazarus and Sommer had promised.

the Santa Fe. But Sommer affirmed that Lazarus's promise would be honored. Indeed, he would do better: it would be "one of the best depots a town the size of Floydada has ever been provided." A contract for construction had been let to the George P. Reintjes Company of Kansas City in May. There were the usual if irksome delays, and the job resulted in predictable cost overruns, but Sommer proclaimed the workmanship to be "first class."[25]

The building was ready for inspection and "formal opening" on February 11, 1929. A. F. Sommer arranged to have only QA&P equipment assigned to the *Plainsman* that day and ordered that its eastbound departure be delayed for one hour so that guests could view the new station building as well as the "crack all-steel train." Hundreds of persons took the opportunity to do just that. Homer Steen, the enthusiastic editor of the *Floyd County Hes-*

The FW&DC began service to Plainview with a spectacular celebration only a few weeks after the QA&P began operations to Floydada.

*perian,* spoke for all when he asserted that the QA&P's station was "one of the finest buildings, both structurally and architecturally, in the entire community" and that it "would meet all requirements of a station to serve a city of 15,000 people." To be sure, there was great pride in Floydada; Sommer received several telegrams affirming that feeling. And there was good reason to be proud, Sommer thought: the building had cost fully $50,000.[26]

The euphoria at Floydada early in 1929 was representative of the general optimism of the time, particularly the deep faith in West Texas and in

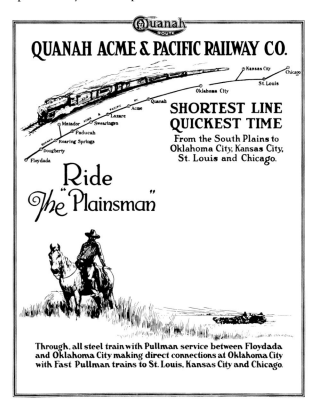

the symbiotic relationship between the carriers and their service areas. Nearby Plainview, for instance, eagerly awaited new service guaranteed by construction to and through that aspiring city by the Fort Worth & Denver City Railway as a part of its South Plains expansion package. The anticipation there ended when the Denver Road opened its line to Plainview about a month and a half after the QA&P initiated service to Floydada. The FW&DC announced the establishment of "direct through freight service" as well as a new passenger train, the *West Texan,* offering overnight service with "standard sleepers and coaches" between Plainview and Fort Worth and Dallas. Collectively, the FW&DC

would, it said, provide "convenient service . . . straight through the heart of the fertile South Plains region" and at the same time "open up a new empire of riches."[27]

It seemed that what was good for the railroads was good for the area and vice versa. This mutual benefit was reflected when the QA&P arranged for a pair of the Frisco's dairy agents to make presentations for area farmers regarding "proof methods of feeding, the care of dairy cows, and economical milk production." There was also more direct evidence of this symbiotic relationship. Lockney and Turkey, villages on the FW&DC's South Plains extension, increased in size and quality with the arrival of the railroad. So, too, did Floyd County and Floydada after the QA&P began service. These new transportation devices, coupled with mechanization and an "inexhaustible supply of water under the Plains," which could be used for irrigation, promised boundless and endless prosperity for the region—or so everyone thought until late 1929.[28]

## CHAPTER II

# Dreams, Designs, and Disappointments

Until business conditions are better we are not justified in building any more lines.—J. M. Kurn to
Charles H. Sommer, March 14, 1930

CHARLES Sommer, like Sam Lazarus before him, was a great booster of the Panhandle-Plains area. His belief in the potential of the region was accentuated by certainty that there was an "inexhaustible supply of shallow water" available there for irrigation. This same intense spirit of optimism similarly engaged others, especially civic leaders of inland villages that still aspired for rail service but also leaders from communities that already boasted such service. All of them constantly entreated railroad managers to build branches and even trunk roads to serve or better serve their needs.

The youthful exuberance of the Panhandle-Plains country was reflected by a pattern of boosterism that had typified western development for decades. All that differentiated it from the rest was the lateness—it persisted well into the automobile era and to the Great Crash of 1929. This optimistic scenario was mirrored by a plethora of publicity pieces. The Lubbock Chamber of Commerce distributed a study entitled *Rainfall Record for Thirty-Five Year Period* covering 1894 to 1925, which was designed to prove that the area was well watered. One Lubbock firm published a series of booklets and broadsides advertising "fertile land ($30.00 to $50.00 per acre), pure water, good health, good schools, and other things that you'll enjoy on the South Plains of Texas." The Lovington, New Mexico, Chamber of Commerce advertised what it labeled "the last of the cheap good lands." Information on "cotton ginnings in bales," showing the spread of cotton plantings to the northwest, was distributed by Southwestern Bell Telephone Company. Numerous agencies provided census data that demonstrated a dramatic growth in the number of farms and farmers plus an equally dramatic increase in land values from 1920 through 1929. And the Chamber of Commerce of Levelland, Texas, contended that there were "unbounded opportunities" in that

"new and prosperous country." Newspapers ballyhooed similarly. The lead article in the *Lovington* (New Mexico) *Leader* for December 28, 1928, enumerated great expectations in that community for general agriculture and ranching based on inexpensive and readily available fuel for pumping water to irrigate area lands—plus the growing possibility of adequate rail service. The *Fort Worth Star-Telegram* of December 30, 1928, carried dual banner headlines: "1928 Sets New Prosperity Records" and "1929 Outlook in West Texas Bright." The latter was a reflection, at least in part, of numerous railroad construction proposals for the region.[1]

Except for its already established lines and the trade areas along them—which were freely and expensively advertised—the Santa Fe was, as it had been throughout the decade in this region, a reluctant participant in the rail expansion movement. It nearly always chose to respond rather than to initiate. It frequently sent survey crews into the field for the purpose of creating rumors; other times it was seeking legitimate information. Naturally its intentions were cloudy. An example was a proposed extension of the Santa Fe's Seagraves Junction (near Lubbock)—to Seagraves line—that would have taken the road into newly developed oil fields around Lovington, New Mexico, nearly ninety miles. It was not built, and there is no evidence that the AT&SF was serious about the venture. Neither is there proof that the Santa Fe intended to drive a new line through the rough country off the Caprock to establish a direct line from West Texas to Dallas and Fort Worth. Santa Fe officials did at one time, however, indicate a desire to secure trackage rights over the QA&P's new line from Floydada to MacBain with the idea of building that company's own road east, thereby forging such a direct route. Under the arrangement there would have been a quid pro quo: the QA&P would have been given trackage rights over the AT&SF from Floydada to Plainview. A rumor also suggested that the Santa Fe would build a north-south line from Canadian (on its "freight main" in the extreme northeastern corner of the Texas Panhandle) through territory generally devoid of rail service to Sweetwater. Such a route, had it been built, would have essentially sealed off the entire region as Santa Fe's domain. In a sense, that had already been accomplished when the AT&SF somewhat unwillingly acquired the ailing Kansas City, Mexico & Orient Railway. It had further sought to protect its historic service area by acquiring the Clinton & Oklahoma Western Railroad in the northeastern Texas Panhandle area.[2]

In March 1928, the AT&SF announced plans to construct a line from Hale Center to Parmerton, sixty-six miles, paralleling its own Lubbock-Texico route and, in large part, the FW&DC's new road from Plainveiw to Dimmitt. One correspondent in the area who was in a position to know told Charles Sommer that Santa Fe officials had forthrightly stated "that their object was to prevent other roads from securing permits to extend their lines into the South Plains Country." On the other hand, one journalist argued that the Hale Center–Parmerton construction would be part of a through route from Dallas to the High Plains. The Denver Road immediately pledged a fight; the QA&P would offer the FW&DC moral support. Sommer thought the Santa Fe's application "had for its purpose principally spite"; he could not see that the line was "in any way justified." The ICC saw it similarly; the application was denied on February 25, 1929.[3]

Still another project involved the Texas–New Mexico Railway, corporate puppet of the Texas & Pacific Railway—itself a part of the Missouri Pacific System. The Texas–New Mexico Railway had earlier secured a permit to open the oil patch northwest of Monahans (on the T&P's main line) with a route through Wink and Kermit. Then, in December 1928, it asked the ICC for permission to extend onward some seventy miles to Hobbs and Lovington, New Mexico. This petition stood in opposition to one filed a few days earlier by the AT&SF to extend its Seagraves branch to Lovington. Another fight between rail titans was promised; the QA&P wished ill for both participants. Lovington, of course, looked forward to receiving rail service— but not from the Santa Fe, a company, said the editor of the *Lovington Leader,* that had "had every opportunity for extending its road into this country but which had never expressed any desire to do so until some other road" proposed to do so. "It has

already sinned away its day of grace" and "should not be permitted to further hinder the development of southeastern New Mexico," bellowed this irate newspaperman. Both applications were authorized, but the Santa Fe declined to exercise its rights, and only the Texas–New Mexico line was constructed.[4]

The Texas & Pacific was involved in another and, to the QA&P, more threatening expansion movement. Some years earlier, the T&P had acquired both the Cisco & Northeastern Railway and the Abilene & Southern Railroad. These acquisitions were not particularly important except that they signaled an ambitious posture on the part of the T&P. Then, in 1928, rumors circulated that it would acquire the more strategically important Roscoe, Snyder & Pacific Railroad, a short line that acted as something of a buffer between the giant MP-T&P and Santa Fe systems. The acquisition was not consummated, but T&P's interest in occupying new territory did not abate.[5]

During the summer of 1930 attorneys for the T&P filed an application with the ICC calling for construction of 333 miles of new line beginning at Big Spring (on T&P's main line) and running north-northwest to Amarillo, with branches to both Lubbock and Vega. It was a massive proposal that engendered equal portions of support and opposition. Sommer predicted "one of the bitterest fights on record" but concluded that the QA&P could not intervene unless "it could, in some way, state its definite position as to the future construction of line westward from Floydada." Failing that, Sommer could only grouse that "the T&P is wanting to horn in" on an area that QA&P had always coveted. He did not believe T&P's avarice ended with this application but that it was part of a grand plan to link up Missouri Pacific lines in Kansas and Texas as well as forge a new route from Texas to the Denver & Rio Grande Western Railroad at Trinidad, Colorado. It was mere speculation on his part. In any event, the ICC eventually ruled that the T&P could build only 126 of the 333 proposed route miles. The T&P was not interested, and the project was dropped. Thus perished what a Dallas writer suggested would have been "the largest single piece of railroad construction in Texas in twenty years."[6]

Another major carrier, the Rock Island, was similarly engaged in one final dream of expansion in the western Texas Panhandle. In April 1930, it projected a seventy-six-mile branch southwestward from its Amarillo-Tucumcari line at Vega, Texas, to Forrest, New Mexico. A railroad representative referred to it as a part of the CRI&P's growing "feeder system," and it may have been. Or it may have represented a defensive strategy. Before plans could be completed, however, the company fell on hard times; construction was never begun.[7]

Not surprisingly, a "paper railroad" represented still another aspect of this broad scenario. In 1928, a charter had been granted to the high-sounding Roswell, Lubbock & Memphis Short Line Railway Company. This firm presumed to build a road from Wellington, along the eastern border of the Texas Panhandle to the Texas–New Mexico border west of Lubbock and planned to use several miles of grade thrown up two decades earlier but never tied and railed. The new company was no more successful than the one that had done the grading. During the years 1927–29 its promoters attempted to sell equities, especially those in a grade from Lubbock to Silverton, to the QA&P. Sommer decided that the property was "so situated that it would be of no use to the Quanah Route."[8]

These same promoters were also behind a scheme that would have linked Snyder, Texas, and Roswell, New Mexico. They contended that when completed the road "would be turned over to operation by a trunk line." This idea spawned great sentiment in support from the affected communities but also great antagonism from the established carriers. Frisco's President Kurn told Sommer to "fight it" since his intention was "to extend the QA&P to El Paso." Nothing came of the Snyder, Roswell & Gulf Railroad, as the company was called, but Kurn's statement on the matter was important in the extreme.[9]

The QA&P's management team was not one to sit idly by. Even before full rail service had been instituted to Floydada, the Sommer brothers spent every available waking moment on plans for a new and dramatic expansion effort for the Quanah Route. The two corresponded endlessly. Charles Sommer, in his methodical way, packaged all recommendations and engineering data obtained from his brother and other sources into a seventy-five-page document entitled "Report on the Examination of Routes West of Floydada, Texas: Proposed Extension of the Quanah, Acme & Pacific Railway Company," which was delivered to President Kurn of the Frisco on January 26, 1929.[10]

Predictably, the Sommer report advocated expansion to the road's historical goal—El Paso. Three routes were evaluated: (1) via Floydada, Petersburg, Abernathy, Levelland, Plains, Lovington, and Artesia to El Paso (378 miles); (2) via Floydada, Petersburg, Abernathy, Levelland, Plains, Loving-

ton, and Carlsbad to El Paso (389 miles); and (3) via Floydada, Hale Center, Cotton Center, Littlefield, and Roswell to El Paso (399 miles). Heavy traffic in potash from Carlsbad, oil from the Artesia field, and agricultural commodities from West Texas offered local traffic incentives. Additionally, Sommer pointed out, through traffic could be attracted to the QA&P-Frisco route because it would be the short line between El Paso and St. Louis (the SP-CRI&P Golden State Route would remain the short line from El Paso to Chicago). Future traffic also existed, he thought, in a potential agreement with the Mexico Northwestern, an independent line that could be tapped at El Paso. The Floydada–Roswell–El Paso option included the possibility of a major spur by way of trackage rights over the Santa Fe from Hale Center to Plainview or, failing that, a new branch between the two places—and perhaps an extension of it westward from Plainview to Olton and maybe even on to Tucumcari, New Mexico. All of these communities could be counted on for support in the form of free rights-of-way and bonuses.[11]

There was general agreement among QA&P and Frisco officials as to what should be done and what the problems would be. Sommer thought that the Roswell route would be the least controversial and predicted that it would generate the greatest amount of local traffic. Kurn agreed and, with the concurrence of his chief engineer, F. G. Jonah, approved the project as long as it was "predicated on El Paso as the ultimate terminal." Any activity, they knew, would aggravate the Santa Fe, which, said Sommer, would "attempt to block any effort of the Quanah Route to build west from Floydada." Nevertheless, he quietly ordered attorneys to draw up preliminary drafts of papers to be filed with the Interstate Commerce Commission.[12]

Communities along the proposed routes had hoped for years to attract the QA&P. Their interest was accentuated when rumors spread in early 1929 that the QA&P was about to move. A writer for the *El Paso Times* proudly observed that the new extension would put that city "in touch with the Great Plains Country." Editorial comment throughout the potential service area expressed similar hopes, and "railroad meetings" occupied the time of leaders in each of the aspiring communities. Sommer was reticent about details. He said only, "Our objective, of course, is an extension westwardly at some future time."[13]

But the usually optimistic Charles Sommer had several concerns about the El Paso extension during

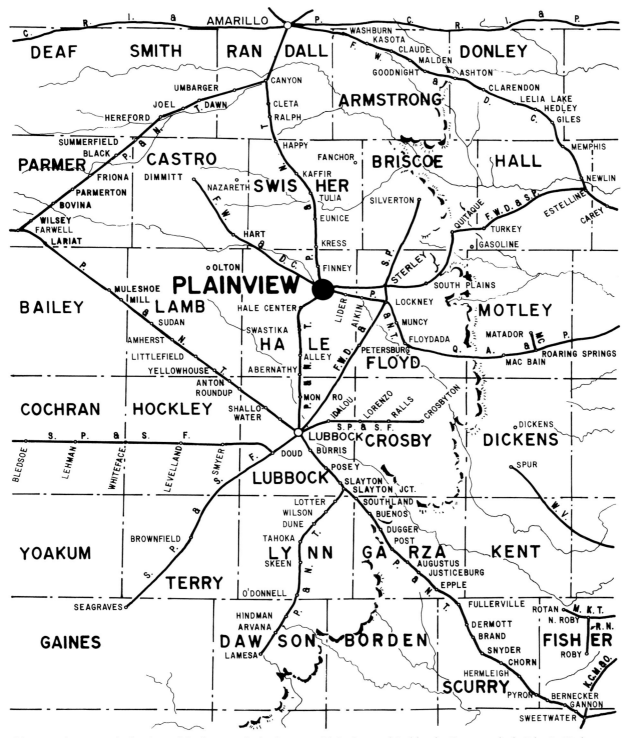

This map gives some indication of the intense rivalry between Plainview and Lubbock. *Cartography by John L. Hodson*

the summer of 1929. He was worried about retaliation on the part of the Santa Fe and perhaps the FW&DC. He was also concerned about circumstances at El Paso. "It is questionable if we will ever want to build to El Paso," he told Kurn, "unless we have some assurance that we can reach the industrial district" of that city. There was great potential in interchange traffic with the Mexico Northwestern, but Sommer thought "the Mexican situation needed clarifying," which might be "a long way off." It is not clear whether Sommer was having second thoughts about El Paso. It is clear, though, that he was thinking of more immediate or short-term expansion gains. "We will never be able to handle wheat in volume until our line penetrates further into" West Texas, he concluded, and such expansions should be accomplished swiftly to fore-stall moves by other roads. He courted community leaders throughout the area immediately beyond Floydada, especially those of Plainview and Lubbock.[14]

Sommer quickly perceived the intense rivalry between Lubbock and Plainview. Each hoped to become the queen city of the area, and of late, Lubbock seemed to have the advantage. The FW&DC's recent expansion, long promoted by Plainview, had, in fact, benefited Lubbock more. Leaders of that community saw the QA&P as a means of cementing its gains; leaders of Plainview saw the Quanah Route as its last hope for supremacy. Representatives of both communities had told Sommer "repeatedly that they have realized their mistake in not encouraging our expansion westwardly . . . rather than supporting the Burlington [FW&DC] . . . which they now" believed "was a mistake." The Denver Road had given them only a "competitive Texas line" instead of "a direct route to St. Louis and the East" such as the QA&P would have afforded.[15]

Sommer looked hard for ways to protect the small road's immediate future and historic goal to build to El Paso—in other words, to keep all options open. Protecting the short term, he increasingly believed, would protect the long term. To do this he urged the construction of thirteen miles of track from Floydada west to a connection with the new FW&DC line and trackage rights over that road to Lubbock—but only if the "Lubbock people were to provide separate terminal grounds for us, without cost, at a location in Lubbock agreeable to us." To balance this, Sommer also urged construction from Floydada on a northwesterly course to Plainview—provided, of course, that the "Plainview people furnish us with suitable terminal facilities, without cost." Delay would be fatal, he maintained, "because the time is not very distant when the Fort Worth & Denver City or the Santa Fe will occupy the only territory in this region available for rail construction, and if they succeed in doing this before we start construction west of Floydada, the Quanah Route will be bottled up."[16]

On January 9, 1929, the *Lubbock Avalanche-Journal* carried a story asserting that the QA&P would soon extend its line from Floydada to Ralls and then into Lubbock via trackage rights over the AT&SF. It sparked a veritable avalanche of rumors in Lubbock and in the area west and southwest of that city. The Lubbock Chamber of Commerce asked Charles Sommer if it could assist in any way. No fewer than 269 persons in the Morton, Texas, area signed petitions calling on the QA&P to build from Lubbock to El Paso by way of their community—which, they said, was "the last of the celebrated Plains country now being developed rapidly by peoples from all sections of the United States."[17]

Charles Sommer asked the Lubbock Chamber of Commerce for direct evidence of how the QA&P could "get into Lubbock, get out, and what it can offer in the way of tonnage." He was assured that there were adequate opportunities for traffic and facilities in Lubbock. The QA&P's new traffic manager, W. L. Richardson, had mixed feelings. He liked the idea of gaining "a connection with the Santa Fe at a main line point" such as Lubbock because it would be useful in attracting overhead traffic, but he was skeptical about the QA&P's ability to compete for local business with the two carriers already serving that community. On balance, he was "somewhat reluctant" to suggest a line that would be built for the sole "purpose of serving Lubbock." Sommer, however, urged construction from Floydada west to the FW&DC with the idea of entering Lubbock over its rails, which, he said, was "fully justified because there is unquestionably a big volume of tonnage at Lubbock and that town is growing by leaps and bounds."[18]

Plainview and the country to the west of it had similarly historical desires for service by the QA&P. In 1927 interest renewed; by 1929 it was at fever pitch. The movement in Plainview was led by Albert G. Hinn, president of the Harvest Queen Mill & Elevator Company. Hinn advocated QA&P's expansion to give West Texas a "main line and short haul to Fort Worth and Dallas, Oklahoma City, and St. Louis." Yet Hinn wanted more than merely the lengthening of the line from Floydada to Plainview; he also wanted a longer northwestward extension to the Southern Pacific at Tucumcari, New Mexico, which, he pointed out, would give the Quanah Route additional important local traffic while satisfying the long-hoped-for El Paso and transcontinental aspirations. Hinn urged a reconnaissance trip to examine the area, and Sommer agreed. Late in January 1929, the two men left

Plainview in the QA&P's "open Chrysler 70, with permanent glass winter top." A few days later Sommer made his report to the SL-SF's Kurn. He recommended construction from Floydada to a point near the Texas–New Mexico border (short of Tucumcari) via Hale Center, Olton, Springlake, and Friona along with a branch to Plainview from Hale Center or, preferably, trackage rights from Floydada to Plainview over the AT&SF.[19]

Sommer ordered W. L. Richardson into the field to secure data on traffic potential, and, predictably, his appearance set off wild speculation. Olton, which featured itself the "Mecca of the Plains," and which was growing at a spectacular rate, was particularly devoted to the QA&P. Richardson's study confirmed potential at Olton and throughout the territory west-northwest of Plainview. A line serving the area would be "the best tonnage producer . . . which might be built on the Plains by the QA&P," he said. Richardson was obviously excited about the potential in local traffic, but he was even more expansive about the need to connect with the T&P at Lovington or the Southern Pacific "somewhere in New Mexico" so that the QA&P might "bid for California traffic." Sommer agreed but focused more on the area west-southwest—a territory "not now served by rail . . . and about the only available area left for new construction." It would be necessary to "occupy the territory" quickly, however.[20]

Other carriers, as Sommer implied, were showing interest in the region. The Santa Fe, although recently frustrated in its expansion efforts, was always a threat. Sommer reported that the AT&SF was ready to file applications for permission to construct new lines from Plainview to Olton, or from Littlefield to Olton, and from Post to Fort Worth. The Texas & Pacific was also contemplating lengthening its Lovington Branch to Roswell. A much grander proposal involved the FW&DC. Early in 1930, the Stamford Chamber of Commerce put forward a campaign—later discussed in detail at a great railroad meeting in Plainview—which called for no fewer than four Denver Road projects involving five hundred miles of line. These included Dimmitt, Texas, to Tucumcari, New Mexico; Plainview, Texas, to Roswell, New Mexico; Spur, Texas, to Plainview; and, Stamford, Texas, directly to Fort Worth. None of these plans had the endorsement

of the railroad involved. Indeed, the president of the Burlington—FW&DC's parent—declared that "we are not in any way interested in it." His statement was a harbinger.[21]

The QA&P was having problems of its own. On February 13, 1929, Sommer had asked W. B. Storey, president of the AT&SF, if his road would allow the QA&P trackage rights between Floydada and Plainview, "including the right to serve industries in Plainview." Storey's chilly reply came a few days later: "It would seem that one company should be able to handle all the business on our line, Plainview to Floydada, and if we give you trackage it would mean two railroads serving a country that will hardly support one." He did not close the door, but Sommer concluded that "unless we can be assured of serving the principal industries in Plainview, there would be no incentive" to extend there. Moreover, a private consultant told Sommer that business there was becoming "dull" and, more important, the recently built lines of the Denver Road had "curtailed the territory tributary [to Plainview] before they were built."[22]

It was a moot question. If the effects of the Depression were slow in coming to West Texas, they certainly were not slow in coming to the SL-SF, the QA&P's parent. As early as March 1930, J. M. Kurn had told Sommer that "until business conditions are better we are not justified in building any more lines." It was a hard pill for the QA&P's president. He was a no-nonsense businessman, but he had always been an ambitious apostle of expansion—especially to El Paso. But he consoled himself that "conditions change overnight," and, furthermore, Kurn had told him that he still intended to "extend the Quanah Route, at the proper time." But that moment seemed increasingly remote. Kurn sent Sommer a terse telegram from aboard the New York Central's train 11 on December 4, 1931: "It is absolutely impossible for us to advance any money for construction at this time." A few months later the Frisco was again in the hands of the courts, a casualty of "hard times."[23]

Few recognized it at the time, but the last vestiges of the railroad construction era were passing. That long and heroic period of the nation's history was a victim of the Great Depression and of changes in transportation services.

## CHAPTER 12

## A Corking Good Job

We will never again be able to build the line from
Quanah to Acme with the cut-off through the
north of Quanah as cheaply as it can be done at
this time.—Charles H. Sommer to J. M. Kurn,
October 7, 1929.

THE country's great railroad construction boom
may have ended—and the QA&P's part in it may
have been disappointingly small—but the final chapter of the Quanah Route's construction era had
not yet been written. Strangely, the concluding
burst of activity did not occur at its western ex-
tremity and did not reflect the company's historic
expansion goals. Rather, the company consolidated
its position by completing its own line between
Quanah and Acme, thereby connecting its two dis-
jointed segments and terminating the long trackage
agreement with the Fort Worth & Denver City.

The mills at Acme and nearby Agatite had for
years provided the QA&P and the FW&DC with
bounteous traffic in wallboard, brown cement plaster, plaster of paris, Keene cement, and dental plaster. It had been Sam Lazarus's interest at Acme that
had given impetus to the QA&P's predecessor—
the Acme, Red River & Northern—and Lazarus
had maintained his association with the Acme Plaster firm until his death in 1926. Then, in 1928, the
Certain-teed Products Company acquired Lazarus's
interest and 95 percent control of the former Acme
Cement Plastic Company. Five years later, it acquired the facilities of the Beaver Board Company
at Agatite. The Certain-teed firm then sought to
forge the two mills into a single working unit. This,
however, presented a problem because the QA&P
performed the usual switching at the Acme mill and
the FW&DC performed like service at Agatite via
its captive company, the Acme Tap Railroad.[1]

In March 1928, George B. Cromwell, assistant
general traffic manager for Certain-teed, told Sommer that it would be necessary to move cars from
one mill to the other to fill mixed loads of plaster
and wallboard. Under current arrangements, to do
this Certain-teed had to absorb a local rate charge

between the two plants. Consequently, Cromwell
proposed that the QA&P alone perform switching.
The Quanah Route, he noted, hauled dirt (gypsite)
from beds along its line southwest of Acme to the
Certain-teed mill, and Certain-teed wanted to continue that arrangement. As a quid pro quo, Cromwell promised that his firm would "make a fair and
equitable division of the traffic" originating at the
two plants "as between the Fort Worth & Denver
City on the one hand and the QA&P-Frisco on the
other." He pointed out that tonnage was nearly
equally divided at the present time and implied that
it would continue to be if the Denver Road accepted his plan.[2]

The response from the FW&DC was negative in
the extreme. Its management pointedly advised
Certain-teed that it alone was the proprietor of the
Acme Tap, much of the trackage within the plant
site at Acme, and the line from Quanah to Acme
that the QA&P used to get between the two communities. The FW&DC implied that the QA&P
was no more than a tenant and if it did not behave
it would lose rights under the old contracts.[3]

Cromwell responded that it would not be a
"good policy for the Denver City or the Burlington
to antagonize the Certain-teed Corporation." At
the same time, he urged that a conference be held
at which "all our interests are freely and frankly discussed." Surely such a meeting would result in
accommodation.[4]

A conference was held—but only railroaders attended. Certain-teed representatives were not invited. Charles Sommer was astonished to be confronted with a demand from the Denver Road
that the QA&P surrender switching rights at Acme
as well as all road traffic between the mills and Quanah. Sommer correctly perceived that the FW&DC

Tonnage in wallboard and other plaster products for years furnished lucrative traffic to the QA&P and the rival FW&DC.

was attempting to freeze out the QA&P at Acme. He recalled for the record that the Acme, Red River & Northern and later the QA&P had been willing to construct a parallel line between Quanah and Acme but had been dissuaded by the Denver Road. Sommer told the FW&DC's representatives that he was perfectly willing to build that line now if forced to do so.[5]

The Denver Road would not budge. Frank E. Clarity, vice-president and general manager, told Sommer that "about the only argument you have in favor of the Quanah Route doing the switching at both of these plants is that it has been doing the switching at Acme for a period of about twenty-five years." Clarity considered the arrangement a travesty. Yet, he said, "it was never too late to correct a mistake or error in judgement." For Clarity the issue was simple: "I cannot for the life of me understand why the Denver should not be permit-

ted to do the switching at the plaster plants, and cannot conceive of any good reason why this switching should be turned over to your line."[6]

The mood among the three participants in the dispute—the two railroads and Certain-teed—became increasingly somber. If Clarity saw no reason for the QA&P to switch the mills, Certain-teed saw several: movement of cars between the mills cost Certain-teed a line haul charge for an intraplant movement; the QA&P's switch engine moved gypsite from the nearby beds to the mills between switching moves at Acme; an official of the QA&P was at nearby Quanah and could be reached by telephone to handle routine as well as emergency problems on a moment's notice; the QA&P/Frisco had routes and rates to points east of the Mississippi River which the FW&DC could not match; and the QA&P had performed this service for years to the satisfaction of Certain-teed.[7]

These arguments got nowhere. C. E. Spens, executive vice-president of the Chicago, Burlington & Quincy (FW&DC's parent), wired Certain-teed that it was "only fair that we should resume operations in the entire district, and we will, therefore, advise the QA&P to this effect, cancellation of existing contracts subject to the termination clauses therein contained." Certain-Teed's traffic manager responded: "We find it difficult to understand your utter disregard of our wishes. . . . Your attitude merely impresses us with the fact that if we must be served by only one railroad, we should exert our utmost efforts to see that it is not the FW&DC." Still, Certain-teed hoped for a change of heart: "We sincerely trust that on second thought you will decide that it is a poor policy to force an industry, whose good will you should desire, into a position of hostility."[8]

There were no second thoughts at either the FW&DC or the Burlington. On November 28, 1928, the QA&P was notified that its trackage agreement—in force since 1913—would be terminated in six months. Frisco's president Kurn urged Burlington president Hale Holden to "cancel the notice and permit the present arrangement to remain in effect." He was not answered by Holden, but, insultingly, by a subordinate who pledged to work with Kurn "in a neighborly way," although he maintained that "you should not ask us to turn over to the QA&P the operation of our properties at Acme."[9]

Officials of the plaster company felt they had been put off by the FW&DC and reasoned that they, in fact, held the trump card because Certain-teed owned many of the tracks at the mill site. The others were owned by the QA&P and FW&DC but rested on land to which the plaster firm had clear title. Thus either one or both of the railroads could be evicted. But Certain-teed wanted, if possible, the goodwill of both roads and exhibited a spirit of conciliation. Another meeting was held and again Certain-teed was not invited. "Their thinking that they can leave us out of consideration is simply stupid," exploded Certain-teed's traffic manager. "If they persist in that thought they may have a rude awakening some day." Nevertheless, the Denver Road's position remained fixed: "Unless we are permitted to do the switching, as requested, the contracts with QA&P should be cancelled," said F. E. Clarity. Moreover, Clarity spurned Sommer's suggestion that still another conference be held. The QA&P's president was exasperated. "I have been unable from the very beginning to understand the attitude of your people in this situation and still feel that their position is the wrong one," he told Clarity.[10]

Before the situation had become impossible, Sommer had ordered contingency plans. His brother A. F. Sommer had suggested that a new line be built between Quanah and Acme—not an extension from the west end of the QA&P's yard in Quanah along the long-held right-of-way on the south side of the FW&DC to Acme but one featuring a new yard fashioned from the former Frisco North Yard in Quanah, running above the Denver Road to Acme, and connecting there with the Quanah Route's line to Floydada. This would avoid the necessity of a second interlocker at Quanah, obviate congestion in the road's tiny yard there, and provide for potential industrial expansion along the company's property. Charles Sommer enthusiastically embraced the idea, observing that the new line would allow easy and direct access to the Certain-teed plant, facilitate an easy crossing of the FW&DC at Acme, and forge a handy connection with the QA&P's yard at that point. Right-of-way for the project was being acquired as quietly as possible.[11]

On February 20, 1929, Sommer advised Orville Van Brunt, Certain-teed's traffic manager, that all hope of compromise had vanished and he had filed papers with the Interstate Commerce Commission requesting permission to construct a line from the North Yard in Quanah to Acme and, if successful, to abandon its trackage rights over the Denver Road from Quanah to the mill site. The "chief purpose and function of the proposed line," the QA&P told the ICC, was "to establish a direct connection between the two parts of its main line." Sommer knew that it would also, as he said to J. M. Kurn, "forever settle our position with respect to the Acme traffic."[12]

The two railroads and the shipper participated in hearings which the ICC scheduled for April 16, 1929. Certain-teed clearly favored the QA&P, but its traffic personnel shrewdly decided that giving "that impression should be carefully avoided." Rather, it appeared "in the case solely for the purpose of protecting Certain-teed's own interest." The Denver Road stated that it alone could handle all traffic in and out of Acme, that there was insufficient traffic to justify two lines, that it was unfair to allow construction of a parallel line, and that its intentions were not to force Certain-teed to route all of its road hauls over the FW&DC. Beyond that it claimed the ICC lacked power to "hear or determine the question of whether" the Denver Road had the right to cancel QA&P's operating privileges. Representatives of the QA&P put forward arguments similar to those it had used at the earlier meetings with FW&DC officials. Additionally, Sommer noted that the Quanah Route had purchased a locomotive to perform the switching and dirt-train work at Acme, and an unfavorable decision would negate this investment and put the crew assigned to the job out of work.[13]

The ICC's hearing examiner, Thomas F. Sullivan, urged maintenance of the status quo except that a new trackage agreement should include more remuneration for the Denver Road. Should the parties reject this proposal, however, he recommended granting QA&P's request for new construction and abandonment of the long-standing trackage rights. Officials of Certain-teed and the QA&P were elated. But the issue was not yet settled.[14]

As early as April, C. E. Spens, the Burlington Route's executive vice-president, had sought compromise. He reaffirmed that intent six months later when he asked Frisco's J. M. Kurn if he would agree to a conference seeking "friendly compromise." Charles Sommer urged firmness. After all, he said, "we will never again be able to build the line from Quanah to Acme with the cut-off through the north of Quanah as cheaply as it can be done at this time." Sommer earlier had hoped for compromise; now he did not. Kurn told Spens: "At this late date the matter should be left to the Commission to decide."[15]

Oral arguments before the ICC were scheduled for October 16, and, surprisingly, a decision was reached less than two weeks later. The regulatory commission saw just one issue at stake—switching service at Acme—and concluded that so simple a question should be "adjusted between the carriers with due consideration for the rights and needs of the shipper." The commission seemed to have more important problems to deal with. The carriers thus were urged to "resume negotiations looking to the continued joint operation of the line between Quanah and Acme." The case would be held open for sixty days.[16]

Sommer's response was to ask F. E. Clarity of the FW&DC for his road's position. The Denver Road softened its stand regarding trackage rights between Quanah and Acme but continued to insist on the unilateral right to switch the mill. Officials of the QA&P and Certain-teed Products found the "new" plan unacceptable and rejected it. The FW&DC offered further conciliation but to no avail. Frisco's Kurn tersely responded: "Let the Inter-

state Commerce Commission settle the matter."[17]

It was clear that the Denver Road now wanted to compromise. It officials had earlier used strangely heavy-handed methods, however, and these were not quickly forgotten. For example, during hearings before the ICC's examiner the FW&DC had complained that "there was something irregular in the relations between" Certain-teed Products and the QA&P, citing the QA&P's failure to assess a $3.50 charge for intraplant movements of cars at Acme. Charles Sommer and Certain-teed's traffic manager contended that there was no authority to charge for such service and observed that the FW&DC, actually the Acme Tap, had refrained from making such charges at Agatite. Officials of the Denver Road subsequently confirmed this and then, after the fact, billed Certain-teed Products— successor to the Beaver Board Products plant at Agatite—for the services. Certain-teed refused to pay; the FW&DC then filed suit against the shipper in the District Court of Hardeman County. Certain-teed's management was neither amused nor impressed; Charles Sommer thought the FW&DC was using the "situation as a club" to force its way on the shipper in the ICC case. Then, just when it was attempting to embarrass Certain-teed in court, the FW&DC sought to flatter the shipper. Certain-teed's traffic manager was advised—in an inordinately clumsy way—that a large order for the firm's products had been placed by the Burlington (FW&DC's parent) but that no further orders would be forthcoming unless Certain-teed altered its position in the Acme switching case. For Certain-teed it was the last straw. Orville Van Brunt responded directly to F. E. Williamson, Burlington's president: "We have never asked for favors in our solicitation of railway purchases but have merely requested a square deal taking into consideration the price and quality of our product and the volume of our freight traffic." The history of the Acme case was clear, Van Brunt exploded: Certain-teed's treatment by the FW&DC was "most inconsiderate and unfair." Certain-teed would, he concluded, divert its traffic "to other and more friendly roads."[18]

Events moved swiftly and properly as far as the QA&P and the plaster company were concerned. In a tersely worded order dated January 25, 1930, the ICC gave the Quanah Route permission to build a new line from Quanah to Acme and to abandon trackage rights over the FW&DC. Sommer perceived it as "a great victory." He was no less exuberant when he learned that Certain-teed had won— "hands down"—in the court case.[19]

Right-of-way long held by the QA&P on the south side of the FW&DC between Quanah and Acme was not employed for the new construction. Rather, new property, acquired by simple deed and warranty deed, provided a new right-of-way on the north side of the Denver Road. A contract between the QA&P and the Lone Star Construction Company was signed on March 20, 1930, for the usual "grading, masonry, bridge building, tracklaying and ballasting" on "approximately six and one-quarter miles" of line. Work began on April 3, but there were the usual delays. Finally, on March 1, 1931, the new line went into operation and arrangements with the FW&DC were terminated. The Lone Star firm finished its work by May 31. A. F.

Sommer told his brother that the construction company had done a "corking good job." [20]

The new track obviated the need for the Acme Tap Railroad, but its death was delayed. On January 1, 1931, the QA&P and the FW&DC entered into an agreement whereby the Quanah Route leased all of the Denver Road's trackage in the plant area at Acme. At the same time, the Denver Road agreed to lease the Acme Tap to the QA&P in the event that Certain-teed wished to reopen its plant at Agatite. This agreement was extended each year until 1937, although the mill was never used again. Finally, in 1938, the line between Acme and Agatite was dismantled; the Acme Tap Railroad was dissolved as a corporation shortly thereafter. [21]

CHAPTER 13

# The Floydada Gateway Case

The bottle has been on ice for some time, and we
will pull the cork now.—Charles H. Sommer to
B. H. Stanage, March 3, 1938

THE QA&P's long-term strategy of reaching El Paso implied a desire to attract a heavy flow of overhead or passover traffic to supplement the company's unpredictable local business. The same justification had been given, if in microcosm, for extension of the Quanah Route from MacBain to Floydada. As early as 1925 Charles Sommer had argued that a connection with the Santa Fe and short-line mileage to existing markets might gather two thousand cars of overhead traffic per year. Such business would move on a regular basis "throughout the year, during the lean months as well as the few heavy months," noted W. L. Richardson, the QA&P's traffic manager. Sommer agreed: it would keep the company "out of the red." In 1925 Sommer had implied and later would state categorically: "Local traffic is not sufficient to support this railroad."[1]

Sommer, of course, had assumed that the Santa Fe would be a willing partner in the movement of traffic via Floydada. Nothing in the record suggests that Sommer was justified in that belief. The Santa Fe traditionally viewed the South Plains as its private province and had fought strenuously to keep out interlopers such as the QA&P. Even though the Santa Fe's monopoly had been broken, its possessive mentality remained.

Sommer's first inkling that major trouble was at hand came during the summer of 1927, when he heard rumors that the Santa Fe would not agree to a connection and interchange at Floydada. In fact, they were not rumors. The QA&P eventually protested, and the Interstate Commerce Commission held a hearing on the matter. The result was a compromise in which both companies agreed to build additional trackage at their own expense. On June 30, 1928, a connection was placed in service. The Santa Fe claimed that it had not attempted to resist interchange with the Quanah Route, but that was

not true. Sommer said he was "unable to understand [Santa Fe's] attitude in the matter." He was in for even ruder awakenings.[2]

As this local problem was being resolved, Sommer asked Frisco officials to use their influence toward the establishment "of rates on interstate traffic" moving via Floydada and the AT&SF. The results were not what Sommer had hoped for. Representatives of the Frisco discovered that the Santa Fe was unalterably opposed to opening any route that might "short-haul" it to and from the Plains country. Officers of the Santa Fe in Amarillo told A. F. Sommer the same thing: "There appears to be no necessity for opening a route in connection with the QA&P." In part, Santa Fe's position reflected a broader pattern, including its negotiations with the Frisco regarding interchange of South Texas traffic via the SL-SF's interior Oklahoma junctions and, in part, it reflected Santa Fe's tradition of demanding receipt of traffic from the East either at Chicago or Kansas City. To open the Floydada gateway, as one Santa Fe official put it, "would establish a bad precedent." Moreover, the Santa Fe was perfectly content with the traditional interchange of interstate traffic moving between the AT&SF and the Frisco at Avard, Oklahoma.[3]

Nevertheless, a trickle of interstate overhead traffic began to move over the QA&P during the summer of 1930. Negotiations were required to determine divisions of rates. The Frisco, in combination with the Quanah Route, asked Santa Fe's agreement to a proposal for "through rates on traffic" moving to California from points on the SL-SF in Oklahoma via Floydada. The Frisco and the QA&P further requested that divisions on traffic moving through Floydada favor Frisco/QA&P by 5 percent over the Avard route. Santa Fe's response was predictable: "This is an unauthorized route as there are no published divisions in effect," said its repre-

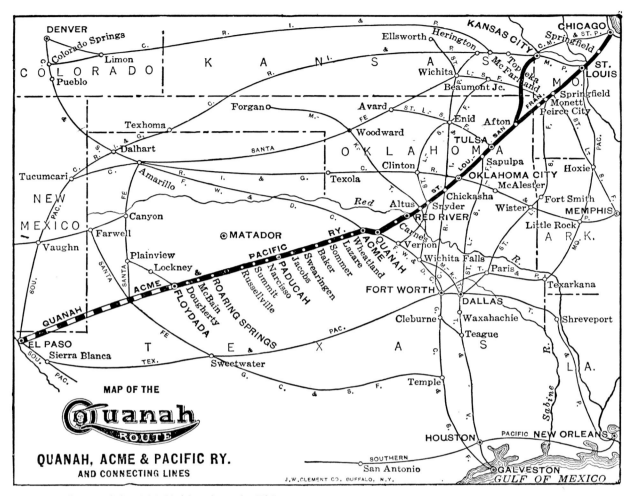

This map illustrated the QA&P's historic goal—El Paso.

sentative. The AT&SF, however, was willing to accept "Avard revenue" on business that already had moved through Floydada but, failing that, it threatened to place a specific restriction in the transcontinental tariffs closing the Floydada gateway. The Santa Fe also demanded that both the Frisco and the QA&P stop soliciting general interstate traffic via Floydada. After consultations, the SL-SF and the QA&P agreed to accept the same revenue split on traffic received and delivered at Floydada as at Avard; the Frisco agreed to stop soliciting California business by way of Floydada; but the QA&P refused to terminate its own solicitations.[4]

Charles Sommer charged that the Santa Fe was "one of the worst carriers in the country to contend with on routes, rates, and divisions." It may have been so. Even the Fort Worth & Denver City was concerned. A Santa Fe official explained the situation to the Denver Road: "Notwithstanding the fact that we received the same revenue west of Floydada as we receive west of Avard for substantially shorter haul, we prefer to handle traffic via Avard for the reason that we consider it cheaper to perform the additional main line service required via Avard than the double branch line service required via Floydada."[5]

There matters stood until March 13, 1933, when the AT&SF—through the Trans-Continental Freight Bureau—announced its intention to close the Floydada gateway. The implications were ominously clear to W. L. Richardson. Should the Santa Fe be successful, the QA&P would lose the meager transcontinental traffic it had attracted, and "the subsequent effect of this needs no explanation." Since the line had been opened to Floydada, 708 cars of transcontinental traffic and 502 additional cars of interstate freight had moved via that point—not impressive but the difference between life and death for the QA&P.[6]

A flurry of telegrams passed between W. L. Richardson and Sommer and between Richardson and his traffic representatives. A hastily arranged conference between QA&P and Santa Fe officials yielded nothing; on April 20 the QA&P filed a complaint with the ICC; and a few days later Sommer requested the personal intercession of Santa Fe's president, W. B. Storey. The Quanah Route's position was simple: the AT&SF was discriminating.[7]

Santa Fe's point, as enunciated through President Storey and company attorneys, was similarly direct. Storey told Sommer that the Santa Fe had determined to "put a stop to this" practice of interchanging transcontinental traffic at Floydada because it moved "from and to territory for which no route and no divisions were authorized." Subordinates echoed Storey, saying that traffic moved unnaturally via Floydada and did so only "by intense personal solicitation and for and on behalf of" the QA&P. Furthermore, they contended, "such service increased transportation costs without benefit to anyone except" the Quanah Route."[8]

Shippers and area chambers of commerce viewed the matter in a less complex fashion. Santa Fe's action was, they said, discriminatory, depriving shippers of routings, the privilege of reconsigning, part unleadings, and the usual transit privileges.[9]

The month of May 1933 was for the QA&P bitter in the extreme. The ICC twice declined to suspend the routing restrictions and, although temporary relief was gained through the federal court at Amarillo, that same body dissolved the restraining order on May 31. The effect was immediate and devastating. Said W. L. Richardson: "It means that . . . our transcontinental rates and routes via Floydada are cancelled on all traffic which is not destined to or does not originate at points on the QA&P proper or the Frisco from Quanah north to Enid and from Quanah north to Sapulpa." Richardson advised his traffic representatives to "discontinue the solicitation of transcontinental traffic for routing via Floydada except to and from these limited points."[10]

Nevertheless, Charles Sommer was not ready to admit defeat. "The Santa Fe's action is about the rankest discrimination that has yet come to my attention," he fumed in a letter to Frank Kell, president of the Wichita Falls & Southern Railway. Sommer had told the QA&P's lawyers that he was "not yet finished with the Santa Fe"; a new formal complaint soon would be filed with the ICC. Support was promised by the American Short Line

If the QA&P lost the Floydada case, it would be condemned to subsist on revenues from short hauls such as cotton, seen here in bales awaiting shipment.

Railroad Association, which complained that it was "quite unfair for Class I roads to take arbitrary action" against smaller companies such as the Quanah Route. The best news of all came, however, from Frisco's President Kurn, who authorized Sommer to hire outside counsel, specifically Robert E. Quirk, formerly chief examiner from the Interstate Commerce Commission, who had been very successful in handling earlier cases for short lines. Quirk would guide the QA&P's efforts, officially styled ICC Docket 26070.[11]

Quirk warned that "through route and division cases for short lines are very troublesome and must be handled with great care." Events in 1934 certainly supported his view. For instance, all looked rosy when the ICC's hearing examiner recommended a decision favorable to the Quanah Route. Richardson reflected the euphoria at the QA&P when he observed that this recommendation was "a blow to the Santa Fe, and to use Pop-Eye's expression, I hope it will blow them down." Sadly for him, however, that optimism soon passed. The hearing examiner, a friend of Quirk's and a man who was thoroughly familiar with the case, died unexpectedly before his personal recommendations could be acted upon. Then, in October, Division Four of the ICC concluded—by a 2–1 vote—that the examiner had erred in his recommendations and moved to dismiss the case. As if that were not bad enough, the QA&P simultaneously suffered a defeat in federal courts over a related case dealing with long hauls on cottonseed and cottonseed products.[12]

Quirk suggested that a petition be filed asking for reconsideration by the entire commission. The president of the American Short Line Railroad Association offered similar counsel. It was, as he pointed out—and Sommer agreed—a matter of

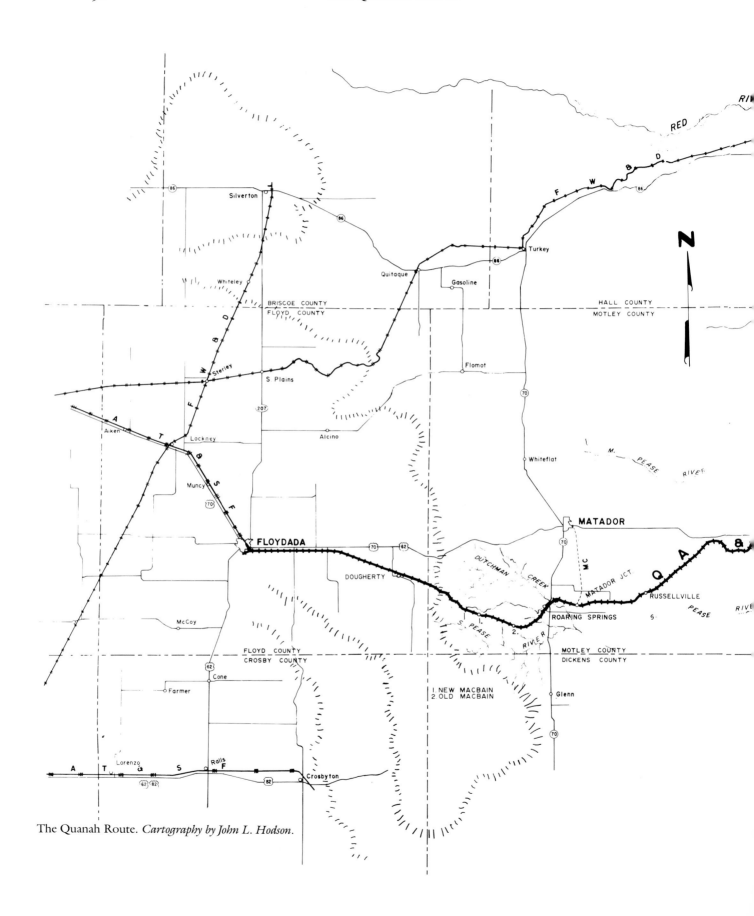

The Quanah Route. *Cartography by John L. Hodson.*

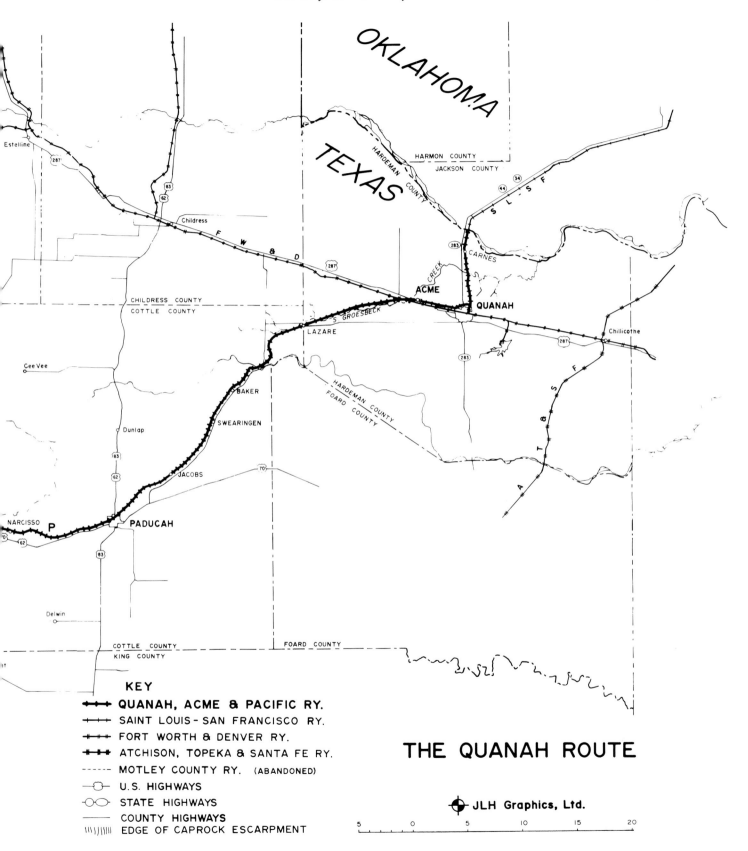

KEY
➤ **QUANAH, ACME & PACIFIC RY.**
┼┼┼ SAINT LOUIS - SAN FRANCISCO RY.
┼┼┼ FORT WORTH & DENVER RY.
■■■ ATCHISON, TOPEKA & SANTA FE RY.
----- MOTLEY COUNTY RY. (ABANDONED)
─□─ U.S. HIGHWAYS
─◯◯─ STATE HIGHWAYS
─── COUNTY HIGHWAYS
\|\|\|\| EDGE OF CAPROCK ESCARPMENT

# THE QUANAH ROUTE

✦ JLH Graphics, Ltd.

5    0    5    10    15    20

great importance to small roads. On December 21, 1934, Sommer ordered his attorneys back to work. Oral arguments were scheduled for June 5, 1925, in Washington.[13]

Quirk promised to stress that the Floydada gateway had not been closed but that, instead, rates applicable via that point were "excessive and unreasonable and discriminated against" the QA&P. This discrimination was reflected in the volume of transcontinental overhead traffic moving via Floydada—only 4 westbound cars and 140 eastbound cars in all of 1934 and 1935. The QA&P would not, he said, seek damage but would, most emphatically, seek relief from discrimination. The AT&SF, he pointed out, accorded more generous treatment to other connecting carriers—the Roscoe, Snyder & Pacific, Rock Island, and FW&DC, in particular.[14]

The QA&P was no more successful this time than it had been earlier. On October 29, 1935, the regulatory agency ruled that the AT&SF's refusal to establish rates and joint rates through the Floydada gateway was not unlawful; the case was again dismissed. It was the QA&P's nadir.[15]

A disappointed Charles Sommer seemed to shake his head in disbelief: "The law holds and so does the Commission that two lines, separately operated but under common control, may be treated as one carrier, yet the effect of this decision is to deny the Frisco and its subsidiary the right to route traffic through its longest gateway to a destination line." It was not in Sommer's character to admit defeat, however, and this case had become a moral crusade for him. Furthermore, the Frisco promised continuing if behind-the-scenes support. It was no surprise, then, when R. E. Quirk filed a petition for reconsideration and rehearing. "We have a hard fight before us," Sommer admitted, "but I am in hopes that we may ultimately convince the Commission that our case should prevail."[16]

Perhaps because of the QA&P's persistence, perhaps because its cause was just, or perhaps for both reasons, the pendulum finally began to swing in its favor. The ICC agreed to reopen the case and, in the process, demanded much more information from the AT&SF regarding its other connections and gateways. "This looks like the first break we have had," exclaimed Sommer. Santa Fe's competitors would be delighted to obtain this traditionally private information, and the larger road would, he was certain, want to protect such data. There was no doubt about it, said Santa Fe's attorney, who was unalterably opposed to disclosure of this information. He had no choice, however, and when testimony was taken by the hearing examiner in Oklahoma City late in October 1936, the AT&SF was forced to make important disclosures, which not only pleased Santa Fe's detractors but materially aided the QA&P's case. In the end, the examiner sustained virtually all of the Quanah Route's complaints. Sommer assumed there was "quite a bit of sputtering" in Santa Fe's law department when the report was released and anticipated that its Chicago attorneys would soon make some "effort to up-set the apple cart." Nevertheless, he said, "at this moment I think we are sitting pretty." Sommer had another reason to be buoyant: the QA&P had received concessions in the cottonseed case.[17]

On February 14, 1938, the ICC finally handed down a decision favorable to the Quanah Route. The regulatory agency required the removal of what it called the Santa Fe's undue prejudice, discrimination, and preference relative to through routes and joint rates with the QA&P via Floydada. Quirk noted that the decision gave the QA&P substantially all the relief it had requested. He also thought virtue had been rewarded: "We have always been right in this case and winning it merely serves to illustrate the practical application of the old adage 'If at first you don't succeed, try, try again.'"[18]

Charles Sommer was less restrained. "It is a signal victory for our rights," he told G. E. Hamilton, the road's attorney in Matador, Texas. Sommer was ready to celebrate. "The bottle has been on ice for some time," he said to an associate at the Frisco, "and we will pull the cork now."[19]

The QA&P had, without question, won a great victory. Yet Sommer was naive if he thought the issue was settled. As Richardson reminded him, "the Santa Fe can go ahead and publish rates in strict compliance with the Commission's order," but that alone was inadequate. As Richardson seemed to anticipate, problems about rates and divisions arose immediately and plagued relations between the two carriers for several months. "Seemingly," said Sommer to R. E. Quirk, "our Santa Fe friends have not yet conceded defeat." A flood of personal letters then flowed between Sommer and H. C. Barron, the attorney who had handled Santa Fe's case. Barron sought compromise, but, with the sweet smell of victory in his nostrils, Sommer sought every advantage. He advised Richardson that divisions on the "Avard basis" (i.e., that the QA&P and Frisco would receive the same divisions of rates as Frisco received via the Avard, Oklahoma, gateway) was "not satisfactory," and he told Barron that if informal negotiations did not soon reach fruition he would institute "a docket involving divisions." Sommer was convinced that the Santa Fe was "frightened at the recent turn of events" and wanted to "make the best settlement" possible. Nevertheless, he agreed to compromises of his own—the matter of divisions, for instance, was referred to traffic personnel and the legal staffs were relieved of that headache. Events moved quickly. On July 15, 1938, the Floydada gateway was reopened with interim rates in effect.[20]

Sommer was again ecstatic—"Santa Fe has hoisted the white flag and we will have to pop the cork in celebration"—and again frustrated, for the AT&SF was intent on dragging its feet in the matter of instituting formal and permanent divisions. Negotiations were handled by Sommer and Richardson, on behalf of the smaller road, and by Paul P. Hastings and various subordinates, on behalf of the Santa Fe. QA&P officials insisted on "at least five percentage points over the Avard basis" and, predictably, the Santa Fe rejected that demand. Richardson pointed out that Santa Fe's haul west of Floydada was 194 miles less than its haul west of Avard, which justified a five-point differential. Sommer wanted to ask for even more because, as he said, "we can still fall back on a basis of 5 percentage points above the Avard basis." Meanwhile, traffic had increased via Floydada and, for the QA&P, a final settlement was imperative to protect maximum revenues. Its position hardened, but so, too, did Santa Fe's. Paul Hastings, vice-president of traffic for the Santa Fe, was blunt: "We are not going to accept less west of Floydada than west of Avard."[21]

In November 1938 and again in April 1939 the QA&P threatened to ask the ICC "to reopen Docket 26070 for the purpose of fixing reasonable divisions." Santa Fe's Hastings thought that divisions should be made by "mutual agreement, if possible," but offered no conciliation. Richardson pointed out that the QA&P was not "asking the Santa Fe for as much revenue as the Santa Fe gave the RS&P at Snyder, the Rock Island at Amarillo, and the FW&DC at Amarillo." Richardson was implying, of course, that the Santa Fe continued to be prejudicial in its affairs with the QA&P—an indictment the ICC had sustained in its decision of February 14, 1938. With that in mind, Sommer gave the AT&SF an ultimatum calling for the divisions listed in table 1. Sommer would not wait long, he said, for Santa Fe's response.[22]

An olive branch was proffered by the AT&SF in June 1939. This softening of position, said Paul

### TABLE 1
### Sommer's Ultimatum to AT&SF

| Between Floydada and | QA&P and connections (%) | Santa Fe (%) |
|---|---|---|
| St. Louis | 39.0 | 61.0 |
| Kansas City | 31.5 | 68.5 |
| Memphis | 35.0 | 65.0 |

Hastings, was because of the "substantial volume of transcontinental westbound traffic" which had been interchanged with the QA&P at Floydada since the summer of 1938. A resolution of the problem was soon arranged, as table 2 shows. The agreement, Sommer gleefully pointed out, was retroactive to the reestablishment of the Floydada gateway, July 15, 1938, and would result in a windfall for the QA&P because most settlements already had been made on the Avard basis. There was even more good news. The Frisco agreed to divide revenues accruing to the two lines according to the above formula with 30 percent going to the QA&P and the remaining 70 percent residing with its parent. A few weeks later, Sommer reported to Frisco's President Kurn that, on nineteen selected carloads, revenues for the Frisco/QA&P had risen, on the average, from $132 per car to $160 per car. This was obvious proof that the struggle had been worthwhile. Even the Santa Fe appeared pleased. Paul Hastings remarked: "I am glad that we have been able to reach this agreement as it will enable us to continue to cooperate with your line in handling transcontinental traffic, and I am hopeful that the nice westbound business you have been handing us will continue."[23]

### TABLE 2
### Resolution of Divisions via Floydada

| To or from | Divisions via Floydada | | Divisions via Avard | |
|---|---|---|---|---|
| | Santa Fe | QA&P/ SL-SF | Santa Fe | Frisco |
| St. Louis | 64 | 36 | 69 | 31 |
| Kansas City | 71 | 29 | 75 | 25 |
| Memphis | 65 | 35 | 69 | 31 |

It was not, however, simply a matter of "peaches and cream." The QA&P learned that continual vigilance was necessary "to keep the Santa Fe honest." Unpleasant incidents would prove to be an ongoing problem in future years.[24]

An inestimable amount of time, energy, and money had been spent by the contesting parties.

Sommer thought the price was justifiable, given the results. There were important corollaries, too. For instance, Sommer found in R. E. Quirk a fine litigator who served the QA&P well in these and future difficulties. More important, Sommer found a monumental talent in his own organization. The QA&P president received much credit for the Floydada decision, but he and most observers gave highest honors to W. L. Richardson, the road's traffic manager. The Quanah Route's Floydada case became famous,—known to virtually all rail managers of the time, and they tied Richardson's name directly to that decision.[25]

## CHAPTER 14

## Dust and Depression

With the farmers it has been "no crops"; with the
grain dealers and businessmen it has been "no business"; and with the railroads it has been "no tonnage." So at least we have all had one thing in common—depleted bank deposits.—A. F. Sommer to
W. H. Edwards, June 9, 1931

THE tag end of the Panhandle-Plains construction boom and the lengthy dispute with the AT&SF over the Floydada gateway were correspondent with the twin verities of the 1930s in the Southwest—the Great Depression and the Dust Bowl.

Dust Bowl conditions appeared first. As early as 1928, Frank Dougherty, founder of the townsite along the QA&P bearing his name, wondered "which was the craziest: to build a railroad in Floyd County or to build a town and elevator." A drought had already settled on the area. "It may rain yet," Dougherty added in a mix of hope and exasperation.[1]

Conditions did not improve. Sommer was "much alarmed at the hot weather" that enveloped the QA&P's service region during the early spring of 1930. "I am no forecaster," he said, "but it looks to me like an early summer, a hot one, and perhaps a dry one." In fact, Sommer was right. By July, Frank Dougherty was proclaiming the harvest in Floyd County the poorest he had ever seen. "It's a tough one to take," he admitted, "but I don't know anything to do but take it." Dougherty reflected grim determination when he told Sommer: "We are plowing up stubble right along and getting ready for another season." Others were less confident. "Things are dry as the dickens down here and we need to start something in order to get the people to take a new heart," reported the secretary of the Chamber of Commerce at Paducah. The only good news, if it could be called that, came when his county and all others along the line of the QA&P were added to the list of drought-stricken counties in Texas and thus eligible for benefits under emergency freight tariffs. At Quanah a committee asked the QA&P for $100 during the fall of 1930 to secure

seed wheat for local farmers who were unable to purchase it. Sommer told the company's directors that business during the past year had been disappointing because of "the wide depression and the almost total crop failure throughout the Quanah region." He understated the case. Although he was pleased to see 1930 pass, the QA&P's president remained "optimistic enough" to believe that "the public will shake off its timid disposition and nervousness" so that confidence might be restored "and start things on an upward trend." Sommer looked forward to "better times in 1931" and thought "it safe to say that we are around the corner."[4]

Meanwhile, the QA&P continued in its "good citizen" role. During the summer of 1936, it was so dry around Lazare that supplies of drinking water became dangerously low. A member of the Hardeman County commission requested assistance from the QA&P, and it was immediately forthcoming. Sommer ordered the railroad to "supply these good people with all the water they need." The water, he said, would be donated by the Roaring Springs Townsite Company, and the railroad would, under special tariff permission, haul it from Roaring Springs to Lazare for one dollar per car.[5]

The Quanah Route took a similar position in moving goods for charitable organizations. From early 1931 through 1934, the QA&P, in cooperation with numerous other railroads, handled, as deadhead freight, several carloads of commodities consigned to the Red Cross and destined for drought victims at various points along the line. On February 9, 1931, the QA&P delivered a shipment of foodstuff from the Henry Field Company of Shenandoah, Iowa, to the Red Cross at Quanah; several days later the local road handled a car of flour donated by citizens of Thurston, Nebraska, to Matador. On another occasion the QA&P and other roads donated transportation for a car of plaster from Acme to a destitute rural school in Arkansas, and they did the same for a carload of feed billed at Dougherty and consigned to the Boles Orphan Home at Quinlan, Texas. In all cases Sommer's response was the same: "We are glad to make such contributions to worthy causes." The record leaves no doubt as to his sincerity.[6]

His hope seemed misplaced. During the early fall of 1928, the Chamber of Commerce at Quanah petitioned the QA&P "to help our farmers by reducing the freight rate on feed bought by them." The problem was real enough. Farmers in Hardeman County had experienced a near failure of their feed crops and needed to import feed. Charles Sommer was genuinely moved and greatly regretted that farmers were faced with such an "unfortunate situation." He prescribed a stiff upper lip: "There is nothing to do but to make the best of a bad thing." Meanwhile, the QA&P would "co-operate in every way possible," he promised. It was vintage Charles Sommer.[2]

But such cooperation would pose problems. The Fort Worth & Denver City and all other regional carriers with which the QA&P shared interchange or connecting traffic would have to adopt a similar policy, and they were slow to do so. A representative of the Denver Road, for instance, blandly asserted that the "railroad was not responsible for the drought." Moreover, he said, conditions were not "as bad as painted" by some in the Quanah vicinity. The position taken by the local road seemed to reflect understanding and compassion whereas the FW&DC seemed cold and removed. There was an element of truth in this assessment, but it did not represent the whole cloth. As both the drought and the Depression deepened, the two carriers—and others too—reduced rates by 50 percent on food and feed moved to the affected counties and on outbound movement of livestock from the same counties. Sommer was perfectly willing to endorse this reduction—and more. He was especially concerned about the small operators and thought the major cattle companies were "better able financially" to assume current burdens and were "taking advantage of the situation" by shipping their animals under the reduced rates. There was nothing to do, however, but honor the arrangement, Sommer concluded.[3]

Continuing dry weather and depressed prices for agricultural products had an immediately deleteri-

The combination of Dust Bowl conditions and hard times drove many residents from farmsteads (like this one between MacBain and Roaring Springs) throughout the QA&P's service area.

ous effect on QA&P revenues. The agent at Floydada told A. F. Sommer in June 1931 that "all the wheat farmers are storing as much of their wheat as they can. They are not rushing the harvest this year like they usually do, that is, they are not running their combines day and night . . . and are not hiring any extra labor." The reason, he said, was "the low price of wheat." One year later the same agent reported that "the combines are running pretty good. . . . However, there is no rush as the farmers do not seem to care whether they ever get their wheat harvested or not." He estimated "that at least 65% of the wheat [would] go into storage." In 1934 Sommer told the QA&P's board of directors that "drought conditions, . . . perhaps the worst of record, aggravated by the continuation of the depression, made further inroads into revenues." His report in 1935 was essentially the same: "The 1935 wheat crop along the Quanah Route was practically a complete failure." In 1936, "Both the wheat crop and the cotton crop were failures." The year 1937 was kinder—a heavy wheat crop and an unusually large cotton crop were produced. Hailstorms reduced available agricultural tonnage in 1938, and in the next season Sommer complained that tonnage in such commodities was down again because of "unfavorable weather conditions . . . further aggravated by the A.A.A. [Agricultural Adjustment Act, which reduced acreage in production]." Conditions were much the same in 1940. Rains returned in 1941, but they came just at harvest time and were heavy; most of the crop was lost, and the QA&P's track sustained heavy damage.[7]

The Quanah Route struggled against long odds

throughout the 1930s. First there was the legacy of the previous decade—an incomplete and seemingly inadequate route structure that terminated at Floydada instead of Plainview, Lubbock, or El Paso. Then there was the unhealthy condition of parent Frisco and the lengthy and expensive case against Santa Fe, which drained the local road. Moreover, the QA&P suffered along with its service area from the combined effects of the Great Depression and the Dust Bowl. Finally, automobiles and trucks were presenting heavy competition. An event involving the village of Dougherty serves to illustrate.

Dougherty was one year old in March 1929. A birthday party was ordered; about a thousand persons from the South Plains participated. The official celebration opened with a concert by the West Texas State Teachers College band and was followed by a barbecue lunch sponsored by the Dougherty Chamber of Commerce. Visitors were also treated to greased pole climbing contests, horse racing, sack races, and more concerts by the teachers college band and high school bands from Crosbyton and Lubbock. Speeches were made by Paul W. Horn, president of Texas Technological College, W. L. Richardson, representing the Quanah Route, and others. A writer from the *Wichita Falls Daily Times* was astonished, as were many observers, "that within a year a town can develop from a wide open space on the bald prairie to a rapidly growing center, with a city plan, fire limits, and protection, sanitary restrictions, water system, telephone system, and graded streets." There was, without question, much that was impressive at Dougherty on March 27, 1929.[8]

Yet the blustery winds of that day were also the winds of change. The largest delegation at the Dougherty celebration had come from Lubbock; they arrived in a caravan of fifteen automobiles. There was deep irony in that, for the civilization of rubber-tires and hardtop roads that those automobiles represented would soon place an onerous burden on the village of Dougherty and on the railroad that had given it life.

There were many additional—and equally ironic—symbols of change. The special consolidated edition of the *Quanah Tribune-Chief* and the *Quanah Times* of July 19, 1925—prepared for the "Plainview Railway Hearing"—contained a major article on the need for "good roads," and on August 16, 1925, the *Fort Worth Record* devoted its entire first page to an endorsement of the Texas Panhandle & Gulf Railroad; page 2, however, was completely given over to articles on automobile sales, traffic jams, and advertisements for Paige & Jewett, Willys-Overland, and Essex motor cars. The *Paducah Post* for November 25, 1926, deplored the failed application of the Texas Panhandle & Gulf, but its lead story dealt with a proposal to pave the Lee Highway, a road that eventually became U.S. 70, largely paralleling the QA&P. In 1928, a brochure prepared by the Gamble Land Company of Floydada contained nearly as much information on Floyd County's roads as on its railroads; more telling was the attending map, which showed Floydada on U.S. 70 but not on any rail line. Four years later stationery for the Paducah Chamber of Commerce bore a map showing that community at the intersection of the east-west Lee Highway and the north-south Great Plains Highway. No rail routes cluttered this cartography. Issues of the *Floyd County Hesperian* in the summer of 1925 seemed to represent the final irony. Included were advertisements from the Ford Motor Company, offering its coupe at $520 and its "stake body one-ton truck" for $515, both f.o.b. Detroit. "Go where you will—whether the road is paved or not," said Ford.[9]

Sommer was frightened by what he saw. "The public fails to realize that the railroads are—next to the production that comes from the soil—the most vital in existence, and that if the railroad fails to function it will naturally follow with a complete collapse of all other industries, and its consequences, that need no explanation." His fears seemed confirmed when, for instance, the Nacogdoches & Southern Railroad was authorized to abandon six miles of its line from LeCerda to Pershing in Nacogdoches County, Texas, during 1926.[10]

Sommer was worried, but he was forced to admit that life was changing. In 1923, he and other railroaders had conceded, in testimony regarding the proposed Texas Panhandle & Gulf, that local traffic was no longer adequate to sustain railroads in the region. A few years later Sommer stated: "Rail transportation today as a public necessity is a different proposition as compared to 15 or 20 years ago. Take for example the Quanah Route. I made buggy trips back in 1908 and 1909 to Paducah, 45 miles from Quanah. It was an all day trip. Now the automobile makes it in two hours or less." More to the point, Sommer observed that persons living in the QA&P's service area now "ride their machines and drive their trucks laden with products and merchandise freely back and forth to trading centers . . . over dirt roads . . . that are well maintained." This new pattern in local transportation obviously cost the railroad a growing portion of its passenger and freight traffic. Some years later, an even more frightened Sommer noted that during "the past fifteen years . . . highway competition has become increasingly severe . . . and has made serious inroads on practically all classes of [freight] traffic." Petroleum products, groceries, livestock, cottonseed, and general merchandise all were, he said, "particularly susceptible to highway competition." He used cottonseed as an example. In 1928, the QA&P handled 864 cars of that commodity but in 1941, only 46 cars. This was not because cotton was no longer grown in the same volume; it was because the railroad had lost the business to truckers. Highway competition also forced railroads to lower "practically all rates with no compensating benefits," complained Sommer.[11]

The president of the QA&P was a fierce competitor but, like most other railroad managers of his time, complained vociferously when he perceived that his opponents enjoyed an unfair advantage. Being forced to compete with unregulated motor transportation was especially unjust. It was small wonder that he heartily supported laws that regulated truck cargo weights and imposed other conditions on motor carriers and that he groused when such laws were not enforced. Railroad industry groups gathered statistics on truck accidents and taxes paid by motor carriers that were used against those who, in the mid-1930s, wanted truck load limits raised. Railroaders were generally successful in keeping such limits down; in fact, by 1939 Texas had the lowest allowable load limit among the states. But one year later A. F. Sommer pointed out that common carrier truckers were "as hard hit [by hard times] as the railroads." The real villains, he said, were the "itinerant truckers." Charles Sommer agreed that there ought to be more cooperation with "legitimate trucking." Nevertheless, he was irked with the Texas Highway Department, which, he maintained, was aided and abetted by the courts and others in "permitting flagrant violations of the trucking laws." Sommer argued for "strict enforcement" and "proper tax on motor vehicles operated for profit," but even with these regulations he was not optimistic, for he had come to believe that "racketeer" truckers would still find a way to "carry on."[12]

Like many other railroad managers of the era, Sommer was unable to come to grips with the problem. In 1930, the trunk railroads of Texas seemed to admit that for less-than-carload shipments, truckers had the advantage of more frequent pickup and de-

Truckers enjoyed public roadways supported by all classes of taxpayers, but railroads had to maintain their own rights-of-way. Here, shoulders are being built near Russellville.

livery service. Three years later Sommer was told by a consultant: "Truckers are going to continue to handle much of the local business, regardless of legislation." The implication was that railroaders were going to have to do more than complain. Sommer paid lip service to the "Fitch System" of rail-truck coordination and asked his traffic manager to examine the possibility of involving the QA&P in motor transportation. But he considered few other alternatives.[13]

Nevertheless, Sommer was both clever and energetic in public relations. When the editor of the *Paducah Post* ran an editorial calling railroads "a home industry" worthy of "community cooperation," Sommer fired off a two-page letter of congratulation. He also took the opportunity to supply the journalist with additional "ammunition." At about the same time, the *Dallas Morning News* carried a letter to the editor which asked rhetorically, "Where Will We Be If Railroads Are Destroyed?" The implied answer was: in sad shape. Sommer wholeheartedly agreed. Proper pubic relations and sympathy for the industry were important, but as the QA&P's general attorney warned, "sympathy will not run a railroad nor pay heavy operating expenses and taxes and compete with automobiles."[14]

Economy, not public relations, precipitated two proposals during the Depression concerning consolidation of facilities—at Quanah and at Floydada. In 1934, the FW&DC suggested that all yards, mechanical facilities, freight houses, and passenger stations at Quanah be coordinated. A lengthy and detailed report was made, but Sommer rejected its recommendations, saying that the Denver Road was attempting to "bring about the abandonment of our new trackage between Quanah and Acme, hoping to restore in some way the old joint trackage arrangement." Sommer's response was likely colored by pride. The Floydada plan, however, was instigated by the QA&P and called for the "the consolidation of station and yard facilities at that point." Before the line had been built to Floydada, Sam Lazarus hoped to get the Santa Fe to lease "one-half interest" in the new QA&P station there. Sommer still hoped for such an arrangement and put the matter directly before the AT&SF in 1933. He also suggested that the smaller road "extend its train to Plainview, handling your [AT&SF] business at a cost below your present operations, same to include agencies and roadway maintenance." The Santa Fe rejected the proposal after brief study and declined again in 1941 after another overture from Sommer. In each case Santa Fe contended that the resulting savings would be inadequate. Santa Fe's decision was likely colored by pride, too.[15]

But pride did not affect Sommer when he analyzed the health of QA&P's Matador branch. Early in 1933, he complained to the road's attorney at Matador, G. E. Hamilton, that shippers were not providing adequate support for the line: "It is simply going to be impossible for the Quanah Route to continue to operate the Branch Line if the citizenship . . . deprives the railroad of its revenue." The QA&P president was particularly upset that Matador merchants were diverting shipments to truckers—many of whom were operating in violation of the law. "The average citizen," charged Sommer, "wants the railroads when he sees them vanishing but apparently fails to appreciate them until the abandonment is threatened." Hamilton agreed: "Their course of conduct has been . . . that the truckers are here, and that they will eventually take the place of the railroads, and that no loss will be sustained by the country."[16]

A few days later, Sommer told Frisco's President Kurn that he had "about reached the conclusion that it might be well to give serious consideration towards filing an application for a permit to abandon the property." It was not possible to use main line locals on the branch because it was laid with fifty-six-pound rail, which would not bear the weight of heavy locomotives. And rebuilding the line to main line specifications was out of the question. Moreover, in the event of abandonment, much of the branch's carload traffic would "to a very large extent find an outlet through our rails at

Roaring Springs." He ordered "an actual survey of . . . out-of-pocket expenses that resulted from operation to Matador."[17]

While the road's accounting department compiled this information, Sommer brooded over the issue and increasingly grew bitter toward trucks and those who used them. Hamilton unwittingly fueled the fire with a lengthy letter written in June 1933: "There is a feeling of resentment by many people against the truck regulation as the unthinking man takes the position that the public highway is free to be used by any man or concern who has anything he wants to haul over it, and if he wants to employ a neighbor to haul his freight for him, he has the right to do it, and that kind of sentiment prompts many good people to give their business to the truck operators, although they know such operation is in violation of the law. But those same people are very much opposed to the railroad ceasing operation." Sommer's patience deteriorated. "It seems to me they should be the last to contribute to truck operations, in their isolated situation . . . I doubt seriously if the town can get along without rail service . . . and," he concluded soberly, "unless there is an appreciable improvement in our traffic on the Matador Branch, we will be compelled, as a matter of preservation, to make application for suspension of operations."[18]

Sommer's worst fears were confirmed when he read the auditor's report. Even apportioning a generous 25 percent of revenue to traffic originating or terminating on the branch (as opposed to crediting the remaining 75 percent of QA&P's division to the much longer haul on the main line) failed to bring black ink to the branch's ledger book. Indeed, out-of-pocket losses had been sizable each year since 1928. Matadorians were told this news at a meeting between railroad officials and local businessmen on January 4, 1934. Matador's businessmen were shocked, and in an attempt to mollify the railroaders they unanimously pledged to use the railroad exclusively for their future freight shipments. Correspondingly, one QA&P official urged economy by reducing train service to a twice-weekly turn from Roaring Springs. Sommer rejected this idea, saying, "The trouble as I see it would be in arranging for a crew and fixing their compensation at a living wage, because, after all, the reduced service would be for the purpose of curtailing operating expenses." By the fall of 1934, Sommer saw "no solution to our troubles other than to completely abandon the property, unless we can get 100% support of the citizenship, and this means the abandonment of trucking patronage."[19]

Such support did not materialize, and on March 14, 1935, the QA&P's board of directors authorized Sommer to apply for abandonment. The matter was kept quiet for the time being, and Sommer did not move immediately to exercise this prerogative. Instead he asked Hamilton for a frank statement of his views. "We do not want to go along indefinitely under the present arrangement," he told the attorney, "and if there is no way in which we can have these good people become conscious of an obligation that will, in the end, benefit them, I see no use fooling around." Hamilton was not optimistic. Matadorians, he said, had lost "sight of the fact that hard times is not the major factor contributing to the railroad's losses, but that they have resulted from the fact that practically everybody has quit patronizing it, and are either hauling their stuff, or are hiring commercial, competing trucks to haul it." In sum, "the people are terribly truck-minded." Therefore, concluded Hamilton, "it might be just as well to go ahead when you become convinced that the company can no longer stand the losses, and take such action as you think best."[20]

There is little doubt that the decision was painful for both Sommer and the community of Matador. On May 17, 1935, necessary materials were filed with the ICC. The news came to Motley County by way of the *Matador Tribune* on May 30. The mood there was a mix of anger and anxiety.[21]

Civic interests at Matador promised a fight. The QA&P's agent there reported that petitions were being circulated and donations were being solicited to pay for legal fees. He told A. F. Sommer that a local grocer had signed the petition in his presence while, ironically, "two large trucks were backed up to his front door unloading." The abandonment issue also evoked a flood of unpleasant recollections regarding railroads and the QA&P in particular. The Quanah Route was charged with having deliberately bypassed Matador and fostered the establishment of Roaring Springs in an attempt to kill the older community. The consequence was what the editor of the *Matador Tribune* called Motley County's "most colossal privately supported enterprise"—the Motley County Railway—"paid for with Motley County money, most of it being supplied by Matador citizens." Others asserted that the QA&P had ultimately purchased the Motley County Railway only for the purpose of extinguishing it.[22]

The Interstate Commerce Commission scheduled hearings for November 18–19, 1935, to be held

TABLE 3
**Decline in Tonnage on Matador Ranch**

| *Received* | 1928 | 1931 | 1935 |
|---|---|---|---|
| Autos | 24 | — | 6 |
| Bagging and ties | 5 | 4 | 2 |
| Brick | 16 | 2 | — |
| Cement | 16 | 30 | 5 |
| Coal | 47 | 19 | 16 |
| Cottonseed cake | 18 | 15 | 12 |
| Feed | 8 | 16 | 13 |
| Flour | 24 | 22 | 5 |
| Gasoline and kerosene | 80 | 70 | 41 |
| Grain | 3 | 7 | 2 |
| Hay | 11 | 13 | 22 |
| Lumber | 56 | 8 | 12 |
| Oil (road) | — | — | 23 |
| Posts | 11 | 6 | 1 |
| Stock | 6 | 35 | — |
| All other carloads | 92 | 23 | 12 |
| *Forwarded* | | | |
| Cottonseed | 171 | 16 | 40 |
| Gravel | 365 | 17 | 0 |
| Stock | 107 | 44 | 26 |
| All other carloads | 30 | 19 | 4 |
| Total | 1,080 | 299 | 262 |

SOURCE: QA&P, Exhibit 4, F1652.

at Matador. QA&P officials, bolstered by support personnel from the Frisco, were prepared. The opposition was not.[23]

Railroad personnel testified that train service had been provided by two daily round-trips from Matador to Matador Junction and return—plus periodic extras—through 1928. In that season, the QA&P had earned a modest profit of $2,061.34 on the branch operation; thereafter, business had fallen off badly and train service had been reduced to a daily turn between Roaring Springs and Matador.[24] The decline in tonnage affected nearly all commodities, as table 3 shows.

Railroaders observed that the once heavy volume of gravel had virtually disappeared when the local supply suitable for concrete purposes was exhausted. There was similar decrease in the volume of another important commodity, cotton. In 1928, the railroad had handled 12,783 bales from Matador, but that number had slipped to 2,769 in 1931 and 3,601 in 1935. Shipments of livestock also had declined, although in recent years there had been a slight upswing because of government drought relief plans such as the Federal Surplus Relief Corporation, which moved area cattle to stockyards at Oklahoma City, Chicago, and other distant points. Less-than-carload shipments represented another category of faltering business; between 1931 and 1934, inclusive, the railroad handled an average of only 282.4 tons per annum to and from Matador. Express and mail revenues remained relatively stable, but the number of passengers handled declined from 385 in 1930 to only 103 in 1934. The railroad earned a paltry $208.74 in passenger revenue on the branch from 1930 through 1934.[25]

That the railroad had attempted to do its best to serve Matador under trying circumstances was affirmed by Charles Sommer and all others who testified on its behalf. Sommer recalled, for instance, that the QA&P had spent heavily to improve the line after its acquisition but had been forced to defer maintenance when traffic declined. Now many repairs were needed, but deficits would have been even greater had proper maintenance been ordered over the years. Company officials cited other evidence of good faith. In an attempt to attract and retain business, the company had reduced rates, as table 4 shows. The railroad had also reduced rates on enumerated inbound commodities. The net result, said Sommer, was that "our revenues were further reduced." Competing for LCL business had been especially perplexing. "In our efforts to cope with the trucking situation, we offered passenger schedule service on merchandise shipments; provided free pick-up and delivery service; and, made drastic reductions in the rates," stated Sommer. There was little doubt that vehicular transportation had seriously damaged the branch's fortunes. Railroad officials had made a record of bus and truck traffic through Matador on several occasions. All this evidence was displayed before the ICC's hearing examiner.[26]

Legal counsel for the protestants and those giving testimony against the railroad were outclassed by those of the carrier. The protestants' attorneys were unfamiliar with and frustrated by the regulatory agency's procedures, and shippers were unsophisticated in their knowledge and expression. The protestants questioned the validity of the railroad's statistics and conclusions; questioned the amount of revenue apportioned to the branch as opposed to the main line; insisted that the current drought was a passing phenomenon and that the service area held great potential; claimed that the Motley County Railroad had been chartered for ninety-nine years and therefore it or its successor was obligated to perform continuous service for that period; claimed that if the line was operated "properly and efficiently . . . it would, under normal conditions, return a dividend on the investment to the

### TABLE 4
### Comparative Rates on Matador Branch

| Commodity | 1926 rate (per cwt) | 1935 rate (per cwt) |
|---|---|---|
| Cotton (to the Gulf) | 99 | 56 |
| Cottonseed (to Quanah) | 25½ | 9 |
| Cattle (to Oklahoma City) | 43½ | 31 |
| Cattle (to Fort Worth) | 41 | 31 |

owners"; and asserted that abandonment would deprive an important county seat and its surroundings of rail service "with consequent injury and financial loss." Lawyers for the protestants brought little contrary evidence to the hearing and instead tried to bring into disrepute the testimony of railroad officials.[27]

The protest did not sway the hearing examiner, who recommended abandonment. The ICC upheld his opinion on April 10, 1936. The regulatory agency found that the branch had lost from $6,607.34 to $14,333.27 per annum from 1929 through 1934; losses would have been greater if usual and proper maintenance had been observed; the total cost of rehabilitation would be over $50,000; and "neither present nor prospective volume of traffic . . . is sufficient to warrant its retention." Abandonment was authorized.[28]

The ruling brought no joy either to the general offices at Quanah or to the executive offices at St. Louis. Rather, the reaction was one of matter-of-fact resolution. Sommer told his brother that "as soon as Mr. Richardson has arranged for the cancellation of all tariffs, we will, immediately after expiration of the 30-day time limit, cease operations." The road's traffic office soon notified "all concerned" that business on the branch was ending. The agent at Matador was informed that his station would be removed from the list of prepaid points on May 15 but that the station would remain open through the month to receive any shipments billed before rates were canceled. The Railway Mail Service arranged to substitute star route service for the closed pouch service that the QA&P offered, and the last revenue run was operated unceremoniously from Roaring Springs to Matador and back on May 31.[29]

The branch's train crew was advised that it would be held on payroll through the dismantling process. That disagreeable chore began on June 29. Meanwhile, contracts were made for the sale of the depot building at Matador (for $200 to the Spot Cash Grocery Company) and for sale of the branch line's ties (for $150 to the branch's locomotive engineer). The toolhouse and coal bin were moved to Quanah, and all other physical properties were razed according to Sommer's orders: "We will not want to leave any evidence of the rail line when we start moving out." This demolition was accomplished expeditiously; it was finished on July 17. As the switch was removed at Matador Junction, the roadmaster in charge of dismantling ordered the locomotive engineer to "tie the whistle down" and then "called the office [at Quanah] to let" officials there "in on the finale."[30]

The mood at Matador was one of bitterness and defiance. Matador's association with steamcar civilization had been, at best, a mixture of love and hate. The editor of the local newspaper wrote of "Matador's old conflict with a hopeless railroad situation." He warmed to his task in a lengthy editorial written a few days before service ended. "When the last train whistles . . . join companions in the oblivion of space . . . [our] . . . obligation will forever be paid—even the last installment of loyalty to the dead nerve of a tottering industry. When the chronic sore on the shoulders of progress is removed, then the journey to greater advancement will be made with reduced effort." The editor affirmed that there was no need to fear the label "inland town."[31]

Denials to the contrary, losing rail service was a serious matter, especially during the 1930s. That the editor of the *Matador Tribune* would spend so much energy denying that fact confirmed it. Yet the impact of motor vehicles was clear enough. The issue of the *Tribune* immediately preceding abandonment carried advertisements from the Matador Buick Company, Sinclair Service Station, Conoco, Phillip Graves's Gulf Station, and FFF Chevrolet Company, and the Ford Motor Company urged Matadorians to "see first what a difference that V-8 feeling makes." In the same issue, the Matador Hardware and Furniture Company contended that "the Railroad Loss is Our Gain"—local merchants would benefit from "lower freight rates than ever before" because trucks would "give equal or better service than the railroad."[32]

One observer thought the Matador abandonment was "an old story, one that has been recorded

Scenes such as this one were increasingly evident along the QA&P as the Great Depression deepened. The QA&P and its constituents suffered together.

already in many communities and that is certain to be told later in many more." He was correct. The case was not unique, but it was of interest because it reflected the trend that had begun earlier and would continue—especially in the years following World War II—as the carriers hastened to rid themselves of branch line mileage. Matador's experience was, indeed, to be replayed countless times thereafter with little variation.[33]

The QA&P was clearly warranted in its application, but Charles Sommer's estimation that trucking was the sole blight on the line's operation was an oversimplification. Changed and changing circumstance was the villain. Admittedly, trucking cut deeply into freight revenues, and the automobile had taken nearly all passenger traffic. Additional carload as well as LCL business had evaporated when the FW&DC built its South Plains line across the northern portion of the branch's service area. An undetermined volume of business was lost to the drought, and government relief policies cut further into agricultural production and its transportation. Finally, changes in land use—fewer cattle in the area, for instance—and the combined impact of the Great Depression and the Dust Bowl drove population from the area and reduced available business. In sum, rail service was less needed in 1936 than when the line had been built only twenty-three years earlier.

## CHAPTER 15

# Cylinder Heads Should Be Polished

Make good time, especially on ballasted track.—
Instructions to locomotive engineer W. H. Norman, May 15, 1930

IN good times or bad, there were trains to run and a business to manage. Charles H. Sommer presided, paying close attention to matters of strategy and finance and maintaining a close liaison with the Frisco. His brother A. F. Sommer, vice-president and general manager, was responsible for operations and engineering. William L. Richardson remained in charge of sales and advertising. This tiny cadre, assisted by subordinate officers and a loyal band of contract employees, undertook the day-to-day routine of the Quanah, Acme & Pacific Railway.

Ownership and control of the QA&P, always confused, was uncluttered after the death of Sam Lazarus in 1926. In 1909, he had owned a clear majority of the road's stock. His share had eroded during 1911, but Lazarus still held approximately 50 percent of the issue. Within three years, however, his portfolio contained only 40 percent of the Quanah Route's stock. This was the situation at the time of his death—even though some sources had claimed that the Frisco owned all capital stock and the equally incorrect assertion that Lazarus was the chief stockholder of the QA&P. The ledger was simplified in July 1926, when the Lazarus estate sold its shares to the SL-SF. Some confusion persisted, though, since the QA&P retained its historic autonomy; the Frisco controlled the property through the ownership of its stock, but control was not exercised and no officer or director of the parent road held similar positions on the Quanah Route. As Sommer explained, the local road was managed independently of the SL-SF, "the latter company in no way attempting to control or operate the QA&P." Frisco's Kurn agreed: "The property is operated independently and is locally managed."[1]

Hard times befell the Frisco in 1933 and, as a consequence of its receivership, all QA&P stock (except the director's shares) passed to the trust of Harrigan & Company in New York City. It would

be returned to the SL-SF upon its reorganization, effective January 25, 1947. It is worth noting that the QA&P survived the Depression and, in fact, never suffered receivership.[2]

The road's carload freight business increased during the 1920s—7,182 in 1920, 12,217 in 1925, and 13,446 in 1929—reflecting a generally robust national economy, development of the railroad's service area, and expansion of the company's line to Floydada. Business fluctuated during the years preceding World War II and was again reflected in carloads handled: 10,471 in 1930, 8,827 in 1935 (the nadir in this and other categories), 9,635 in 1940, and 12,431 in 1941. Such statistics mirrored the vagaries of the Great Depression and its accompanying drought, the diversion and then restoration of QA&P's transcontinental traffic, and the growing war-related business late in the period. Major classifications of cargo included plaster and plaster products, grain, cotton, cottonseed products, livestock, sand, and gravel, lumber, crude petroleum, refined petroleum, and coal. The relative importance of these goods varied over time. Coal, for instance, ranked second in tonnage in 1920 and declined thereafter as area consumers switched to alternate fuels. The movement of sand and gravel followed the development of area townsites, the construction of vehicular roadways, and mirrored the local economy. Cottonseed products were particularly susceptible to truck competition and became less important in the QA&P traffic mix in later years. The movement of petroleum—crude and refined—escalated but was generally restricted to the Quanah–Red River line.[3]

Throughout the 1920s and 1930s, products flowing from the Acme mills supplied both significant tonnage and revenue for the QA&P. Except for the trying times of the mid-1930s, this traffic maintained top ranking among all classes. Virtually all of

Throughout the 1920s and the 1930s, products flowing from mills like this one supplied life-sustaining revenue for the QA&P.

this business was interchanged to the FW&DC for westbound movement at Acme or was taken to Quanah for eastbound carriage by the Denver Road or the SL-SF. (The QA&P, of course, received revenue as far as Red River on all tonnage moving via the Frisco.) Plaster was hardly a romantic commodity, but it was steady and remunerative traffic, and it paid the bills.[4]

A second commodity of historic importance to the QA&P's traffic mix was cotton and cotton-related products. The shipment of these goods began as soon as the line was built west of Acme. In time, trucks reduced the carrier's tonnage in cottonseed, but bales of cotton in carload lots were shipped in large numbers every year. Throughout the 1920s and into the next decade every agency station except Acme billed cotton. Of these Paducah led, followed by Roaring Springs or Matador. Most of this traffic moved on transit rates to Quanah for compression and then to the Gulf for export via the FW&DC. In 1928, for example, 930 cars of compressed cotton were delivered to the Denver Road. An interesting corollary in the 1920s was the movement of laborers into the producing area. More than two thousand cotton pickers were transported in one season, generating welcome passenger revenue but forcing the Quanah Route to look for additional equipment because its passenger roster was inadequate for such a rush.[5]

The movement of grain reflected growing conditions in each season, but grain usually ranked high among the various classes of business. In tonnage, it was sixth in 1920, seventh in 1930, and fourth in 1940. Agents, particularly those west of Roaring Springs, regularly advised the Quanah of-

fice about crop conditions and the progress of harvest. The agent at Floydada told W. L. Richardson in 1931 that the Farmers Grain Company there had received the first load of wheat on June 11, the average yield appeared to be nineteen to twenty bushels per acre, and the QA&P would handle the first carload out of Floydada that season. The devastating drought that followed was mirrored in the number of cars handled—244 in 1931, 122 in 1932, 202 in 1933, 125 in 1934, and only 66 in 1935. Many persons left the QA&P's service area during these difficult years, but others stayed on in grim determination. "This is the best *next year* country we know of," was one observer's cryptic statement of confidence. Another was harsher: "We have three rains every year: One after a wheat failure; one after a feed failure; and, one after a cotton failure."[6]

The rains, always sporadic, ultimately returned—if haltingly—and the land again produced wheat in large volume. Most of the resulting traffic was handed to the Denver Road for delivery to terminal elevators at Fort Worth or Gulf ports. When the FW&DC failed to provide adequate service or when it failed to appear appreciative, however, the QA&P diverted-wheat to the Missouri-Kansas-Texas Railroad (Katy) at Altus, Oklahoma. This routing was indirect and wasteful of ton miles, but the Katy offered good service and was pleased to have the business. Moreover, the QA&P earned more revenue because the cars moved via Red River, and parent Frisco also gained a portion of the division for its twenty-nine-mile haul from Red River to Altus.[7]

If one had to offer a short definition of the QA&P's service area it would be cattle country. This was reflected in the railroad's traditional traffic mix. As soon as the line was built to Paducah, cattlemen began to avail themselves of the new rail service. In 1910, drovers pushed a herd all the way from the Parramore Ranch in Stonewall County to the Paducah loading pens. At about the same time, the Swenson brothers purchased the famous Spur Ranch south of the QA&P and a less well-known spread on the Tongue River between Matador and Paducah. Swenson cattle soon moved in great numbers aboard cars loaded on the Quanah Route. Other large operators such as the Matador Land & Cattle Company also used the line extensively. Its manager did not stretch reality when he said that arrival of the QA&P marked "the commencement of a new era in the history of the Matadors." Entire trainloads of animals were shipped from QA&P pens to distant ranges in Montana, and entire trainloads were unloaded at the same pens as the Matador firm shifted livestock among its many theaters of operation under a rate system that was lower for range animals than for market cattle. When the White & Swearingen firm decided to place its ranch lands on the market for settlers in 1925, its livestock was herded into the pens at Swearingen. Still another cattle firm, S. Burke Burnett's 6666, used the QA&P on a regular basis. A representative shipment made by the Burnett company on October 17, 1929, consisted of ten cars of stocker cattle—fifty-two head in forty-foot cars and forty-eight head in thirty-six-foot cars—consigned to a party at Hominy, Oklahoma.[8]

The QA&P always labored to secure slaughter livestock for movement to Oklahoma City over Fort Worth and all other packing centers. This policy, of course, guaranteed important revenue for the Frisco as well. In 1928, the QA&P advertised twenty-four hour livestock service from Floydada to Oklahoma City on Tuesdays and Saturdays. Business was brisk. Although Oklahoma City was favored for slaughter animals, the QA&P unhesitatingly entered into rate agreements with all comers for any movements, especially for range cattle and horses in carloads lots.[9]

The volume of livestock handled during the 1920s was impressive. In 1920, 954 carloads were handled, representing 13.3 percent of the total freight for the year. By 1922 the number had risen to 1,329 cars. Business was brisker after the Quanah Route completed its line to Floydada. In 1929, 56 carloads of sheep, cattle, hogs, horses, and mules were received from the AT&SF at that point and moved overhead or to destination via the QA&P. Conversely, shippers on the Quanah Route could now avail themselves of a western outlet. Westbound stock was mostly destined for consignees on the AT&SF or FW&DC in West Texas, although some went all the way to California.[10]

The livestock business, always important, was even more prized by the railroad during the Dirty Thirties. In 1930, the QA&P handled 1,669 carloads, representing 15.9 percent of its total; in 1940 only 868 carloads were moved, representing 9.0 percent of all loaded cars. Most of this originated at or terminated at pens along the QA&P, although the road did handle some overhead traffic. For instance, cattle consigned to the yards at Oklahoma City and horses billed to Memphis were received from the Santa Fe at Floydada. Additionally, slaughter cattle loaded on the FW&DC in West Texas and bound for Oklahoma City, as well as mules billed from FW&DC points in New Mexico

and consigned to a firm in Memphis, Tennessee, rolled over QA&P rails from Quanah to Red River.[11]

The railroad billed numerous single-car as well as LCL livestock shipments, but its major interest understandably centered on multiple-car orders and consignments by the major ranches in its service area. There were several such shipments each season. A few examples are representative: twenty-nine cars for Swearingen and thirty-one cars for Narcisso received from the Santa Fe in 1932; forty-five cars loaded at four sites on the QA&P by the Matador Land & Cattle Company in 1932; twenty-three shipped from Narcisso by the Pitchfork Land & Cattle Company in 1933; twenty-two cars dispatched by Miller & Son from Swearingen in 1935; three thousand head shipped from Narcisso in 1939 by the Four Sixes Ranch; and twenty-five cars billed at Swearingen by the Triangle Ranch in 1939. These usually moved in special trains to or from FW&DC, Frisco, or Santa Fe connections. Outbound shipments were destined for points as diverse as Toledo, Ohio; Los Angeles, California; MacMillan, Idaho, Oklahoma City, Oklahoma; Burden, Kansas; and various other ranges in Texas. A particularly interesting shipment involved one of the last, or perhaps even the last, herd of longhorns in Cottle County, loaded at Swearingen during 1936 for transport to the Lohman Ranch at Foraker, Oklahoma. Employees and officials alike took pride in this traffic.[12]

The QA&P understandably tried to attract traffic that would yield revenues both for itself and its parent, the Frisco, but it was not always possible to gain the long haul over the SL-SF. In one case, the routing on fifty cars of cattle from Narcisso to Omaha was controlled by a party who refused to allow passage via Kansas City and agreed to use the Frisco only for delivery to the Rock Island at Chickasha, Oklahoma. Even this represented a concession on the part of the consignee; heretofore his shipments from QA&P points had moved via the FW&DC to a connection with the Rock Island at Waurika, Oklahoma. Try as they might, QA&P officials could not dissuade this man from his preference for the Rock Island. In 1940, the Pitchfork Ranch ordered thirty-five cars for cattle sold to finishers at Oakland and Walnut, Iowa. "At the last moment," groused W. L. Richardson, "the Rock Island appeared on the scene and offered the shippers a 22-hour schedule from Chickasha to destinations." He had to admit, ruefully, that the cars had twenty-five and a half hours of "free time left" when they were delivered to the Rock Island at Chickasha. Richardson was badgered by Charles Sommer and Frisco officials to secure longer hauls on such shipments, but he bluntly told them that "in view of the better service"—service that obviated the need to unload animals in transit for feed, water and rest—"it was impossible" to do better than handle such shipments to Chickasha.[13]

Tension between railroad officials and shippers always characterized the livestock business. Sometimes difficulties resulted from misunderstanding or ignorance of the other's problems. Shippers' requests for operation of special trains for stock shipments could cause dissension. One rancher, for instance, became irate when the railroad would not run a special train to handle his three-car shipment from Swearingen to Quanah. Yet revenue for such special service would not have matched expenses. Charles Sommer accordingly set a new policy that special trains would run from Swearingen if there was enough freight for ten cars and from points farther west if there was enough for twenty cars. A. F. Sommer complained that cattlemen seemed to think "that the carriers should always adjust train service to their convenience." Nevertheless, he favored running special trains, especially if they could be loaded on Sundays—"an awfully good time to get these shipments off of our hands." But ranchers could not always move their animals to shipping points on a schedule convenient for the railroad. Most shippers wanted to get their animals to market not later than Wednesday because buyers tended to withdraw late in the week. Moreover, because of range conditions—as well as market conditions—it was often either impossible or foolish to ship large numbers at one time. A case in point involved R. C. Miller & Son, who ordered twenty-two cars for loading at Swearingen in 1935. These cars were to carry cattle to Spur, Texas, via Quanah and the FW&DC. But rain descended on the ranges shortly after the order was placed, it washed away fencing around the holding pasture and the cattle scattered. Ranch hands labored to round them up, but it was tedious and time-consuming. The original and subsequent loading and connecting schedules were broken at cost to the QA&P and especially the FW&DC in deadheading crews to protect the shipment. Railroad officials were furious, but as one of the ranchers said, it was impossible to communicate adequately under the circumstances. One QA&P official agreed. "These parties are not the usual high-strung cowtraders that we encounter so often, but just old cowmen who had more cattle on their

hands than they knew how to handle."[14]

Other problems attended shipping cattle. One that the railroad had no control over was the $5 brand inspection fee imposed on all cattle shipped from the railroad's pens in Cottle County. Independent-minded ranchers did not blame the railroad for this fee but threatened to drive their cattle to another county on the Wichita Valley (FW&DC) unless the tax was suspended. Nor did the railroad have any control over the economy or the weather. When John MacKenzie complained of the "deplorable condition" of the loading pens at Russellville, Charles Sommer felt constrained to tell him that "we have been passing through a period of depression which along with a series of droughts has forced us to watch our expenditures carefully." The two businessmen seemed to find mutual understanding on that point.[15]

Nevertheless, the strain between the railroaders and the cattlemen did not subside. Shippers along the entire length of the QA&P complained that they could not get their animals to Fort Worth in under forty-eight hours from the time they "loaded out" because QA&P trains arrived at Quanah either too late or too early for direct connection with Fort Worth–bound FW&DC trains—bringing a charge from the Fort Worth Stock Yards Company that the Quanah Route was arranging its schedules to give preference to "Oklahoma City and other northern markets." To respond to these complaints, Charles Sommer asked officials of the Denver Road if some accommodation might be made. He seemed to imply that the FW&DC should rearrange its schedules; the Denver Road, however, suggested that the QA&P adjust its own service. Sommer brooded about the matter. There was no justification for more than one regularly scheduled train in each direction on the QA&P. These trains were responsible for all local work west of Acme and had to protect the Santa Fe connection at Floydada and the Frisco connection at Quanah. They were also responsible for the accommodation of livestock movements. In the end, Sommer was forced to tell disgruntled shippers that "while we would like very much indeed to accommodate shippers with respect to connecting trains, in handling live stock, it is unfortunately impossible for us to meet all situations, and we have attempted to adjust our schedules so all interests will be served." Other complaints derived from derailments, excessive shrinkage, and the application of federal law requiring that livestock be delivered within thirty-six hours of loading or be unloaded, fed, and watered at railroad pens. On the QA&P, the thirty-six hour law was not as crucial as the incompatibility of connections at both Floydada and Quanah. Unloading and reloading stock at Floydada delayed QA&P trains and added to overtime claims by crews; at Quanah, it interfered with routine switching operations.[16]

G. E. Hamilton worried openly about the possibility of losing the livestock traffic to trucks. Many cattlemen, he said, in 1933, had already "equipped themselves with big trucks and they are hauling thousands of cattle to Fort Worth . . . ; they are all soon going to get weaned away from the railroads, and when that traffic once departs, it will be hard to win back." A dramatic shift to trucks was, to be sure, under way, as is indicated in comparative deliveries of cattle, calves, swine, and sheep to Fort Worth: trucks delivered 76,949 head in March 1932 and 90,859 in March 1933; 96,994 and 52,173 head, respectively, were delivered by rail.

Truckers did have distinct advantages. They were not forced into arbitrary schedules, were not affected by connections, and could expeditiously accommodate small consignments, and cattle hauled in trucks were not as susceptible to weight loss as were those shipped by rail. These advantages especially benefited the "little fellow," who in the past had been forced to appeal to his neighbors to help fill out a carload.[17]

Railroad managers could be faulted for not recognizing the threat to their livestock business and not responding to it earlier. Yet within limitations that were simply a part of railroading, they did seek to compete. Early in 1933, FW&DC's John A. Hulen agreed with QA&P officials "that we should make every effort to hold the business and the friendship of the cattle people." This pledge was made good during the following fall when the Denver Road inaugurated a new train, originating on its South Plains line, to serve the needs of livestock operators. An excellent connection was made at Quanah with the QA&P so that shippers on the local road, like those on the FW&DC, might enjoy overnight delivery to Fort Worth. The new service apparently was better received by shippers on the FW&DC than on the QA&P because only twenty-eight cars were interchanged at Quanah during the 1933 shipping season. Nevertheless, both companies were happy to announce that the train would run again for the 1934 season, beginning in August. Other carriers also attempted to meet competition. The Frisco announced in 1933 that if the QA&P delivered to it at Quanah "five cars or more," and if

those cars had "33 hours or more of free time" (within the provisions of the thirty-six hour law), it would handle them to Kansas City "without unloading for feed, water, and rest." The AT&SF, in cooperation with the Rock Island, instituted twenty-four-hour service from the South Plains to Oklahoma City via Amarillo. Finally, the Oklahoma National Stock Yards Company and the Oklahoma City Junction Railroad cooperated with the QA&P and the Frisco in advertising a special program of "livestock in small lots at carload rates" to be loaded on Mondays and Wednesdays, effective September 29, 1937. This service was aimed at small operators in an attempt to meet truck competition, and it worked well, generating thirty-four additional carloads of business during the 1937 season and twenty-two cars the following year.[18]

The issue of claims was always thorny. Two examples illustrate. On November 25, 1929, the Matador Land & Cattle Company shipped 505 head of cattle in eighteen cars from Matador to Kansas City. Eight animals died en route. The superintendent of claims for the Frisco argued that they were "old worn out cows . . . very thin and weak . . . and apparently perished because of . . . inherent weakness." But the QA&P agent who oversaw the loading pledged that "the cars were not overloaded and the cattle apparently were in good condition and able to stand shipment." The carrier was liable, and Frisco paid the claim. In another instance, involving three carloads billed from Narcisso by the Swenson Land & Cattle Company, ten animals perished before arriving at Kansas City. In this case, the Frisco claim agent asserted that the animals had died "apparently due to inherent weakness of the animals" and/or because calves and grown animals had been loaded without any partition to separate them. The QA&P's representative contended that shippers customarily loaded cows and calves without partitions but confirmed that the cows were "all old and poor when loaded." A notation to that effect had been made on the livestock contract. This claim was denied. Another problem involved the number of animals loaded per car. Railroaders sought to protect against claims resulting from overloading by noting that exception on the contracts and waybills.[19]

There is no doubt that some shippers engaged in duplicity and that rivalry between railroaders and ranchers was ancient. Railroad officials were especially annoyed when shippers ordered more cars than necessary, when they drove cattle overland and did not rest them before loading, when they had not "cut out the culls" before loading time, when they delivered cattle to the pens hours or even days after they had promised, or when they failed to show up at all. All these actions delayed the trains, resulted in missed or delayed connections, added per diem charges, and necessitated the payment of overtime rates for train crews. Not all shippers were so thoughtless or unprincipled; A. F. Sommer referred to the offenders as "curbstone dealers." Nevertheless, tension was evident, and it was exacerbated by the traditional distrust between railroad employees and cowhands. One patron, who accompanied a shipment to market in 1937, rejoiced that "a vast change had taken place from the old days when we would have a fight almost every time we went to market," and a longtime QA&P agent recalled that cowhands, especially those from the Matador ranch, "were sometimes very tough customers."[20]

A. F. Sommer's contempt for cattlemen in general and some in particular grew over time. A complaint from Tom Burnett (son of the late S. Burke Burnett) caused Sommer to throw up his hands in exasperation. "I thought we had become emancipated from this class of cattlemen," he bellowed. Sometime later he lost his temper with another cattleman who had ordered cars but had trucked his stock instead. Sommer pointed out that tariffs allowed the carriers to assess a penalty for those who ordered cars without using them, and he urged that the QA&P adopt such a policy. The road's traffic manager wrote a two-page letter arguing against it, however, saying that enforcement of the rule might antagonize shippers so they would not use the railroad. This incident also reflected the growing alienation between the road's operating and traffic departments and personally between A. F. Sommer and W. L. Richardson. Then, an incident in 1938 brought the matter to a head. A commission agent with whom Sommer had had earlier difficulties ordered six cars for loading at Dougherty but did not have the animals ready when the train arrived. The train left without the livestock. Sommer fired off a letter to the buyer in which he said that he was "always glad to accommodate a shipper" and was "not unmindful of the business that you have given us and we are appreciative of it." But, he said, "you are familiar with our train operations, that is we have only one local train which leaves Floydada . . . about 10:30 in the morning, and certainly there should be some way that you could arrange to have your cattle to the pens and ready to load when our train arrives." Sommer's bluntness was characteristic. A reply was not long in coming: "You need not

tell me you won't hold your damned train another time." The shipper sent a copy of his letter to Frisco officials and promised to avoid or short-haul the QA&P from then on. Sommer sent an order to all agents spelling out "deadlines for stock to be loaded" at every station along the line. Livestock handling was further restricted when, on May 6, 1939, QA&P trains began operations "on public schedules." It seemed that A. F. Sommer could now afford his abrasive position; the Depression was lifting and the QA&P was receiving a growing amount of transcontinental freight. The place of livestock in the road's traffic mix would continue to decline gradually.[21]

The QA&P enjoyed an impressive volume of miscellaneous carload freight, including packing house product (PHP) cars operated from Fort Worth by Armour & Company, from Oklahoma City by Wilson & Company, and from Wichita by Jacob Dold Company. These were known as route cars or peddler cars, requiring a seven-thousand-pound minimum loading, were operated on a once-a-week basis until the late 1930s, and carried items for grocery stores in communities along the line. For a while, the railroad also received carloads of butter from the Floydada Creamery, which were consigned to the Springfield Ice & Refrigerator Company at Springfield, Missouri, or moved to destinations as far away as Chicago. And although it contributed little revenue to the QA&P, solicitation resulted in a large volume of gasoline and other petroleum products moving from refineries at or near Wichita Falls to northern and eastern points via Quanah. The petroleum traffic resulted in considerable income for the Frisco. Finally, with the end of prohibition, the Quanah Route received a periodic carload of beer, usually Schlitz from Milwaukee or Pabst from East Peoria, for delivery to the thirsty residents of West Texas. The carrier was required to report all such business and was subject to a myriad of regulations by the state of Texas.[22]

Other constituents simply sought to slake their thirst with water—a commodity that was shipped in carload lots from Roaring Springs. The quality of water at Quanah and in much of the road's service area was, to say the least, poor. In some places it was nearly impossible to find, and frequently it was unfit for human consumption or even for use in boilers. The water at Roaring Springs, however, was very good. As early as 1930 the railroad built water-loading racks on the south side of the main line near the depot. The railroad used much of this water, shipping it to isolated section houses and in some cases to trackside tanks. Water for commercial purposes was shipped to the ice company at Quanah; to Paducah for distribution in five-gallon or wagonload lots to individuals for human consumption or to the many cotton gins that used it for cooling purposes; to Paducah for the ice company and for the Paducah Bottling Company; and to Acme for use by the mills. The rates for water and for transportation were extremely reasonable. In 1938, for example, the cost per eight-thousand-gallon tank of water delivered to Paducah was a mere $20, which included the cost of the water and transportation. For the five summer months of 1937, the QA&P received $1,657.15 in freight revenues from this traffic.[23]

The volume of LCL business reflected the condition of the local economy and the battle with trucks for business even more than did the volume of carload business. Late in 1928, the Frisco initiated a through package car from St. Louis to Quanah offering delivery the third morning after shipment. Additional package cars were later operated from Kansas City and Oklahoma City to Quanah. All three cars broke bulk at Quanah and, of course, contained lading destined for merchants there as well as cargo that was drayed to the FW&DC for further shipment on that road or was loaded on a line car headed for Floydada. Then, for a brief period, a St. Louis-to-Childress car was added in cooperation with the FW&DC. Hard times and truck competition affected LCL traffic, and W. L. Richardson was reduced to pleading with local agents to hunt for business lest the cars be discontinued. His fears were confirmed when the Childress car was removed, but he was pleased to see the establishment, as replacement, of a Quanah-to-Floydada line car loaded at St. Louis. In all cases he energetically sought to retain business moving over the Red River line. The operating department cooperated; Frisco crews were told that, in the event of trouble, they were to "see to it that they go into Quanah with the three merchandise cars." These were to be spotted at Quanah between the QA&P and FW&DC stations so that "transfer men could start working on the merchandise without delay." It was a busy scene. On December 28, 1933, alone, 5,848 pounds of merchandise were transferred to the FW&DC from the three package cars. Richardson had his hands full trying to keep volume up while at the same time orchestrating the efforts of three railroads at Quanah.[24]

Richardson also attempted to drum up business at on-line communities by alerting them to next-

### TABLE 5
### The Downward Trend in LCL Traffic

| Station | 1933 | 1936 | 1941 |
|---|---|---|---|
| Quanah | 935,665 | 657,148 | 621,035 |
| Paducah | 1,551,177 | 1,055,240 | 974,143 |
| Roaring Springs | 378,190 | 346,243 | 220,036 |
| Floydada | 412,955 | 430,744 | 374,211 |

day delivery on goods ordered from Quanah wholesale houses. Each westbound local carried the package car from St. Louis, the line car from Quanah, and the PHP cars. All were placed immediately ahead of the caboose. Each was unloaded by train crews and agents at the various way stations.[25]

Charles Sommer required detailed reports on everything, including monthly LCL business. Those he saw during the 1930s were not encouraging. Statistics for LCL illustrate the downward trend (table 5). Sommer asked Richardson to explain the drop in volume. Richardson cast his cold eye on the matter and responded with a single word: trucks. They offered more frequent service and lower tariffs and were more energetic in their solicitations. He could offer no suggestion as to how the railroads might compete. He thought the carriers had been well advised in 1932 by J. R. Turney of the St. Louis Southwestern Railway when he counseled a new package car system embracing a multimodal approach. The current system, Turney had said, was as "out of place as a corset at the seashore." Railroaders had not listened. Instead, they had clung to the old ways of handling small lots and package shipments—much to their collective detriment.[26]

A periodic and rather romantic source of revenue came from the movement of show trains and show cars. Paducah, "one of the best tent show towns in West Texas," was frequently visited by these troupes. Small shows with two or three cars—Jones Brothers Circus and Christy Brothers Show—as well as large ones with twenty to twenty-five cars—Cole Brothers, Gentry Brothers, and Delmar Shows—played there in years before the Depression. After the line reached Floydada, shows traveled to that community as well—Christy Brothers in 1928, Al G. Barnes in 1929, and Harley Sadler Shows in 1933. Some shows stopped only at Quanah and others moved overhead to or from the FW&DC via Red River. Among these were Bill H. Hames Shows, Brunks Comedians, and the Eureka Whaling Company's Exhibit Car 22. Single-car or small movements occasioned little fanfare, but the larger ones required contracts, meticulous planning, and an advance car handled in regular service a day or two

# FRISCO
## LINES

# LOW FARE
# EXCURSION
### TO
# OKLAHOMA
# CITY
# SUNDAY, FEB. 24

**ALSO LEAVING CERTAIN STATIONS FEB. 23rd, AS INDICATED BELOW**

**SCHEDULE**

| STATION | Train 404 | | Train 410-10 | | ROUND TRIP FARES |
|---|---|---|---|---|---|
| Lv Quanah | 10:10 pm Feb. 23rd | | 7:45 am Feb. 24th | | $4.00 |
| Lv Eldorado | 10:43 pm | " | 8:22 am | " | 3.50 |
| Lv Creta | | | f 8:35 am | " | 3.25 |
| Lv Olustee | f 11:10 pm | " | 8:52 am | " | 3.25 |
| Lv Altus | 12:55 am Feb. 24th | | 9:16 am | " | 3.00 |
| Lv Headrick | f 1:20 am | " | 9:44 am | " | 2.75 |
| Lv Snyder | 2:05 am | " | 10:15 am | " | 2.50 |
| Lv Indiahoma | f 2:33 am | " | f 10:42 am | " | 2.50 |
| Lv Cache | f 2:50 am | " | 11:00 am | " | 2.25 |
| Lv Lawton | 3:20 am | " | 11:33 am | " | 2.00 |
| Lv Fort Sill | 3:38 am | " | 11:45 am | " | 1.75 |
| Lv Elgin | f 4:05 am | " | 12:04 pm | " | 1.50 |
| Lv Fletcher | f 4:16 am | " | 12:11 pm | " | 1.50 |
| Lv Cyril | 4:31 am | " | 12:20 pm | " | 1.50 |
| Lv Cement | 4:43 am | " | 12:35 pm | " | 1.25 |
| Lv Norge | f 5:07 am | " | f 1:01 pm | " | 1.00 |
| Lv Chickasha | 5:22 am | " | 1:20 pm | " | 1.00 |
| Lv Amber | f 5:38 am | " | f 1:43 pm | " | 1.00 |
| Lv Tuttle | 6:00 am | " | 2:03 pm | " | 1.00 |
| Ar OKLAHOMA CITY | 6:50 am | " | 2:50 pm | " | |

f — indicates stop on signal to take on passengers.

Tickets sold at these fares will be good going to Oklahoma City only on train 404 as shown in the above schedule.
Returning, tickets will be good on any train leaving Oklahoma City prior to 1:00 pm, Monday, February 25, 1929.

**TICKETS GOOD ONLY IN COACHES AND CHAIR CARS**

Ticket Offices at certain of these stations are not open at night or on Sunday; passengers from such stations should buy tickets during the day, Saturday.

## VISIT THE
## SOUTHWEST AMERICAN
# LIVE STOCK
# SHOW

## ASK THE FRISCO AGENT
### FOR ADDITIONAL INFORMATION

J. W. Nourse
Passenger Traffic Manager

---

before the circus train.[27]

The nature and quality of passenger service offered by the Quanah Route during the 1920s, at least until the Floydada extension opened in 1928, is surrounded by mystery. The *Official Guide of the Railways* from 1920 through 1925 shows daily round-trip passenger service, but the QA&P's A-3 (gas-electric motor car) had not successfully or dependably handled A-4 (passenger trailer car) because of heavy westbound grades and had disappeared by the summer of 1922. The A-3 was likely leased and then sold to the Frisco; the A-4 was converted into a work train bunk car in 1923. Mixed train service began in mid-1922, possibly earlier, and was operated on a daily-except-Sunday basis from that time. This was the QA&P's "passenger service." Schedules remained much the same as before; there was a daylight run from Quanah to Roaring Springs and back. Connections were made at Roaring Springs with a "Daily Automobile Line" to Floydada.[28]

The community of Paducah, which had strained relations with the QA&P throughout the history of the road, complained that the absence of Sunday service deprived it of mail service on that day as well as a means by which to receive cotton pickers on a daily basis. The railroad, through Charles Sommer, responded that service had been reduced because of inadequate revenues on Sunday runs, "to afford the crews a recreation that they are justly entitled to," and to provide time to work on the road's locomotives. In fact, the issue was solely economic. Times were hard for the company and passenger revenues were down. During the first nine months of 1923, the railroad handled an average of only 33.8 passengers per day and earned a mere $52.11 on a daily average.[29]

Nevertheless, a formal complaint was filed by the Cottle County Chamber of Commerce with the Railroad Commission of Texas citing several alleged shortcomings, including the absence of daily service. Mixed train service, the Chamber asserted, was "at its best very unsatisfactory." Patrons were especially irked when train crews tended to switching chores before pulling the train up to station platforms for unloading. Moreover, the trains were rarely on time and frequently very late. The citizens of Cottle County felt that "the QA&P Railway Company should be made to give adequate and satisfactory passenger service over their line." Could not motorized service be instituted, they wondered? The state's regulatory agency wondered the same. A hearing was scheduled.[30]

Charles Sommer was embarrassed. He hated criticism and was especially galled at having his good name—and the QA&P's reputation—besmirched at the Railroad Commission offices. All he could do in this case, however, was make the best possible presentation. The experiment with the gas-electric car had been a miserable failure, he said. The car had been too small to handle the volume in drummers' sample trunks and other baggage and express and had not been able to handle a trailer because of grades. He would be happy to acquire motorized equipment again, though, as soon as a manufacturer could provide adequate equipment for the QA&P's needs. Beyond that he reiterated the company's position: Sunday revenues would net red ink—traffic on Sunday never had been good, and now the railroad was faced with competition from "jitneys and busses." But he would see to it that the oil lamps in the coaches were replaced with more "modern" Pintsch gaslights, and he would advise crews to unload passengers before doing the station work. These concessions were not enough. Explicit pressure from Paducah and implicit pressure from the regulatory agency mounted. On October 6, 1924, the railroad reinstituted Sunday passenger service, but continued with mixed train service during the rest of the week.[31]

As Charles Sommer had predicted, the volume of passengers was not adequate to support Sunday operations. Expenses exceeded revenues by a two-to-one margin, as was shown in the number of passengers carried—only 269 for the fourteen Sundays of March, April, and May 1925, or an average of 19.2. A. F. Sommer thought the only reason patrons wanted the service was to receive mail and "the funny papers." He urged that "we take it off and argue the question later." Sunday service was suspended.[32]

No great stir resulted, and, in the main, the Railroad Commission of Texas found the company's service adequate. An inspector in 1924 found the trains on time and crews conducting their business in a courteous way. In addition, he volunteered that the track was the best he had seen "laid on dirt." The inspector complained, however, that the station at Swearingen had "no negro waiting room," there was "no water keg" at that facility, fires had not been lit in waiting rooms of several stations, many waiting rooms were dirty, and agents and brakemen failed to wear caps and badges as prescribed by law.[33]

The country was experiencing a flush of optimism in 1928, which on the QA&P was accentuated when workers completed the new line from Mac-Bain to Floydada. Charles Sommer was caught up in the enthusiastic spirit. During the summer of 1928, he convinced the Frisco to extend through passenger service from Oklahoma City to Floydada. Two sets of equipment, both owned by the Frisco, would be required; one set would be stenciled "Frisco" and the other "Quanah, Acme & Pacific." The parent road would use its power between Oklahoma City and Quanah and the QA&P its engines for the western portion of the run. Sommer told his brother to use locomotives 25 and 27 and to decorate them "to the extent that the tender and panel under the cab is striped with a small gold leaf line" and the same to be applied "to the sand box and dome over the boiler." Additionally, he said, the "cylinder heads should be polished" or painted aluminum. By mid-September the two roads agreed that the trains would consist of a baggage car, combination mail-baggage car, "partition" coach, chair car, and standard sleeper. All equipment was to be steel; the sleeper represented Pullman's car line 3434. The schedule, inaugurated on October 1, called for an overnight trip from Oklahoma City to Quanah (with two hours dead time at Altus to encourage inbound sleeping car traffic), a morning run to Floydada, an early evening departure, and an overnight return to Oklahoma City. Easy connections were available, as always, at Oklahoma City for Tulsa, Kansas City, St. Louis, and other points on the Frisco. Maximum speeds on the QA&P were raised from forty to forty-five miles per hour in deference to the "spit and polish" of this new "varnish."[34]

Sommer had told his brother at Quanah always to give the train's locomotives "a neat appearance" because he was "inclined to the belief that a good-looking locomotive is an asset in advertising." Indeed, Charles Sommer was shrewdly perceptive in such matters. Not surprisingly, he responded to compliments on the train's name—the *Plainsman*—by ordering employees to use this designation instead of the more mundane trains 1 and 2 "whenever an opportunity offers."[35]

An important collateral development involved negotiations between the QA&P and the Railway Mail Service (RMS) for the purpose of establishing a Railway Post Office (RPO) route that had been going on since 1925. They came to fruition when the RMS established the Quanah & Floydada RPO simultaneously with inception of the *Plainsman*. This new service lent the train an additional element of prestige and extended en-route sorting to

One set of passenger equipment, shown here at the engine facility in Quanah, was stenciled "Quanah, Acme & Pacific" for use on the *Plainsman*.

the entire region. Now patrons could wait until the last minute, take letters to the train, and hand them to a clerk who postmarked and dispatched them in the finest time-honored way. Such "mail drops" were especially heavy at Floydada.[36]

Express and baggage service was similarly extended to Floydada over the QA&P. The earlier contract with Wells Fargo & Company was superseded by one with American Railway Express on September 1, 1920, and still another on March 1, 1929, with Railway Express Agency. The usual baggage tariffs were filed, supplemented by a special local and joint tariff for the interstate transportation of milk and cream. This was designed to attract shipments to processing plants located on the SL-SF in Oklahoma and Missouri. It was not very successful because most buyers had prior agreements or producers sold directly to local creameries.[37]

President Sommer hoped that the train, "while not profitable," might at least become "self-supporting." In fact, its early operation did result in profit, reflecting public acceptance of the new service and the diligent efforts by all employees to make it successful. The Texas Motorways Com-

pany even initiated bus service from Lubbock that connected with arrivals and departures of the *Plainsman*. Advertisements placed in Plainview and Lubbock newspapers generated additional business, especially sleeping car traffic, and agents such as Robert Medlen at Floydada drummed up interest among college students in service offered by the *Plainsman*. Rates were reasonable: $7.00 in coaches and $9.00 in sleepers for the round-trip from Floydada to Oklahoma City and return. For lower berths, one paid an additional $3.75, for upper berths an additional $3.00. Even these inexpensive fares were reduced when the QA&P instituted a two-cent per mile rate at the end of 1932.[38]

The initial exuberance diminished quickly, though, after the Crash of 1929 and the onset of the Great Depression. As early as December 1929, the Frisco contemplated taking off the chair car in order to reduce the train's consist, and seven months later the car was indeed removed. For the QA&P, profitable operation of the *Plainsman* ended, with only three monthly exceptions, in February 1930. The train had generated passenger revenues of $3,008.23 in January 1929 but only $291.32 for February 1932. The decline reflected a broader pattern. In 1924, revenue from local and interline tickets sold at Quanah (including those for Frisco trains) had totaled $37,223.43; in 1930, the total was a disappointing $12,900.34.[39]

The Frisco quietly made plans to discontinue its part of the service. When Sommer learned this, he labored hard to have the decision reversed, but to no avail. The through train operated its last run on June 20, 1931. Thereafter an overnight layover at Quanah was required for passengers headed from points on the QA&P to points on the Frisco. An immediate gasp of disappointment arose from communities along the QA&P and from passengers themselves, especially those who had become accustomed to the comforts of the *Abilene* and the *Canarsie,* sleepers usually assigned by Pullman. All Sommer could do was to point out that the trains had not paid out-of-pocket costs and to pledge that the QA&P would continue to operate the trains—still designated the *Plainsman*—on the same schedule although without the direct Frisco connection and Pullman service—at least temporarily. Depressed revenues also dampened his enthusiasm for the 2-cent rates. They were canceled and were replaced with the standard 3.6-cent rate.[40]

The *Plainsman* offered useful service for those traveling from one local station to another as well as for those traveling to distant points. For instance, it provided a means by which QA&P patrons could reach Fort Worth and other major Texas communities via Quanah and the Denver Road. (For only fifty cents, Gulley Transfer Company would convey a passenger and baggage between depots at Quanah.) Occasionally, especially during the happier years of through service by the *Plainsman,* the QA&P provided an even more cosmopolitan outlet. In 1931, as an example, two Floydadians used the QA&P's cars on the first leg of a long journey to attend the Rotary International Convention in Vienna, Austria. On even rarer occasions Quanah Route passenger trains operated in a heroic manner; on December 17, 1935, a victim of an automobile accident was transported in the baggage car of the *Plainsman* from near Lazare to medical care at Paducah.[41]

However important they may have been to the transportation or psychological needs of its service area, the trains earned more and more red ink. During the period from 1930 to 1935, these losses grew from a few dollars to as much as $1,000 per month. Revenue from tickets sales plummeted: $291.32 for February 1932; $84.41 for June 1933; $80.37 for May

1935; and $47.92 for February 1939.[42]

An anguished discussion began early in 1932 among Sommer, his brother, and W. L. Richardson over what to do about the "passenger train problem." A variety of suggestions were made: to handle LCL and PHP on the *Plainsman;* to acquire motor vehicles to handle mail and express; to acquire motorized equipment especially designed to handle mail, express, and high-class LCL but to discontinue passenger service; to entice the Frisco to reestablish through overnight service to Oklahoma City; and to turn the *Plainsman* into a mixed train. There were serious objections to each of these alternatives, and the QA&P continued to operate its passenger trains in the usual manner. Charles Sommer was emphatic that the mail contract be protected and responded vigorously whenever complaints were heard regarding the nature of service or time schedules offered by the Quanah Route. Even the editor of the *Paducah Post* recognized the line's problems: "Railroads are not as important as they were in days gone by," he said in 1937, but "we had better consider the question of whether or not we want a railroad before we decide on having the mail taken away from this common carrier." The matter was not that serious, but Sommer did state that "any appreciable reduction in our mail earnings might force us to discontinue" the trains.[43]

In an attempt to ease the drain on the company's financial resources, Sommer did order cuts. The first of these resulted in the suspension of Sunday passenger service, effective September 10, 1939. He anticipated complaints and was not disappointed: "Immediately a big howl went up from the citizens along the line because there was no mail on Sunday"—even though "there is really no point in these people getting their mail on Sunday except as a matter of habit." Nevertheless, one postmaster sought to have the railroad's mail contract canceled. Sommer was irked but determined. At considerable pain to his ego, he ordered the discontinuation of the *Plainsman* at the end of its run on December 9, 1939. Thereafter, passengers, mail, and express would be handled on a mixed train schedule calling for a daily-except-Sunday turn leaving Quanah at 4:15 A.M. and returning 2:35 P.M. Steam-heated passenger equipment was returned to the Frisco and exchanged for combine 122 and coach 923, each equipped with ancient coal stoves and guaranteed to agitate patrons who had been accustomed to more modern devices.[44]

The Post Office Department's Railway Mail Service also had complaints. The new westbound service was satisfactory, it said, but not the eastbound, because dispatches needed to be made so early in the day. The area superintendent pointed out that the RMS liked to offer patrons the option of same-day response to delivered mail. Local postmasters and patrons agreed that such service was needed. The superintendent soon received what he called "bitter complaints" regarding service under the mixed train schedule and obliquely threatened to suspend the contract for Railway Post Office space. This did not happen, surprisingly, although on April 11, 1940, a portion of mail normally moving via the Quanah & Floydada RPO was diverted to a star route.[45]

Elsewhere, the QA&P was responsible for Frisco's passenger operations at Quanah and earned revenue on all such business between Quanah and Red River. Service there was similar to that on the QA&P during the 1930s—up and down, mirroring hard times. The Frisco's own service was upgraded in 1928 to correspond with and to complement the *Plainsman*. A through St. Louis sleeping car was added at about the same time to Frisco's other daily train to Quanah, arriving there at 8:15 P.M. and leaving at 7:45 A.M. By August 1930, the day train was down to the modest consist of a combination car, combination baggage and Jim Crow car, and one coach. Less than a year later, of course, the Frisco broke the QA&P's direct connection by discontinuing its night trains. Thereafter, only the day train survived, and in abbreviated form. It was motorized during 1932 or 1933, in the form of Brill cars trailing a combination mail and baggage car. QA&P officials frequently besieged Frisco officials to improve the quality of service to Quanah but with no success. One Frisco superintendent bluntly told A. F. Sommer in 1936 that the current passenger run was "not paying expenses" and, in his opinion, "what the people in this territory want is an adequate service they can use in inclement weather when the busses and trucks cannot be depended on, but when the weather is favorable they do not use railroad transportation." Indeed, instead of upgrading service the Frisco downgraded the train to mixed status late in 1939, returning it to passenger train status in mid-1940, probably to provide adequate passage for traffic moving via Fort Sill, on the Frisco near Lawton, Oklahoma. Boardings and revenue statistics tell the story of declining use. In November 1927, 1,316 passengers were handled on what the QA&P called its Red River line; only 432 were handled in April 1930. These passengers paid $1,273 for such service in April 1929, but only $127 in April 1930. Sales of local and interline tickets at

Quanah for 1930 totaled $12,900.34; for 1941, a mere $1,392.54.[46]

If the public's interest in regular passenger services was slackening, its interest in excursions was not. The QA&P participated in innumerable reduced-rate agreements and handled dozens of special movements in the 1920s and 1930s. These took the form of local outings from one location to another along the Quanah Route as well as spectacular special trains moving overhead. Special tariffs were issued for the District Convention of the American Legion at Quanah, the last roundup at the OX Ranch near Swearingen, a softball game at Paducah and a return engagement at Quanah, the Cottle and King County Pioneer Jubilee at Paducah, and "educational excursions" such as the one on which two hundred elementary school pupils took the train from Paducah to Narcisso.[47]

The QA&P also participated in a spate of interline agreements. Examples included frequent excursion rates to Oklahoma City and Dallas and Christmas and New Year excursion fares to all stations in Texas. Special rates were given for the Texas State Fair, the Southwestern Exposition and Fat Stock Show, Pageant of Pulchritude, Texas gubernatorial inauguration, Biennial Session of the Grand United Order of Odd Fellows and Household of Ruth, Texas Parent-Teachers Association meeting, and the annual Farmers' Short Course at Texas A&M College. The QA&P was also eager to assist local groups that were making trips to distant points. One such group was the Floydada Band, which in 1929 moved to Dallas aboard a special car on regular trains of the QA&P and FW&DC.[48]

The handling of special trains presented challenges but also opportunities for profit and publicity. In 1929, the Dallas Chamber of Commerce routed its Annual Good-Will Tour over the QA&P. The nine-car train made brief stops at local stations en route from Floydada to Quanah. A year later, the Oklahoma City Chamber of Commerce included the QA&P line for its tour, traveling on a ten-car train. QA&P officials went to great lengths to provide a smooth run, and engineer W. H. ("Bill") Norman was instructed "to make good time and especially so on ballasted track." A. F. Sommer and W. L. Richardson joined prospective shippers in the observation car to point out the fine condition of the QA&P's property. The same meticulous attention to detail was given the movement of schoolchildren to the Centennial Exposition at Dallas in October 1936. Locomotive 27 headed a special train of seven coaches which loaded a total of

The QA&P frequently operated special trains for special events.

558 persons from Floydada, Roaring Springs, and Paducah. These were forwarded to Dallas as part of another special train on the FW&DC. Tired but happy children (and their equally tired but probably not as happy sponsors) were returned several days later over the same route and in the same style. Although it did not require a special train on the QA&P, the Texas Centennial Celebration designated October 4 as Railroad Men's Day and, although a special train was not required on the QA&P, the neighboring Denver Road did operate one from Childress. Employees from all area railroads were encouraged to ride free "as prescribed by pass rules"; sixty-four QA&P employees availed themselves of this opportunity and made the round-trip aboard a Frisco coach provided gratis by the QA&P and handled in the same way by the FW&DC.[49]

The government frequently required special movements. Few involved the Quanah-Floydada line; virtually all required use of the Red River line and represented an interline arrangement with the FW&DC. One of these involved "one kitchen car, three baggage cars, and three coaches with approximately 89 CCC men en route from Tabernash, Colorado to Cache, Oklahoma." A Civilian Conservation Corps party of eighteen men moved in the reverse direction, from Hobart, Oklahoma, to Memphis, Texas. The government also paid transportation charges in connection with the movement of candidates for training at the Citizens Military Training Camp at Fort Sill, Oklahoma, in which five men from Paducah participated in 1939. In most cases these movements were made on regularly scheduled trains.[50]

Providing special trains for football games was another regular part of the QA&P's traffic routine

in the early 1930s. They were a headache for railroaders but seemed necessary for public relations. All required the same minimum fares: at least two hundred tickets at one dollar each. At least two of these excursions were run from Roaring Springs to Floydada to accommodate the team and fans from Matador, but usually trains were operated in conjunction with annual meetings of football teams from Paducah and Floydada. The first for which there are records was in 1930 when 512 passengers rode a special from Floydada; Charles Sommer rejoiced that the resulting revenue was "around $2.00 per train mile." The net from operation of the 1932 train was reduced by a broken window and the loss of twelve light globes and one ax from the coaches. Charles Sommer ordered QA&P officials to ride the 1933 train from Paducah to Floydada and to advise him of "any wanton destruction." A. F. Sommer reported that the crowd was "most orderly . . . even though Paducah won." Nevertheless, he said, "these excursions are getting to be quite a problem."[51]

He ordered that the 1934 train be operated at no more than twenty-five miles per hour to prevent catastrophe should some passenger pull the air, and he told the conductor to "keep all vestibules closed" and lock "the door of the rear coach" to keep passengers off the platform. His apprehension was well founded. More than four hundred persons crowded into the three coaches and one baggage car, and before the train had returned to Paducah "a first-class drunken melee" broke out, with damage to all cars. Light switches were turned off, bulbs were broken, the air was pulled, and wooden door panels were kicked out despite the best efforts of the crew, railroad officials, and the sheriff from Paducah. Damage, said A. F. Sommer, "was not done by high school kids, but by the grown ups . . . the erstwhile citizens." Indeed, he continued, "the ringleaders in tearing things up" were the ones who should "have influence in maintaining some semblance of order." These football excursions, he reported to his brother, had become "an occasion for a general drunk by the town's people." Charles Sommer referred to the incident as "mob-like violence" and issued orders that no such excursions be operated unless "sponsored by responsible organizations which will guarantee proper policing and handling of these rowdies." It was a moot issue. The highway between Paducah and Floydada was paved before the next game was scheduled.[52]

Charles Sommer, like Sam Lazarus before him, liked to tour the line aboard the 6666 on "president's specials." Both did so frequently. It was good

Charles Sommer loved nothing more than to tour the line aboard the "Four Sixes," shown here in Quanah in the 1930s.

to "show the flag" and to show the property to board members and shippers alike. Others also toured the line in business cars. The Frisco's President Kurn did so in 1924 aboard his car, and officials of the FW&DC and Burlington did likewise in 1925 to view the property with an eye toward buying it. Also in 1925, M-K-T car 406 took hunters from Dallas to Narcisso.[53]

The QA&P's stable of motive power and rolling stock underwent changes during the two decades following World War I (see table 6). Locomotive 17, a decrepit old mill, had been scrapped in 1920. All of the road's locomotives were converted from coal-fired to oil burners in 1922, and when the QA&P acquired the Motley County Railroad it similarly converted numbers 19 and 103 to burn oil. The road's locomotive fleet was further modified by the lease of Frisco's number 605, a 4-6-0, in 1923, and by the acquisition of a used 0-6-0 from the SL-SF in 1930. The new switcher, Frisco's 3670, became QA&P's 33. More changes followed. The elderly number 19, retired in 1931, was scrapped in 1935. The same fate befell number 23, retired and scrapped in 1939, and number 103, retired in 1939 and scrapped the next year. As a consequence, the Quanah Route owned only three road locomotives, numbers 25, 27,

and 101, and two switch engines, numbers 31 and 33, when World War II broke out. Frisco's number 605 had long since been returned to its owner, but the QA&P in the late 1920s initiated a policy of leasing 2-10-0s from the SL-SF. Several of these, usually one or two at a time—including numbers 1617, 1620, 1622, and 1629—were under lease at various times.[54]

QA&P employees, enginemen and shopmen alike, took pride in the road's motive power. Locomotive 27, usually assigned to the *Plainsman*, was a favorite of both. After shopping in 1938, one writer said: "She looks good enough to pull anybody's passenger train." Each locomotive had its own personality, and the whistles on each were different. Many considered the melodious reports from the whistle on number 101 especially fine. Enginemen had great affection for the road's own locomotives, but they also liked the Frisco's 1600s; they rode well, pulled well, and steamed well.[55]

The company's rolling stock inventory was appreciably reduced over the years. After its A-3 was sold to the Frisco, QA&P leased passenger equipment from that road. It also leased freight equipment. In 1922, it owned forty boxcars, eleven flats, and three tanks. Many of these were converted to

The QA&P acquired the 103 in 1925 and wrote it off the books in 1939. *Harold K. Vollrath collection*

Snow in abundance is not common on the Southern Plains, but a blizzard in February 1940 filled cuts near MacBain. Locomotives 1620 and 27 give it their best. *E. B. Marsalis collection*

TABLE 6
**QA&P Motive Power, 1922**

| Number | Wheel arrangement | Date purchased | Manufacturer |
|---|---|---|---|
| 23 | 4-6-0 | June 1909 | Baldwin |
| 25 | 4-6-0 | May 1910 | Baldwin |
| 27 | 4-6-0 | May 1910 | Baldwin |
| 31 | 0-6-0 | February 1916 | Baldwin |
| 101 | 2-8-0 | July 1915 | Baldwin |

TABLE 7
**Performance Record, 1922–1941**

| Year | Carloads | Operating revenue | Operating ratio | Net income |
|---|---|---|---|---|
| 1922 | 9,210 | $437,177 | 60.82 | $ 10,616 |
| 1925 | 12,217 | $656,105 | 49.13 | $136,126 |
| 1929 | 13,467 | $736,519 | 62.56 | $ 56,923 |
| 1930 | 10,471 | $471,295 | 71.31 | $ 73,837 |
| 1934 | 10,122 | $315,502 | 86.76 | ($182,239) |
| 1936 | 8,827 | $272,037 | 103.81 | ($238,437) |
| 1940 | 9,635 | $380,567 | 70.32 | ($117,592) |
| 1941 | 12,431 | $483,046 | 62.39 | ($ 50,925) |

A. F. Sommer was especially proud of this Chevrolet, modified for inspection purposes.

maintenance-of-way equipment, and the rest were retired as they became obsolete. The road did acquire three cabooses as well as bunk cars and water cars for bridge and building crews. The company was always parsimonious about expenditures for roadway equipment, but after unsuccessful bouts with snow, the shops built, in 1940, a fifty-ton snowplow, number 031. It was fashioned from the tender of locomotive 23, scrapped earlier. Motor Inspection Car 100 graced the rails in 1915 and 1916, and in 1939 the company equipped a Chevrolet sport sedan for inspection use. A Chrysler touring car was acquired in 1928 "for general use by management," and in the same season an Essex coach model was purchased for the traffic department.[56]

The performance of the QA&P, shown in traffic and revenue statistics, reflected the roller-coaster nature of regional and national economic conditions between the wars (see table 7). The road's modestly expanded service area was another factor of importance. The road earned $717,245 in net income for the years 1922–29, inclusive, but in the twelve years following 1929 the company lost $1,596,433. The years 1935 and 1936 were particularly difficult, with net operating deficits. Not surprisingly, the QA&P paid dividends in 1930 amounting to $450,000, but not again during the decade.[57]

## CHAPTER 16

# An Activity Necessary to War Production

With the restoration of our transcontinental rates through Floydada, and the return of "normal" times, no telling where we might go.—*QA&P Employees' Magazine,* May 1938

THE major variables that confronted the QA&P during the 1930s were the Great Depression, the Dust Bowl, and the Floydada case; in the years immediately following, the principal elements affecting the company were World War II and the restoration of transcontinental traffic. For the Quanah Route it seemed as if night had turned to day. During the 1930s its officials had constantly struggled to keep the road alive. Now, in the first half of the 1940s they faced a daily battle to supply manpower and equipment adequate to handle the traffic offered.

As soon as transcontinental rates were restored in 1938, W. L. Richardson sought to attract traffic that earlier had moved via the Floydada gateway. Schedules showing service from Los Angeles and San Bernardino to St. Louis, Chicago, Birmingham, Fort Worth–Dallas, and Oklahoma City were distributed to traffic representatives and shippers. "Our service," promised Richardson, "favorably compares to the best." He pledged that all eastbound carloads, whether perishable or "dead freight," would move on perishable schedules.[1]

Frisco officials had helped the QA&P regain transcontinental rights via Floydada, but there were difficulties between the two companies. Frisco's other western gateway—Avard, Oklahoma—was a constant problem. In 1939, Charles Sommer finally had Frisco's general traffic manager, J. R. Coulter, convinced that joint revenues accruing on loads via Floydada were higher than those derived from traffic via Avard. Coulter advised his sales force accordingly. A few months later, however, Coulter was boosting Avard for California traffic because of its shorter mileage. The Frisco's connecting service at Quanah was a more immediate problem for the QA&P. Almost simultaneously with the QA&P's victory in the Floydada gateway matter, Richard-

son learned that Frisco's management had "set its foot down on any increase in service at this time because business is too thin." Traffic moving overhead on the QA&P as well as that interchanged between the FW&DC and the Red River line at Quanah went into a precipitous decline. Sommer blamed it on "schedules out of Quanah" on the SL-SF. But Sommer and Richardson were forced to accept the situation, and the need for QA&P's parent to effect even more operating economies early in 1940 further reduced services, especially on eastbound movements. Better and more frequent train operations via Red River had to wait for America's involvement in World War II.[2]

Meanwhile, Richardson labored to increase traffic moving to or from the Denver Road at Quanah. In 1940, the QA&P delivered 2,740 cars to the FW&DC and received 1,592 from it. Despite this impressive volume, officials of both companies continued in their periodic wrangling. A salesman for the FW&DC told Richardson that he hoped the QA&P in 1940 would increase its contribution to the larger road's "welfare, so as to more nearly equalize our relative value, one to the other." His was a strange logic.[3]

The Japanese attack on Pearl Harbor and the hysteria that followed had an immediate effect on the QA&P. Railroaders everywhere were sternly directed by the army not to disseminate information regarding the location of troop staging areas. Sommer ordered that "no information be given out or the subject discussed at any time as to the handling of freight or anything else connected with the operation of the Army." The government further suggested that "suspicious persons" loitering about the "vicinity of telegraph offices be duly reported," that safeguards to property and equipment be undertaken and that critical material be conserved.[4]

The national upsurge in business resulting from war also affected the QA&P. Richardson enthusiastically urged his forces to keep their "patrons constantly informed of the service available via Frisco–QA&P–Santa Fe" as contrasted with the delays that were occurring on other routes as the result of clogged terminals. "We are not congested," affirmed the Quanah Route's traffic manager. He reminded shippers that the QA&P route offered fifth-day delivery on California business. At the same time, Sommer urged Frisco officials to "preserve as far as possible our long haul, maximum revenue transcontinental route" by soliciting traffic for the Floydada gateway.[5]

The volume in general overhead freight quickly rose and so, too, did block movement of passover traffic. Early in 1942, twenty-three carloads of "huts" were transported from Quanah to Floydada in a single movement by Extra 1622; as part of a shipment of oil refinery equipment to the Soviet Union in 1943, the QA&P handled twenty-one carloads of pipe; and shortly thereafter fifty-six carloads of trucks, moving in fifty-foot automobile cars from Fort Wayne, Indiana, to San Diego, California, were handled by the QA&P. There followed a "red hot" movement of sixty-three carloads of dump trucks built by the Galion All Steel Body Company at Galion, Ohio, and destined for Port Hueneme, California. Sommer urged forces at Quanah to be on their toes because this movement would be watched "with much interest" from the time it left St. Louis until it reached Floydada. He especially wanted sufficient power available to get the train over the line without doubling the hills. Sometimes large shipments trickled across the country a few cars at a time, as when the QA&P participated in the movement of two thousand carloads of fabricated houses from points in Ohio to a California

port. The shipment moved at the rate of sixteen to twenty cars per day.[6]

Many multiple-carload and passenger movements were commissioned by the government. In 1939, two chair cars were required to take candidates from Quanah to the Citizens Military Training Camp at Fort Sill, Oklahoma, and in the fall of 1941 the QA&P delivered "16 CCC men" to Floydada aboard the regular equipment of train 1. The majority of these passenger movements, however, were on behalf of the military and involved only the Red River line. Most were to or from installations in Oklahoma—Fort Sill, Tinker Field (Oklahoma City), and Altus Air Force Base—and moved via the FW&DC at Quanah.[7]

Early in the war, QA&P officials were given detailed information regarding each special military movement. For instance, one movement called Main 7077 involved four hundred officers and enlisted men, who, along with their baggage, were transported from Fort Sill to Camp Roberts, California, aboard fourteen cars shortly after the Pearl Harbor bombing. Later on, however, each participating railroad issued "transportation orders" covering only its portion of the movement, and thus the origin and destination of most "Main Trains" were not generally known. But because several of these special movements originated or terminated on the SL-SF, QA&P employees did have that information. These movements included eight cars from Fort Sill in 1943 with "4 white officers and 165 colored men"; 996 men aboard twenty one cars bound for Will Rogers Field in 1943; and 20 officers and 314 men from Tinker Air Force Base on fourteen cars in 1944.[8]

Military passenger business continued throughout the war years and shortly thereafter. Just days after atom bombs had been dropped on Hiroshima and Nagasaki, the QA&P handled 316 troops from Fort Sill on a westbound extra consisting of eleven cars. These soldiers avoided the horrors of combat because the war came to a conclusion before they arrived on the West Coast. Others had not been as fortunate; they were the "disabled members of the Armed forces." Beginning in mid-1944, railroads willingly gave these victims special attention as they returned to their homes from military hospitals. Railroaders knew them as "star cases" because their orders and tickets were stamped with the impression of a star. It was the government's way of quietly and privately identifying them as persons in particular need.[9]

The heavy volume of business was not without

Passover traffic boomed as World War II escalated. Number 1, with engines 723 and 1619 coupled, struggled with a heavy train of merchandise and war material as it wound its way between Narcisso and Russellville. *Francis Gunter collection*

its problems, especially for the Quanah-Floydada line of the QA&P. Important nonflammable overhead traffic moved on mixed trains 1 and 2, which made direct connections with the Santa Fe at Floydada. Other westbound transcontinental traffic was handled by the local freights, although it suffered a twelve-hour delay at Floydada because the AT&SF operated a single turn per day. This angered shippers but, unless the volume of business justified running extras, QA&P and Santa Fe officials saw no other solution.

A second major problem involved motive power: there was simply too little of it. Neither the QA&P nor its parent company had felt the need to expand their respective locomotive fleets during hard times, and neither had had the financial means to do so. The result was a calamitous power pinch during the war years. With a leased SL-SF 1600 or two, plus its own modest motive power holdings, the QA&P was able to cover regularly scheduled operations, but there was near panic in the Quanah offices when tonnage required doubleheading, when an extra movement was necessary, or when mechanical failures occurred. Ordinarily, the road's two 0-6-0s handled routine switching chores at Acme and Quanah, and the "20s"—numbers 25 and 27—handled trains 1 and 2. That left locomotive 101 plus leased 700s or 1600s for the locals and all other assignments. Both Sommer brothers pleaded with the Frisco for more power but had to acknowledge that the parent firm was in dire need of every locomotive it had. One way of coping with excess westbound tonnage was to "steal" Frisco locomotives that brought it to Quanah for use on Floydada turns. In that way the QA&P was able to move the tonnage without acquiring additional power. There was hell to pay, however, if these locomotives were not ready for the Frisco when its trains were ordered and/or the crews rested.[10]

Communication between the traffic and operating officials of the QA&P and the Frisco and the attendant problem of paperwork caused further difficulties. The QA&P found it nearly impossible to get accurate information on inbound nighttime freight movements because the Frisco had precious few second- and third-trick operators between Oklahoma City and Quanah, and it often miscalculated in calling QA&P crews, which added costs. Less understandable were periodic lapses in communication between the two roads. In 1942, QA&P officials were astonished when "10 cars of military impediments"—"hot stuff," as one of them put it—showed up without advance notice. Paperwork also presented a problem. In the routine of railroading at that time, a "passing record" had to be made at each interchange point before the cars could proceed over the connecting line. This required copying all information from every waybill, a chore that on the QA&P was done at both

A. F. Sommer was loath to order extra trains, but they were frequently required. Here, Extra 723, doubleheaded with a 1600, has reached Floydada with a train of mixed freight, including flammable materials.

Quanah and Floydada. The lean work force of the Quanah office—clerks and officers alike—frequently had to work after hours or on days off to accommodate this tradition. It was a tedious and expensive business that imperiled the expeditious movement of lading.[11]

W. L. Richardson worked hard to secure business for the QA&P, and he was exuberant when it was well handled. In 1943, when the Quanah Route moved one train of seventy-eight cars carrying cargo for the Soviet government—billed from Terre Haute, Indiana, to the port of San Francisco—he was beside himself with glee. Revenue gained by the little road for that service alone amounted to $8,000—"not bad for one train," he chortled. Yet when all did not go as planned he complained bitterly. "The average shipper is just naturally skeptical of using a short line for *service*," he told Sommer. Richardson hated anything less than perfection, and when the QA&P got a "black eye" because of poor or inadequate service he took it personally. "The bad thing about losing traffic," he observed, was "that it is usually so hard to get it back." It was Richardson, after all, who had to face the shipper, and his position could be easily understood.[12]

On the other hand, the operating difficulties faced by A. F. Sommer were also quite real and his views also could be easily understood. He was confronted with the responsibility of operating a railroad that was short of both motive power and manpower and locked between strong carriers— the Frisco and Denver Road at Quanah and the Santa Fe at Floydada—that frequently treated the

Even the locals were occasionally doubleheaded. Here, train 52 hurries into Acme. *E. B. Marsalis photograph*

Quanah Route in high-handed ways. Beyond that Sommer was charged with running an efficient operation. "Frankly," he said, "it puts me between the devil and the deep blue sea."[13]

The headaches and frustrations of QA&P officials in this hectic time might be epitomized by the troubled record of Extra 1628 West for February 19, 1943. Early on that date, with very little warning, the SL-SF delivered two trainloads of Studebaker trucks, lend-lease material for the Soviets. Finding himself short of both power and crews and needing to protect scheduled service, A. F. Sommer chose to put the two trains together and doublehead locomotives 1628 and 1613. Frisco officials were angry because the 1613 was theirs. Delay resulted from the need to service the Frisco locomotive, which had just arrived with one of the trains, and to make one original and four carbon copies of each waybill. "We had three typewriters going," Sommer later recalled. Finally, after a three-and-one-half-hour delay, Extra 1628 left Quanah. All went well—briefly. The train failed on Pease River hill, had to double, and then "pulled out two draw bars" a mile east of Roaring Springs. Sommer blamed the locomotive engineers but admitted that neither of them had had "much training in the handling of air on trains of this length." The disabled cars were set out and the train moved on, but it was clearly jinxed. Neither locomotive had a large tender so the train stopped at every tank on the line to take water, causing more delay. Then, three miles east of Floydada, both engines ran so low on fuel that crews found it necessary to "cut and run" for oil. While fueling the locomotives at Floydada, the engineers got down to lubricate their respective charges and were astonished when the locomotives "walked

off" because of a "leaky throttle" on the 1613. Before they could be stopped, sad to say, the oil crane had been pulled down. Meanwhile, the trailing westbound local—creeping through fog—nearly "rear-ended" the caboose of Extra 1628 because its "green brakeman" (actually a section hand who had been drafted into emergency train service) had not gone back to "flag." Extra 1628 finally delivered its train to the Santa Fe "shortly after midnight."[14]

Richardson was in a rage over the incident. His forces had solicited the business with what he claimed was a pledge from A. F. Sommer's operating department to move heavy trains out of Quanah within an hour after delivery from the SL-SF. In the case of Extra 1628, countered A. F. Sommer, much of the operation had been beyond his control. Charles Sommer was forced to arbitrate between his two headstrong lieutenants. He promised that the QA&P would "make every possible effort to expedite the movement of traffic reaching Quanah in extra trains" and, for that matter, "all transcontinental traffic."[15]

Other problems that were even harder to control involved the liability of being identified as a short-line railroad and ongoing relations with the Frisco. The QA&P wanted to portray itself as an independent company, yet it identified itself with the larger Frisco. Independence was useful in maintaining managerial autonomy and generating liberal divisions, but there was utility—especially for soliciting traffic—in showing closely coordinated service with the parent company. Yet there were problems in establishing coordination even within a parent-child relationship. In November 1944, a little over half of QA&P's transcontinental business moved by way of the Frisco from St. Louis to Quanah. Richardson complained that the Frisco moved this tonnage on a random basis instead of collecting it all in one or two westbound trains. Early in 1945, he discovered that in one twenty-four-hour period ninety-nine cars for Quanah had moved in no fewer than eight trains, and the elapsed time from St. Louis to Quanah ranged from thirty-four hours and five minutes to fifty-seven hours and thirty-five minutes. Delay cost business, Richardson growled. He observed that the Office of Defense Transportation hesitated to authorize use of routes that were not time-efficient compared to alternatives and had urged carriers and shippers alike to "increase the car supply eliminating delays." Surely, Richardson argued, it would be wise for the SL-SF to forward Quanah cars in daily trainload lots.[16]

The 1628 headed a troubled train on February 19, 1943. *Harold K. Vollrath collection*

At the same time, Richardson was confronted with another nagging problem. He tried as best he could to monitor traffic moving via Frisco's Avard gateway because he worried that SL-SF traffic representatives ignored or gave second preference to the Floydada routing and solicited "along the line of least resistance irrespective of the features of long haul routing, maximum revenues, or divisions." Charles Sommer agreed and urged the Frisco to provide reliable connections at Quanah. The parent road was burdened with other questions—the heavy traffic of war, a shortage of power—but, nevertheless, its attitude seemed obtuse. As a consequence, the SL-SF's Oklahoma City–Quanah line was slighted with a resulting delay to traffic. By late 1944 the War Department concluded that the Avard gateway was more time-efficient than the Floydada gateway by twelve to twenty-four hours, and the QA&P lost "Navy symbol oil trains," which heretofore had moved via Floydada. All these developments posed a growing dilemma for QA&P management.[17]

The Frisco was not alone in causing anxiety for the QA&P. Relations with the Santa Fe had improved little if at all, in part because of Santa Fe's historic position regarding the Floydada gateway and, in part, because of its own problems in coping with wartime volume. The primary issue of contention during these years was the connecting service on Sundays. Even before the war the QA&P had urged the larger road to institute daily operations, but it had not done so. Consequently, priority traffic arriving in Quanah too late to reach Floydada before Santa Fe's departure on Saturdays was routinely diverted to the FW&DC. This was irksome, and it deprived the Quanah Route of revenues on overhead traffic that it had so assiduously solicited. Charles Sommer pointed out to the Santa Fe's traffic department in 1941 that the rate of interchange at Floydada had greatly accelerated and asked if the line might consider establishing Sunday service. The AT&SF declined but promised to order an extra when the QA&P could promise at least twenty cars of "manifest freight." A. F. Sommer thought that solution inadequate. He wondered if the Santa Fe would allow the Quanah Route trackage rights to Plainview from Floydada on Sundays only. In that way tonnage could be made available for further handling without added expense to the AT&SF. Nothing came of it. Charles Sommer concluded that it was the same old line: "They have done everything they possibly could to retard improvement through that gateway."[18]

The answer was not so simple, although Sommer had a point. Traffic moving via the Santa Fe from Floydada had to move over a dogleg route of

There were times when mechanical failure rather than human failure resulted in distress. Such was the case on October 29, 1944, when train 431, *The Red Raven*, derailed near Carnes, north of Quanah, damaging and delaying transit of naval radar equipment, among other lading.

TABLE 8
**Floydada Interchange**

| Year | Eastbound | Westbound | Total |
|------|-----------|-----------|-------|
| 1937 | 103 | 631 | 734 |
| 1938 | 162 | 675 | 837 |
| 1939 | 609 | 1,372 | 1,981 |
| 1940 | 872 | 1,602 | 2,474 |
| 1941 | 1,174 | 2,493 | 3,667 |
| 1942 | 1,586 | 5,884 | 7,470 |
| 1943 | 2,294 | 6,482 | 8,776 |
| 1944 | 2,910 | 10,332 | 13,242 |
| 1945 | 2,125 | 11,599 | 13,724 |

TABLE 9
**World War II Growth at Floydada Interchange**

| Month/Year | Eastbound | Westbound | Total |
|------------|-----------|-----------|-------|
| December 1941 | 116 | 382 | 498 |
| August 1945 | 156 | 765 | 921 |

branches and secondary main lines whether by Plainview, Lubbock, and Texico or by Plainview, Canyon, and Texico. As a matter of routine, interchange business at Floydada was handled by Santa Fe's daily-except-Sunday mixed train and was subject to delay at Plainview, Lubbock, or Canyon. The AT&SF could have improved scheduling by instituting through service and by adding a Sunday train but chose not to do so. Furthermore, there is ample evidence that it attempted to discredit the Floydada gateway, as Charles Sommer said, on "every basis, whether real, fancied or false." The Santa Fe, he said in 1945, "spare no effort to tell the shipping public that the route is unnatural, subject to delays, involving branch line service, using every reason they can to disparage the route, to convince the shipper that the Floydada gateway is objectionable."[19]

Despite all its difficulties, the QA&P moved an impressive volume of traffic over its rails during the years following the Depression. Total passover business, including that credited to the Red River line, increased from 4,156 cars in 1937 to 6,819 in 1941. Similar growth occurred on the Quanah-Floydada line following the restoration of interstate rates. Dramatic changes came even before World War II; the volume of traffic increased every month during 1941. It was a harbinger of happier times. The volume of business interchanged at Floydada increased from a total of 3,667 cars in 1941 to 13,724 in 1945. (See table 8). Monthly volumes fluctuated; the eastbound monthly high was established in February 1944 with 416 cars, and the westbound

high was made in April 1945 with 1,526 cars. Comparative statistics regarding interchange at Floydada for December 1941 and August 1945 demonstrate the growth that occurred during World War II (table 9). In 1941, the QA&P's passover traffic amounted to 53 percent of total cars handled; in 1945, it accounted for 76.9 percent of all carloads.[20]

All of this was accomplished with an incredibly spare work force. The QA&P was never a company to hire more than necessary. During the Depression it had cut the force to the barest minimum, but when prosperity returned it found that there was competition for employees. This problem was compounded by the drain on manpower resulting from the Selective Training and Service Act of 1940.

Although the War Department acknowledged that certain railroad jobs were crucial, it would not authorize blanket exemptions for railroaders. Instead, it classified occupations according to the critical nature of the work and projected shortages in that area. Beyond that, local boards were given broad powers in determining exemptions. In 1940, the greatest need, the government said, was for material procurement. The Selective Service System then classified railroad transportation as an activity necessary to war production and support of the war effort. At least for a time, railroaders were not affected by the draft in great numbers because nearly all of them qualified for occupational deferments.[21]

The conscription law provided that any person who vacated a permanent position to enter military service was to be considered on furlough or leave of absence and, should he eventually reapply for his

A. F. Sommer was under great pressure for crews to handle through as well as local traffic. Here the Acme turn is about to leave for another round of switching at the mills. *J. M. George photograph*

position, was to be restored to it or to a position of like status and pay and with no loss of seniority. The Western Association of Railway Executives affirmed this policy on September 20, 1940. Charles Sommer, however, was uneasy about agreements made at the national level or those mandated by government. He saw them as enroachments on managerial prerogative. He asked other carriers for copies of the agreements they were making and quarreled for a while with one labor organization about the matter. Nevertheless, the QA&P amended its personnel policies to reflect the law on April 9, 1941.[22]

In 1942, a flap developed between Sommer and the Brotherhood of Maintenance of Way Employees over the issue of physical examinations for discharged veterans. The union felt that examinations given by the armed services as a part of separation were adequate and that it was unnecessary for

the railroad to order another before the employee was reinstated. Sommer saw it otherwise; the carriers, he said, might be forced to take back a physically defective person, he argued. The Class I railroads, including the Frisco, agreed with the union. So did the American Short Line Railroad Association. Sommer again swallowed his pride and went along.[23]

There were few problems in maintaining the work force in 1942, but during the season following the QA&P had trouble finding and retaining brakemen and section laborers. In the past, Sommer had not been willing to authorize draft exemption requests for men in these positions, but on April 26, 1943, he made a new policy: "Effective at once deferments will be asked for all classes of employees on the ground that they are essential to the operation of the railroad." Local boards, he said, should be mindful of the QA&P's obligations as a common carrier and its contribution to the war effort "through the transportation of essential war materials." He noted that the local line suffered in recruiting adequate replacements because of its remote location and because endangered railroad employees could easily find exempt farm jobs in the immediate area. By the summer of 1943, the problem was acute in the railroad's shops, on its track gangs, and in maintaining a pool of junior trainmen. The "turnover on our track gangs has been terrific," reported A. F. Sommer. By that time, the railroad had filed requests for occupational deferments for more than half of its work force.[24]

The labor problem did not improve during the last two years of conflict. Local boards were under much pressure, and so, too, were the carriers. The QA&P and the Hardeman County board represent a microcosm. In February 1944, the Hardeman board needed to provide 65 men to meet the current quota but had only 13 men available, 9 of whom could not pass physical examinations. The board saw no other choice than to reclassify some employees at the Acme mills and on the QA&P. Sommer was aghast at the prospect of losing more men. He pointed out that 19 railroad employees already had been drafted, the number of QA&P employees in Hardeman County had slipped from 119 in 1941 to 81 in 1944, and at the same time, the railroad had expanded its gross ton miles three times over. The railroad could not lose many more employees and still function. It was not a difficulty unique to the Quanah Route; it was a nationwide problem. Indeed, the Office of Defense Transportation had asked the Selective Service System for relief in meeting the manpower shortages.[25]

The enigma was acute during the month of March 1945. J. Monroe Johnson of the Interstate Commerce Commission stated that the army should discharge any railroad employee who was not already overseas. "He is of far more use working on his job on the railroad than he is at the fighting front." The problem was crucial for the QA&P, which that month faced the loss of two brakemen, two station agents, and one pumper. The railroad fought valiantly for their deferment. Those registered in Hardeman County, where, said A. F. Sommer, "we have always had cooperation," received exemptions. Those registered in Motley County, where there had been historic rancor regarding the railroad, were not as fortunate. Sommer was disheartened: "Anyone familiar with our situation and the demands on us to handle war traffic should quickly realize that they are doing a disservice to

Conscription of men for the war threatened to break up operating crews. Shown here at Floydada on January 8, 1940, are, left to right, J. W. Shaw, H. O. Wells, E. B. Marsalis, I. C. Huckaby, and D. C. Riley. *E. B. Marsalis collection*

the government by failing to give reasonable consideration to requests of this nature."[26]

There is little doubt that the QA&P suffered from the consequences of inadequate manpower. Section men were used as brakemen and, in a few cases, officials were, too. It was impossible to find qualified telegraph operators. The press of war was the primary culprit, but Charles Sommer knew that the road's "location and scanty population" added to its problems. He observed that the Class I roads were "waiving the age limit of employment in that men over 45 and as old as 60" were "eagerly sought." But such a liberal policy would have been ineffectual on the Quanah Route because there was no available pool of men of any age to draw from. Labor problems contributed to what Sommer called "war jitters," affecting nearly "everyone with some kind of vexation in consequence of the war." All he could do was prescribe "a little degree of tolerance."[27]

QA&P officials also feared the possibility of receiving their own draft notices, as did the road's secretary-auditor, J. W. Sampley, early in the war. Sommer hastily asked the QA&P's local attorney,

G. E. Hamilton, for advice. Hamilton was not optimistic: "Local boards are made of local men and
they are sometimes prompted by sentiments such
as: 'My boy, and my neighbor's boy both had to
go, so I think no high-collared railroad official
should be exempted, so I move we send him along
with the rest and let the railroad rustle up some
woman to do his work.'" Sampley, however, was not
drafted. The issue was similarly vexing for W. L.
Richardson, who was offered a commission in the
army. For him to accept, said Sommer, "would be
a very commendable thing . . . but, on the other
hand, if there is no obligation on your part, then
there is a question in my mind whether it is the best
thing for you to do." Sommer admitted that he
would prefer to have Richardson stay on the job,
and he did. In this instance and in others when
QA&P officials were considered for commissions in
the army's railway battalions, Sommer was in a
quandary. Should he recommend members of his
already thin official cadre or should he seek to
protect the company by urging each member to
stay on the job? In all cases he chose the latter
course, but there is no evidence that he ever refused
to write strong endorsements when requested to
do so.[28]

Sommer had similarly mixed feelings over requests for exemption on behalf of the company's
traffic representatives. His initial position was that
none would be made. Richardson agreed initially
but soon changed his mind. By the summer of 1942,
Richardson was advising his representatives to tell
their local boards that they were "engaged in defense work . . . necessary for the prosecution of the
war effort." Following the issuance of Occupational
Bulletin No. 21 (a slightly revised and expanded list-
ing of recommended exemptions) by Selective Service director L. B. Hershey on September 17, 1942,
Richardson counseled his men to list their positions as traffic-rate clerk. Sommer thought his traffic manager was stretching the issue but promised
to learn the Frisco's policy. Richardson's position
hardened: "According to my understanding, an employee is considered necessary so long as he is employed by an industry which is considered necessary." That was too much for Sommer. "No request
for deferments will be made for our soliciting
forces," he told Richardson in 1943. It was a bitter
pill for the QA&P's energetic traffic manager, and
it was equally bitter for his forces. They had, as one
said, "been on the fence," not knowing whether to
enlist, seek employment in exempt positions, or remain with the Quanah Route. Some resigned and

some were drafted.[29]

Sommer's attitude toward hiring women was
likely characteristic of American railroad management at the time. During the Depression the
QA&P's position had been particularly severe.
"The employment of married women in all departments will be prohibited," the road's president had
decreed in 1932. The rule, he said, excluded "wid-
ows still maintaining their husbands' names, but
who are *wholly* dependent on themselves for support." Even when the labor supply tightened, Sommer was determined not to modify the policy. He
reluctantly admitted that it might be necessary to
hire women, even as station agents, but he would
do so only "as a last resort." He understood that
several of the Class I roads had hired women and
related the story of a recent visitor who had told
him of seeing women working on track gangs in
Pennsylvania. Sommer was astonished: "I was told
that these women were largely Slavs and other
huskies of Balkan origins, and that they drive a
spike or tamp a tie as well as a man." On March 5,
1943, he felt compelled to announce that, "for the
duration of the war, it will be permissible to employ, in the General Offices where their services can
be made of use, married women whose husbands
have been inducted into the military services." This
policy would not apply, however, to "employees
who marry and whose husbands are not in military
service at the time of their marriage." The policy
change had little impact. The number of female employees rose from seven in August 1941 to twelve in
January 1944.[30]

Maintenance of the road's track structure in the
face of serious manpower shortages became acute
early in the war and got no better as time passed.
The QA&P, like other area roads, hired Mexican
laborers. The Brotherhood of Maintenance of Way
Employees objected, first as a matter of policy, and
later more strenuously when Mexican laborers were
allowed to work on section gangs "with white employees." The union pointed to the current agreement, which provided that "Mexican gangs shall be
considered and treated as a separate unit, and . . .
shall not have interchangeable seniority rights in
white gangs." The QA&P had violated this provision, but Sommer was adamant: "It is our intention
to employ anyone who applies for work on any of
our gangs." The union was willing to renegotiate
the contract to allow "intermingling Mexicans and
white gangs," but Sommer hedged. He thought
that this would force the Mexicans to join the
union or lose their jobs, which would create a

closed shop, "exactly what we do not want to happen," he told his brother.[31]

Neither side viewed the issue from a moral or ethical viewpoint during the early stages; both considered only its practical implications. The railroad's position was simple: "We must always have a free hand in dealing with the employment of Mexicans." The union's position was equally simple: "Until such time as this rule is changed, we must insist that it be lived up to." Then, early in 1943, the union brought up the matter of discrimination and suggested again that the rule be changed to give Mexicans equal rights with whites employed in the maintenance-of-way department. A. F. Sommer was agreeable, but his brother was cautious, even obtuse. A. F. Sommer pointed out that the arrangement would allow each man to "bump in anywhere their seniority permitted," although this would require the company to provide separate bunk cars for the Mexicans because whites, he was sure, "would not want to domicile with Mexicans." On balance, however, he favored the rule change.[32]

The issue became heated late in 1943. The union continued to hammer on the matter of discrimination, citing various executive orders. Sommer sought the aid of the American Short Line Railroad Association. Its general counsel believed the union was attempting "a not-very-well concealed subterfuge to accomplish a selfish purpose"—to eliminate the QA&P's "Mexican labor by having the Mexicans 'bumped' by white labor by reason of interchangeability of seniority." Sommer refused to accept the rule change, and the union responded by referring the matter to mediation. In the end the union won, but the entire episode reflected Charles Sommer's jealous devotion to managerial prerogative and his periodic inability to discern changed circumstances.[33]

The continuing migration of blacks into the QA&P's service area posed an additional if essentially theoretical problem for labor policy. A. F. Sommer thought that "Negro help" might be recruited at Quanah and Paducah, but since the "Negro situation" was "still quite an issue" west of Paducah, he thought the road might find itself "in trouble if it should at any time put a Negro gang and move it west of Tongue River to do any work." Charles Sommer brought up the issue in a conference with union representatives and was assured that "while blacks and whites are being intermingled on some roads" the union did not like it. But the union did not object to segregated gangs.[34]

Toward the end of the war, Charles Sommer wondered if the manpower shortage might be ameliorated by the use of German prisoners of war from a camp in nearby Childress. More than two hundred of these men were already laboring successfully on behalf of the Quanah Cotton Compress Company at various locations, and Sommer thought they might be used as conveniently for track work. A request for the use of prisoners was placed with the War Manpower Commission in May 1945, but the Brotherhood of Maintenance of Way Employees objected. The use of war prisoners, it said, "would not be in the best interests of anyone" and would be "a slap in the face to our boys who have fought the Nazi fanatics so nobly and have suffered untold misery in stamping out the persecution of the peoples of Europe." Sommer disagreed: "I think that working these prisoners would make them more conscious of the mischief they have created than permitting them to idly enjoy the comforts of a prison camp" and, furthermore, "these prisoners would receive only $.10 per hour for their work, while the prevailing rate of pay would be turned over to the Government." The union would not budge and, of course, the issue soon became moot.[35]

The railroad's participation in the war effort took additional forms. Even before the conflict began, the QA&P cooperated in a salary allotment plan for the purchase of United States Defense Savings Bonds. Shortly before America's entry into the conflict, A. F. Sommer reported that over $400 had been saved by Quanah Route employees during the five months since the plan was begun. G. E. Hamilton was an active booster, saying that there were two good reasons for every person to participate: it was a convenient way "of laying up a little nest egg" and it would "take off the biting edge of hard times that always tramp hard . . . following war among nations." The attack on Pearl Harbor accelerated voluntary participation, and management sent letters to each employee urging his new or continued involvement. Some simply could not afford it. One trainmen told A. F. Sommer that the recent increase in wages had been offset by inflation: "My obligations have so far taken all that I earn," he said, but he would try to purchase "a few defense stamps." A locomotive engineer declined for similar reasons but pointed out that his school-age son purchased stamps every week. Participation by various classes of employees in mid-1942 ranged from 10 percent for extra gangs to 100 percent for mechanical forces, and the percent of payroll assigned to bonds varied from 1.27 for extra gangs to

How could the QA&P prepare for the postwar era? One way, argued W. L. Richardson, was to keep the plant in good shape and to advertise the fact. Here the 1620 is all dolled up to pose on the freshly painted bridge at Acme. Note the two QA&P boxcars trailing immediately behind the 1620.

6.94 for the bridge and building gangs.[36]

A few months later, A. F. Sommer complained that only 96 of the firm's 160 employees were purchasing bonds through the Payroll Savings Plan. This, he groused, was a mere $563 of an approximately $18,000 monthly payroll. The Treasury Department soon called on QA&P employees for a monthly quota of $1,800—not very much, A. F. Sommer thought, in support of those who were "risking their lives to see that our shores are not invaded and that we are permitted to continue our way of living." He was forceful, even pushy. "All employees should think this over and be prepared to definitely commit themselves," he advised. The QA&P itself proudly participated in several local bond drives; the company pledged $20,000 for the 1943 drive in Motley County and $25,000 for the 1944 drive in Floyd County. All told, the railroad acquired $450,000 in par value bonds of various series during the war.[37]

The railroad, its officials, and its contract employees all suffered from shortages, escalating prices, and other war-related problems. The price per barrel of oil, used for firing the road's locomotives, rose from 44 cents in 1939 to $1.12 in 1943. Taxes paid by the road also rose, from $200,517.95 in 1943 to $376,748.29 in 1944. The war effort drained trans-

portation resources, and the government actively discouraged travel. Passenger space, especially Pullman accommodations, became scarce early on, and even top QA&P officials were forced to ask friends on other roads to intercede on their behalf when they wanted to travel. A Katy official arranged for Pullman accommodations from Whitesboro, Texas, to St. Louis for A. F. Sommer in 1942. Sommer was pleased to gain the sleeping car space and considered himself especially fortunate to find that, after the soldiers had been fed, he was allowed to have a meal on the diner. The personal intercession of a friend on the Denver Road, however, did him little good in 1943. He was told that first-class accommodation on the FW&DC's train 1 was sold out a month in advance. Nevertheless, it did profit one to have friends in high places or to have others in a position of dependence. For instance, A. F. Sommer periodically received complimentary cases of Coca-Cola from the bottler at Paducah. The soft drink was hard to come by in World War II, and Sommer was glad to receive the gift. He promised that carloads of water would be faithfully delivered from Roaring Springs to the bottler's spur in Paducah.[38]

For the management and employees of the Quanah Route, there were no longings for a

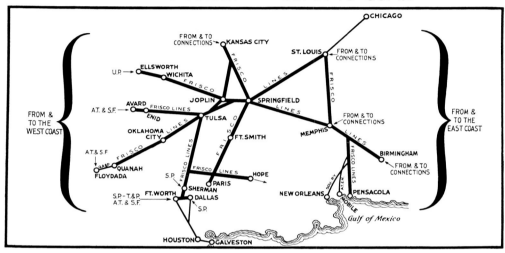

This Frisco ad showed that Charles Sommer and W. L. Richardson had finally persuaded the QA&P's parent company to support the Floydada gateway.

golden past—they held no nostalgia for the 1930s, and they had absolutely no wish to return to those "good old days" when the first world war ended. A heavy and profitable business in overhead traffic had been attracted during the war years, and QA&P officials, especially W. L. Richardson, urged that the company take steps to retain such business in the postwar era. Very early in 1943 he and Charles Sommer had urged the Frisco's chief traffic officer to promote the Floydada gateway among government traffic managers, who would, at the end of the war, return to private companies and be responsible for traffic routings. Meanwhile, Richardson stressed the need to provide proper and adequate service and to be prepared for the "reconversion" to peacetime conditions. "Routes without service certainly will not get very far," and, he said, neither would railroads that failed to change with changing times.[39]

For the QA&P retaining overhead business was vital. From 1941 through 1945, the Quanah Route generated 60 percent of its total traffic from government or war-related consignments. Both Charles

Sommer and W. L. Richardson understood that it was necessary to maintain a high volume of passover traffic in the future; local business alone would not sustain the QA&P. Both men thought that, on balance, the road had done a creditable job in handling government business and believed that the contacts they had made would favor the road with private postwar traffic. Moreover, they had finally persuaded the Frisco to support the Floydada gateway; the parent company had promised to establish new through train service to be known as the T-C Train (transcontinental) or the California Flash. There was, to be sure, an immediate and predictable downturn in passover traffic at the end of hostilities, but Richardson predicted, shortly after V-J Day, that as "reconversion" got under way "commercial traffic should gradually improve." He hoped that commercial passover traffic would reach "an average of 1,000 cars monthly." With the war over, he pushed the matter with his representatives. "It has now become an age of outselling our competitors," he told them.[40]

CHAPTER 17

# *Working on the (Short Line) Railroad*

It must be a great pleasure to be in charge of
a small, loyal organization such as you seem to
have.—O. M. Colston to Charles H. Sommer,
February 1, 1939

THE QA&P provided jobs as diverse as superintendent of terminals, section laborer, general agent,
pumper, president, track inspector, general attorney, warehouseman, porter, and stationary fireman.
The greatest percentage of employees were section
hands. Next were members of bridge and building
gangs, extra gang laborers, clerks, stenographer-
clerks, bridge and building carpenters, and roundhouse employees. The vast majority of the company's help was recruited locally, especially from
Hardeman County, with lesser numbers coming
from Cottle and Motley counties. Few claimed
origins other than Texas.[1]

On the other hand, during the early years the
company hired—as a matter of course—large numbers of men who had "railroaded elsewhere." Many
were boomers who worked a short while and then
moved on in their traditional style. Others came to
stay. Nevertheless, there was a monumental turnover in help, especially in the period before 1920.

This pattern suggested informality and mobility
among the crafts. One chap, who arrived on the
property after serving as a brakeman on the Frisco,
worked on the QA&P's bridge gang, then became
agent at Swearingen, and finished his employment
as a conductor on the Matador Branch. Another
fellow started as cashier at Matador, then became
agent at Roaring Springs, moved to the road's traffic department, and finally transferred to the official
ranks of another road. More traditional was the career of Francis M. Gunter, who started as a section
laborer, became station helper at Roaring Springs,
and retired as agent at Floydada in 1980. Other
longtime employees followed similar patterns.
B. H. Stone began his railroading career on an extra
gang and forty-eight years later retired as a locomotive engineer. Another veteran, Joe W. Shaw,
started in 1910 as a bridge and building carpenter,

switched to the roundhouse as a boilermakers'
helper, then went on the road as a fireman, and
eventually was promoted to engineer.[2]

The number of employees and the company's
compensation budget rose after 1910 as the road
pushed west. In 1917, the company had a monthly
average of 144 employees and paid out $114.218.98
for wages and salaries. Four years later, a monthly
average of 164 employees received $197,847.84.[3]

Wages increased very little from 1910 until a scarcity of labor combined with government awards
drove them up during World War I. In 1917, representative wages were as follows:

| | |
|---|---|
| Passenger engineers | $4.00 per day |
| Freight conductors | $4.25 per day |
| Boilermakers | $.50 per hour |
| Section laborers | $.16-1/2 per hour |
| Agent (Paducah) | $110 per month |

Rates for all classes were up by 1920, but when
the road was returned to its owners after government operation, QA&P management determined
to make reductions (see Chapter 6). The issue
served to focus Charles Sommer's inherent pater-
nalism and his simultaneous dislike for unions and
decisions made by "distant boards." That is not to
say that his views were without merit. Indeed, the
road's earnings early in the 1920s did not pay "actual running expenses." Employees, however, also
had a complaint: their wages were cut while the
cost of living dropped only slightly. Reductions
ranged from 2.9 percent to 28.6 percent, depending
on the class of labor or the position in question.[4]

On balance, employees likely made slight gains
in real income between 1917 and 1929. For instance,
in 1921 passenger engineers received $200 per
month, boilermakers made 72 cents per hour, and
section men drew 37-1/2 cents per hour. Raises dur-

ing the 1920s were both rare and thin: boilermakers received a mere 2 cents per hour increase before the Great Depression set in.[5]

In the early years health care for employees was provided by a local physician at Quanah who agreed to furnish "all necessary drugs, dressings, hospital accommodations, and his services." For this package employees paid monthly dues according to a simple scale: those earning less than $40 per month paid 50 cents and those making more than $40 per month paid $1.00. In 1920, the QA&P added a comprehensive death and dismemberment insurance plan through the Metropolitan Life Insurance Company. Each participant paid 35 cents per week, with the railroad picking up the balance of premiums. This informal arrangement sufficed until more expansive plans were inaugurated in the 1940s.[6]

QA&P management astonished but pleased its employees in 1924 by authorizing a Christmas bonus based on 20 percent of the November payroll. In all, seventy-eight employees shared $2,243.15. Sommer pointed out that 1924 had been kind to the road and that the bonus was "a small way to show our appreciation to the efforts and the assistance of our employees who have helped to make possible the successful operation of the property." His brother A. F. Sommer endorsed the idea: "I believe that we will get this back many times in better cooperation and a closer feeling toward the company." The good news quickly reached the *Quanah Tribune-Chief*, whose editor assured his readers that the QA&P's interest in its employees "made them the most loyal railroad men in the Southwest." Charles Sommer, who usually thrived on publicity, was irked; he told his brother that the bonus should have been "strictly confidential between us and our employees."[7]

Similar bonuses were issued every Christmas season through 1929. In each of those years Charles Sommer made the affair more auspicious, ordering specially printed notices and envelopes, but in all cases eschewing outside publicity. Sommer faced a dilemma in 1929, however. Income was down, but he hated to disappoint employees. In the end, he determined to "go ahead, considering the excellent cooperation we have had." A total of $4,321.05 was distributed among 178 employees. One of these, a section laborer at Narcisso, thanked Sommer and added: "I am pleased to be an employee of a company operated by people of the highest standard of humanity." Sommer was touched. He commented that "this check apparently hit home and I am glad

it gave him a little pleasure." Privately, he told his brother that he had "strained a point in paying the bonus this year because we got a bad jolt [decline in traffic]." Nevertheless, he thought the expense had been worthwhile. *Railway Age,* the trade journal, agreed. It ran an editorial on December 28 praising such bonus payments.[8]

The number of employees in 1939 and the company's wage payments were less than in 1930, a result of the hard times of the Depression decade. In 1930, the road had a monthly average of 216 employees; in 1939, the number was 129. In 1930, the firm's annual payroll stood at $289,946.71; by 1939, it had slipped to $185,945. Salaried employees received a 5 percent pay cut early in 1931, and all employees had their checks slashed by from 5 to 10 percent on February 1, 1932. Sommer was reluctant to effect these unpleasant changes but felt constrained to do so because of the "current crisis"; the cuts were received without rancor. As business improved, Sommer ordered a restoration of 2.5 percent on July 1, 1934, another 2.5 percent on January 1, 1935, and remaining 5 percent three months later.[9]

Labor relations were calm during the 1930s, perhaps because of universal adversity. In any event, all employees seemed to "pull in harness." Sixty-one railroaders from the QA&P donated from 50 cents to $2.50 each to the Empty Stocking Fund at Quanah during the bleak Christmas season of 1930. Six years later a large delegation of employees participated in a celebration of railroad week at Quanah and the company's shop employees fabricated the likeness of a locomotive, mounted it on an automobile, and entered their "engine" in the parade.[10]

The "all-of-us-are-in-it-together" psychology resulted in formation of the QA&P Booster Club. Its purpose was to get more business for the railroad, and its motto was "Every QA&P employee a Solicitor." Members (all employees were members) were given cards stating that they were a part of the QA&P family and were urged to hand these cards to local merchants when making purchases. In that cryptic way the railroaders would, they thought, remind businessmen to use the railroad instead of trucks.[11]

All of this was reflected in the *QA&P Employees' Magazine,* initiated, edited, and published by employees. The magazine's function, as defined by Orvis Weathers, the first editor, was to "create a closer relationship among the employees, to make them feel more like one big family, and to arouse an enthusiasm for more earnestness and sincerity in our

work for the road." Not surprisingly, management enthusiastically supported the venture. After all, the notion of family was very close to Charles Sommer's heart; he always referred to the labor force as "the boys." Sommer was delighted when outsiders expressed "deep interest" in the publication, and, more important, as one said, recognized "the spirit of the employees that has prompted and supported it." The Christmas issue for 1935 was especially impressive, and Sommer nearly burst with pride when one person told him "he doubted if there was another magazine in the United States—railroad, industrial, or otherwise—that had for its foundation the support, loyalty and untiring efforts of the employees such as the QA&P's." Additional compliments flowed in. A vice-president for Pure Oil told Sommer that "it must be a great pleasure to be in charge of a small, loyal organization such as you seem to have."[12]

The growing attention that the magazine generated proved, however, to be a mixed blessing. Sommer increasingly involved himself in its affairs with the result that the magazine became more sophisticated. Its mailing list was expanded to five hundred in 1938. The editorship passed from contract employees to junior-level officials, who viewed the president's suggestions as directives. In the process the *QA&P Employees' Magazine* became a mouth piece for management. Certainly employees saw it that way. The magazine passed from the scene before World War II.[13]

The Great Depression resulted in a flood of applications by men from all over the country who were looking for work. Some of these were boomers, but the majority were simply out of a job. Most, like W. D. Wilson of Chicago, were told that "because of general business conditions, we are being pressed to find employment for men who have been with us for many years and, therefore, there is no possibility of having anything for you in the near future." When openings did occur, local applicants were favored. So, too, was the gender that traditionally held a position. Thus a man

from Vernon who applied for a position in the general office was rejected because "the job has always had a young lady on it." Some carriers, like the nearby Wichita Falls & Southern Railroad, sought to place their excess trainmen on the QA&P, at least temporarily, for the "wheat rush." Particularly pathetic were the cases of senior men who had lost jobs when their employers went out of business or had been released because of business conditions. For instance, the QA&P could find no room for a telegrapher who had twenty-six years' experience on the Fort Smith & Western and had to disappoint a longtime storekeeper for the Tonapah & Goldfield.[14]

There is no question that management took a personal interest in company employees. The railroad encouraged employees to take advantage of educational opportunities through the International Correspondence Schools of Scranton, Pennsylvania, and provided a payroll deduction plan for those who enrolled. It also demanded that its employees—current and prospective—be fingerprinted. By mid-1942, Charles Sommer could report that every person had been processed. In some instances, unsavory characters were discovered, especially among extra gang and bridge and building employees. The time from the date of fingerprinting to the receipt of information was frequently several weeks and even several months, however, and during that time many of these persons had established credible work records on the QA&P. Nevertheless, they were declared unwelcome when their records were discovered, deepening personal tragedy for many.[15]

Such personal interest sometimes resulted in benefits for employees. One veteran conductor, who started with the road when it had been the ARR&N, became so deaf and feeble that he was used only "on extra runs where it was just a matter of moving an engine over the road," but because of his long service he received a modest monthly salary or, as A. F. Sommer put it, a "kind of pension." Eventually the man retired, but he was not forced to do so and, the Depression notwithstanding, he was kept on the payroll. The same concern was given to the crewmen or the Matador branch when that line was retired. "If it is at all possible to provide work for these boys," C. H. Sommer told his brother, "we must do it." And when a conductor told A. F. Sommer that he had no money to handle unexpected expenses connected with the illness of one of his children, Sommer promptly advanced him $20 against his next check. "We are

W. H. ("Big Bill") Norman, here looking sheepish in the cab of number 27 after a minor derailment near Acme. *B. H. Stone collection*

only too glad to accommodate our employees in this manner," he said, "but would prefer that you not say anything about this to the other employees." More serious was the plight of a roadmaster who suffered a debilitating illness that eventually forced him to leave the company's service. Charles Sommer called him "a loyal worker who is ready to go at anytime" and ordered that the company pay for him to have a medical examination at the Frisco's hospital in St. Louis. He also advanced him more than $500 against a future salary that he knew the man would never earn. The same personal interest was manifest when an employee retired. A case in point involved W. H. Norman, an engineer, who had started his career as a fireman for the ARR&N in 1902. When Norman retired in 1945, C. H. Sommer said that the Quanah Route was "losing one of its most faithful and valued employees." In a warm, personal letter, Sommer told Nor-

man: "Your service over these many years, and as one of our oldest employees, has been one of prudence, thoughtfulness, and attention to duty, and nobody knows better than I do the interest you have always displayed in putting your best foot forward for the company."[16]

As in any business, complaints were made to management about the affairs of individual employees. In some instances the employee was found to be at fault and was dealt with in a stern manner; in other cases, management perceived that employees were falsely charged and stood resolutely behind them. Thus when an extra gang foreman burglarized a home near Paducah, and when a brakeman stole "a pair of nylons and some silk underclothes off a clothesline at Lazare," the men were dismissed. When the agent at Dougherty was the victim of a malicious attack because of his opinions as a member of the school board there, however, the road's management unstintingly supported him.[17]

The company followed a similar if somewhat more cautious policy regarding complaints from companies or individuals to whom debts were owed by employees. Some of these involved the firm's salesmen who passed bad checks in their respective territories, especially during the Depression. Sommer told Richardson to handle the matter: "It gives us a bad name and if we do not stop it, it will be tantamount to approval—something which is against our policy." Richardson admonished the offenders, but there is no evidence that any of them were fired. The QA&P was more cautious when local employees were involved. Those levying complaints almost always threatened to withhold patronage from the railroad, but unless the employee had failed to pay for "life necessities" the Sommer brothers were unwilling to involve themselves or the company in the matter.[18]

This policy developed fine focus as the result of a cause célèbre involving a station employee who, just before the onset of the Depression, bought a lot in Floydada from the owner of a large wholesale lumber company in that community. Soon thereafter the man was forced to move to another location on the railroad, was unable to keep up his payments on the lot, and could not reconvey the property because the seller stubbornly refused to exercise his rights under vendor's lien clause. The lumberman called the railroader a man of "Bolshevik disposition." From an economic point of view the issue was clear—the seller was trying to enforce a contract made at pre-depression prices that would, in Depression times, make him a lot of money. Yet he had protected himself with a lien that he did not wish to exercise because, of course, the property had depreciated in value. The railroad employee had acted in good faith, had paid the taxes, and sought compromise. Consequently, QA&P management and its legal counsel agreed that the company would not involve itself. The lumberman was irritated and, in spite, routed his cars away from the QA&P and demanded that the man be fired before he would restore business to the local road. Charles Sommer stood resolutely for principle even though the road lost business. Said Sommer: "I would under no circumstance lend myself to handling the problem as he has suggested, not in these times nor in any other time in a similar situation."[19]

QA&P managers clearly showed compassion when they thought it was required, but they were also capable of making swift and decisive judgments when they calculated that an employee's dismissal was in the company's interest. The reasons for dismissal varied: a brakeman stealing from baggage and express shipments, a section man taking a motor car without permission, a station agent who "got his hand in the till," an engine watchman for chronic bad judgment, a clerk for incompetence, a hostler for drinking while on duty, and a section foreman who left his gang for the purpose of "entertaining a fishing party." In some cases, the person accumulated a thick file showing a variety of problems; in others, especially among maintenance-of-way forces, one serious incident could bring dismissal.[20]

If QA&P records are any indication, it was hard to go through a railroad career—especially in the operating crafts—without receiving at least one reprimand or assembling demerits for infractions. A leverman assigned to the tower in Quanah overslept one morning because he had stayed up too late listening to the "Walter Winchell Program"; a humorless A. F. Sommer threatened disciplinary action if the incident was repeated. A brakeman was fired twice, in each case for insubordination, but stayed until retirement as an "emergency man." Indeed, a number of men were rehired after they had been fired. This was the case of a section laborer who was dismissed for fighting while on duty and for an engineer—a notorious "low water man"—and his fireman, although their carelessness resulted in a boiler explosion that ripped locomotive 33 in 1931. Disciplinary measures seemed most predictable and hardest for track and bridge and building gangs, less so for all other crafts.[21]

Of course, not every employee stayed until retirement. Indeed, most who received employment on the QA&P eventually resigned—normally because the person could not benefit from steady work on the railroad, because of low pay, or because he found a better position elsewhere.[22]

Virtually all who left the company requested a service letter, and since the law—at least since 1930 and likely before—made it illegal to blacklist or to discriminate, these were issued routinely. Some were humorous: "Services as conductor were satisfactory although his conduct toward lady passengers which led to his resignation was not satisfactory." Most were direct: "His services were satisfactory"; "His services were entirely satisfactory"; "He attempted to discredit the management before the Railroad Administration." In a few instances, long-gone employees asked for a letter of reference

The tower in Quanah

showing service or circumstances other than the truth. The railroad, of course, retained its personnel records, and its officials responded to such requests with brief replies stating the person's occupation and dates of service.[23]

Although blacks made up an increasing percentage of the population in the QA&P's service area, they were rarely employed by the railroad. Until recent times, those hired were used in traditionally servile positions and were victims of classic racism. In the road's earliest days, a black was hired as porter on the passenger train, blacks were assigned to business car 6666, and blacks served as porters or janitors in the general office building at Quanah. In the 1960s, a single black worked in train service.

One incident suggests the status of blacks on the QA&P and also implies standard racial attitudes at Quanah during the years of World War II. Throughout the summer of 1944, there was concern at that place over one J. Vance Jenkins, porter on the Frisco's passenger train that tied up each evening in Quanah after its arrival from Oklahoma City. A. F. Sommer told his brother that Jenkins was organizing the blacks into "an Eleanor club'"

and was "generally spreading information and mingling among the colored people at Quanah while there between runs." This had led to bad publicity for the railroad, and C. H. Sommer asked the Frisco's special agents to investigate. They discovered that Jenkins was working to establish a National Association for the Advancement of Colored People chapter and that he was encouraging the black community to demand a janitor for the two-room "colored school" as well as concrete sidewalks, gravel streets, better sanitary conditions, and even telephone service. White leadership of Quanah was upset, as were the "good negroes," especially the pastor of the "colored Baptist church," according to the investigators, because they believed Jenkins would do more harm than good. The sheriff of Hardeman County was particularly offended. He stated that "they usually took care of their negro problems in Texas and had no difficulty in doing so." The sheriff and Frisco's special agents must have been successful in whatever tactics they employed, for the record divulges no further reference to this man. Charles Sommer thought the matter "had been given excellent handling."[24]

Of all classes of railroad employees, the most admired—or the best known, at least on a small operation—were locomotive engineers, conductors, and station agents. Representative examples from the QA&P include Elton B. Marsalis (engineer), Floyd H. Hodo (conductor), and Robert Medlen (agent).

Born on July 10, 1908, Elton Marsalis was the son of Leonard B. Marsalis, an engineer on the QA&P and one of the two engineers who piloted the first passenger train in Floydada in 1928. Young Marsalis, like two of his brothers, hired out on the QA&P in engine service. He served on the roundhouse crew in 1925, was promoted to fireman in 1926, to engineer in 1930, and retired in 1973.[25]

Like Marsalis, Floyd H. Hodo also began his railroad career in the QA&P roundhouse during the mid-1920, but, unlike Marsalis, he went into train service in 1927. He was known as a good switchman and conductor and also as an adept practitioner of "caboose cooking." Hodo was fond of recalling that three of his children went to college on money earned from the QA&P. He retired in 1972.[26]

Of the company's station agents, Robert Medlen was the best known and most respected. He developed an interest in railroading at Anson, Texas, where he hung around the depots, and he hired out on the Motley County Railway, serving as agent for that company at Matador in 1916. He transferred to the QA&P in 1917 as cashier and then agent at Quanah, then agent for the QA&P at Matador (after the Motley County Railway became part of the larger road), and had the honor of opening the new station at Floydada when the line was extended to that point. He was respected by salaried employees, officials, and the general public; local citizens frequently asked him to write letters of recommendation for them. Medlen was a member of the Floydada Rotary Club, the Chamber of Commerce, and the school board. Like Hodo, he frequently pointed out that he had been able to send all of his children to college on money earned from the Quanah Route. When Medlen retired in 1960, the railroad hosted a farewell party for him and the *Floyd County Hesperian* ran a feature story. One official observed that Medlen had been "an able, conscientious, energetic, and loyal employee." It was no exaggeration.[27]

No class of employee enjoyed more adulation than did locomotive engineers. Indeed, a clear and understandable mystique surrounded them, especially during the age of steam. Perched high above

Far left, Floyd H. Hodo, who was adept at "caboose cooking"; left center, H. O. Wells; right center, Joe W. Shaw, who started with the QA&P in 1910 as a bridge and building carpenter and retired as a locomotive engineer; and far right, Elton B. Marsalis.

the rail in locomotive cabs, engineers were masters of all they surveyed. Some, however, seemed more regal than others. On the QA&P, for instance, Bill Norman always got up from his seat box and rolled a Bull Durham cigarette whenever he passed certain mileposts and whenever a collision was imminent between his charge and a vagrant steer. There were several fine engineers on the Quanah Route—L. E. Marsalis, Fred Watson, and Bill Norman, among others. Their skills were attributable, in part, to their previous experience in the QA&P's roundhouse. Watson, in particular, was respected for his mechanical ability; he was known to set up wedges and even reduce the main rod on a locomotive when trouble developed far from the shops. Nevertheless, engineers traditionally earned memorable status by their devotion to "fast running" or their talents as "whistle artists." The QA&P's "high steppers" included Watson, Joe Shaw, and Earley Jones; the "whistle artists" were Norman, Watson, and Jones. Indeed, one QA&P employee far from home during World War II "yearned to hear Earley Jones' whistling." Fred Watson, who earned the nickname "Whistling Watson" during steam days, died in the engineer's seat of a diesel locomotive in 1958.[28]

The devotion of Charles Sommer to the company's locomotive engineers and, for that matter, to all classes of employees is clear enough; his dislike for the railroad brotherhoods to which they belonged is similarly clear. He took a personal if paternalistic interest in all employees; he thought unions were unnecessary on small roads and counterproductive for the entire industry. And in this regard, as in many others, he postured the QA&P as a tiny independent or as an integral part of a Class I system as he thought the situation required. Nevertheless, the QA&P signed contracts with all of the brotherhoods by the mid-1930s.

There were frequent problems between the QA&P and the Brotherhood of Maintenance of Way Employees, perhaps because of the high turnover among employees of this class or the absence of talented and constant union leadership at the local level. In any event, a contract between the QA&P and this brotherhood—covering rates of pay, work rules, and working conditions—was signed on July 9, 1937. The general chairman of the union called it "a very liberal agreement" and no doubt Sommer saw it similarly. That was the problem. Sommer felt that this and all other such contracts limited his managerial prerogatives. There was so much acrimony over contested issues that some of them were taken to the Emergency Board of the National Railway Labor Panel, the National Railroad Adjustment Board, and even a federal district court. Sommer was outraged in 1946 when the union accused him or "chiseling" the road's maintenance-of-way personnel by failing to abide by a recent national wage settlement. Sommer pointed out that QA&P was not a party to the national agreement, but the union threatened a strike. Relations between track labor and management were strained until well into the 1950s.[29]

Sommer was equally opposed to establishing a contract with enginemen and trainmen but equally unsuccessful in preventing it. Early in 1935, he met with local employees, I. C. Huckaby representing the trainmen and W. O. Lucas representing the enginemen. These two urged that the QA&P adopt the Frisco's rates of pay and working conditions. Sommer disagreed: "There is no real need for a lot of complicated working agreements on a short line like ours because our operations are simple and cannot in any way be related to conditions obtaining on a trunk line." The issue was referred to the National Mediation Board for a decision. As Sommer

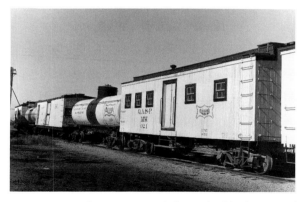

Maintenance-of-way personnel charged with the care of right-of-way at remote locations such as the Tongue River breaks between Narcisso and Russellville were housed in gang cars. *Fred M. Springer photograph*

viewed it, Section 2 of the National Labor Act did not require the execution of written contracts. Furthermore, he saw no need to make changes because current procedures, which had been policy for twenty-five years, were working well. No written contract had existed before; he saw no need for one now. He had always "dealt leniently and fairly with the crafts," he had "personal contact with all of the men" and he had "ironed out any differences when they existed." For Sommer the idea of written contracts was utterly abhorrent; such formality violated his paternal instincts; and he was hurt by the notion that "the boys" would feel the need for them.[30]

Yet times had changed, and as T. H. Steffens, a friend and president of the Sand Springs Railway, pointed out to Sommer, "the organizations [unions] now have the law on their side." Contracts were drawn between the Quanah Route and the Brotherhood of Locomotive Firemen and Enginemen and the Brotherhood of Railroad Trainmen effective June 1, 1936, but the men thus covered gained little—at least initially—because these agreements merely put into writing "present rates of pay and working conditions." On the other had, the employees now had an effective bargaining device and designated spokesmen which they quickly but judiciously used. In 1938, local representatives requested that the QA&P "adopt standard rates," but Sommer reminded them that traffic was down, the Depression was still having a severe impact, and the company could not pay such rates. The representatives were fair-minded and did not push the matter until better days, in 1943, when they renewed the effort. Sommer would not budge, and the national

Mediation Board was again drawn into the local road's affairs. One year later, the board ordered the QA&P to settle on the basis of "80 per cent of standard." The old contracts were revised accordingly.[31]

Other agreements were drawn eventually, with less hoopla, with the Order of Railroad Telegraphers; the International Brotherhood of Firemen, Oilers, Helpers, Roundhouse and Railway Shop Laborers; the International Association of Machinists; the International Brotherhood of Boilermakers, Iron Ship Builders and Helpers of America; and the Brotherhood of Railway Carmen of America.[32]

It would be wrong to characterize labor relations on the QA&P as acrimonious; it would be equally incorrect to label them as harmonious. In 1946, the QA&P had no fewer than seven cases before national mediation boards; only five members of the American Short Line Railroad Association had more. Nevertheless, there was a persistent spirit of family. When one member had a problem, as did the station agent at Paducah in 1951, officials happily joined with contract employees to "take up a collection." And during hard times contract employees at the roundhouse—after accepting the ten percent wage reduction—voluntarily reduced their daily hours to seven so that two fellow workers could be kept on the payroll.[33]

Employment numbers fluctuated throughout the

### TABLE 10
### Wage Scales, 1940–1944

| Position | 1940 ($) | 1942 ($) | 1944 ($) |
|---|---|---|---|
| Mixed train engineers | 6.55/day | 0.95/hr | 0.95/hr |
| Mixed train conductors | 5.67/day | 0.84/hr | 0.84/hr |
| Boilermakers | 0.79/hr | 0.90/hr | 0.95/hr |
| Section laborers | 0.34/hr | 0.44/hr | 0.55/hr |
| Agent (Paducah) | 165/month | 190/month | 208/month |

SOURCE: Various data, F51 and 1662.

1940s. Reflecting the hangover of the Depression, only 129 were on the payroll in 1940. Two years later, the number stood at 145, but in 1945 it slumped to 123, suggesting a thin labor pool in the service area brought about by the draft. Good times followed, and when the decade closed the company employed 190 persons. The payroll reflected this increase to some extent, but it mirrored more accurately a rise in average annual wages and salaries: 1941, $204,763; 1945, $295,925; and 1949, $649,261.[34]

Wages for representative positions or classes during the first half of the 1940s rose as shown in table 10.

## CHAPTER 18

# Managing the (Short Line) Railroad

A short line like the QA&P has only two things
to offer shippers who can use other routes—
friendship and service.—W. L. Richardson to the
QA&P sales force, July 5, 1949

FOR a small operation, the QA&P featured an astonishingly talented management team. The company also attracted the active interest of a number of persons whose names are firmly ingrained in the lore of the Southwest.

The early life of the QA&P was touched by two men whose names are well known to students of southwestern history. One of these was Samuel Burke Burnett, an important Texas cattleman, and the other Quanah Parker, a Comanche chief. Burnett shipped cattle on the QA&P from his famous Four Sixes Ranch, was a QA&P director, and owned business car 6666 before the railroad acquired it from his estate. The community of Quanah, seat of Hardeman County, Texas, was, of course, named for Quanah Parker, a prominent Indian who once made war against the white interloper but eventually came to accept the inevitable. The QA&P trademark or corporate emblem was designed in the likeness of an Indian, which Quanah Parker claimed was his likeness and which was so intended by the railroad. Charles Sommer attempted to memorialize Parker's strong links with the QA&P in a booklet entitled *Quanah Parker: Last Chief of the Comanches* and published by the company. There is much room for skepticism, however. Sommer quoted Parker as saying that he had invested $40,000 in the QA&P. There is evidence that he donated $5 to an early community fund drive in support of the railroad, but there is no record that he owned stock in either the Acme, Red River & Northern or the QA&P. It is possible that he contributed to the bonus that was given by the city of Quanah to launch the expansion to Paducah in 1909, and it is also possible that he purchased bonds issued by the railroad, although that is unlikely. In any event, Quanah Parker's name was inextricably linked with that of the QA&P.[1]

This 1910 portrait of Quanah Parker was used as a QA&P promotional shot.

The work of Samuel L. Lazarus has been recited earlier and will not be recounted here except to note the words of Charles Sommer at his death: "I have lost the best and dearest friend that I ever had. He was a wonderful man, and to me typified the real American citizen. He was liberal and he was broad." Lazarus was also a remarkably talented entrepreneur in the classic mold.[2]

Lazarus's successor was Sommer himself. Born at Galveston on October 2, 1878, Sommer went to work for the Gulf, Colorado & Santa Fe Railway as an office boy in the auditor's department during 1895. He was transferred to Houston ten years later. There he represented the Santa Fe in construction of the Houston Belt & Terminal Railway. As a result of his work in Houston, Sommer came to the attention of Sam Lazarus, who hired him in 1906 as vice-president of the Acme, Red River & Northern. He served in that office for the QA&P until Lazarus died in 1925. The board of directors then abolished the position of vice-president, combined its responsibilities with those of the president, and appointed Sommer to the post.[3]

Although he did not complete a high school program and did not have an opportunity to pursue a college degree, Sommer developed interests usually associated with those who had such benefits. He played the violin and cello in the Galveston Symphony, played the viola in the Houston Symphony, was organist at St. Joseph's Church in Houston, and was a lifelong devotee of the opera. As a youth he was also a talented athlete, interested in swimming, bowling, and baseball. As an adult he had two hobbies—collecting stamps and, in his words, "railroads and more railroads."[4]

Sommer was a man of immense talent, if periodic contradiction. He was hard-driving and energetic; one subordinate remembered him as "always in a hurry." He could be defensive, swift to judge, and his righteousness tended toward self-righteousness. Yet he had the capacity to compromise, was influenced by logic, and could be compassionate if made aware of full circumstances. He pushed very hard for the QA&P and for the railroad industry in general, but there is no evidence that he ever engaged in illegal or unethical conduct. Indeed, even as the little railroad struggled for its existence he insisted on maintaining "what the law requires—on that we must rest our case." He could be generous. When the Veterans of Foreign Wars post at Matador requested that the QA&P donate a lot for it to build on, Sommer explained that as an officer of the company it was not within his province to grant such a request. Nevertheless, he purchased the lot with his own funds and then deeded it to the organization. He could be vindictive. He was, he said, "in favor of extreme and drastic handling where the offender is of the Bolshevik type." He advocated harsh treatment—"the rougher the better"—for those who went absent without leave during World War II and, later on, was incensed by "that fellow Robeson [Paul Robeson, the black opera star] who goes around the country outraging the sentiments and loyalty of us Americans, and yet seems to have a

Charles Sommer

preference for remaining in this country for safety and protection."[5]

As vice-president and then as president, Sommer conducted executive duties with enthusiasm and skill. This could be either a liability or an asset. He was torn between wanting to be involved in all aspects of the company's routine and the need to let his talented and egocentric subordinates play active and productive roles in the management of the company. He had to be especially careful in balancing the needs and aspirations of two lieutenants—his brother A. F. Sommer and W. L. Richardson. Sommer had a genius for handling them. He could pacify the high-flying Richardson, and he could be sternly businesslike with his brother. It was a great testimony to Sommer's skills that he could get these two to "pull in harness."[6]

Sommer enjoyed being president of a railroad. It

gave him recognition, an outlet for his bountiful talent, and an opportunity to travel. In 1936, he held no fewer than 153 transportation passes—from the Alton Railroad to the Yosemite Valley Railroad as well as from the Hudson River Day Line and the Pullman Company. He enjoyed a salary that allowed him to vacation in Canada and in Arizona.[7]

Sommer—"Mr. QA&P," *Railway Age* called him—retired as president on December 31, 1951, but pledged to "do business at the old stand—426 Frisco Building in St. Louis—for a while." He retained a seat on the QA&P's directorate. Death claimed him at the age of eighty-two, on January 13, 1961.[8]

The QA&P's board of directors memorialized Sommer as "an outstanding railroad man of more than fifty years." Furthermore, said the board, "His life in every way reflected the qualities of a true gentleman, a fine associate in business, and honesty at its best and will be sorely missed by all his associates. His kindly human qualities and gracious manner were an inspiration to all who knew him and his passing occasions a sense of personal loss." A subordinate put it simply: "Charles Sommer was a very able short line railroad President."[9]

His brother, Anthony F. ("Tony") Sommer, was not as complex and was more predictable. Born in 1887 at Galveston, he, too, began his railroad career on the Gulf, Colorado & Santa Fe, as a blueprint boy. Unlike his older brother, A. F. Sommer secured a college education, earning a bachelor of science degree in civil engineering from Purdue University. Following his graduation in 1914, he became a draftsman for the QA&P, then was promoted to resident engineer, and to vice-president and general manager in 1918. Although a competent engineer and a reasonably good operating man, A. F. Sommer was not as effective or as popular as his brother. He was perceived as arbitrary, unbending, and without humor by employees and by much of the public. A former conductor called him "a hard rock."[10]

W. L. Richardson came to the road in 1927 after previous railroad service with the Kansas City Southern, Texas & Pacific, Southern Pacific, and Fort Smith, Subiaco & Rock Island. On the QA&P he served as chief clerk to A. F. Sommer before his appointment as general agent, then traffic manager, and finally executive vice-president. He retired in 1961.[11]

Richardson was aloof, exacting, and—for Quanah, Texas—"high brow." He was also hardworking, talented, a fine salesman, and "a good idea man."

A. F. Sommer

"His mind was always working," is the way one associate remembered him. Richardson, of course, was the prime mover behind the QA&P's successful rate cases and Floydada gateway case. Later he was architect of the road's nationally respected traffic department and the successful program to attract overhead traffic. His approach to salesmanship was simple: active solicitation coupled with reliable service. Subordinates saw him as "difficult"; shippers viewed him as attentive to their needs; community leaders at Quanah respected him for his attempts to draw industry to the area.[12]

Unquestionably the most admired and respected official on the QA&P was Quin K. Baker, who arrived on the property shortly after the sudden death of A. F. Sommer late in 1945. Born in Welda, Kansas, on October 18, 1894, Baker graduated from the University of Kansas in 1916 with a degree in civil engineering. Immediately thereafter he took a job in the engineering department of the Frisco and moved up the ladder to become assistant superintendent at Fort Scott. From there he moved to Quanah as vice-president and general manager of the QA&P. Later, upon the resignation of Charles H. Sommer, Baker became the road's president and general manager effective January 1, 1952. He simultaneously became a member of the directorate.[13]

Baker was as respected away from the property as he was on it. Eventually he became chairman of the executive committee of the Texas Railroad Association, a member of the board of the American Short Line Railroad association, and an active par-

W. L. Richardson

Quin K. Baker

ticipant in the affairs of the American Railway Engineering Association. At Quanah, he served on the boards of the Chamber of Commerce, Memorial Hospital, and Industrial Foundation and was an elder in the Presbyterian church. As the result of his efforts on behalf of the National Indian Hall of Fame, he was named honorary lieutenant governor of Oklahoma in 1959.[14]

Quin Baker's style was open and accommodating. He was popular with contract help as their comments attest: "They don't make them better"; "You always got a square deal"; "He sought advice from us"; "He was a Christian Gentleman"; "He was tops." A veteran station agent who was about to retire told Baker: "The best thing that ever happened to the QA&P was when you came along." Others felt the same. A member of the official family recalled his capable dealings with shippers, employees, Frisco officials, and community leaders. Indeed, he said, Baker was "one of the best short line executives in the nation."[15]

Other members of the official family include O. L. Bell, general attorney, 1952–70; Stanley M. Blashuk, traffic manager, 1957–61; Roy Bridge, secretary and auditor, 1931–40; Charlene Crisp, who started as a clerk in 1937 and retired as treasurer and auditor in 1980; D. W. Curnutt, superintendent of the shops, 1912–46; O. C. Dettenhaim, bridge and building foreman and then roadmaster, 1943–66; Leo A. Elliott, secretary and treasurer, 1964–69, and vice-president, 1966–69; G. E. Hamilton, local attorney and then general attorney, 1912–62; Clifford E. Harris, chief clerk, a variety of positions,

and, eventually, treasurer, 1931–65; Claude J. McCready, superintendent of the shops, 1946–73; Charles R. Sherwood, assistant traffic manager and then traffic manager, 1940–57; John W. Sampley, valuation accountant and then secretary and auditor, 1930–64; J. W. Sowell, general counsel and then vice-president, 1970–80; and L. A. Thomas, vice-president and general manager, 1964–66.

The responsibility for attracting business fell, of course, to W. L. Richardson, who was named to head the QA&P's traffic department after it was established collaterally with opening of the extension to Floydada. The QA&P was already pledged to cooperative solicitation of transcontinental business in conjunction with the Frisco, but Sommer did not look for much parental assistance in this regard. As Richardson pointed out, "If the Frisco had only one route in connection with the solicitation of transcontinental traffic, and if that one route were in connection with the QA&P, then there would be no need for separate QA&P representation." The presence of the SL-SF route via Avard precluded such cooperation, and as a consequence, Sommer was willing to authorize several off-line agencies staffed by QA&P representatives.[16]

By mid-1930, offices had been established at Detroit, Louisville, St. Louis, Tulsa, Houston, San Francisco, and Los Angeles; agencies at New Orleans, Chicago, New York, Kansas City, Buffalo, and Amarillo were created later. Representatives worked under contracts that called for payment of $3 to $5 for each carload of business they attracted. This arrangement proved inadequate for some, such as the representative at Buffalo, who resigned in 1931 because he could not "make his gasoline expenses out of it." Others quit when they found positions yielding regular salaries, but most found ways to supplement their earnings from the QA&P. Several held similar positions with other—but not competing—railroads such as the Minneapolis, Northfield & Southern; Kansas, Oklahoma & Gulf; and Chicago & Illinois Midland.[17]

Richardson's traffic department was wounded by the Great Depression and suffered greatly during the time when transcontinental tariffs were suspended. Yet it did not perish; rather, it matured. Representatives were "placed on a salary basis" in 1935, and when transcontinental rates were reestablished in 1938, the QA&P put five of its fourteen representatives on full-time contracts. The rest worked for two or more roads, drawing salaries from each. By 1948 all representatives were employed fully by the Quanah Route. Annual salaries went up as the QA&P increasingly participated in the movement of prime overhead traffic (table II). During the next decade the QA&P entered into wage deduction arrangements that allowed traffic men to purchase new automobiles that they could use for both business and personal needs. Salaries also rose. By the end of the 1950s, entry-level positions were filled at $500 per month, a rate that ensured that the local road would attract an accomplished sales force. In 1960, it numbered twenty six—fifteen general agents, four traffic managers, four traffic representatives, two commercial agents, and one vice-president-traffic—located in sixteen cities around the country.[18]

Richardson constantly sent letters and circulars to his representatives in which he complimented, complained, informed, criticized, cajoled, and exhorted. In the main, however, he relied on the power of positive thinking. "When you succeed in selling QA&P routing to a shipper, you have definitely done him a favor," said Richardson to his sales force in 1949. A short line, he continued, "has but two things to offer shippers who can use other routes—friendship and service." When shippers objected to using short lines, representatives were to remind them that the QA&P was a part of the Frisco family; when they objected to the congestion of the trunk carriers, salesmen were to remind them of QA&P's independent status and personalized attention. Richardson argued that the Quanah Route's service was "equal to the best and superior to several other transcontinental routes." Consequently, he expected his forces to produce. As in-

### TABLE II
### Salaries of Sales Representatives, 1939–1948

| Location | 1939 ($) | 1940 ($) | 1948 ($) |
|---|---|---|---|
| Dallas | 960 | 1,160 | NA |
| Los Angeles | 2,100 | 2,100 | 4,800 |
| New York | 600 | NA | 4,578 |
| Pittsburgh | 300 | 510 | 4,578 |

ducement he promised to "authorize office help" for representatives generating "100 active monthly accounts."[19]

Richardson also urged local station agents to be alert for opportunities. During the mid-1930s, they were instructed to spend a part of each day soliciting local shippers and thanking them for previous business. With the end of war in sight, Richardson urged an even more devoted interest to needs of local patrons and reminded agents to seek "industrial development" at their stations. Only Robert Medlen at Floydada, however, was given an account for solicitation expense.[20]

Charles Sommer and QA&P's traffic manager were adept practitioners of the "you scratch my back and I'll scratch your back" approach. Both men reminded officers of large roads and small pikes alike of what the QA&P afforded them in open routings. Representatives of the large carriers usually acknowledged, "with thanks," but promised little. The small roads, however, frequently pledged reciprocity. "We short lines have to stick together," said the traffic manager of the tiny Des Moines & Central Iowa Railway.[21]

There were times when relations with foreign roads seemed more pleasant than those with the QA&P's parent. Although Richardson urged his representatives to cooperate with the Frisco's sales personnel—to facilitate "a freer exchange of information and gain a larger volume of traffic"—he frequently found that SL-SF salesmen were ignorant of their road's ownership of the Quanah Route. Many of them perceived the local road as merely one of Frisco's friendly connections. That issue, although a constant problem, was not as serious as others. One example will suffice. In 1953 the QA&P promoted new outlets for Roaring Springs water among distributors in Oklahoma and Texas. The Eureka Springs Water Company, a firm located on the Frisco in Arkansas, complained that such competition might be harmful to its interests and threatened to reduce shipments on the SL-SF if the parent road did not pressure the QA&P to discontinue promotions of Roaring Springs water. Richardson defended his action: "We are constantly trying to develop the territory tributary" to the QA&P; but an important Frisco official accused him of promoting "selfish interests." In the end, the Frisco official prevailed.[22]

On the other hand the two companies did work together successfully on such major undertakings as joint promotional dinners held at Detroit in 1953 and Memphis in 1955. Important shippers and friendly colleagues in the rail industry—150 in the case of the Memphis affair—were sent engraved invitations requesting their attendance for a splendid evening of cocktails, hors d'oeuvres, and dinner featuring filet mignon. The two railroads split the bill; for the Memphis dinner the QA&P paid $1,372.22.[23]

The QA&P enthusiastically advertised itself in a variety of ways. As early as 1916 the road signed advertising contracts with the *Motley County News, Roaring Springs Echo, Paducah Post,* and *Quanah Tribune-Chief.* Later it placed advertisements in the *Floyd County Hesperian* and in publications as diverse as the *Texas Booster, Sheriff's Association Magazine,* and Quanah High School's yearbook. The Frisco also advertised for the QA&P as a part of its regular campaign on Radio KVOO at Tulsa.[24]

Charles Sommer argued that the name of the company was "too localized," that it did not "lend itself to a geographic location" which the public could easily identify. Those who did identify it, he complained, frequently viewed the Quanah Route as "just another short line," perhaps even "a jerk-water" road. For these reasons, Sommer stoutly supported an expanded advertising budget that he administered with W. L. Richardson. Early attempts were heavy-handed, but experience proved a good teacher. Both men agreed that it might be necessary to "fudge" a bit. For instance, before promotional photographs were made of them at Quanah or elsewhere on the local road, Frisco locomotives, steam and diesel, were restenciled to show QA&P rather than Frisco ownership. In 1939, A. F. Sommer even had a QA&P herald cut to mask the SL-SF emblem under the headlight table of locomotive 1626. In 1949, photographs were made of a streamlined SL-SF Pacific-type locomotive in front of the Quanah Route's general office building. These were then "doctored" to assert QA&P ownership. The pictures, said Richardson, would "acquaint a lot of shippers with the modernity of the QA&P."[25]

Photographs were used in a wide range of promotional literature, including postcards. As many as five thousand of these were printed in 1930. They were used by the railroad, among other purposes, to advise shippers and consignees of the date their lading passed over the QA&P. Photographs were also employed to illustrate the road's annual holiday greeting, a tradition that was begun during World War II. In 1951, fourteen thousand Christmas cards were mailed to shippers and friends of the company and its officials.[26]

Other promotional items included Sommer's book on Quanah Parker, magnifying glasses, cigarette lighters, calendar cards, pen and pencil sets, canasta playing cards, score cards, whisk brooms, book matches, wooden pencils, metal paper clips, and scratch pads. Most of these were dispensed by Richardson's traffic forces, but Sommer claimed a significant portion for his own uses. He regularly sent such items to top officials of other rail lines, especially short lines, and also to persons who had granted him favors or were in a position to do so—the head of the pass bureau at the New York, New Haven & Hartford, Willard V. Anderson at *Trains Magazine,* a Pullman conductor on the *Olympian Hiawatha,* and shippers whom he knew personally. He also sent items to those of no special rank who had requested them. The Railway Express messenger working on Rock Island trains 51 and 52 through Oklahoma City asked for a magnifying glass because he worked "nights under poor lights"; one was promptly sent to him.[27]

The two advertising devices that likely had the greatest impact on shipper's attitudes were the road's circulars and blotters. Production of these began in the late 1930s, shortly after transcontinental rates were restored, and they were issued on a periodic basis. Blotters were commercially printed and of standard size; circulars were home-produced mimeographs on 8-1/2 × 11 stationery. After World War II, both items were printed and mailed on a scheduled basis. Attractively printed in black and red they featured maps showing the route of the QA&P in exaggerated style relative to its major connections and ballyhooed the Frisco-QA&P-AT&SF transcontinental route as well as advantages of FW&DC routings for northwest Texas via Quanah. The press run for circulars stood at three thousand in 1946 but escalated to five thousand just a year later. The messages they bore reflected Richardson's skill as a wordsmith and his flair for turning a flowery phrase. Bi-monthly calendars were included as a part of the blotter format during 1948. Two years later, the style was modified to include clever cartoons in a QA&P setting. The

All departments cooperated to assert QA&P ownership of Frisco equipment. It helped in the road's advertising campaign and solidified pride in all employees.

same artwork was used for the circulars by early 1949. Production and distribution of the blotters ended in the late 1950s, a casualty of ballpoint pens; issuance of the circulars had stopped somewhat earlier.[28]

Blotters and circulars attracted positive attention for the QA&P. The road's traffic representatives felt that at least 50 percent of recipients read the circulars and used the blotters, and most felt that they "kept the name of the railroad before traffic managers." A few shippers complained that the messages contained too many "fancy words," but others felt that these words were an attraction. "Your delightful advertisements are as good as a subscription to the *New Yorker*," cooed John W. Barriger, president of the Monon Railroad. One major trunk line, the Southern Pacific, however, complained that maps on blotters and circulars failed to include its transcontinental options; Richardson felt that SP's complaint simply proved the effectiveness of QA&P's advertising. That the circular/blotter campaign resulted in new traffic is undeniable. An official of the Belfast & Moosehead Lake Railroad wrote to Richardson on the day he received a new circular to advise that he had just routed two Cali-

fornia shipments via the QA&P; the traffic manager for the New England Confectionary Company spent two-thirds of a letter applauding another circular and ended up by noting that he had just shipped two carloads of candy over a route favoring the QA&P; a vice-president of the Handy Sand Company of Evansville, Indiana, promised to ship over the Quanah Route if the company continued to supply him with "those clever bulletins"; and a similar message came from the traffic manager of the Tyler Furniture Company in Niles, Michigan. Sommer's judgment was categoric: "We have found that these cartoons have helped us immeasurably in securing traffic."[29]

Richardson did not believe that advertising alone could secure and retain business. He fully understood that personal contact and, above all, reliable service were primarily responsible for that. One shipper used the QA&P because its traffic manager was "an old friend" of Charles Sherwood (Richardson's assistant), and Schlitz Brewing used the Quanah Route because its traffic manager was a friend of Quin Baker. Others were simply impressed with the QA&P; one shipper said that he had never seen such an aggressive railroad. Another complimented

Blotters were issued monthy and were immensely popular.

the railroad's advertising campaign and added: "You are on the right track—and we believe that goes for your service, too!" On the West Coast, Pacific Coast Borax Company said: "We have found your representation and your service to be all that could be asked for." On the East Coast, Virginia-Carolina Chemical Corporation said: "We are very glad to favor the QA&P with our tonnage." There is no doubt that the QA&P practiced what it preached. Its service was of a personalized nature—just as its advertising promised.[30]

During the course of its history, the QA&P was also fortunate to receive much unsolicited publicity from the local as well as regional and even national press. The *Dallas Morning News* ran a two-column story dealing with Quanah Route Day at the Texas State Fair in 1910. During the period of expansion, the company was constantly in the limelight in the area press, and after World War II regional and national publications dealt with the QA&P as an integral part of transcontinental rail movements. Particularly delightful was the *Chicago Daily Tribune* "Winnie Winkle" cartoon for November 24, 1950; it featured "Uncle Roscoe" running to catch "The

Limited"—a freight train of FW&DC and QA&P cars. The local road also benefited from a radio broadcast originating in Amarillo by Laura V. Hamner in 1950.[31]

The Quanah Route similarly attracted the attention of railfan magazines and the trade press. Representatives of *Trains Magazine* expressed interest in doing a story on the road in 1948, but Sommer was suspicious of their intentions. He recognized that *Trains* was "quite a popular magazine," although he felt that it discriminated in favor of the Class I carriers and ridiculed the smaller roads. He worried that *Trains* might cast the QA&P in the "Grass Route Railroad" category, which, of course, he wanted to avoid. Sommer ordered Quin Baker and W. L. Richardson to cooperate, nevertheless, by supplying data and illustrations. There was no such hesitancy, however, when *Railway Age* evinced a desire to do a story on the Quanah Route. Sommer and Richardson were flattered in the extreme and did everything possible to generate a positive impression. The article appeared in the September 1, 1952, issue and, like another that would appear in *Trains* a decade later, reflected well on the QA&P.[32]

CHAPTER 19

## *Acts of God and Man*

It looks like courts and juries will absolutely ignore
the testimony of railroad witnesses, and decide a
case on mere shadows of evidence.—John P. Marrs
to T. K. Hawkins, June 17, 1924

FOR a transportation company, the "plant" of which is spread over many miles, and which services a multiplicity of communities and constituencies, the chances for misadventure resulting from the acts of God and human error are incalculable. This proved just as true for the QA&P as for the New York Central, the Southern Pacific, or any great system.

Nature has always been, in turn, a blessed provider and a stern adversary for those living on the Great Plains. The QA&P was unavoidably affected by natural disasters. Flash floods, for instance, were a constant threat during the days before upriver dams. In 1913, an important bridge was knocked out of line after raging waters reached as high as the stringers, but this did not deter nearly a dozen patrons from a stranded passenger train who walked across it and rode a freight train on to Quanah. Thirteen years later, members of the Texas Kid Rodeo Company complained vociferously when its entourage was stranded at Matador following a deluge that washed out parts of the branch. The main line was similarly blocked for over a week in 1935 while a pile driver from the SL-SF repaired bridges following spring floods. One season later train 1 was saved from destruction by an alert citizen who spotted a washout between Acme and Lazare. High water affected operations again in 1943, 1946, and 1949. In an effort to remedy these problems, the QA&P did extensive work between Lazare and the Pease River and replaced bridges at crossings of the Pease and Tongue rivers and Dutchman Creek.[1]

Sandstorms, particularly during the Dust Bowl period, also had deleterious effects on the railroad's operations. These storms were particularly wrathful in 1935 west of Paducah and near Roaring Springs and around the Caprock escarpment two

years later. Some seventy stock cars were bedded with sand from a single wind-filled cut during the summer of 1937.[2]

The constant wind is a fact of life on the Plains, and when it is dry, dust storms are common. Less frequent phenomena are blizzards. Those in 1938 and 1940 astonished QA&P railroaders and stymied operations. The 1938 storm came late, in April, and entrapped train 1 near Lazare on one day and, although doubleheaded, near Narcisso the next. It was the worst winter storm in forty years, according to old-timers. Two years later, in February 1940, another storm had an even more unpleasant effect on QA&P operations. Snow derailed a tender truck behind the locomotive on train 1 between Russellville and Roaring Springs; the westbound local freight was already stalled at MacBain. The line was closed for five days, and the embarrassed QA&P had to borrow a snowplow from the Denver Road.[3]

Another of nature's marvels, fire, visited property of the Quanah Route as well as that of its trackside neighbors. Flames ripped through the road's planned community, Roaring Springs, in 1918, destroying several downtown structures, including the "picture show." Grass fires, and the potential for them, were omnipresent threats. Consequently, fire guards—sometimes up to six furrows in width—were plowed along the right-of-way and on adjacent lands to prevent the spread of fires, one of which burned over two hundred acres of grassland and caused much excitement among hands on the Swenson property near Narcisso. Fires destroyed cotton loaded in a boxcar at Floydada, the outhouse at Dougherty, and, in 1949, two bunk cars at Sommer. Sadly, the 1949 conflagration took the life of an extra gang laborer.[4]

Nature found still another, if unpredictable, way

A flash flood on June 6, 1941, resulted in a decision to strengthen the bridge over the Tongue River with a steel girder.
*E. B. Marsalis collection*

to confound operations on the QA&P. Although its route worked westward on a line that demanded only a gradual rise in elevation, east to west, there were some significant grades that were always difficult. The most tedious of these was Pease River hill, westbound, where heavy trains often "fell down" and had to "double." On one occasion, during the days of steam power, a train killed a hog at the top of the hill, and its carcass was dragged down the track by a coyote, greasing the rails en route. The next upbound train and those following for a few days suffered the embarrassment of being unable to get up the hill on the slick rails.[5]

Accidents, especially derailments, always have been an unpleasant element of railroading. The QA&P was not spared. The incidence of these, major and minor, increased during World War II as traffic burgeoned. A broken rail at Carnes derailed train 431 on October 29, 1944, and a sun kink (warping of the track structure) undid the same train at Red River on April 22, 1945. On the line west of Quanah, Extra 101 suffered derailment of a car loaded with steel near Sommer on December 27, 1943. This would have been incidental except that this car and another tipped over as crewmen attempted to rerail it, killing a roadmaster and a conductor and injuring a brakeman. The QA&P had to borrow the FW&DC's wrecker to clear the line. The Denver Road's derrick was also summoned following derailment of eight cars in the consist of train 2 near the Pease River bridge on July 7, 1948. Fortunately, there were no injuries in this case. It was much the same when train 1 "rear-ended" Extra 1619 on February 26, 1949; minor damage resulted, but nobody was hurt. In 1957, joyous citizens of Cottle County flocked to the scene of a derailment west of Paducah where a car loaded

with California wine spilled its contents.[6]

Grade-crossing mishaps were another unpleasant occurrence. In most cases, motor vehicles plunged into the side of a moving train, were hit broadside, or were driven off the roadway to prevent collision. Incidents of this nature, particularly in the early days, usually resulted in more property damage than personal injury or death. There were unfortunate exceptions, however, such as in 1937 at Paducah when train 2 hit a pickup truck that was driven in front of the train, killing three, and in 1954, when, again at Paducah, three teenagers were killed and two others were seriously injured after their automobile struck a westbound freight train.[7]

Accidents involving machines did less damage and were not as severe in their impact on life and limb. In 1930, two motor cars, one bearing the pumper from OX Tank and the other carrying men from a bridge and building gang, collided on a curve near Jacobs. Happily, injuries were minor. Less fortunate were eight men who were riding a motor car that was struck by a pickup truck at a Floydada grade crossing in 1959. Seven of the eight were injured, one seriously. There was no personal injury and very little property damage as the result of a bizarre incident that took place in 1944. On March 20, a track inspector reported that the company's telephone line was down near MacBain; he was unable to determine how it might have happened. The matter was not serious, but it was intriguing. After a month of snooping, QA&P officials discovered that Army Air Corps personnel had accidentally done the damage when retrieving a glider plane from the Childress Army Air Field that had gone down near the QA&P right-of-way.[8]

Still other untoward events involved locomotives. During the winter of 1949, train 1 was delayed

Nature embarrassed the QA&P during the great blizzard of February 1940, when snow stalled the westbound local freight at MacBain.

Winston M. Estes, son of QA&P conductor T. M. Estes (right), memorialized the Hawkins affair in a novel. *E. B. Marsalis collection*

at the Quanah station after water along the track froze wheels of locomotive 187 to the rail; another locomotive was summoned to "break the equipment loose." A bemused Quin Baker told Charles Sommer that "the 187 was not mean enough." In 1931, locomotive 33 was labeled "too mean" when its boiler exploded in the Quanah yards. Fortunately, the blast went forward through the smokebox; crewmen were astonished but unhurt. And in 1920, QA&P officials had been mortified when Frisco locomotive 733, entrusted to the QA&P for safekeeping while it lay overnight in Quanah between runs, "ran away from the roundhouse, passed the General Office Building, and entered the FW&DC's main line." The itinerant locomotive came to rest—it ran out of steam—just west of the Kansas City, Mexico & Orient crossing at Chillicothe. Red-faced officials dispatched the QA&P's locomotive 101 to retrieve the wanderer. A. F. Sommer blamed an inexperienced hostler who apparently failed to shut the throttle all the way and may not have put the reverse lever "on center."[9]

Because of its remote location and because it was not parallel to other lines, detours were rare. Through trains had privileges from Quanah to Plainview over the Denver Road; another agreement provided reciprocity between Quanah and Acme. As a consequence, QA&P rails between those points hosted the Denver Road's fine *Texas Zephyr* on at least one occasion. The KCM&O also used QA&P trackage, at least from Red River to Quanah, for the purpose of detouring away from derailments on its line between Altus and Chillicothe via Quanah and the FW&DC.[10]

The Quanah Route was periodically visited by burglars and vandals, the incidence accelerating dur-

ing the Depression. The company's freight houses and LCL cars were particular targets. The depot at Matador was burglarized in 1932, and thieves made off with cash, the express company's pistol, an automobile battery, and two tires. Items taken in various burglaries at Quanah and Paducah included lard, snuff, spices, cigarettes, shoes, coffee, liquor, earthenware, cured meats, and various other food products and consumer goods. Stock cars at Roaring Springs were rifled of journal box packing, coal was stolen from the pumphouse at OX Tank, and itinerant cotton pickers once even chopped off tie ends to be used as fuel. The company's attorney, G. E. Hamilton, concluded that "dire want is making criminals of many poor people now, who would, under normal conditions not think of violating the law." Yet, he said, "such felonious acts cannot be permitted to go by without effort to locate and punish those guilty."[11]

The QA&P was also victimized from within. On September 23, 1931, the staff of the general office building and the entire management team were astonished and disheartened when an official of the company since 1907, T. K. Hawkins, shot himself to death in an anteroom adjoining his office. The reason was quickly apparent. The sixty-four-old Hawkins had written a letter to C. H. Sommer the day before in which he admitted that he had embezzled several thousand dollars over the years. He had done this, he said, by "swapping drafts" and had used the proceeds for "speculating," a venture in which he had been "without any luck." The railroad eventually charged, in Texas courts, that an area bank that had handled Hawkins's transactions should have know, as Sommer said, that the monies

Number 187 in charge of train 2 at Quanah on October 23, 1948. This same locomotive froze to the tracks during the winter of 1949. *Preston George photograph*

"were trust funds belonging to the railroad." The QA&P accepted $25,000 in settlement from the surety company; the bank was asked to make up the balance of the railroad's loss—$50,000, plus legal costs. After five years in the courts the QA&P lost. The matter was a cause célèbre in Quanah and was memorialized in fiction by Winston M. Estes, son of T. Marvin Estes, a QA&P conductor, in his novel *Another Part of the House.*[12]

A constant problem for the railroad, especially during the first three decades of its existence, was livestock on the right-of-way. The early position of Sam Lazarus was that claims resulting from collisions between livestock and trains should be paid "if there was any liability at all" because he did not want to "antagonize settlers and shippers" Local officials responded with a policy of paying "market price" for cattle—about four cents per pound in 1911. The rate of "slaughter" rose dramatically, how-

ever, and the company was forced to reassess its policy. Many cases were settled out of court because, as one official said, "it is cheaper to pay them than to stand a law suit." Moreover, it was almost impossible for the railroad to win suits of this nature. Texas law was specific: "Each railroad shall be liable to the owner for the value of all stock killed or injured by the locomotives and cars of such railroad company." Furthermore, the railroad had difficulty winning cases of any type in its service area. "It looks like courts and juries will absolutely ignore the testimony of railroad witnesses, and decide a case on mere shadows of evidence," said one disgusted railroad attorney after he had tried and lost what he thought was an "airtight case" involving a "cow killing." Another QA&P lawyer, G. E. Hamilton, pointed out that plaintiffs would claim the value of an animal "just under $100, and therefore too small to permit appeal beyond the county court."

He and other QA&P officers concluded that the company had "no possible chance of beating this kind of case in a Justice of the Peace Court." Local sentiment—"frontier justice"—was against it; the livestock owner had every advantage. A flood of payments resulted: for the loss of a Jersey cow that "passed through the defendant's [railroad's] fence into a field of sorghum and overate herself, dying from the effects"; for two horses that became frightened and ran into the barbed wire fence damaging themselves to the point of requiring destruction; for a bay mule killed on a bridge; and for three hogs killed by train 2.[13]

Railroad officials knew that they were victimized by livestock owners and those who claimed to be such and, as a result, they were as concerned with strays as with animals whose ownership was know. For instance, when a stray horse roamed the property near Lazare in 1930, the company's attorney urged its immediate removal: "If the train should kill him his 'master' will show up promptly with a claim for the death of a Thoroughbred, Steeldust, or Hamiltonian horse." In other cases railroaders were convinced that livestock owners sometimes dragged dead animals to the right-of-way and then filed bogus claims against the railroad.[14]

There were, of course, circumstances that were beyond the control of either the rancher or the railroader. Livestock, particularly cattle, were frequently spooked by the sound of locomotive whistles and the noise of passing trains and often manifested their anxiety by tearing through right-of-way fences. This made difficult work for railroaders and stockmen and placed the lives of the animals in jeopardy. That same right-of-way, though, became particularly attractive when rains failed and the ranges dried up because railroad property remained lush by comparison, and no fence could keep stock from answering instincts of survival.[15]

## CHAPTER 20

# Tradition, Trauma, and Transition

I might also say at this time that consideration
should be given to an extension of our line to Lubbock at the earliest opportunity.—Charles H. Sommer to C. C. Kratky, August 27, 1946

THE circumstance of the Quanah, Acme & Pacific
Railway during the immediate postwar period was
predictably mixed. It had enjoyed a heavy and profitable freight business during the war years, but, as
Charles Sommer told the company's directors, the
"property was badly run down" because of the
heavy pounding it had taken and because labor and
materials had been in short supply. Business remained good following the end of hostilities and
could be expected to improve; yet treated ties and
new or relay rail of ninety-pound section remained
scarce. Nevertheless, Sommer and Quin Baker, the
vice-president and general manager since the death
of A. F. Sommer in 1945, pressed an improvement
program. In 1949, the QA&P installed thirteen miles
of ninety-pound rail, an impressive 37,858 ties, and
completed ballasting of the main line with chatt.
This work was necessary, W. L. Richardson pointed
out, to retain the impressive volume of overhead
traffic now moving via Floydada. Indeed, this traffic
was the company's greatest source of revenue, followed in importance by gypsum products billed at
Acme, cotton, wheat, and maize. Altogether, revenues produced $241,959 net income for 1949, and
the QA&P paid all back interest owed the Frisco.
But Sommer and Baker understood that several
changes soon would be required to keep the road
profitable.[1]

One persistent thorn was the QA&P's passenger operation. Regular passenger service between
Quanah and Floydada had resulted in nearly continuous red ink during the Depression because of
the paucity of population in the QA&P's service
area as well as the public's growing devotion to
the automobile. The number of autos registered in
Hardeman County alone had grown from 1,709 in
1923 to 3,341 in 1928, and these numbers had increased even in hard times. To offset revenue short-

falls, the Quanah Route replaced passenger trains
with mixed service effective December 11, 1939.[2]

Debits from passenger offerings (i.e., tickets, mail,
express, miscellaneous), remained, but by crediting
freight revenues from mixed service, trains 1 and 2
earned net profits. These trains provided humble if
friendly service for the few persons who chose to
use them, and local folks still came down to visit
with passengers while mail and express were loaded
and unloaded and the train crew performed switching duties. And the trains still stopped for the convenience of patrons—even at undesignated stations
such as "Ginsite," a few miles west of Paducah. Sad
to say, however, the passenger car was empty rather
more often than not.[3]

Mixed train operation was a necessary compromise, but it also yielded constant problems. Scheduling, hardly designed to interest passenger volume, was arranged to expedite passover freight
between the Frisco and the Santa Fe at Floydada and
to provide easy connection for mail and express at
Quanah from the Denver Road's Dallas-to-Denver
passenger train 8. But heavy head end business
and monumental passenger numbers occasioned by
World War II meant that number 8 was frequently
late, and the QA&P in these instances ordered its
number 1 off to Floydada with remunerative freight
for the AT&SF but without mail and express. In
other cases, the QA&P waited for the FW&DC's
number 8 or for a tardy Frisco freight, although this
made the Quanah Route's number 1 late on its appointed rounds. In either instance, the QA&P's decision enraged the Post Office Department, the
Railway Express Agency, and their patrons. Postmasters complained that when number 1 was off
schedule rural carriers could not complete their
routes until after dark, and in at least one case Bor-
den ice cream from Amarillo consigned to Hall's

Drugstore at Paducah suffered irreparable damage when it failed connection at Quanah.[4]

Partial relief came in 1943 when the QA&P determined to run numbers 1 and 2 "as straight passenger trains, except when we have freight cars to move." It was not double-talk, although departure times were admittedly confusing. When the train handled freight, it left Quanah at 4:30 A.M.; when it carried passengers only, departure was set at 6:15 A.M. In this way, A. F. Sommer argued, postal and express schedules could be protected. Carloads of freight handled by these two trains reflected the change, ranging from 371 in September 1943 to only 27 two months later.[5]

W. L. Richardson urged that the company alter schedules and again acquire a gas-electric motor car to provide requisite passenger service. In part, Richardson was motivated to protect and expand the lucrative overhead freight business and, in part, he sincerely believed that the QA&P was "not getting its share of the existing passenger traffic." The war, after all, resulted in rationing of both gasoline and rubber tires. But while "other railroads and the busses" were "doing a land office" business, the "QA&P had practically no" demand west of Quanah. "The reason," said Richardson, was "plainly because of the present service. Adjust the service to the point where the public can use it, and it will be used." But the potential was inadequate, Charles Sommer concluded.[6]

Consequently, the QA&P continued to provide what really amounted to mixed train service from Quanah to Floydada. Revenue from all passenger service predictably turned up during the war and then, just as predictably, turned downward thereafter. The record from the Quanah station illustrates. In 1940, sales there amounted to a mere $1,311, rising to $9,627 in 1944, and then dropping to only $3,465 in 1948. These totals, of course, included tickets sold for the Red River line and Frisco connection. During the first three months of 1947, 358 persons rode numbers 1 and 2, but only 222 were revenue-producing, and in the twelve months following April 1947, the two trains yielded only $858.98 in ticket sales.[7]

To advance freight interests over passenger made perfect sense to Charles Sommer, but it was a continuing frustration for the Post Office Department, which advised the company in May 1948 that it was contemplating the cancellation of en-route sorting performed by the Quanah & Floydada RPO. Sommer was thoroughly alarmed. The mail contracts, as Richardson observed, had been "one of Mr.

Sommer's pets for a very long time." Richardson meant, of course, that the QA&P's president had been "present at the beginning" and retained a deep nostalgia for passenger trains. At the same time, though, Sommer and Richardson both understood that without mail revenues, passenger operation west of Quanah would be an intolerable loser—a fact, however, that the Railroad Commission of Texas might choose to ignore in any discontinuance hearings.[8]

Management considered options, of which there were four: relinquish the mail contract and seek discontinuance of the mixed trains; offer full passenger service using a motor car; offer full passenger service using a traditional steam train; or establish truck service to hold the mail contract. Sommer quickly dismissed the first and last options, and the second was eliminated when the Frisco advised that it could not supply a motor car of the type required. Thus on July 27, 1948, the QA&P reinstituted "full" passenger service between Quanah and Floydada. The Post Office had already determined to cancel the mail contract, but a remarkably concerted local campaign in support of the railroad plus the establishment of real passenger trains forced an abrupt reversal of that decision.[9]

None of it made any difference. By April 1949, Sommer reluctantly concluded that there was "no prospect of increasing our revenue from passenger train operation to the point where we could break even." He also decided to "forego any consideration of attempting roadway bus transportation," but he toyed endlessly with the possibility of reinstituting mixed service. Quin Baker, always diplomatic with Sommer, gingerly counseled otherwise. Sommer gave in. "We take considerable pride in this small passenger train and the service it renders," Baker told T. E. Shoemake of the Railway Mail Service, but "at the same time, this will not pay the expenses and we have lost money every month for the last year." Indeed, the service attracted an average of only 1.2 passengers per train; net losses from August 1948 through July 1949 aggregated $29,560. Papers were filed with the Railroad Commission of Texas asking permission to remove the trains. Hearings at Paducah late in 1949 produced only scattered opposition. Approval came shortly thereafter; the last runs were scheduled for February 18, 1950.[10]

The *Fort Worth Star-Telegram* called it "the passing of an era," but Douglas Meador in the *Matador Tribune* was more expansive. "There was a plaintive note in the engine's whistle," wrote Mea-

Quin Baker, striding away from the train toward the photographer, was unemotional as the end came for passenger service west of Quanah. *E. B. Marsalis collection*

dor, "the melancholy pain of departure—spurred by the spasm of death." Quin Baker was joined by many others from the Quanah offices and by several retirees, including engineer Bill Norman and conductor C. L. Graham, who had handled the first train into Swearingen back in 1910. Up ahead, the careful hand of Elton B. Marsalis was on the throttle of locomotive 695; his father had served as engineer on the first QA&P passenger train into Floydada. The mood was varied. The laughter of children contradicted the sober talk of gray-haired oldsters who exchanged stories of times gone by and speculated nervously about a world devoid of passenger trains. Conductor T. Marvin Estes recalled that he had met his wife of more than forty years when she used the QA&P to get from Acme to school in Quanah. But most of all, Estes kept his own counsel, Douglas Meador reported, standing on the back platform watching "two ribbons of steel unroll from the spools of time." Two days later, auditor J. W. Sampley completed the final tally sheet on trains 1 and 2—still labeled the *Plainsman* on his archaic forms. The last runs, Sampley dryly recorded, had handled 102 "free" passengers and 59 "revenue" patrons yielding $43.17.[11]

Charles Sommer could not bring himself to make the last runs. Perhaps he had too much of an emotional investment in the trains. But he was there in spirit. As early as 1927 he had told Congressman Marvin Jones that "the private automobile and the bus lines have simply played havoc with our passenger traffic." To preserve local service he had persuaded the Frisco to expand through service to Floydada as soon as QA&P rails reached that place. The result was the *Plainsman*—"Sommer's train," with much of the equipment proudly stenciled "Quanah, Acme & Pacific" on the letterboards. But the *Plainsman* died an early death when the Frisco's J. M. Kurn ordered a reduction in train miles and cut off the Oklahoma City–Red River segment. As a consequence, Sommer lamented, "We had to pull off our end of the run." In reality, only by attaching the combination RPO-express car and coach to

freight trains had service to Floyd County survived this long.[12]

The Quanah Route, of course, continued as a nominal purveyor of passenger service over the 8.1-mile segment of line between Red River and Quanah. Traffic there for the Frisco's continuing service to Lawton, Oklahoma City, and beyond was better than west of Quanah, but—except for the war years—showed little vitality (see table 12).

The Frisco accordingly petitioned to remove the trains in 1953, gaining permission two years later. Collaterally, the QA&P obtained authorization to end its participation following the arrival of train 409 on July 17, 1955.[13]

Sommer had an equally strong attachment for steam locomotives, especially those owned by the QA&P, but in the matter of dieselization he would have little choice. When the United States entered World War II the Quanah Route owned five loco-

TABLE 12
**Passengers and Passenger Revenue, Red River Line**

| Month/Year | Total passengers in and out of Quanah over Red River Line | QA&P revenues |
|---|---|---|
| November 1937 | 132 | $ 20.80 |
| November 1938 | 126 | $ 21.42 |
| November 1939 | 77 | $ 13.20 |
| November 1940 | 101 | $ 16.16 |
| November 1941 | 124 | $ 19.53 |
| November 1942 | 1,901 | $322.04 |
| November 1943 | 1,890 | $348.72 |
| November 1944 | 2,038 | $387.85 |
| November 1945 | 945 | $180.06 |
| November 1946 | 414 | $ 76.36 |
| November 1947 | 233 | $ 45.22 |
| November 1948 | 175 | $ 37.21 |

Crew members on the last QA&P passenger trip west of Quanah included, left to right, T. M. Estes, conductor; E. B. Marsalis, engineer; Horton Murphy, fireman; and J. W. Reynolds, brakeman. *E. B. Marsalis collection*

motives—25 and 27 (4-6-0s), 101 (2-8-0), and 31 and 33 (0-6-0s); all were elderly and were held together only through the tender devotion of the road's mechanical force. The torch awaited 25 in 1945, 26 in 1946, and 33 and 101 in 1947. Thereafter only switcher 33 legitimately carried QA&P colors, although leased Frisco 4-6-0s, 2-8-0s, and 2-10-0s often were stenciled for the home road, carrying bolted plates admitting SL-SF ownership. Sommer and Baker both liked the arrangement. They were familiar with steam, and they liked to exercise control over their motive power inventory. Moreover, the road's labor agreements held down costs of doubleheading when tonnage required, and the lease arrangement with the Frisco was generous in the extreme—only $5 per locomotive day.[14]

The Frisco was also happy with this arrangement. It had begun its dieselization program and had plenty of steam power of the type required by the QA&P. Between 1945 and 1950, the Quanah Route ordinarily leased two 4-6-0s and three 2-10-0s at a time, although the smaller road drew addi-

tional power during wheat rushes and when there were unexpected surges in overhead traffic.

Diesel salesmen, as might be expected, came calling at Quin Baker's office at Quanah and at Charles Sommer's suite in St. Louis. The two men toyed with the idea of acquiring units for the QA&P's account. Sommer, frightened by potential disaster occasioned by war in Korea, sought a decision on internal combustion, but the parent's president, Clark Hungerford, insisted on systemwide dieselization using Frisco units. The parent initially assigned diesel power to Quanah from West Tulsa only for expedited trains, but on July 31, 1950, when the QA&P found itself embarrassingly short of steam power, three Alco units (5221, 5310, 5220) handled forty-five loads to Floydada. Two weeks later, three General Motors products (5037A, 5113B, 5003A), accompanied by Frisco's vice-president of operations, took sixty-one loads to the AT&SF. All of this brought a smile to the face of Charles Sommer, who was amazed by the ability of diesel power to lift tonnage over the QA&P's difficult profile be-

Revenues slipped on the SL-SF/QA&P passenger operation between Quanah and Oklahoma City. In 1946, two coaches were required (seen here near Creta, Oklahoma, on June 1), but by 1955 the consist was down to one coach (between Red River and Quanah). *Preston George photograph*

Charles Sommer and Quin Baker liked the arrangement allowing the QA&P to lease power from the Frisco. Here, the 1620 hurries twenty-four cars of Quanah-bound freight near Indianhoma, Oklahoma, in May 1946. *Preston George photograph*

Diesel products from Alco and GM astonished old heads by easily lifting heavy tonnage over the QA&P's difficult profile. The reign of steam was at an end.

The vanquished shunted aside. *J. M. George photograph, E. B. Marsalis collection*

tween Lazare and the Caprock, by reductions in over-the-road train times, and by savings in labor.[15]

Yet the parent road could not immediately supply enough units to dieselize the QA&P. During the winter of 1950–51, diesels were used only when westbound tonnage otherwise required doubleheading 1600s. By early spring, however, steam trains were assigned solely to the triweekly local to Floydada, and on May 21 Quin Baker announced that all service was now diesel-powered. When 2-10-0 number 1624 was returned to the Frisco on June 11, Baker reported to Sommer that "this leaves us without any steam locomotives." The Frisco assigned a pool of recently acquired EMD GP-7 road switchers to a West Tulsa–Oklahoma City–Quanah–Floydada pool, among them numbers 546, 547, and 564 lettered for but not owned by the QA&P. These and all others employed on the QA&P were rented on a unit-mile basis. Full dieselization was interrupted, though, when floods elsewhere diverted so much business to the Frisco that steam reappeared again for about two weeks in July. But that was the end of it. Water tanks and fuel oil facilities were indecorously retired and dismantled to end forever the gallant era of steam on the Quanah Route. At the end of February 1952, the Frisco announced that the entire system had been dieselized.[16]

If Charles Sommer waxed nostalgic over passenger trains and steam locomotives, he was totally without emotion on the matter of the QA&P's tenuous route structure and limited service area. Sommer, of course, had long advocated extension of the QA&P to El Paso for the purpose of opening a broad new territory and forging an attractive short-mile route for overhead traffic moving to and from California via the Southern Pacific. Those plans, which had been considered since 1910, had been frustrated by recession and depression, indecision and hesitancy among senior officers of the Frisco, and war. In the late 1920s, Sommer had made a personal reconnaissance and had "reported favorably on several routes, but," as Sommer recalled, "the whole matter was compromised at that time with an extension to Floydada, much to my regret." He was referring to the sad reality of meeting the Santa Fe at the end of one of its branches instead of making a secure junction with a main artery. Local traffic, he had always known, could not sustain the road, and passover business via Floydada suffered because of the Santa Fe's philosophy, which bordered between indifference and hostility. Even now the Santa Fe refused to schedule regular Sunday service.[17]

When the 1624, with drive rods removed, was delivered to the SL-SF, Quin Baker could announce that QA&P's service was entirely diesel powered. *J. M. George photograph, E. B. Marsalis collection*

The possibility of extending the QA&P to El Paso "over a route through the oil fields of West Texas and New Mexico and through the potash beds" surfaced again after World War II, but by mid-1950 Sommer was forced to admit "that it is definitely out of the picture and no interest is manifested [by the Frisco] in such a project." That did not mean, however, that Sommer had given up on gaining for the QA&P a more suitable western terminus. Lubbock remained enticing. Indeed, he told Quin Baker, "there is no question in my mind—and I have known this for twenty years—that we missed the boat by not building into Lubbock. . . . I have used everything at my command to interest the powers that be, especially during Mr. Kurn's regime, but I could not interest anyone in the potentialities that were clear to me if only we could extend our line as far as Lubbock." Sommer pointed out that this would obviate the Santa Fe's constant complaint about moving transcontinental traffic over its doglegged route to Floydada, would favor the Quanah Route in its campaign to increase overhead business, and would expand opportunities for local billings. After all, Sommer exclaimed, "Lubbock has grown by leaps and bounds and bids to outrival Amarillo." On August 27, 1946, Sommer urged the Frisco's trustee to consider "an extension of our line to Lubbock at the earliest opportunity."[18]

Actually, Sommer had asked for preliminary construction estimates as early as the summer of 1940 for some thirteen miles of line west from Floydada to Barwise, on the Fort Worth & Denver City, thirty-one miles above Lubbock. The war intervened before action could be taken, but thereafter

GP-7 locomotives 546, 547, and 564 were lettered for but were not owned by the QA&P. *Everett L. DeGolyer, Jr., photograph*

Redundant now that steam had disappeared, water facilities and eventually even the roundhouse at Quanah would be retired.

Sommer directed Baker to study the prospect of getting in and out of Lubbock "with an independently constructed line" or, as an alternative, "using the FW&DC" from Barwise or Petersburg. "Primarily," Sommer reminded Baker, "our interest is to afford an interchange with the Santa Fe." Sommer had already gotten a tentative agreement from the Denver Road and had made favorable arrangements in Lubbock for the interchange of traffic with the AT&SF.[19]

Meanwhile, Sommer asked W. L. Richardson for his views. Richardson was confident that sufficient new business could be attracted to justify the extension but worried "about the attitude of the ICC toward an application to build a new line *which would not produce new traffic but which would mainly take existing traffic from other carriers* [FW&DC and AT&SF]." That concern led him to suggest "going beyond Lubbock" because such additional expansion would "enable us to show *public convenience and necessity* by being able to give rail service to a large territory presently without it." Richardson knew that this dream would not become reality. Regarding possible problems with the Santa Fe if the QA&P reached Lubbock, Richardson joined with legal counsel in asserting that the Floydada gateway case and others favored the QA&P in retention of a through route, that is, the interchange of transcontinental traffic at Lubbock as opposed to Floydada.[20]

More firmly convinced than ever "that there are unlimited opportunities in which to greatly increase our volume of traffic via the Quanah Route through a direct connection at Lubbock with a main line of the Santa Fe," Sommer again pressed the matter. Early in 1952, he formally urged Frisco president Clark Hungerford to authorize the extension he had so long held dear. The effervescent Sommer missed no opportunity to press the issue among officers and directors of the Frisco, shippers, public officials, and opinion makers. Yet he had to admit to the Lubbock Chamber in August that plans were "moving slowly." Sommer hoped that an expansive tour of Lubbock and environs and a reception for Hungerford as well as other top officers would "put the icing on the cake," but it did not work out that way.[21]

The fly in the ointment proved to be Theodore H. Banister, vice-president of traffic for the Frisco. Banister thought extension to Lubbock might benefit the QA&P but not its parent. Sommer was utterly confounded and wondered if Banister considered the QA&P "a foreign railroad." In the end,

Sommer thundered, all revenues went into "one pocket" because it was "the Frisco system that we have all been working for." It fell to Richardson to make the case with Banister. Yet having Richardson handle the situation had its problems. By this time he was the Quanah Route's executive vice-president, but he was required to defer to the parent road's Banister. Both were proud men with massive egos; collision was inevitable. Then, too, Sommer's perception of the Frisco's attitude toward the QA&P— a "down the nose" view—was essentially accurate. Managers of the larger company never seemed to grasp the reality that the QA&P, as an independently managed yet totally captive extension of the parent, contributed an outsized division on interline billings. In any event, Banister did not take kindly to Richardson's reminder that what was good for the Quanah Route was "certainly good for the parent." Banister's response was icy: "I am not prepared to change my views." Sommer was exasperated. "I GIVE UP!," he exploded in a letter to Richardson.[22]

But it was not in Sommer's character to give up. Even after his retirement as an officer, he remained on the QA&P board, was kept fully informed on all matters, and remained a force within the Frisco Building at St. Louis. As late as 1954, he joined Baker and Richardson to pore over maps looking for some way out of the trap at Floydada. Collectively they persuaded Clark Hungerford to consider four options: construction from Floydada to Barwise (12.3 miles) with trackage rights to Lubbock over FW&D; construction from Floydada to Petersburg (15.5 miles) with trackage rights to Lubbock over FW&D; trackage rights to Plainview over the AT&SF and construction from Plainview to Muleshoe (60.7 miles) with trackage rights over the AT&SF into Clovis, New Mexico; or trackage rights to Plainview over the AT&SF, trackage rights over the FW&D from Plainview to Hart, construction from Hart to Farwell, Texas with trackage rights over the AT&SF into Clovis, New Mexico. Sommer reminded Hungerford that Sam Lazarus had gained a written promise from Santa Fe president E. P. Ripley in 1912 to allow the QA&P access to Plainview. It mattered not at all. Banister remained obdurate, and his view prevailed in Frisco councils. Even Sommer had to admit at the end of 1954 that the issue was "dormant for the present." In fact, the matter was not dormant, it was dead. The ramifications were awesome for the QA&P's future.[23]

Sommer had known significant disappointments

during his long career—the worst being the QA&P's inability to escape its dead-ended route structure—but there was much that was impressive in his stewardship. He had seen the road safely through the terrible days of the Depression, the life-threatening Floydada gateway case, the chaos of the war years, and the many transitions since 1945. Employment had gone from 121 in 1938 to 207 in 1951; the number of carloads handled had dropped from a pre-Depression high of 13,446 in 1929 to 8,704 in 1935 but stood proudly at 35,613 in 1951; and freight revenues had bottomed in 1935 at a paltry $241,900 but rebounded to a vibrant $2,766,931 in 1951. Moreover, Sommer had authorized an impressive policy of line improvements, had kept the operating ratio at an enviable 50.93 for the six years following World War II, and had maintained a healthy surplus. Payment of dividends to the parent was resumed in 1951. In short, Charles Henry Sommer bequeathed a healthy and prosperous property when he turned over full managerial reins to Quin Baker effective January 1, 1952.[24]

## CHAPTER 21

# *The* Belle Epoque

I would like to suggest that instead of using the
nickname you mention ["Quit Arguing & Push"],
that you substitute "Quick As Possible."—Charles
H. Sommer to Laura V. Hamner, June 8, 1949.

DURING the 1950s and into the early 1970s the
Quanah, Acme & Pacific reaped the happy harvest
of Charles Sommer's long labors. The years 1952–
64, when Quin Baker served as president, were especially rewarding. Indeed, the QA&P in 1962
was reclassified by the Interstate Commerce Commission as a Class I carrier—reflecting the road's
impressive growth in volume of business and
revenues.[1]

The Quanah Route's long-standing determination to play a major role in transcontinental passover business was rooted, of course, in a selfish
but understandable purpose: survival. All four
counties in the QA&P's abbreviated service area
had reached their maximum populations between
1920 and 1940. Agricultural production in the area
had turned up following the Depression and, with
increased irrigation around Dougherty and Floydada, promised even more growth in the future. All
of it, however, was susceptible to competition from
trucks, which benefited more and more from a net-
work of farm-to-market roads and an expanded system of federal highways. For example, two state
roadway projects were completed in Hardeman
County in 1946–48, one serving Lazare, a station
on the QA&P at which wheat and cotton shipments immediately declined as a consequence. At
the same time, W. L. Richardson was properly concerned over the loss of long-haul billings. He noted
in 1949 that trucks could make delivery from
Quanah to Los Angeles in forty-eight to fifty
hours. Clearly, the QA&P could not live on local
business.[2]

That did not mean that the Quanah Route ignored its service area and local customers. Indeed,
company officers and agents along the line took an
almost "mother hen" approach to carlot as well as
LCL shippers. The trend of LCL business on the

QA&P, however, mirrored what was happening everywhere. Better public roads led to greater competition from trucks, which produced ton miles for
such business more efficiently and often offered
customers greater flexibility than the rails. Set-out
and "way" cars were still employed by the Quanah
Route to distribute the little LCL business that remained, and pickup and delivery at Quanah, Paducah, Roaring Spring, and Floydada were provided
under contract with local drayman. Yet there was
less and less need for these services. Combined
volume of LCL shipments at those four stations
dropped from 161,986 pounds for August 1948 to
only 102,573 pounds in 1949.[3]

The movement of wheat from farms tributary to
the QA&P presented a more optimistic picture.
When the annual crop was harvested, a great rush
occurred. As one company officer put it, the "combines worked day and night, and so much grain
was gathered that the problem of transporting it
to the elevators became acute—every known type
of vehicle being pressed into service." It was much
the same with the railroad. Empty boxes were
spotted at elevator spouts, and at the peak of activity a "tramp switcher" worked Dougherty,
Boothe Spur, and Floydada. During the age of
steam, a 1600 handled twenty-five loads eastbound
to Roaring Springs, twenty cars to Quanah, with a
Quanah–Roaring Springs turn shuffling the resi-
due. The wheat rush was hectic. Most cars moved
to Fort Worth or to the Gulf for export via Quanah
and the Denver Road or, to gain maximum haul for
the QA&P/Frisco, Altus, Oklahoma, and the Missouri-Kansas-Texas. But trucks were encroaching
on this profitable business, too. The Lon Davis
Grain Company of Floydada reported that two-
thirds of its 1959 wheat crop moved by truck.[4]

Cotton provided local as well as overhead revenue. Every station boasted loadings before World War I, and Dougherty and Floydada were added to this list after completion of the Floydada extension. Before World War II, however, Carnes, Lazare, and Swearingen dropped out. Gins at Floydada, Roaring Springs, and Paducah accounted for the greatest volume. Most shipments were billed to the compress at Quanah and the rebilled to Gulf ports for export via Quanah and the FW&D or Altus and the M-K-T. Quin Baker was pleased to tell W. L. Richardson that 82 percent of the 1960 production from QA&P's service area had reached Quanah by rail and that 92 percent of the compressed cotton had gone forward in the same fashion. Richardson had good news of his own. Cotton from California and Arizona was moving to southeastern mills via Floydada and the Quanah Route.[5]

Richardson's active mind found additional opportunities for agricultural traffic near Floydada when producers from the Rio Grande Valley undertook to grow carrots, onions, peppers, and other produce in West Texas. The first carload of carrots left for Memphis, Tennessee, on October 23, 1948. Thereafter the company built an attractive vegetable shed that was leased to processors; ice for refrigerator cars came from the Floydada Ice Company at $10 per ton. Volume was good for a few years, but truckers eventually captured nearly all of the fresh vegetable business. The shed was sold in 1966.[6]

Another commodity that continued to show up on traffic reports was water, which moved from Roaring Springs to Paducah for the Coca-Cola plant, to a distributor there who sold it door-to-door for drinking and laundry purposes, and to company section houses and for locomotive use at Paducah and OX Tank. Occasionally, during exceptionally dry periods, the QA&P also moved water to Quanah to maintain greenery around the company's office building. And in 1953, when a critical shortage developed at the Certain-teed Products plant in Acme, the road handled emergency shipments to satisfy industrial and personal needs. Ten company-owned tank cars were retained for this purpose, but they were scrapped after the city of Paducah developed its own supply system and the QA&P terminated use of steam locomotives.[7]

The histories of the livestock industry and the QA&P had been intertwined since the inception of the railroad. Typically, yearling cattle moved from local ranges in the spring and stocker sheep arrived early in the winter, but drought—such as occurred in 1946—resulted in the heavy movement of live animals to Iowa, Illinois, and other states in the upper Midwest during summer months. Isolated cars of stocker and slaughter animals moved in all seasons, although most of this business now went by truck. Further changes would come. By 1950, only six major livestock shippers still used the railroad; the shipment of livestock in LCL lots had ended in 1942.[8]

For the Quanah Route and for the railroad industry in general, the handling of livestock was always a mixed blessing. Large consignments, moving as a unit from origin to destination, were good business, but isolated billings could be bothersome. Moveover, as slaughter movements increasingly passed to truckers, the rails were left with only seasonal movements; meanwhile, rolling stock, pens, chutes, and watering facilities were left unused, and when faced with the need to repair or dismantle, managers often chose the latter. The result was complaints from shippers, who ironically had brought about the problem by turning more and more to rubber tires and hardtop roads. It was a vicious cycle, and it was compounded by other problems. Ranchers frequently delivered their animals to the pens after the train had left, or failed to show up at all, sticking the railroad company with car rental payments. If animals were loaded at Narcisso, Russellville, Dougherty, or MacBain, agents from open stations were required to take typewriters, seals, billing materials, and even portable telephones to these remote locations to accomplish their duties. Federal requirements for feed, water, and rest after thirty-six hours of confinement were certainly appropriate to provide humane treatment of animals but were expensive for the carriers and pointed up their relative disadvantage compared to trucks—especially for isolated carload lots. And there were endless claims with attendant bureaucratic paperwork. All in all, livestock carriage was "not ordinarily considered a good freight tonnage," as even W. L. Richardson had admitted as early as 1933.[9]

The QA&P did not actively discourage local livestock shipments or overhead livestock business, but neither did it encourage them. By 1950, livestock accounted for only 1.3 percent of all carloads, and before another decade passed facilities were removed at Lazare, Swearingen, and Roaring Springs. Moreover, Quin Baker insisted on an exact accounting for every movement. He discovered, as a result, that on a $6,116.40 billing of thirty carloads from Russellville to Pukwana, South Dakota, in 1964, the QA&P earned net of a mere $134.92.

TABLE 13
**Shipments from Acme, 1947–1950**

| Year | Total cars | QA&P | Percent |
|------|-----------|------|---------|
| 1947 | 6,553 | 5,060 | 78 |
| 1948 | 6,918 | 5,810 | 85 |
| 1949 | 5,782 | 4,862 | 84 |
| 1950 | 7,753 | 6,721 | 87 |

SOURCE: Compiled from data in letters of CHS to Clark Hungerford, Mar. 13, 1947, Feb. 3, 1948, Feb. 9, 1950, and Feb. 16, 1951.

The decline in volume and profitability continued. Remaining facilities at Narcisso, MacBain, Russellville, and Paducah were retired between 1969 and 1973, and all service ended with cancellation of regional and transcontinental tariffs in 1972 and 1973.[10]

The movement of livestock was deeply rooted in the life and times of the QA&P, but even more important historically, and infinitely more rewarding in net revenue, was the handling of plaster products from Acme. Although the QA&P was forced to share shipments with the Denver Road, a great majority was billed by the Quanah Route (see table 13).[11]

The number of loadings dropped in later years as gypsum deposits elsewhere were tapped, as car capacity was increased, and as truck competition accelerated. This was extremely profitable business—intrastate divisions ranged from 11.3 percent to 26 percent depending on destination—and W. L. Richardson did everything possible to protect it. In his own inimitable way, he lectured Quin Baker as well as Frisco personnel, for example, on the matter of providing bulkhead flatcars. Railroaders tended to dislike making expenditures for "special equipment" but, in Richardson's words, had "paid dearly through traffic losses for their failure to recognize and keep step with progress." The Frisco, he complained, "has been one such line." But eventually the SL-SF did yield, and bulkhead flats were made available for wallboard shipments at Acme.[12]

Revenue adequate to make the QA&P a profitable and healthy railroad with a positive future simply could not be derived from local business, however. With that knowledge, the company's management had for more than two decades labored with tenacious diligence to attract overhead traffic as "meat and potatoes" over which "gravy" from local loadings might add a pleasant relish. The Santa Fe, which had done nothing since the ICC order of 1938 to assist the Quanah Route in promoting interchange via the Floydada gateway, remained as intransigent as ever following World

War II. Finally, however, the AT&SF agreed late in 1950 to provide Sunday service on a regular basis, and William Richardson immediately ordered a broad advertising campaign alerting shippers of reliable seven-day-a-week service via Floydada. Volume picked up immediately. A total of 23,018 overhead loads (15,010 westbound, 8,008 eastbound) passed over rails of the Quanah Route in 1953. Even the Frisco, which had always been lukewarm to the QA&P's aspirations, came around. As 1954 dawned, the SL-SF assigned EMD F-3 and F7 locomotives to through runs all the way from St. Louis to Floydada. The purpose, as Richardson gleefully noted, was to "further improve service."[13]

The task of overseeing the QA&P's improved fortunes fell to the shoulders of the able and affable Quin Baker. He relished it. Many officers at the Frisco jealously complained when it seemed that he had carte blanche from the parent company. Baker grinned and shrugged off that assertion but quietly poured every penny he could find into the property. Retirement of the old waybill press at Floydada in 1952 represented a perfect symbol of change. The installation of carrier telephone circuits and printer service between the Frisco and the QA&P was followed by acquisition of teletype machines at Quanah and Acme; a base radio station at Quanah aided in communication with trains and with maintenance forces; and Quin Baker parked his company-owned Oldsmobile in front of the impeccably maintained Mission Style general office building at Quanah.[14]

Nothing, however, was more important to Baker than improvements to roadway. They were many and varied, ranging from the replacement of short trestles with pipe and fill to the installation of dragging equipment and hot-box detectors. All major bridges were strengthened and otherwise modernized, and chatt became the uniform ballast. Rail in the main track was 90- and 100-pound per yard with 115-pound section for the westernmost forty-one miles—all checked on a regular basis by Sperry Rail Service. Moreover, passing tracks at Roaring Springs and Narcisso were extended, and tie plates and rail anchors added strength and stability to the main track. Procedures changed, too. In 1946, the QA&P had used one bridge and building gang and two extra gangs and had six to twenty section laborers at a half-dozen locations. By the mid-1950s, though, the Frisco did the QA&P's bridge work under contract, and most track maintenance was done by machine.[15]

Baker often personally solicited business for the

W. L. Richardson constantly urged the SL-SF to provide bulkhead flats like this one to compete with the Denver Road for wallboard billed at Acme.

The QA&P used two GP-7s on its daily-except-Sunday turn between Quanah and Floydada, one here passing through Paducah, but business boomed when the Santa Fe finally agreed to daily service into and from Floydada.

QA&P. For instance, he reminded a shipper at Quanah—with tongue in cheek—that "we are poor folks . . . and need the 'biz.'" Yet it was the formal responsibility of W. L. Richardson to fill the trains—a task he undertook with verve. With his talented assistants, Charles R. Sherwood and then Stanley M. Blashuk, Richardson monitored the company's sales force, formulated promotional campaigns, and looked endlessly for opportunities to expand the road's traffic base. This included keeping tabs on available routings and the flow of business among all carriers. Before the era of mega-mergers, this was a prodigious task. The movement of a carload of newsprint from Pine Falls, Manitoba, to Los Angeles in 1958 represents only one example among infinite possibilities. The complex routing and carrier participation were as follows: Pine Falls–Winnipeg (Canadian National); Winnipeg–Duluth (Duluth, Winnipeg & Pacific); Duluth–Minneapolis (Great Northern); Minneapolis–Albia, Iowa (Minneapolis & St. Louis); Albia–St. Louis (Wabash); St. Louis–Red River (Frisco); Red River–Floydada (QA&P); and Floydada–Los Angeles (AT&SF). Richardson made sure to advise his counterparts elsewhere about billings made on the QA&P that favored their roads, and most of them reciprocated.[16]

It is impossible to know whether the quality of the QA&P's overhead service got better as traffic volume grew, or if volume grew as service improved. It is clear, though, that both were impressive through the 1950s and 1960s. The name *Red Raven* once had been used for trains handling expedited traffic from St. Louis to Floydada, but in 1950 that identification was changed to the *Flash*. Other and more notable changes came in 1959 when the Frisco, QA&P, and Santa Fe agreed to through

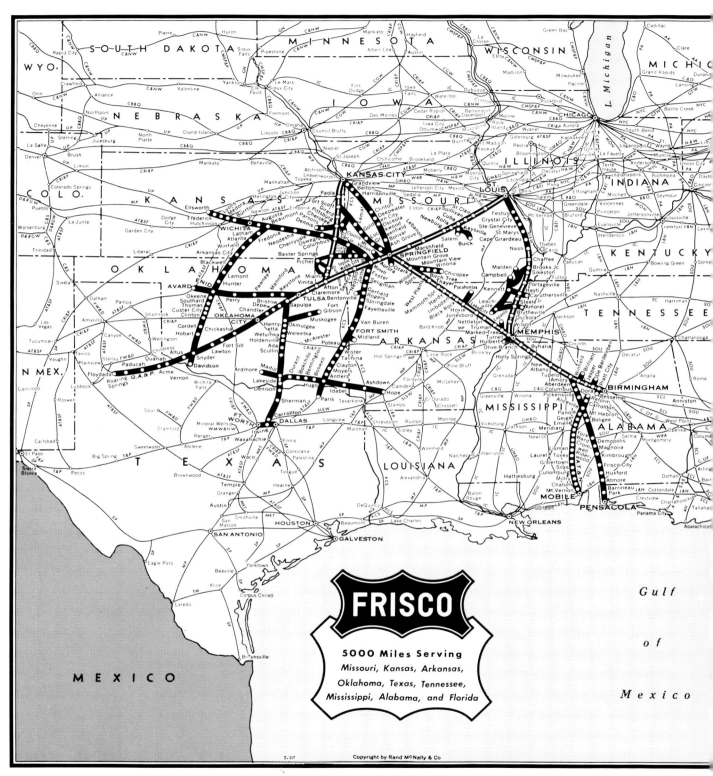

By the early 1960s, QA&P managers had finally persuaded the Frisco that the Floydada gateway should be used for the longest system haul.

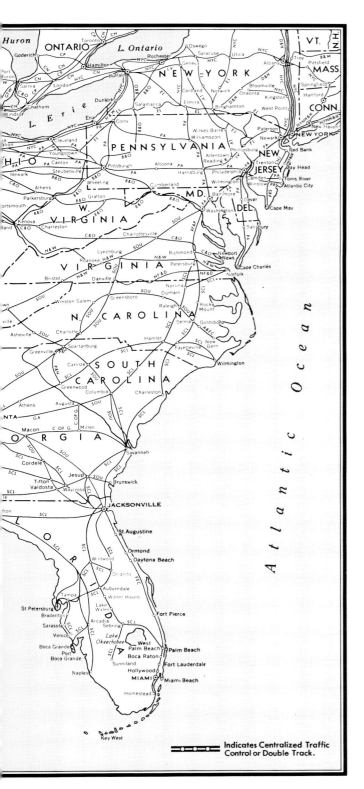

Indicates Centralized Traffic
Control or Double Track.

schedules (power and cabooses changed at Floydada) for two trains in each direction daily. These
became the celebrated QLA (St. Louis–Quanah–
Los Angeles) and the QSF (Birmingham–Quanah–
San Francisco) westbound, and the lesser-known
CTB (Clovis-Birmingham) and number 3310 eastbound. Regular triweekly local schedules survived
into 1963; thereafter such service was provided by
extra trains or by number 3310. A daily turn from
Quanah met the needs of Acme.[17]

Once committed to the Floydada gateway, the
management of all three participating roads eagerly
proctored performance. When the QLA used two
hours and fifty minutes for the 110-mile run from
Quanah to Floydada on September 29, 1962, Quin
Baker thought "we should have done a little better." After all, he pointed out, the QLA of one day
earlier had handled a heavier train in only two
hours and fifteen minutes. Usually, the QA&P did
a good job in getting trains over the line, but admittedly there were exceptions. The AT&SF always
took note. "Knowing your interest in expediting
this business," mocked a Santa Fe operating officer
after one embarrassing performance, "I am quite
sure you will expedite your train so that it will reach
Floydada on time or better." More often than not,
the Frisco was the slowpoke—at least until the
Santa Fe got its attention. Thereafter, Frisco's operating department issued new orders: "Everyone
should see that this train [QLA] is given preferred
handling at all times with no delays and absolute
minimum time spent moving through terminals."[18]

Meanwhile, Richardson looked for still more
business—especially for eastbound movements to
balance the predominantly westward flow. He
found, for example, that potash from Carlsbad,
New Mexico, to connections at Memphis, Tennessee, afforded lucrative revenues for the QA&P and
its parent. At the same time, Richardson pledged to
locate revenue loads for the thirty-five Damage-
Free boxcars that the QA&P leased from General
American Transportation Company in 1955. Richardson's forces also managed to attract a regular
shipment of perishables from California and Arizona. In that way, tiny Quanah, Texas, became " a
regular icing station for all eastbound perishables
via Floydada" and an "emergency icing station for
westbound traffic." That business stopped in 1959,
when volume turned down and more mechanical
refrigerator cars entered service.[19]

One factor remained constant, however: the
problem of getting perishables or any other time-
sensitive traffic through St. Louis. Richardson com-

The QLA usually filled at Tulsa.

plained bitterly in 1957 when the Terminal Railroad Association of St. Louis—itself owned by the Frisco and other trunk roads—failed because of slow reicing to make eastern connections eighteen times out of thirty during one test month. Important business was lost as a consequence. Richardson exploded. "If nothing can be done" to remedy the situation, he explained, "then we shall discontinue the solicitation of this traffic and turn our efforts in other directions." This failure was "at the expense of the TRRA as well as the Frisco and the QA&P." These was no response.[20]

One increasingly important element in the Quanah Route's traffic amalgam—automobiles—was neither transcontinental nor local in nature. The movement of autos by rail was almost negligible by the mid-1950s. Old-fashioned boxcars were inadequate for this haulage, and the industry was shamefully slow in meeting competition. The Great Northern and the Grand Trunk Western had ex-

perimented with handling automobiles on flatcars during the early 1920s, but the idea did not catch on. By 1959, however, the Southern Pacific, the Frisco, and perhaps others were moving truck trailers loaded with automobiles as a part of Trailer-on-Flat-Car (TOFC) business. For the Frisco, this commenced when the Chrysler Corporation began shipments of its 1960 model products from Valley Park, near St. Louis, to Irving, Texas, near Dallas. The new service, Frisco's Clark Hungerford asserted, was "very remunerative to us and it has been of great help to the automobile people." And, added T. H. Banister, "all of this business is new to the rails and does not represent business transferred from boxcars." At the same time, the SL-SF ordered trilevel racks capable of handling twelve conventional or fifteen compact autos.[21]

Even as it prepared to haul automobiles to the metropolitan Dallas area, the Frisco quietly ordered the Quanah Route to make provisions for

The SL-SF planned for the future by improving track structure. Here, the CTB passes through Eldorado, Oklahoma, where a steel gang is installing welded rail.

The QA&P leased thirty-five of these Damage-Free box-cars in 1955.

W. L. Richardson continued to authorize advertising for the QA&P's account, but increasingly the parent road took over such activities.

automobile-handling facilities at Floydada, which would serve as a distribution point for much of West Texas and New Mexico and would give the Frisco/QA&P a line-haul of 830 miles for Chrysler products assembled at St. Louis. The first shipments—Plymouths and Chryslers—arrived on September 24, 1959. Dallas & Mavis Forwarding Company and United Transport provided over-the-road delivery. An unloading ramp for trilevel flats was installed in 1960, and more capacity was added in 1965 and 1968—by which time the QA&P boasted a handsome property featuring five unloading tracks and a large fenced-in holding area. In 1963, the Floydada terminal handled an average of 1,955 vehicles monthly, but that increased to 3,000 in 1969. Moreover, Chrysler vehicles were joined by those from General Motors, American Motors, and International Harvester; Ford was conspicuous by its absence.[22]

Operations during these years of the company's *belle epoque* were a perfect example of efficiency. The exchange of trains and crews between the Frisco and the QA&P in North Quanah took only minutes, and speed of passage across the road's rugged profile was a routine matter. Part of this efficiency reflected management's long-term dedication to making the QA&P a well-respected link in the transcontinental chain, and part represented

Floydada received the first shipment of automobiles in 1959. Expansion followed in 1965 and 1968.

a policy of avoiding per diem charges under car rental agreements.

Procedures called for tonnage of the QLA to be handed to the Santa Fe before midnight. The power was fueled by a Floydada concessionaire, meals were delivered to the crew, eastbound blocks were assembled from the transfer tracks, and—often within thirty minutes or less—the CTB hurried toward Quanah with time-sensitive lading for the Frisco. Elapsed time for the 220-mile turn, Baker noted, was under eight hours. Track conditions warranted a 49-mile-per-hour authorization, he beamed.[23]

The QSF arrived in Floydada a few hours later. Carloads of autos were immediately spotted for unloading, and then the crew exchanged tonnage with the AT&SF before going to eat. Locomotives were fueled, the now empty auto racks gathered, the train put together, and number 3310 headed east doing local work en route. All of this, Baker proudly pointed out, was accomplished with one set of lo-

comotives, one crew, and in compliance with the hours of service law (twelve hours maximum).[24]

The automobile business was lucrative but hardly without problems. Soon after the Frisco signed contracts with Chrysler, new vehicles were showered with sulfuric acid from overhead bridges near St. Louis—presumably the work of disgruntled teamsters. Occasionally sophisticated thieves stole batteries, radios, or hub caps, but on balance the QA&P suffered few claims and little damage from vandals. On one occasion, however, local youths who had a taste for fine automobiles stole a Cadillac from the Floydada lot and showed it off around town for a few hours. Much more irksome for railroaders and truckers alike were autos that arrived with dead batteries, flat tires, or empty gasoline tanks. Other expensive delays to unloading resulted when ignition keys for all autos or one car were lost or misplaced.[25]

Big-time railroading, the QA&P's management learned, had other liabilities. Claims were natural in

The results of the March 8, 1961, derailment of the QLA at Roaring Springs. "Ship It on the Frisco," emblazoned on the side of one car, seemed cruelly misadvised on this day.

the course of business. During the years when the QA&P handled LCL, these were as diverse as pilferage of cookies at Floydada, broken chinaware at Paducah, and damaged picture frames at Quanah. These were small casualties, but they always generated endless and expensive paperwork. Damage sometimes occurred on carload traffic, too. Shortage in wheat on one car billed from Dougherty to Fort Worth in 1963 cost the QA&P $3.24; damage to three sacks of onions shipped to Boston from Floydada in the same year amounted to 28 cents; and the absence of two valve handles and one cigarette lighter on John Deere tractors from Waterloo, Iowa, to Paducah resulted in a bill for $3.52. Other cases were more serious. Fires started by sparks thrown by hot brake shoes ignited floorboards of a boxcar carrying tinplate in 1958 and on a car bearing canned goods a year later. Claims were, respectively, $670.80 and $1,465.28. On another occasion, Cargill Incorporated complained bitterly and with good reason when the entire contents of a tank car

loaded with soybean oil disappeared between the loading facility at Minneapolis and Quanah, where QA&P carmen discovered the problem. The loss was $7,000.[26]

The possibility of great damage and awesome claims was part and parcel of running fast and heavy freights. Fortunately, however, the QA&P suffered few serious derailments. The worst, at least in dollar value, occurred on March 8, 1961, when a semitrailer truck collided with the speeding QLA at the east edge of Roaring Springs. The accident took place in broad daylight at a crossing with clear visibility, but the truck driver and the person accompanying him—both of whom died instantly—apparently did not see the train until they crashed into it. The velocity of impact turned over the outside rail, throwing the hind three of four diesel units and the first twelve of the train's cars off the track. Locomotives and cars were stacked into a space of only 150 feet along the right-of-way; miraculously, none of the crew members was injured.

A shoofly was constructed and wreckers were borrowed from the Frisco and the FW&D to pick up the mess. Officials estimated the loss at $291,500, not to mention two lives.[27]

Claims and losses resulting from derailments notwithstanding, the Quanah Route turned in an extremely impressive performance during the years 1951–73. Total carloads handled rose from 30,909 in 1952 to, as an example, 49,139 in 1961—this in an age when car capacities and thus payload were increasing. In 1966, the QA&P originated or terminated 150,855 tons of freight and bridged another 1,072,830 tons. Indeed, by 1969 about 250 cars daily were interchanged at Floydada. The primary commodities handled by the road during these years were agricultural products, food, paper, chemicals, plaster products, autos, and forwarder loadings.[28]

All of this was accomplished with marvelous efficiency and resulted in splendid profits. Total compensations for officers and contract employees rose to $769,997 in 1961 from $745,631 ten years earlier but dropped to $656,214 in 1971 because fewer employees were needed as a result of technological improvements in motive power, rolling stock, track maintenance, and office procedures and the transfer of certain responsibilities to the parent company. In all, average employment dropped steadily from 169 for the years 1951–60, to 75 for 1961–70, to only 57 for 1971–73. The company's operating ratio reflected this decline: 46.13 for 1951–60; 40.18 for 1961–70; and an admirable 33.58 for 1971–73. Most important, the Quanah Route earned $19,908,214 in net revenue for the years 1951–73, inclusive. Dividends paid to the Frisco ranged from 300 percent in 1951 to 3,500 percent in 1965 (as paid on $150,000 par value of stock, $600,000 in 1951, and $5,250,000 in 1965).[29]

The Quanah, Acme & Pacific Railway was in good physical condition, owned a fine reputation among the shipping public, claimed an extremely handsome division on transcontinental business that it handled on a mere 118 miles (Red River–Quanah–Floydada), and was earning impressive net profits. It had proved itself. The past was prologue, was it not? The future looked bright, did it not?

CHAPTER 22

# Valhalla

Bill's letter sets out good reasons in rebuttal, besides the Quanah Route will be heading straight
for disaster without its transcontinental traffic. The
local business will never sustain the property.—Charles H. Sommer to Robert Quirk, August 12, 1954

CONDUCTOR F. L. Pierce swung aboard the caboose, waved a friendly greeting to the Frisco crew
that had brought the train to Quanah, and then
lifted his radio to tell the head end that he was
aboard: "Highball, QLA." Almost instantly engineer R. L. Choat affirmed, "Highball, QLA," and
widened on the throttle of locomotive number 714.
Exhaust poured from four units, rose upward, and
then flattened as the train gathered speed. A few
minutes later, the FW&D diamond at Acme mut-
tered in complaint beneath weight of the passing
train as it roared off toward the southwest in a val-
iant race with the setting sun. Back in the caboose,
Pierce studied the train list, wrote up his reports,
and gazed at a passing landscape he had seen hundreds of times before. Only two hours and thirty-
five minutes after leaving Quanah, Pierce turned
over both train and waybills to the Santa Fe, which
hustled the tonnage out of town just fifteen minutes later. Meanwhile, Pierce walked to the depot,
signed the train register, and exchanged pleasant-
ries with agent Francis Gunter; the rest of the crew
turned the power, picked up lunches, and doubled
the train together. After a mere thirty minutes,
Pierce again raised his radio: "Highball, CTB." It
all went like clockwork, a matter of routine. But
this was hardly an ordinary trip. Pierce had delivered the last QLA to Floydada; now he was in
charge of the final CTB to use that gateway. The
date was August 1, 1973.[1]

Pierce and all others of QA&P persuasion must
have shaken their heads in disbelief. How could circumstances have changed so quickly? In fact, the
roots of monumental changes implied by these last
runs were as deep as they were ominous. Some
were slight and subtle, some were bold and obvi-

ous, some were internal, some were external.

The Frisco, as might be expected, was the author
of many modifications affecting the QA&P. During
the 1960s, it was a company in flux. Frisco's management style in that decade, said *Modern Railroads*, was "oriented to operating the railroad as a
business, geared to making profits. Its management
stresses youth, training, and initiative. Above all, it
is a management that stresses teamwork." The
Frisco was, without doubt, trimming to become a
leaner, more aggressive purveyor of rail transportation. The emphasis, it was clear, would be on
change, not tradition. Already, for example, the
parent had demanded and obtained new mono-
grams for its principal subsidiaries—on the QA&P
the image of Quanah Parker was now encased in
the Frisco's familiar beaver pelt. More important,
some of these subsidiaries disappeared, merged
into the parent. The St. Louis–San Francisco of
Texas passed in 1964, the Alabama, Tennessee &
Northern in 1971.[2]

Other changes involved the QA&P directly.
None was more important that the forced retirement of Quin Baker because of age—he was seventy on September 30, 1964. It was bad for the
QA&P, and it was bad for Baker. He had no hobbies; railroading, as his wife said, was his life. Without his job he was lost; a heart attack claimed him
on April 12, 1965. Baker was the only "resident
president" in the company's history. Upon his retirement the position passed to L. W. Menk, who
was already chairman of the board and president of
the Frisco, then to J. E. Gilliland in 1965, and to
R. C. Grayson in 1969. Nominally in charge of the
QA&P after Baker's retirement was L. A. Thomas,
then Leo A. Elliott from 1966 through 1969, and

QA&P presidents after Quin Baker included L. W. Menk   (1962–65),   J. E. Gilliland (1965–69),   and R. C. Grayson
(1969–80).

Jim W. Sowell thereafter. None had a semblance of
the power exercised earlier by Charles Sommer and
Quin Baker.[3]

Other internal modifications similarly diminished the QA&P's independence; the Frisco's approach was much like chopping off a dog's tail an
inch at a time. When W. L. Richardson retired in
1961, the road's sales department was broken up;
shippers were advised thereafter "to direct all in-
quiries regarding routes, rates, and schedules to
Frisco traffic offices." Advertising functions were
assumed by the parent, but these lacked the crea-
tivity of the previous three decades. Another major
change occurred at the end of 1964 when all accounting functions and personnel were transferred
to the Frisco's offices at Springfield, Missouri. After
L. A. Elliott retired in 1969, there were only four
officers left at Quanah: Jim Sowell, vice-president
and general counsel; Charlene Crisp, treasurer, auditor, and assistant secretary; Charles Hurt, train-
master; and Robin Morris, roadmaster.[4]

Nevertheless, when the AT&SF unloaded welded
rail between Plainview and Floydada during the
early 1970s, it gave the impression that the Floydada gateway had gained a permanent niche in the
Santa Fe's transcontinental strategy. Before that rail
could be installed, however, Santa Fe and Frisco
officials huddled to discuss two crucial questions.
Would the Frisco be willing to deliver its Birmingham–Memphis–Springfield–West Coast/St. Louis–
Springfield–West Coast business to the AT&SF via
Avard, Oklahoma? And would the Frisco agree to
divert its Floydada automobile business to Ama-

rillo via Avard? The Frisco's route to Avard, Santa
Fe officials pointed out, ran 175 miles west from
Tulsa to a junction with the AT&SF's main freight
route at Avard and was shorter and less subject to
delay than the Floydada gateway route. The Avard
route, Frisco representatives averred, would require
massive and expensive improvement to handle
time-sensitive traffic and, moreover, the SL-SF was
extremely reluctant to yield control of its highly remunerative automobile traffic to the Floydada distribution center. Santa Fe planners responded that
the Frisco was presently forced to maintain two
routes west, to Avard and the QA&P to Floydada,
when one would easily suffice. Frisco counterparts
conceded privately that one of the two lines was
redundant and that neither one was awash in local
business; economies would certainly result if one
could be abandoned. Haggling continued. The impressive investment at Floydada and the fine automobile business to that location loomed large for
the Frisco, but the AT&SF, now as always, preferred not to handle overhead volume through
Floydada, hoped to avoid the heavy capital investment in new rail for the Plainview-Floydada
branch, and favored Avard over Floydada even
though interchange in Oklahoma would require
considerably more ton miles to earn the same revenue. In an attempt to pressure the SL-SF, Santa Fe
officials threatened to seek alternate eastern connections for passover traffic, but Frisco negotiators
were unmoved. Ultimately the larger road sweet-
ened the pot with improved divisions on overhead
traffic via Avard and very attractive divisions on au-

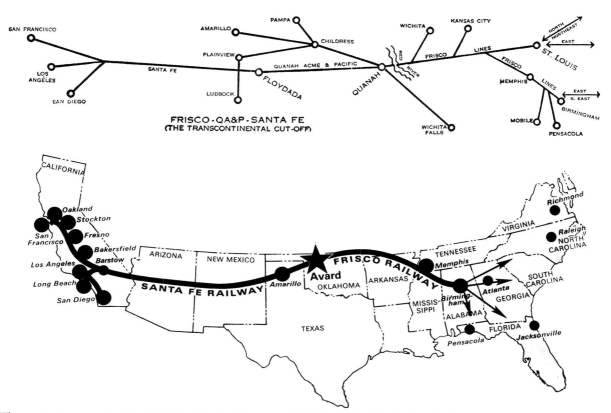

The route structure via Floydada that Charles Sommer and W. L. Richardson had worked so hard to implement would pass to the QA&P's arch rival Avard in 1973.

tos moving via Avard and billed to Amarillo for distribution. A deal was struck to that end early in 1973. The QLA and then the QSF would be rerouted; the Avard gateway would live, the Floydada gateway would not.[5]

There was irony in this decision. When the Floydada route was reopened for through business during the late 1930s, Richardson and Sommer had gained greater divisions via the QA&P than the SL-SF received via Avard. The Frisco's J. R. Coulter in 1939 advised his company's salesmen of this "in order that they might solicit for gateways which will produce greatest earnings for the Frisco." Richardson thought there was an explicit understanding on the part of the parent that its earnings were greater "from transcontinental traffic which is routed in connection with the QA&P via Floydada." Indeed, the Frisco system—that is, SL-SF and the QA&P—received 36 percent on tonnage to and from Pacific Coast points and St. Louis moving by way of Floydada, compared to 31 percent via Avard. In fact, however, Coulter and later T. H. Banister were lukewarm to QA&P routings. "There is no disposition on our part to divide efforts or to con-

fuse the solicitation of transcontinental," Banister told Richardson, "but we have to keep the overall picture before us at all times." This schizophrenic approach on the part of the parent explains the QA&P's response—enlargement of its sales force to eighteen representatives around the country by 1949. These men, Charles Sommer had pledged, would "work as harmoniously with Mr. Coulter's office as possible, but independently," working always to gain routings that would give "Frisco the longest haul." In other words, QA&P salesmen always were obligated to recognize the symbiotic relationship between the parent and its subsidiary—even if the parent did not always respond in kind. Eventually, of course, the QA&P had won out over Avard; regularly scheduled service even disappeared between Enid and Avard in 1967. Now the tables would be turned.[6]

Word of this change leaked out early in 1973. A meeting at Floydada sponsored by local authorities was designed to convince the Frisco to change its mind. The concern at Floydada, strange to say, was only indirectly linked to the future of rail service by the QA&P after removal of the through trains. Im-

George Adams received the last bills from train 3310 on August 31, 1973. *Photograph by the author*

mediately at stake were the jobs of forty truckers employed by the auto carriers and loss of $1 million in payroll. The Frisco's decision, company representatives replied, was firm, although they promised to run a local train to Floydada three times per week and more often during the harvest season. They also pledged to help Floydada find new industries that would be advantageous to the railroad and to the community.[7]

Meanwhile, plans went forward to divert the QLA, QAF, and their eastbound counterparts. The last runs of the QLA and CTB were made on August 1, 1973, and the final QSF departed Quanah at 9:55 P.M. on August 30. Two hours and fifty minutes later, conductor Guy R. Adams presided over delivery of forty-one loads and fourteen empties to the Santa Fe. Three cars of autos were unloaded, the five units were fueled, the crew ate one final late-night meal at King's Restaurant, and at 3:25 A.M. on August 31, engineer B. H. Stone switched on the headlight of locomotive 688 and started the last number 3310 toward Quanah. The end of QA&P's transcontinental participation came at 6:45 A.M. at Quanah when bills for eighteen

loads and twenty-eight empties aggregating 2,537 tons were turned over to agent George Adams. It was not quite the end, as it turned out, because problems on the Avard line forced the Frisco to detour four large trains in each direction during mid-October. But there would be no repeat performance.[8]

This overwhelming trauma was followed almost immediately by a bizarre episode that implied phoenixlike resurrection of the QA&P to a line again carrying important traffic. On August 9, a Fort Worth & Denver train running on that company's South Plains Branch, spinning off the main line at Estelline and running southwesterly to Lubbock, had derailed and done heavy damage to a tunnel near Quitaque. Trains were temporarily rerouted over the Santa Fe, but the FW&D quickly bargained with the Frisco to run one train daily in each direction between Wichita Falls and Lubbock over the QA&P from Acme to Floydada and the Santa Fe from Floydada to Lockney to regain FW&D rails. Regular detours began on September 4.[9]

Negotiations with the Denver Road then matured for its purchase of 104 miles of the QA&P between Acme and Floydada. On December 3, 1973, the QA&P's board of directors authorized this sale for $3.6 million, payable in common stock of the Burlington Northern, FW&D's parent. Both local and trade press promptly reported the sale as an accomplished fact. Meanwhile, Paul F. Cruikshank, president of the Denver Road, met with regional officials of the Santa Fe to arrange long-term trackage rights over twelve miles of the AT&SF's now extremely light-density branch between Floydada and Lockney. Cruikshank's efforts were quickly rewarded at that level, and the matter was referred to the Santa Fe's general office in Chicago for confirmation. Senior officials there, however, proved to be recalcitrant. Charles Sommer, had he been alive, would not have been the least bit surprised. "They [the Santa Fe] had not been on friendly terms with the Fort Worth & Denver," Sommer had written in 1929, "since that line built into the Plains country." Such hostility had permeated the Santa Fe's corporate culture and, as late as five decades after the era of expansion had ended, raised its ugly head to prevent this important cooperative venture. For want of agreement on rights over only a dozen miles of line, the transfer of QA&P trackage to FW&D passed to the realm of what might have been. (Ironically, thirteen years later the AT&SF would seek a buyer for the entire Plainview-Floydada branch.) The Denver Road, with no other choice, repaired the Quitaque tunnel to open its line between Estelline and Lockney. The last detour train—Extra 5746—rolled 4,127 tons from Acme to Floydada on January 1, 1975.[10]

This strange and disappointing episode in the QA&P's history had one particularly unpleasant footnote. On January 20, 1974, the FW&D's train number 186, Extra 6307 on the QA&P, suffered a massive derailment in the rough breaks of the Pease River between Lazare and Swearingen. Sixty-two of the train's eighty cars piled up in eight hundred feet of earthen cut. Federal investigators later estimated that Extra 6307 was making seventy miles an hour when it went into a six-degree curve restricted by operating rules to thirty miles per hour; the entire crew was likely asleep at the time. Damage to the track was $18,000, to equipment $478,192, and to lading unknown. The QA&P was fully indemnified.[11]

The Quanah Route slimmed down in response to its tightly circumscribed purpose of delivering only local service. Two-thirds of the road's trainmen and enginemen followed traffic routed via Avard and moved to Enid, Oklahoma. Two full crews survived, at least initially, to protect triweekly service to Floydada and the five-night-per-week Acme turn. Station forces remained stable: an agent and an operator at Quanah and agents at Paducah and Floydada; Acme had been closed on November 10, 1967, and Roaring Springs had followed on December 31, 1971. Maintenance-of-way forces were reduced to only seven men—adequate to keep the track structure in shape for service that was reduced by the end of 1974 to that provided by one crew performing weeknight switching at Acme and road work to Floydada "as needed."[12]

This reduced service was reflected immediately in the company's income accounts. The year 1973 had been generous in yielding agricultural shipments, 1974 much less so. Billings of wallboard from Acme fell off, too. The QA&P handled a mere 486,416 tons of freight in 1974, but with its plant in good condition and with only thirty-three persons on its payroll, the company's operating ratio remained at a very respectable 39.7. In addition, the QA&P paid its parent a handsome dividend of $3.15 million.[13]

The Frisco responded to this apparent good news on April 7, 1975, by having the QA&P board authorize application for abandonment of the entire 104-mile line west of Acme. Frisco's marketing forces had determined quantitatively what Charles Sommer had known intuitively: "The Quanah Route would be headed straight for disaster without its transcontinental traffic." That business was gone forever, and the local business—mostly cotton, wheat, milo, and a scattering of fertilizer and implements amounting to only about thirteen hundred cars annually—could not sustain the QA&P. Thus senior officers of the Frisco wanted the line "abandoned at the earliest possible time to avoid financial losses." The few remaining shippers, local authorities whose civic pride was wounded by the threatened loss of service, and railroad labor vowed a fight. The Interstate Commerce Commission ultimately agreed to hear the case at Paducah.[14]

The proceedings opened before administrative law judge Geraldine B. Keyes on November 10, 1976. The protestants hired Ray Farabee, a state senator from Wichita Falls, to represent them. Farabee was admittedly unaccustomed to working before the ICC and was visibly unsure of himself at the outset but gained confidence over the next several days. There was actually little that he and the protestants could do, though, except to plead for continued rail service. Billings to and from the affected stations, they had to admit, had dropped to

Of the two remaining train crews, one was assigned to triweekly service between Quanah and Floydada. Here it picks up grain at Boothe Spur, January 20, 1976. *Photograph by the author*

Wallboard moved westward from Acme to the AT&SF at Floydada, empties returning via the same route. In a few weeks, wheat in the foreground would be harvested and shipped from elevators at nearby Dougherty. *Photograph by the author*

only 1,101 cars in 1975. Many decried loss of the life-sustaining overhead business, but Frisco representatives pointed out that the Avard gateway offered less elapsed time on transcontinental traffic because it was eighty miles shorter than the Floydada route and that the interchange there, unlike Floydada, was not at the end of a stub branch of the Santa Fe.[15]

The protestants' most effective ammunition was provided, ironically, by the Frisco itself. Farabee found inconsistencies and omissions in company testimony, and in some cases the railroad simply failed to do its homework. Moreover, Geraldine Keyes proved formidable; she was especially unimpressed by the arrogance of Frisco's attorneys, who initially talked down to her and underestimated her knowledge and verve and who—when they attempted to cover their tracks—made the fatal error of pandering to her. When company witnesses told Keyes that maximum authorized train speeds had been reduced because track conditions had deteriorated, she evinced skepticism and demanded a first-hand look. A caboose hop was ordered, and Keyes found that the line was easily good for Federal Railroad Administration Class III standards, that is, thirty-five miles per hour. The Frisco's credibility was, for her, further damaged. Keyes found the QA&P to be a profitable operation, its plant in good shape, and she concluded that it served "a substantial public need in connection with the movement of agricultural commodities to and from the stations located on the line and beyond." The full commission upheld her judgment on October 12, 1977. It was not so much that the protestants won as that the Frisco lost. But the story did not end there.[16]

Life for the QA&P and for those who worked for it remained uncertain. Traffic levels between Acme and Floydada remained stable—1,117 carloads for 1976 as opposed to 1,161 in 1975—and the company still received impressive divisions on business handled between Red River and Quanah. Most of this traffic was for interchange with the FW&D, but volume was down appreciably. The Frisco replaced heavy rail with lighter section between Red River and Altus, Oklahoma—much to the alarm of local shippers who perceived it as the first step to abandonment.[17]

Other developments implied both disaster and opportunity. The QA&P deeded the former station building at Roaring Springs to a local civic group and undertook to find acceptable uses for the brick structure at Floydada and the general office building at Quanah. The Floydada station had been locked up some years earlier in favor of a new one adjacent to the automobile facility, and the Quanah office was closed at the end of 1978 when all functions were moved to spartan quarters alongside the wye in North Quanah. Sad to say, however, negotiations failed, and both handsome buildings swiftly fell into disrepair.[18]

The script that the Frisco wrote for the now moribund Quanah Route was predictable. The local road's surplus was drained through dividends payments ($652,500 from 1975 through 1978), the track structure could not continue indefinitely without cyclical maintenance, and the potential for an expanded traffic base was nil. Not surprisingly, then, the Frisco again early in 1978 filed papers to abandon the line west of Acme, it fumbled again, and the application was denied on procedural grounds.[19]

All of this captivated the imaginations of several people who studied the possibility of purchasing the QA&P. One of these was Mickey Nunley, president of the Roscoe, Snyder & Pacific Railway, who pointed out that profitability depended on the establishment of overhead business. Nunley found the Frisco mildly receptive to establishment of through schedules and tariffs, but the Santa Fe promised nothing more that tri-weekly connections at Floydada. Moreover, Nunley worried that deregulation of the American railroad industry, then being considered by Congress, might "have a very negative affect on all short line railroads." Consequently, said Nunley, "until this issue is resolved in Washington, an intelligent business decision cannot be made." He was right. Congress did pass the Staggers Act, as it was known, to deregulate the industry. The Roscoe, Snyder & Pacific would be a victim of that legislation, perishing in 1984.[20]

Much more important to the Frisco than the QA&P's abandonment case by this time was its own future as an independent company. On February 1, 1977, the Frisco and the larger Burlington Northern had announced that they were "commencing joint studies into the feasibility of unification." That news raised only a few eyebrows within the industry because this was, in a phrase of the trade press, the era of megamergers. Nevertheless, the path to combination proved serpentine. Opposition came from medium-sized roads, especially the Missouri-Kansas-Texas. Finally, though, on April 17, 1980, the ICC gave its blessing; on November 21, 1980, the merger was consummated. The St. Louis–San Francisco Railway disappeared into a sea of green and white, although the QA&P,

After 1978, the former general office building at Quanah fell into disrepair. *Harold W. Ferguson photograph*

Reverend, best friend and mascot at the QA&P general office building in its last days. *Photograph by the author*

Traffic levels in 1978 warranted only one crew to care for the switching at Acme and usually one train a week carrying wallboard, grain, and cotton to Floydada. Floydada recedes in the horizon as the weekly train heads east. *Photograph by the author*

Playing dominoes was a ritual for crews waiting for departure time at Floydada. This would be the final game. Floyd County Hesperian *photogrqaph*

strange to say, lived on as a wholly owned subsidiary of the Burlington Northern.[21]

Although nothing loomed larger in the eyes of Frisco managers than prospective merger with the Burlington Northern, they had determined by mid-August 1978 to make another run at abandonment of the QA&P. The ICC appointed an administrative law judge to hear the case, but hearings were suspended when the wisdom of compromise dawned on Frisco attorneys. To this end, the SL-SF arranged with the AT&SF for service of on-line industries at Floydada; promised to donate land or otherwise grant concessions to affected shippers; and agreed to "pay 75 cents per bale substitute service on cotton trucked from Roaring Springs to Quanah for subsequent shipment by rail." The entire package was predicated on the willingness of protestants to drop their complaints and on permission of the ICC to abandon the line from Paducah to Floydada, 67.2 miles. The Frisco promised, in addition, that the QA&P would offer train service to Floydada for ninety days following receipt of abandonment authority and promised not to file on the Acme-Paducah segment for at least

five years. There were no protests to the amended proposal. The ICC decision came early in 1981; it was served on February 10. Abandonment was granted. Local wags laughed that the QA&P would again be called the "Quit at Paducah," as it had been six decades earlier before expansion had taken the road on to Roaring Springs and MacBain.[22]

At least the anxiety of waiting for a decision was over. There was confusion about when the last run to Floydada County would be, but there was no uncertainty as to disposition of Floydada's relatively new steel depot, which was disassembled, loaded, and billed to a Frisco station in Oklahoma. It was ready to move when Extra 1382, a caboose hop and the final train from Quanah, arrived at Floydada at sunrise on May 5, 1981. The crew tied up for eight hours rest but reassembled early to play dominoes in the caboose, to reminisce about the QLA and the QSF, and to ponder together the changes their lives had taken since the big trains had been diverted to Avard. The decision to maintain service to Paducah, they knew, would result in but one trip per week, and the mill at Acme did

The Frisco itself disappeared as a corporate entity when merged into the much larger Burlington Northern on November 21, 1980.

The demise of the QA&P is reflected in the faces of (*left to right*) Clyde King, engineer; William Clawson, conductor; Fred Pierce, brakeman; Dee Smith, fireman; and Larry Tidmore, brakeman. *Photograph by the author*

not provide enough business for a regular job at Quanah. Some contemplated retirement, some considered relocation, others pledged to "hang on to see what happens." Somebody recalled that Charlene Crisp had retired and that as a consequence Jim Sowell was the only company officer at Quanah. It made no difference, they agreed, since the QA&P as they had known it was already dead.[23]

Then it was time to go. A few keepsake pictures were taken, and enginemen joked about the QA&P sign that somebody had pasted under the cab window of the locomotive. There was no need for punctuality, but perhaps out of years of tradition, all were aboard at the appointed hour: 3:25 P.M. Soon the laughably short train was rolling effortlessly at thirty miles per hour on a grade elevated adequately to remind one of the QA&P's heritage as a dedicated high-speed freight railroad. On both sides of the right-of-way were beautifully verdant blankets—fields that thirty days later would yield a bountiful harvest of wheat. The train reached Boothe Spur at 3:43, Dougherty at 3:58. Except for the gracious chatter of songbirds, it was almost ghostly silent at Roaring Springs when Extra 1382 interrupted briefly at 4:25, passing the handsome station and rolling through town in regal style on well-anchored 115-pound steel with ties deeply bedded in chatt. Conductor W. C. Clawson stood on

the back platform of his caboose, as he had leaving Floydada and passing through Dougherty, looking in vain form somebody to wave farewell. Not even the free whistling of engineer C. H. King brought out a solitary soul to witness passage of this last train. Clawson dolefully deserted to the inside as the train rumbled over Shorty Creek trestle, churned upgrade toward Russellville, and disappeared forever around a curve. There was work to do at Paducah and Acme, cotton and wallboard to pick up. Meanwhile, the Santa Fe's Extra 3604 was already spotting empty boxes at docks formerly served by the QA&P at Floydada. The old order had passed; the new had begun.[24]

Clawson and his fellows were essentially correct in their assessment that the Quanah Route had drawn its final breath. The official death notice did not appear, however, until later in 1981, when the Burlington Northern issued a cryptic obituary: "The Quanah, Acme & Pacific Railway was merged into BN effective June 1. The QA&P had been a wholly owned subsidiary of the Frisco. The line in northern Texas served as a major link between the Frisco and the Santa Fe. Its importance diminished in the mid-1970s, however, when the Frisco established a new gateway in Avard, Oklahoma. At the time of merger it had fewer than 20 employees."[25]

Thus perished the adventure that had begun so

many years before as the Acme, Red River & Northern, that evolved into the Quanah, Acme & Pacific, that failed in its dreams of expansion to El Paso or even Lubbock, and that enjoyed but a few years in the sun as a well-respected participant in moving freight to every part of the land. Now only ghost trains pause to load cattle at Narcisso, to pick up cars of water at Roaring Springs, or to gather important lading from the Santa Fe interchange at Floydada. Happy to say, however, no signals are set against their movement; for them there are no restrictive orders.

The laughably short last QA&P train from Floyd County was seemingly swallowed up by the immensity of the country west of MacBain. *Photograph by the author*

Nary a resident at Roaring Springs noted the passing of the final train. *"Sic gloria transit." Photograph by the author*

*Eddie Guffee photograph*

*Eddie Guffee photograph*

# Notes

The following abbreviations will be used in the notes:

AFE      Authority for Expenditure
AFS      A. F. Sommer
CEE      C. E. Ensminger
CHS      C. H. Sommer
DED      D. E. Decker
F      QA&P File Number
GEH      G. E. Hamilton
ICC      Interstate Commerce Commission
NF      No File Number
QB      Quin Baker
REQ      R. E. Quirk
RPC      Record of Property Change
RRCT      Railroad Commission of Texas
SL      Sam Lazarus
WLR      W. L. Richardson

Unless stated otherwise, all documents cited were located in QA&P files when the author was researching them.

## CHAPTER 1

1. Walter Prescott Webb, *The Great Plains*, pp. 145–56.

2. *Texas Almanac, 1961–1962*, p. 585.

3. *Hardeman County, Agricultural and Industrial Edition*, p. 83.

4. Carl Coke Rister, *The Southwestern Frontier*, p. 301; James Wilson, *Agricultural Resources of the Texas Panhandle*, p. 22.

5. Richard C. Overton, *Gulf-to-Rockies: The Heritage of the Fort Worth & Denver—Colorado and Southern Railways, 1861–1898*, pp. 31, 93–108.

6. Ibid.; Jonnie R. Morgan, *The History of Wichita Falls*, pp. 29–30.

7. Overton, pp. 93–108.

8. Ibid.

9. Bill Neal, *The Last Frontier: The Story of Hardeman County*, p. 57; *Hardeman County, Agricultural and Industrial Edition*, p. 3; Overton, p. 129.

10. Neal, p. 43.

11. *Hardeman County, Agricultural and Industrial Edition*, p. 83.

12. Neal, pp. 84–85, 249. There is considerable confusion about the owners and even the exact corporate designations of the mills at Acme and Agatite. Among those listed in a variety of sources are Quanah Plaster Company, Eureka Cement Plaster Company, Texas Cement Plaster Company, Agatite Cement Plaster Mill, Lone Star Plaster Mill, and American Cement Plaster Company.

13. *Reedy's Mirror* 23 (Dec. 18, 1914): 93; *St. Louis Globe-Democrat*, Mar. 6, 1926.

14. "Biography of Sam Lazarus by Charles H. Sommer," F185; General Land Office of Texas, Abstracts of Land Titles, 7:84, 163–64, 8:138; Margaret Elliot, "History of D. B. Gardner's Pitchfork Ranch of Texas," *Panhandle-Plains Historical Review* 18 (1945): 12–79, esp. 36–37, 54.

15. Elliot, pp. 12–79; J. R. Williams, *The Big Ranch Country*, pp. 25, 110; Laura V. Hamner, *Short Grass and Longhorns*, p. 127.

16. Neal, p. 45; "Biography of Sam Lazarus"; *Reedy's Mirror* 23 (Dec. 18, 1914): 93.

17. Charles S. Potts, "Railroad Transportation in Texas," *Bulletin of the University of Texas, Number 119, Humanities Series 7* (1909): 68.

18. ARR&N, Minute Book, pp. 1–8; Don L. Hofsommer, "The Acme, Red River & Northern: An Early Texas Short Line Railroad," *Red River Valley Historical Review* 5 (Fall 1980): 17–26.

19. Hofsommer, "Acme, Red River & Northern," pp. 17–26; Charles H. Sommer, "History of the Quanah, Acme & Pacific Railway Co.," *QA&P Employees' Magazine* 1 (Dec. 1934): 4; SL to John Summerfield, June 4, 1903, F33; St. Clair Griffin Reed, *A History of the Texas Railroads and of Transportation Conditions under Spain and Mexico and the Republic and the State*, p. 429.

20. ARR&N, Minute Book, pp. 8–10. In his brief biography of Lazarus, Charles H. Sommer argued that Lazarus was "associated with the building of the Frisco line from Sapulpa to Oklahoma City and later to Quanah, Texas." Whether he was or not, it seems clear that Lazarus was already wielding much influence with the SL&SF; see Reed, pp. 429, 533.

21. ARR&N, Minute Book, pp. 13–22.

22. John Summerfield to SL, June 2, 1903; SL to Summerfield, June 4, 1903, both in F181.

23. CHS to GEH, June 9, 1932, F1288; Neal, p. 249; Memorandum of Agreement . . . ARR&N, Salina Cement Plaster Co., Acme Tap Ry., and FW&DC Ry., Mar. 31, 1903, F1340; Memorandum of Agreement, FW&DC Ry. and ARR&N, Apr. 25, 1903, F1340; Memorandum of Agreement, QA&P Ry., FW&DC Ry., and Acme Tap Ry., Dec. 12, 1911, F1340; ARR&N, Time Table No. 1, July 10, 1903, author's collection.

24. John Summerfield to SL, Sept. 3, 1903, F33.

25. J. L. Allhands, *Railroads to the Rio*, p. 208; *Quanah* (Texas) *Tribune-Chief*, Jan 31, 1903; J. L. Allhands to QB, Nov. 2, 1956, F213-2; Reed, pp. 533, 538. The Oklahoma & Western Railroad Company was sold to the SL&SF on July 18, 1907.

26. Reed, pp. 423–33; Potts, p. 67–71; Ira G. Clark, *Then Came the Railroads: The Century from Steam to Diesel in the Southwest*, pp. 236–43; William Edward Hayes, *Iron Road to Empire: The History of 100 Years of the Progress and Achievements of the Rock Island Lines*, pp. 167–217.

27. *Reedy's Mirror* 23 (Dec. 18, 1914): 93; "Biography of Sam Lazarus."

28. ARR&N, Minute Book, passim; *Poor's Manual of the Railroads of the United States*, 1908, p. 2005.

29. SL to Allison Mayfield, Feb. 13, 1908; Mayfield to M. Marx, Feb. 19, 1908; Marx to CHS, Feb. 24, 1908, all in F7.

30. F7.

31. Ibid.

32. Ibid.

33. Ibid.

34. Ibid.

35. ARR&N, Minute Book, pp. 31, 49–51.

36. Ibid.

37. Ibid.

38. RRCT, Circular No. 3046, General Order, Recognizing the Quanah, Acme & Pacific Ry. Co., Mar. 17, 1909.

## CHAPTER 2

1. Vernon Gladden Spence, *Colonel Morgan Jones: Grand Old Man of Texas Railroading*, pp. 148–49.

2. *Quanah Tribune-Chief,* Mar. 3, 10, 1910.

3. Ibid., Mar. 3, April 21, June 20, 1910.

4. Ibid., Apr. 21; Neal, p. 69; Reed, p. 535. The Texas collection at Baylor University, Waco, has considerable material on the QSD&R.

5. F7.

6. F13, passim; J. C. Lofton to SL, May 24, 1910, F13; Keith L. Bryant, Jr., *History of the Atchison, Topeka & Santa Fe Railway,* p. 198; J. S. Edwards to SL, Apr. 22, 1910, F13.

7. A. A. Soward to SL, Mar. 16, 1910; Arthur B. Duncan to SL, May 24, 1910; R. C. Andrews to SL, May 12, 1910; *Quanah Tribune-Chief,* Jan. 27, 1910; J. A. Graham to SL, Mar. 31, 1910; E. L. Bedell to SL, Mar. 9, 1910; H. D. Slater to SL, May 10, 1910; S. H. Wither to SL, May 9, 1910; R. R. Holland to SL, Apr. 12, 1910; Harry K. Baughn to SL, Mar. 29, 1910; S. H. Wither to SL, May 9, 1910; R. R. Holland to SL, Apr. 12, 1910; Harry K. Baughn to SL, Mar. 29, 1910; S. W. Holden to SL, Apr. 28, 1910; John I. Hinkle to SL, Mar. 29, 1910; S. W. Holden to SL, Apr. 28, 1910; John I. Hinkle to SL, Mar. 18, 1910; DED to A. B. Duncan, May 26, 1910. All of the foregoing correspondence is in F13.

8. Quanah, Texas, Chamber of Commerce, brochure, 1909.

9. Contract, ARR&N and J. B. Goodlett and T. E. Ledbetter, Oct. 27, 1908; Amended contract, same parties, Feb. 26, 1909; ARR&N, Minute Book, p. 65.

10. ICC, *Valuation Report,* 41:816; Neal, p. 42.

11. *Lubbock Avalanche,* Dec. 25, 1908; DED to CHS, Feb. 8, 1909, F13.

12. ARR&N, Minute Book, p. 65; *Lubbock Avalanche,* Apr. 1, 1909; Contract, QA&P and citizens of Paducah, Texas, Mar. 24, 1909; Secretary's Agreement No. 10, *Lubbock Avalanche,* Sept. 29, 1910, citing an unidentified issue of the *Paducah Post.*

13. Amendment to the Articles of Incorporation, ARR&N, p. 1; QA&P, Right-of-way and Track Map, June 30, 1911; CHS to DED, Feb. 3, 1909, F7.

14. CEE to F. M. Sands, Aug. 16, 1909, F13; Contract, QA&P and FW&DC, Sept. 24, 1909, QA&P Secretary's file 4; CHS to GEH, June 9, 1932, F329 and 1288.

15. *Quanah Tribune-Chief,* Jan. 6, 13, 18, 1910; Architect's Plans and Drawings, Quanah office building, QA&P Roadmaster's office, Quanah; QA&P, Right-of-way and Track Map, June 30, 1911.

16. *Quanah Tribune-Chief,* Jan. 6, 1910; Engineering Report, pp. 10–16.

17. QA&P Minute Book 1, pp. 18–19; QA&P Stock Certificate Book 1; Neal, p. 189.

18. Amendment to the Articles of Incorporation, ARR&N, Jan. 21, 1909, p. 1; *Poor's Manual,* 1910, p. 2677; QA&P, Minute Book 1, pp. 19, 30; ICC, *Valuation Report,* 41:811; Contract, QA&P and Pacific Construction Company, Mar. 8, 1909, F1479.

19. Contract, QA&P and Pacific Construction Company, Mar. 8, 1909, F1479.

20. Allhands, *Railroads to the Rio,* pp. 210–11; CEE to *Manufacturers Record,* Mar. 19, 1909.

21. Neal, p. 254; QA&P, Right-of-way and Track Maps, June 30, 1911.

22. CEE to E. S. Price, Apr. 3, 1909; SL to CEE, June 5, 1909; G. W. Johnson to CEE, July 11, 1909; F. M. Sands to CEE, July 24, 1909, all in F88.

23. CHS to F. M. Sands, Aug. 13, 1909; T. K. Hawkins to CHS, Aug. 17, 1909; CHS to Hawkins, Sept. 1, 1909, all in F333.

24. *Quanah Tribune-Chief,* Jan. 6, 1910; Neal, p. 56; Engineering Report, p. 10; QA&P, Right-of-way and Track Maps, June 30, 1911.

25. Engineering Report, p. 10.

26. CHS to WLR, Sept. 12, 1951, NF; G. S. White to SL, Aug. 27, 1909, NF.

27. G. S. White to SL, Aug. 27, 1909, NF; Carmen Taylor Bennett, *Our Roots Grow Deep: A History of Cottle County,* p. 177.

28. Bennett, p. 177; Engineering Report, p. 11; QA&P, Right-of-way and Track Maps, June 30, 1911.

29. CHS to F. M. Sands, Aug. 13, Nov. 12, 1909, F3; CHS to CEE, Nov. 29, 1909, F71.

30. CHS to Hon. Allison Mayfield, Dec. 20, 1909, F3; T. K. Hawkins to CHS, Nov. 26, 1909, F84; Hawkins to CHS, Dec. 15, 1909, F71.

31. P. E. Jordan to T. K. Hawkins, Oct. 28, 1909, NF; Bennett, p. 34; *QA&P Employees' Magazine* 2 (Mar. 1936): 5.

32. QA&P Right-of-way and Track Maps, June 30, 1911; Engineering Report, p. 11; T. K. Hawkins to CHS, undated [Jan. 1910]; CHS to W. F. Sterley, Dec. 18, 1909, both in F71; *Official Guide of the Railways,* Feb. 10, 1910, p. 565.

33. CEE to CHS, Dec. 13, 1909, F71; CHS to Allison Mayfield, Dec. 20, 1909, F6; *Quanah Tribune-Chief,* Jan. 13, 1910, citing an unidentified issue of the *Paducah Post; Quanah Tribune-Chief,* May 12, 1910.

34. Neal, p. 254; Bennett, p. 177.

35. Bennett, p. 177; *QA&P Employees' Magazine* 2 (Mar. 1936): 6.

36. Bennett, p. 177; *QA&P Employees' Magazine* 3 (Feb. 1937): 3.

37. *QA&P Employees' Magazine* 2 (Mar. 1936): 5; Bennett, p. 210; B. B. Paddock, ed., *History of Texas,* 2:767.

## CHAPTER 3

1. CEE to CHS, Dec. 24, 1909, F13; *Quanah Tribune-Chief,* Jan. 13, 1910; CHS to AFS, Mar. 2, 1916, F52.

2. *Quanah Tribune-Chief,* Jan. 17, Apr. 21, 1910; W. M. Pearce, *The Matador Land and Cattle Company,* p. 132.

3. Atchison, Topeka & Santa Fe Railway, *Excerpts from the President's Annual Reports to the Stockholders with Special Reference to the Construction History of System Lines, 1873–1916,* known internally as *Santa Fe Splinters,* System AT&SF, 1:80, found in office of the Valuation Engineer, System AT&SF, Topeka, Kansas.

4. James Marshall, *Santa Fe: The Railroad That Built an Empire,* pp. 426–27, 432–33.

5. *Lubbock Avalanche,* Mar. 24, 1910. For an exceptionally fine study see Carl Harper, "Movement toward Railroad Building on

the South Plains of Texas, 1907–1914."

6. *Lubbock Avalanche,* Mar. 24, 1910.

7. Ibid.; Donovan L. Hofsommer, *Katy Northwest: The Story of a Branch Line Railroad,* pp. 19–20; Harper, pp. 49, 62; *Lubbock Avalanche,* Dec. 25, 1908.

8. CHS to SL, May 23, 1910, NF; QA&P, Minute Book 1, p. 47, and 2, pp. 63, 119.

9. *Lubbock Avalanche,* Feb. 24, 1910; QA&P, Minute Book 1, pp. 27–28.

10. QA&P, Minute Book 1, p. 41; *Lubbock Avalanche,* May 4, June 22, 1911; *Quanah Tribune-Chief,* May 11, 1911; QA&P, Minute Book 1, p. 65, and 2, pp. 53, 59–61, 65.

11. CEE to CHS, May 18, 19, 1910; SL to CEE, May 11, 1910, all in F13.

12. CHS to SL, May 23, 1910; O. S. Ferguson to DED, May 10, 1910; DED to Ferguson, May 13, 1910; CHS to DED, May 18, 1910, all in F13.

13. *Lubbock Avalanche,* Feb. 10, 1910; Julian M. Bassett to SL, Apr. 4, 1910, F13; CEE to CHS, June 22, 1910, F13; Marshall, pp. 434–35.

14. *Lubbock Avalanche,* Feb. 24, 1910; DED to SL, May 26, 1910; CHS to SL, undated [1910], both in F13.

15. CEE to CHS, Feb. 6, June 22, 1910, F13.

16. CEE to SL, Feb. 6, 1910, F13.

17. DED to SL, May 9, 1911; SL to CEE, May 29, 1911, both in F13.

18. SL to A. Sanger, July 1, 1910; SL to CEE, May 11, 1910; SL to S. H. Cowan, Aug. 1, 1910, all in F13.

19. Pearce, p. 133.

20. SL to Murdo MacKenzie, Jan. 31, Apr. 1, 1910; SL to W. F. Hull, Feb. 8, 1910; SL to Sam H. Cowan, Feb. 9, 1910, all in F13.

21. Pearce, pp. 134–35.

22. Ibid., pp. 133–35.

23. QA&P, Minute Book 1, p. 89; Contract 244, QA&P and Matador Land and Cattle Company, Sept. 21, 1911, all in QA&P Secretary's files; Pearce, p. 135.

24. Pearce, pp. 136–37; QA&P, Minute Book 2, pp. 141–51.

25. Pearce, p. 134; *Quanah Tribune-Chief,* Jan. 6, 1910.

26. E. H. Bunnell to CHS, June 25, Aug. 20, 1928, F1479; QA&P, Minute Book 1, p. 53, and 2, p. 25; QA&P Stock Ledger, pp. 53–55; *Poor's Manual,* 1912, p. 1214.

27. *Poor's Manual,* 1912, p. 1214.

28. *Quanah Tribune-Chief,* Nov. 9, 1911.

29. QA&P, Minute Book 2, pp. 63–73; ICC, *Valuation Report,* 41:805; QA&P, Annual Report to the ICC, 1914, p. 31; QA&P, Report to the ICC, "Securities Issued or Assumed as of June 27, 1920," Sept. 2, 1920.

30. QA&P, Minute Book 2, pp. 107–13.

31. AFS to CHS, June 9, 1922, Dec. 9, 1925, F39; J. A. Knox to CHS, Oct. 29, 1912, F13; *Lubbock Avalanche,* Nov. 21, 1912.

32. Bennett, p. 86; *Quanah Tribune-Chief,* June 20, 1913.

33. J. A. Knox to CHS, Apr. 29, 1913; CHS to Robert Cray, May 5, 1913, both in F71.

34. Pearce, p. 137; *Quanah Tribune-Chief,* May 22, 1913; QA&P, Annual Report to the ICC, 1914, p. 83; AFS to CHS, Dec. 9, 1925, F39.

35. ICC, *Valuation Report,* 41:808; Engineering Report (revised), pp. 2, 12; *QA&P,* Right-of-way Map, Apr. 1931.

36. T. A. Hamilton to E. N. Brown, Sept. 17, 1919, NF; ICC, *Valuation Report,* 41:807, 321; QA&P, Annual Report to the ICC, 1914, p. 71; QA&P, Right-of-way Map, Apr. 1931.

CHAPTER 4

1. *Lubbock Avalanche,* Oct. 28, 1909, May 12, 1910.

2. *Hale County Herald,* Apr. 28, May 12, 1911; CEE to SL, Feb. 6, 1910, NF; AFS to CHS, June 9, 1922, F39.

3. *Lubbock Avalanche,* Mar. 14, Oct. 3, Nov. 14, 1912.

4. QA&P, map with projected extensions and comments thereon, June 25, 1913.

5. QA&P, "Map of Territory of Quanah, Acme & Pacific Railway Showing Direct Lines between El Paso and St. Louis," Feb. 1914; CHS to AFS, Feb. 18, 1914, F13.

6. *Quanah Tribune-Chief,* Jan. 8, 15, 31, 1914.

7. Ibid., Apr. 20, 1914; *Lubbock Avalanche,* Aug. 1, 1912; *Floyd County Hesperian,* July 15, 1915. The last mention of the QA&P's El Paso line plans appeared in the *Lubbock Avalanche* for Mar. 5, 1914. Charles H. Sommer, "History of the Quanah, Acme & Pacific Railway," published in various issues of the *QA&P Employees' Magazine,* 1932–51, p. 1, and rough draft, F213-2; *Poor's Manual,* 1916, p. 1941.

8. Clark, 236–42; Hayes, pp. 167–217.

9. *Poor's Manual,* 1914, p. 1388; *Railway Age* 62 (Jan. 19, 1917): 124; *Poor's Manual,* 1918, p. 1244; ICC, *Valuation Report,* 41:810; QA&P, Annual Report to the ICC, 1922, p. 108; QA&P, Stock Certificate Book 1, Certificates 1–77.

10. *Poor's Manual,* 1918, p. 1244.

11. CHS to J. W. Murphy, Feb. 2, 1935, F191; ICC, *Valuation Report,* 41:821; W. C. Nixon to SL, Aug. 13, 1914; Avery Turner and G. H. Scheyler to SL, Aug. 1, 1914; Agreement between Receivers of St. Louis, San Francisco & Texas Railway and Quanah, Acme & Pacific Railway, July 25, 1914, all in F191.

12. *Quanah Tribune-Chief,* Jan. 13, 21, Feb. 17, July 4, 1910.

13. CHS to AFS, Feb. 11, 1916, NF; SL to T. A. Hamilton, Apr. 25, 1919, NF; QA&P, Map of Narcisso Townsite, May 2, 1918; Engineering Report (revised), p. 11; QA&P, Right-of-way and Track Maps, Apr. 1931; Don L. Hofsommer, "Town Building on a Texas Short Line: The Quanah, Acme & Pacific Railway, 1909–1929," *Arizona and the West* 21 (Winter 1979): 355–68.

14. Bennett, p. 149.

15. Engineering Report (revised), pp. 11–13; SL to T. A. Hamilton, Apr. 25, 1919, NF; CHS to AFS, July 29, 1927, F308.

16. Pearce, pp. 137–38; SL to T. A. Hamilton, Apr. 25, 1919, NF.

17. Pearce, pp. 137–38; CHS to AFS, Feb. 20, 1915, NF.

18. QA&P, Roaring Springs Station Plat, May 1927; Engineering Report (revised), p. 12.

19. QA&P, Minute Book 2, pp. 143–49.

20. Ibid.; SL to T. A. Hamilton, Apr. 25, 1919, NF; Pearce, pp. 139–40.

21. Pearce, pp. 138–39. Corporate records show that a total of $10,650 was received by the railroad as donations to complete construction (Schoolar, Bird & Company, Public Accountants, Dallas, "Report on the Motley County Railway," Oct. 21, 1918, to the Board of Directors of the Motley County Railway, p. 3; the report is hereafter referred to as MCR).

22. Motley County Railway, Annual Report to the ICC, Dec. 31, 1925; a statement of purpose and list of contributors drawn by the Law Office of Hamilton & Davis, Childress, Texas, undated [1913], F1116; Motley County Railway, Articles of Incorporation, p. 1.

23. Contract between the Motley County Railway and Frank Fennen, June 24, 1913, F1116; Engineering Report upon the Motley County Railway, Dec. 30, 1922, p. 2.

24. Memoranda of Agreement, QA&P Ry. and Matador & Northern Railway, undated [1912], NF; DED to CHS, Aug. 16, 1913, NF; CHS to DED, Aug. 23, 1912, NF.

25. DED to CHS, Nov. 20, 1913, NF; Contract between QA&P and Motley County Railway, Nov. 20, 1913, QA&P Secretary's file 126.

26. DED to CHS, Nov. 25, Dec. 6, 1913, NF.

27. Ibid., Nov. 20, 1913, NF; SL to A. B. Echols, Nov. 17, 1913, NF; Echols to SL, Nov. 22, 1913, F591.

28. Engineering Report on the Motley County Railway, Dec. 20, 1922, pp. 2, 8–10.

29. Robert Cray to CHS, Feb. 24, 1914, F591; Contract between the QA&P and the Motley County Railway, Nov. 23, 1914 (bond).

30. Robert Medlen, interview with author, Jan. 16, 1976.

31. Statement showing cars received and delivered to Motley County Railway at Matador Junction, F591.

32. H. O. Stephens to CHS, July 28, 1917; CHS to Robert Cray, Aug. 18, 1917, both in F591.

33. Contract between the QA&P and the Motley County Railway, Sept. 29, 1917; ICC, *Valuation Report,* 41:821.

34. MCR, pp. 1–4, A-1.

## CHAPTER 5

1. CHS to T. K. Hawkins, Feb. 4, 1909, NF; QA&P AFE 3; Contract with Southern Iron & Equipment Co., Apr. 23, 1909; CHS to T. K. Hawkins, Aug. 21, 1909, NF; F. M. Sands to CEE, July 12, 1909, NF.

2. QA&P, Minute Book 2, p. 187; QA&P, Contract with the Baldwin Locomotive Works, July 24, 1915, Secretary's file 90; Engineering Report upon the Quanah, Acme & Pacific Railway, account 51; AFE 5.

3. QA&P, Minute Book 2, p. 187; Engineering Report, account 53.

4. CHS to T. K. Hawkins, Feb. 4, 1909, F7 and 187; CHS to F. M. Sands, Oct. 11, 1909, F3.

5. QA&P, Contract with General Electric Company, July 19, 1912, Secretary's file 58; QA&P, Minute Book 2, pp. 187, 201; Engineering Report (revised), p. 17.

6. QA&P, Contract with S. Burke Burnett, Jan. 5, 1917; QA&P, Minute Book 2, p. 223; Engineering Report (revised), p. 21; CHS to T. K. Hawkins, Oct. 21, 1922, F790; *Quanah Tribune-Chief,* Feb. 24, 1918.

7. *Official Guide of the Railways* 42 (Feb. 1910): 565; 43 (Feb. 1911): 703; 46 (Apr. 1914): 1308; 51 (Oct. 1918): 1122.

8. SL&SF, Time Table, Jan. 15, 1905, p. 15; Robert Cray to CHS, Feb. 29, 1916, F708; Alexander Hilton to SL, Jan. 4, 1916, NF.

9. QA&P, Contract with J. H. Simpson, Mar. 25, 1913, Secretary's file 62; QA&P, Contract with O. F. Hood, Apr. 1, 1914, Secretary's file 16.

10. Joseph Stewart to CHS, Jan. 15, 1910, F122A; Post Office Department to CHS, Sept. 19, 1913, Secretary's file 95; QA&P, Contract with United States Express Company, Feb. 20, 1910, F22; QA&P, Contract with Wells Fargo & Company, July 1, 1914, Secretary's file 77.

11. Blanche Scott Rutherford, *One Corner of Heaven,* p. 185; Bennett, pp. 148, 244; Robert Medlen, interview with author, Jan. 16, 1976; *Quanah Tribune-Chief,* Feb. 3, 1910.

12. *Quanah Tribune-Chief,* June 2, 1912; SL to J. W. Arnett, May 2, 1910, F13.

13. *Quanah Tribune-Chief,* Aug. 20, 1912; Neal, p. 254; *Quanah Tribune-Chief,* Oct. 16, 1913; Elton B. Marsalis, interview with author, Jan. 25, 1976.

14. Bennett, pp. 34–46, 71, 84.

15. Douglas Meador, *Trail Dust,* p. 22.

16. Engineering Report (revised), p. 2; Various statements, F44; *Poor's Manual,* 1910, p. 1108; and 1916, p. 1875.

17. *Poor's Manual,* 1912, p. 1709; and 1916, p. 1730; *Official Guide of the Railways,* Apr. 1914, p. 1308; Oct. 1918, p. 593; Various statements, F88.

18. ICC, Brief of the Fort Worth & Denver City Railway, Finance Dockets 7464 and 7465, May 4, 1929, p. 3; Reed, pp. 399, 522; on the Acme Tap Railroad, see ICC, *Valuation Reports,* 134: 738–39.

19. QA&P, various contracts and memoranda with the Fort Worth & Denver City Railway and Salina Cement Plaster Co., 1909–14, Secretary's files 3, 41, 66, 67.

20. Correspondence, passim; A. Henley to CHS, Oct. 6, 1913, all in F604.

21. D.B. Keeler to SL, Dec. 11, 1913; SL to Joab Mulvane, Dec. 13, 1913, both in F604.

22. *Poor's Manual,* 1915, p. 1020; 1910, pp. 1911, 2676; and 1917, p. 1875.

## CHAPTER 6

1. John F. Stover, *American Railroads,* pp. 187–97.

2. Ibid.; Annual Report of the Quanah, Acme & Pacific Railway Company to the Railroad Commission of Texas, 1918, p. 3.

3. Stover, pp. 187–97; ICC, Finance Docket No. 12964, vol. 159, pp. 522–89; *St. Louis Globe-Democrat,* Dec. 22, 1929; QA&P Final settlement between the Director General of Railroads and the St. Louis–San Francisco Railway and Other Corporations, Oct. 7, 1921, Secretary's file 160.

4. Stover, pp. 187–97.

5. Ibid.

6. QA&P, Wage Schedules . . . Jan. 1, 1918, and Jan. 1, 1920, NF; CHS to AFS, Dec. 14, 1920; Chamber of Commerce of the United States, *The Railroad Strikes,* a printed statement, July 10, 1920, both in F919.

7. CHS to AFS, Dec. 24, 1920, July 10, 1922, both in F919.

8. AFS to all agents, July 27, 1922; AFS to CHS, July 28, 1922, both in F961; *Railway Age,* Sept. 30, 1922; AFS to all QA&P shop employees, July 27, 1922, F961; CHS to AFS, Oct. 24, 1922, F961; AFS to CHS, Oct. 26, 1922, F919.

9. *Official Guide of the Railways,* Apr. 1921, pp. 553, 1057; CHS to T. E. Leckie, Dec. 26, 1919, NF.

10. RRCT, "Special Notice," Apr. 27, 1921, NF; CHS to John P. Marrs, May 2, 1921, F603; GEH to CHS, May 7, 1921, NF; CHS to GEH, May 13, 1921, NF; QA&P Division Sheet No. 5 between the Motley County Railway and all other lines, June 21, 1921.

11. American Railway Association, Circular 2483, Aug. 11, 1924, NF; CHS to GEH, Aug. 19, 1924, NF; CHS to AFS, Sept. 4, 1924 (telegram), NF; CHS to A. B. Echols, Sept. 5, 1924, NF; American Railway Association, Circular 2492, Oct. 3, 1924, F205.

12. J. E. W. Thomas to CHS, Sept. 8, 1924, NF; T. K. Hawkins to CHS, June 18, 1921, F75-A; CHS to AFS, Nov. 10, 1924, F603; AFS to CHS, Oct. 31, 1924, NF; J. E. Powell to AFS, Nov. 6, 1924, NF.

13. *Motley County News,* June 10, 1925; Motley County Rail-

way, Directors' Resolution, Apr. 9, 1925, Motley County Railway Minute Book; Motley County Railway, Contract with the Quanah, Acme & Pacific Railway, Apr. 9, 1925, F1116.

14. CHS to AFS, June 22, 1925, F1116; John P. Marrs, July 8, 1925, F603.

15. CHS to AFS, Feb. 6, 1926, F1107; *Quanah Tribune-Chief,* Dec. 7, 1927; ICC, *Finance Reports,* 124:302–303; CHS to GEH, Apr. 27, 1927, F1178.

16. GEH to AFS, May 16, 1925; Secretary of the Matador Chamber of Commerce to George B. McGinty, Dec. 14, 1926, both in F31.

17. Robert Medlen to AFS, Feb. 4, 1926, F31; H. C. Mulroy to GEH, Feb. 23, 1927, NF; John P. Marrs to CHS, July 8, 1925, NF; GEH to CHS, July 7, 1925, NF; *Motley County News,* June 10, 1925.

18. Motley County Railway, VO3 Report 1924, 1925; Engineering Report upon the Motley County Railway; AFS to CHS, Dec. 9, 1926, F232; *Motley County News,* June 10, 1925; *Annual Report of the Motley County Railway to the Interstate Commerce Commission,* Dec. 31, 1925.

19. *Annual Report of the Motley County Railway to the Interstate Commerce Commission,* Dec. 31, 1925; GEH to CHS, Mar. 9, 1927; AFS to CHS, Feb. 12, 17, 1926, Mar. 12, 1927; CHS to AFS, Feb. 15, 1926, all FN; AFS to CHS, Feb. 17, 1926, F232.

20. CHS to JMK, Feb. 11, 1927, F1116.

## CHAPTER 7

1. Bryant, pp. 194–99; Richard Saunders, *The Railroad Mergers and the Coming of Conrail,* pp. 44–57; Albro Martin, *Enterprise Denied: Origins of the Decline of American Railroads, 1897–1917,* pp. 1–21.

2. Clark, pp. 258–62.

3. GEH to SL, Oct. 2, 1924, NF; "The Texas Panhandle Reviewed," a five-page typed manuscript by F. B. Kirby, secretary of the Quanah Chamber of Commerce, n.d. [1925?], F453; Marshall, pp. 432–33.

4. Application of the Texas, Panhandle & Gulf Railroad, requesting a hearing for a certificate of public convenience and necessity, July 20, 1923, F984.

5. JMK to CHS, Sept. 4, 1923, Frisco file 1653–109; W. F. Evans to CHS, Aug. 29, 1923, F984.

6. ICC, Finance Docket 3134, announcement of Oct. 19, 1923; *Paducah Post,* Sept. 13, Nov. 1, 1923; CHS to AFS, Nov. 17, 1923, F984; *Dallas Morning News,* Nov. 28, Dec. 1, 1923; *Fort Worth Star-Telegram,* Nov. 28, 1923.

7. Statement by D. E. Jordan, Dec. 1, 1923, F984; *Dallas Morning News,* Nov. 28, Dec. 2, 1923.

8. Statement of W. F. Sterley, given at the Fort Worth hearing, F984; *Fort Worth Star-Telegram,* Sept. 7, 1923.

9. *Dallas Morning News,* Nov. 29–30, 1923.

10. T. W. Kinsley to F. G. Jonah, Sept. 10, 1923; H. R. Safford to CHS, Dec. 8, 1923, NF; CHS to Safford, Dec. 10, 1923, both in F551.

11. Testimony of Charles H. Sommer before the hearing at Fort Worth, F984.

12. *Fort Worth Star-Telegram,* Dec. 1, 1923; *Dallas Morning News,* Dec. 1, 1923.

13. *Dallas Morning News,* Dec. 1, 2, 4, 7, 1923.

14. *Fort Worth Star-Telegram,* Jan. 27, 1924; *Wichita Falls Record News,* June 17, 1924; R. C. Gowdy to CHS, Jan. 28, 1924, F551.

15. James Hutton Lemly, *The Gulf, Mobile & Ohio: A Railroad That Had to Expand or Expire,* passim; John P. Marrs to CHS, June 17, 1924, F984; CHS to H. R. Safford, Dec. 10, 1923, F551; SL to JMK, June 19, 1924, F1354; JMK to SL, Feb. 19, 1925, F1111.

16. CHS to H. R. Safford, Dec. 10, 1923, F551; SL to JMK, June 19, 1924, F1354; John P. Marrs to CHS, Nov. 26, 1924, F1354.

17. A. E. Harp to CHS, Jan. 21, 1924; CHS to Harp, Jan. 24, 1924; Harp to CHS, Jan. 30, 1924, all in F1354; GEH to SL, Oct. 2, 1924, NF; John P. Marrs to CHS, Aug. 24, 1924, NF; *Dallas Morning News,* Aug. 25, 1924; *Wichita Falls Times,* Aug. 24, 1924.

18. Ross Simpson to E. N. Brown, Mar. 4, 12, 1925, NF; Simpson to AFS, Mar. 7, 1925, NF; Mileage Statistics, F1111.

19. Hayes, p. 209; Julius Grodinsky, *Railroad Consolidation: Its Economics and Controlling Principles,* pp. 45–46. The Frisco undertook expansion of its own during this time, by purchase and by construction. See *History of the Frisco,* p. 30.

## CHAPTER 8

1. *Quanah Tribune-Chief,* Apr. 3, 1925; Application of the Fort Worth and Denver South Plains Railway, Finance Docket 4769, Apr. 7, 1925, F1075.

2. Return of SL, Finance Docket 4769, May 18, 1925, F1075; *Wall Street Journal,* June 4, 1925.

3. Application of the Pecos & Northern Texas Railway, Finance Dockets 4747 and 4756, F1075.

4. John P. Marrs to CHS, May 25, July 8, 1925, F1075.

5. *Quanah Times,* Apr. 5, 8, 1925.

6. Ibid., Apr. 18, 1925.

7. JMK to SL, June 29, 1925, F1111.

8. SL to Murdo MacKenzie, July 2, 1925; SL to GEH, July 7, 1925, both in F1075; JMK to SL, July 9, 1925, F1111; QA&P, Minute Book 2, pp. 349–51; Application of the Quanah, Acme & Pacific Railway, July 14, 1925, F1111.

9. *Floyd County Hesperian,* July 16, 1925; Letter of Agreement, SL to Mr. W. M. Massie and others, July 17, 1925, NF.

10. *Quanah Tribune-Chief,* July 17, 1925; *Quanah Tribune-Chief* and *Quanah Times,* Special Consolidation Issue, July 19, 1925.

11. ICC, Notice of Proceedings, Finance Dockets 4769, 4747, 4756, June 29, 1925; *Dallas Morning News,* June 15, 28, 1925; John P. Marrs to CHS, June 16, 1925, F1075.

12. *Dallas Morning News,* June 28, July 7, 8, 26, 1925; *Fort Worth Star-Telegram,* July 26, 1925; *Quanah Tribune-Chief,* July 28, 1925; CHS to J. P. Marrs, July 10, 1925, F1075.

13. *Dallas Morning News,* July 26, 1925; *Fort Worth Star-Telegram,* July 26, 1925.

14. *Fort Worth Star-Telegram,* July 24, 1925; George B. McGinty to SL, July 21, 1925, F1111.

15. *Quanah Tribune-Chief,* July 24, 31, 1925; *Fort Worth Record,* July 24, 1925.

16. *Dallas Morning News,* Sept. 23, 1925; CHS to B. H. Strange, Feb. 25, 1925, F984; *Fort Worth Record,* Aug. 10, 16, 1925.

17. SL to Thomas P. Littlepage, Sept. 2, 1925, F1111; AFS to CHS, Apr. 10, 1925, F131; *Dallas Morning News,* Oct. 30, 1925; CHS to Cecil Smith, Aug. 15, Sept. 17, 1925; CHS to J. P. Marrs, Aug. 15, 1925, all in F1075.

18. QA&P, Minute Book 2, pp. 353–57; Various petitions, F1111; SL to GEH, Sept. 26, 1925, F1111; *Quanah Times,* Oct. 18, 1925; ICC, Notice, Finance Dockets 4959, Sept. 29, 1925.

19. CHS to AFS, Aug. 10, 1925, NF; CHS to Cecil Smith, Aug. 26, 1925, F1111; *Dallas Morning News*, Sept. 23, 1925; Return of Fort Worth & Denver City Railway to Questionnaire No. 2, Finance Dockets, 4959 (1925); Return of the Atchison, Topeka & Santa Fe Railway to Questionnaire No. 2, Finance Dockets, 4959 (1925); J. W. Barwise to Cecil Smith, Dec. 28, 1925, F1111; CHS to SL, Sept. 4, 1925, F111.

20. *Quanah Tribune-Chief*, Jan. 6, 1926; Sam Rayburn to Cecil H. Smith, Jan. 12, 1926, NF; Smith to CHS, Jan. 30, 1926, F1111; RRTC to ICC, Feb. 1, 1926, F1111; *Dallas Morning News*, Mar. 4, 1926; CHS to Cecil H. Smith, Mar. 19, 1926, F1111.

21. *St. Louis Globe-Democrat*, Mar. 6–9, 1926; *St. Louis Post-Dispatch*, Mar. 6–9, 1926.

22. Application of the Pecos & Northern Railway, Finance Dockets 5372 (1926); Cecil H. Smith to SL, Feb. 25, 1926, F1111; *Dallas Morning News*, Mar. 25, 1926; Return of the Quanah, Acme & Pacific Railway to Questionnaire, Finance Dockets 5372 (1926); CHS to Cecil H. Smith, Feb. 27, 1926, NF; *Fort Worth Star-Telegram*, Apr. 16, 1926; CHS to AFS, Apr 28, 1926, F1128; Testimony for Record [Finance Docket 5372] by CHS, F1128; Cecil H. Smith to CHS, May 29, 1926, NF; Three statements, F1128; J. G. Pepkin to Cecil H. Smith, May 28, 1926, NF; Cecil H. Smith to Hon. Sam Rayburn, May 13, 1926, NF.

23. ICC, Report of C. E. Boles, Finance Docket 3134 (1926), mimeographed, 43 pp., F984; *Fort Worth Star-Telegram*, Mar. 19, 20, 1926.

24. *Dallas Morning News*, Mar. 23, 25, 1926; *Fort Worth Record-Telegram*, Mar. 20, 1926; *Floyd County Hesperian*, Mar. 25, 1926.

25. ICC, Order, Finance Dockets 3134, 4747, 4756, 4769, 4959, Apr. 19, 1926; Reply of the Fort Worth Denver South Plains Railway, Finance Dockets 3134 et al., Apr. 2, 1926; Reply of Dallas Chamber of Commerce, Finance Dockets 3134 et al., Apr. 1, 1926; ICC, Notice, Finance Dockets 4747 et al., Mar. 26, 1926; ICC, Notice, Finance Dockets 3134 et al., June 17, 1926; ICC, Notice, Finance Docket 5372, July 3, 1926; Cecil H. Smith to CHS, July 6, 1926, all in F1111; Charles D. Mahaffie to CHS, June 30, 1926, NF.

26. CHS to JMK, July 2, 12, 1926, F1111.

27. CHS memorandum, Mar. 23, 1926, F984.

28. CHS to Cecil H. Smith, Mar. 23, Apr. 5, 1926, F1111; Smith to CHS, Apr. 13, 1926, F1111; O. L. Slaton to Smith, Apr. 29, 1926, NF.

29. GEH to CHS, Mar. 22, 1926, F1111; Cecil H. Smith to CHS, May 29, 1926, NF; CHS to JMK, July 12, 1926, F1111.

30. CHS to Cecil H. Smith, Apr. 5, 12, 1926; CHS to JMK, July 12, 1926; JMK to CHS, Apr. 1, 1926, all in F1111; *Dallas Morning News*, May 18, 1926.

31. CHS to JMK, July 23, 1926; GEH to CHS, July 28, 1926, both in F1111; *Railway Age* 81 (July 31, 1926): 209.

32. CHS to JMK, Nov. 19, 1926, F1111; ICC, Order, Finance Dockets 4747 et al., Nov. 8, 1926; *Railway Age* 81 (Nov. 27, 1926): 1033–37; *Dallas Morning News*, Nov. 20, 1926; ICC, *Finance Reports*, 117:233–80.

33. *Fort Worth Star-Telegram*, Nov. 19, Dec. 2, 1926, July 2, 1927; *Dallas Morning News*, Nov. 20, Dec. 22, 1926.

34. *Fort Worth Star-Telegram*, Nov. 19, Dec. 17, 1926; *Paducah Post*, Nov. 25, 1926; *Dallas Morning News*, Nov. 20, 27, 1926; ICC, Order, Finance Dockets 4769 et al., Dec. 13, 1926.

## CHAPTER 9

1. AFS to CHS, Aug. 30, 1926, NF; CHS to JMK, Sept. 8, 1926, NF; *Dallas Morning News*, Aug. 20, Sept. 15, 1926; JMK to CHS, Sept. 15, 1926, F1154; "Application of the Ardmore, Vernon & Lubbock Railway Company for a Certificate of Public Convenience and Necessity and for Authority to Construct and Finance a Line of Railroad . . . ," Aug. 20, 1926, F1154. A charter was also later obtained from the state of Texas.

2. JMK to CHS, Sept. 18, 1926; CHS to GEH, Oct. 15, 1926; GEH to CHS, Oct. 29, 1926, all in F1154; *Dallas Morning News*, Oct. 31, Nov. 5, 1926; *Fort Worth Star-Telegram*, Nov. 7, 1926.

3. ICC, Notice of Hearing, Finance Docket 5798, Aug. 2, 1927; CHS to AFS, Aug. 9, 1927; G. F. Stephens to CHS, Sept. 5, 1927, both in F1154; *Dallas Morning News*, Aug. 5, 1927; CHS to JMK, Sept. 10, 1927; JMK to CHS, Aug. 16, 1928, both in F1154; *Wichita Falls Record News*, Feb. 7, 1929.

4. Hayes, pp. 208–18; Grodinsky, pp. 45–56.

5. Reed, pp. 428–30.

6. CHS to JMK, Mar. 22, Sept. 3, 1926, F1111; CHS to JMK, Sept. 7, 1926, F1207; CHS to JMK, Dec. 9, 1926, F1153; JMK to CHS, July 11, 1927, F1207.

7. CHS to JMK, July 16, Aug. 10, 1927, F1207.

8. CHS to JMK, Mar. 23, 1928; GT&W, Income Account, 1924–25, both in F1207.

9. JMK to E. N. Brown, June 22, 1928; J. E. Gorman to E. N. Brown, Aug. 16, 1928, both in F1207.

10. Joint Management Team to J. E. Gorman, Oct. 24, 1928, F1207.

11. Agreement between the St. Louis–San Francisco Railway Company and Joseph J. Jermyn covering purchase by the Frisco Company and capital stock of Gulf, Texas & Western Railway Company, Nov. 22, 1928, F1207; *St. Louis Globe-Democrat*, Dec. 21, 1928; *Fort Worth Star-Telegram*, Dec. 21, 1928, Jan. 8, 1929; *Lubbock Avalanche-Journal*, Jan. 9, 1929.

12. *Fort Worth Star-Telegram*, Jan. 11, 1929; W. H. Abernathy to CHS, Dec. 19, 1928, F1207; *Fort Worth Star-Telegram*, Dec. 18, 1928, Jan. 10, 1929; Orville Van Brunt to CHS, Dec. 21, 1928, F1207; Ben B. Cain to CHS, Nov. 26, 1928, F1207; E. W. Clark to CHS, Jan. 12, 1929, F549; M. P. Leaming to O. H. McCarty, Jan. 10, 1929, F1207.

13. T. H. Wilhelm to Carl S. Guin, Apr. 2, 1929, F1351; CHS to JMK, May 8, 1929, F1186; AFS to CHS, Mar. 25, 1929, F1351; R. L. Gillentine to A. P. Pearce, Feb. 9, 1929, F1351; H. G. Clark to CHS, Mar. 20, Apr. 4, 1929, F1351; *Dallas Morning News*, Mar. 23, 1929; *Fort Worth Star-Telegram*, Apr. 11, 1929; ICC, *Finance Reports*, 111:137–46; *Rock Island Magazine*, July 1929, p. 6.

14. *Fort Worth Record*, May 6, 1929; *Childress Daily Index*, May 5, 1929; *Fort Worth Star-Telegram*, May 7, 1929; H. G. Clark to CHS, May 1, 1929, F1351.

15. G. A. Simmons to CHS, Apr. 20, 1929; Carl S. Guin to T. H. Wilhelm, May 2, 6, 1929, all in F1351.

16. *Fort Worth Star-Telegram*, July 17, 19, 1929; CHS to M. G. Clark, May 31, 1929, F1351; W. H. Abernathy to A. M. Bourland, July 11, 1929, F1351; *Dallas Morning News*, July 19, 1929; H. G. Clark to CHS, June 4, 1929, F1351.

17. ICC, *Financial Reports*, 158:231–33; Hofsommer, *Katy Northwest*, pp. 87–92; *Fort Worth Star-Telegram*, Dec. 19, 1929; ICC, Finance Docket 7370 et al., orders, Apr. 14, 1930.

18. *Quanah Tribune-Chief*, Apr. 22, 1930.

19. *Fort Worth Star-Telegram*, Apr. 26, July 3, 6, 1930; *Quanah Tribune-Chief*, July 11, 1930.

20. CHS to A. P. Pearce, July 15, 1930, F1351; *Fort Worth Star-Telegram*, Aug. 22, Sept. 5, 1930; *Quanah Tribune-Chief*, Sept. 5, 23, 1930.

21. CHS to AFS, Sept. 9, 1930, F1351; *Fort Worth Star-Telegram*, Aug. 22, 1931; *Vernon Record*, Aug. 28, 1930; J. E. Gorman to

Mason Harwell, Feb. 26, 1931, F1351.

22. *Wichita Falls Daily Times,* Feb. 22, 1931; Hayes, p. 221; *Quanah Tribune-Chief,* July 4, 1930; *Fort Worth Star-Telegram,* July 3, 1930; Reed, pp. 430–31; *History of the Frisco,* pp. 23, 31; F. Hol Wagner, Jr., *The Colorado Road: History, Motive Power, and Equipment of the Colorado & Southern and Fort Worth & Denver Railway,* p. 195.

23. *Wichita Falls Daily Times,* Jan. 30, 1925; CHS to AFS, June 7, 1926, F1107; CHS to AFS, Feb. 15, 1929, F551.

24. CHS to E. T. Miller, June 25, 1929, F1050; QA&P, Application, Aug. 17, 1929; QA&P, Return to Questionnaire No. 1, Finance Docket 7783, Oct. 17, 1929; John Sharp to CHS, Sept. 7, 1929, F549; CHS to Sharp, Sept. 10, 1929, F549.

25. CHS to AFS, Aug. 24, Sept. 6, 1929, NF; James Williams to CHS, Dec. 3, 1929, NF.

26. CHS to AFS, Nov. 9, 1929, F1365; CHS to W. T. Montgomery, Nov. 27, 1929, F548; ICC, *Finance Reports,* 158:95–97; CHS to G. A. Simmons, Mar. 12, 1930, F1365; E. J. Beard to CHS, Feb. 18, 1930, F1365; CHS to JMK, Mar. 20, May 7, 1930, F1365; CHS to GEH, May 2, 1930, F1365.

## CHAPTER 10

1. *Texas Kicker* (Floydada), Sept. 12, 1890; *Floyd County Times,* Apr. 24, 1891.

2. *Texas Kicker,* Oct. 24, 1890; *Lubbock Avalanche,* Oct. 16, 1908, July 1, 1909, Mar. 17, 1910; Rutherford, p. 223; *Plainview News,* Dec. 17, 1920.

3. Contract between the QA&P and the Citizens of Floyd County, Texas, July 16, 1925.

4. W. M. Massie to CHS, Nov. 20, 1926; CHS to Massie, Nov. 24, 1926; CHS to GEH, Nov. 26, 1926, all in F1111; CHS to F. M. Dougherty, Nov. 27, 1926, F1172; CHS to C. B. Dorchester, Nov. 27, 1926, F1111.

5. *Fort Worth Star-Telegram,* Dec. 4, 1926; CHS to AFS, Dec. 20, 1926, F1111.

6. CHS to AFS, Jan. 17, 1927; CHS to GEH, Jan. 17, 1927, both in F1111; SL to Murdo MacKenzie, July 11, 1925, NF.

7. CHS to AFS, Feb. 19, 1926, F1195; W. M. Massie to CHS, Jan. 27, 1927, F1111.

8. Clarence E. Gilmore to CHS, Feb. 16, 1927; CHS to Gilmore, Feb. 28, 1927, both in F1111.

9. *Amarillo Daily News,* Mar. 11, 1927; GEH to AFS, Mar. 5, 1927; JMK to CHS, Mar. 5, 1927; CHS to C. P. Rutledge, Mar. 10, 1927, all in F1111.

10. *Quanah Tribune-Chief,* Mar. 18, 1927; CHS to JMK, Apr. 20, 1927, F1111; Contract between the QA&P and the Lone Star Construction Company, May 6, 1927, Secretary's file 266; AFE 166.

11. Purchase Order No. Q 1340, May 25, 1927; AFS to CHS, June 16, 1927, F1316; *Floyd County Hesperian,* Sept. 29, Oct. 20, 1927.

12. *Engineering News-Record,* Dec. 6, 1928; CHS to George B. McGinty, Oct. 7, 1927, F1111; ICC, Order, Oct. 19, 1927.

13. CHS to JMK, Sept. 29, 1927, F1316; *Floyd County Hesperian,* Sept. 29, 1927; CHS to L. G. Mathews, Nov. 1, 1927, NF.

14. Murdo MacKenzie to SL, July 14, 1925, NF; QA&P, Right-of-way Maps, Jan. 1929; GEH to CHS, Jan. 10, 1928, NF; CHS to GEH, Jan. 12, 1928, NF; *Floyd County Hesperian,* Mar. 29, Nov. 22, 1928, Jan. 24, 1929.

15. CHS to F. M. Dougherty, Feb. 10, 1928, NF; "Tracklaying and Surfacing" (Floydada Extension), F551; *Engineering News-Record,* Dec. 6, 1928.

16. *Floyd County Hesperian,* Oct. 20, 1927; CHS, memorandum, Jan. 5, 1928, F1316; CHS to George B. McGinty, Mar. 20, 1928, F1111; ICC, Order, Finance Docket 4959, Apr. 9, 1928; Charles Mahaffie to CHS, Aug. 31, 1928, F1111.

17. ICC, Order, Finance Docket 6388, July 27, 1927; QA&P, Report to ICC, Finance Docket 6388, Dec. 31, 1927; W. T. Montgomery to CHS, Dec. 26, 1928, NF.

18. *Railway Age* 81 (July 31, 1926): 209, and 81 (Nov. 27, 1926): 1033–37, AFE 166; T. K. Hawkins to CHS, Dec. 21, 1928, F71; QA&P, Contract with F. F. Boothe, June 10, 1931, F1484.

19. F. M. Dougherty to CHS, Nov. 19, 1926; CHS to GEH, May 24, 1927; GEH to CHS, June 23, 1927; CHS to Dougherty, Dec. 2, 1927, all in F1172; CHS to Ethel Cogswell, Apr. 18, 1928, F1282; QA&P, Right-of-way Map, Jan. 1927; Hofsommer, "Town Building on a Texas Short Line," pp. 355–68.

20. *Floyd County Hesperian,* Mar. 1, 1928; F. M. Dougherty to CHS, Mar. 22, 1928, NF.

21. *Floyd County Hesperian,* Mar. 1, 1928; *Fort Worth Star-Telegram,* May 7, 1928; Original Plat of the Town of Dougherty . . . Floyd County, Texas, Mar. 21, 1928.

22. *Floyd County Hesperian,* Mar. 12, 1928; CHS to JMK, May 1, June 5, July 2, 1928, F1316; CHS to AFS, July 16, 1928, NF; W. E. Grissom to AFS, Aug. 14, 1928, F51-9.

23. CHS to AFS, June 21, 1928, F31-5; CHS to S. S. Butler, Sept. 7, 1928, F1338; *Floyd County Hesperian,* Mar. 8, 1928; H. C. Knickerbocker to CHS, Sept. 26, 1928, NF.

24. Ed Bishop to CHS, Sept. 20, 1928, F1261; *Floyd County Hesperian,* May 28, 1940, July 15, 1965; *QA&P Employees' Magazine* 1 (Oct. 1935): 21–24.

25. AFE 166; CHS to JMK, Feb. 25, 1927, F1111; *Floyd County Hesperian,* Dec. 1, 1927; CHS to GEH, Jan. 12, 1928, NF; CHS to the Ware Company, May 24, 1928, NF; CHS to JMK, Sept. 6, 1928, F1316.

26. AFS to CHS, Feb. 6, 1929, QA&P file FE; *QA&P Employees' Magazine* 1 (Oct. 1935): 34; *Floyd County Hesperian,* Feb. 7, 14, 1929; Various telegrams, Feb. 11, 1929, F1294; AFS to CHS, Feb. 12, 1929, NF.

27. *Fort Worth Star-Telegram,* July 2, 1927; *Plainview News,* Nov. 15, 1928; *Plainview Evening Herald,* Nov. 20, 1928.

28. *Floyd County Hesperian,* Dec. 5, 12, 1929; *Fort Worth Star-Telegram,* Feb. 20, 1927; *Wichita Falls Daily Times,* Mar. 22, 1929.

## CHAPTER 11

1. Lubbock Chamber of Commerce, *Rainfall Record for Thirty-Five Year Period* (1929); *Farm Life on the South Plains of Texas* and brochure/broadside from the South Plains, Inc., Lubbock (1929), F1354; Lovington, N.Mex., Chamber of Commerce, *The Last of the Cheap Good Lands* (1928); Southwestern Bell Telephone Company, *Cotton Ginnings in Bales* (1928); *Agricultural Data on the Counties of the Texas Panhandle* (n.p., n.d. [1926?]); Levelland, Tex., Chamber of Commerce, *Facts and Figures Concerning Levelland and Hockley County* (1928); *Lovington Leader,* Dec. 30, 1928; *Fort Worth Star-Telegram,* Dec. 30, 1928.

2. *Amarillo Daily News,* Nov. 24, 1928; *Fort Worth Star-Telegram,* Dec. 17, 1928, Jan. 26, Feb. 2, 14, 1929; Sept. 13, 1930; Joint Management Team to J. E. Gorman, Oct. 24, 1928, F1207; Marshall, pp. 296–98; *Wall Street Journal,* Nov. 6, 1928.

3. *Dallas Morning News,* Mar. 11, 12, 1928; E. S. Rowe to CHS, Mar. 15, 1928, NF; *Fort Worth Star-Telegram,* May 6, 22, 1928; *Lubbock Avalanche,* May 22, 23, 1928; CHS to GEH, June 23, 1928, F1292; *Plainview Evening Herald,* Jan. 29, 1929; *Dallas Morning News,* Feb. 26, 1929.

4. *Fort Worth Star-Telegram,* Nov. 12, Dec. 6, 1928; *Dallas Morning News,* Dec. 6, 1928, Sept. 5, 1929; *Lovington Leader,* Dec. 14, 1928.

5. *Dallas Morning News,* Oct. 29, 1926; *Fort Worth Star-Telegram,* Dec. 16, 23, 1928.

6. John W. Murphy to JMK, Aug. 27, 1930, F1432; *Dallas Morning News,* Aug. 26, 1930; *Fort Worth Star-Telegram,* Aug. 26, 27, 28, 29, 31, Sept. 5, Nov. 1, 6, 8, 9, 1930; CHS to JMK, Sept. 5, Oct. 10, Dec. 20, 1930, F1432; Charles Reinken to CHS, Aug. 30, 1930, F1432; *Fort Worth Star-Telegram,* June 25, 1931; *Dallas Morning News,* Aug. 26, 1930.

7. WLR to CHS, Apr. 30, 1930, F549; *Amarillo News,* Apr. 30, 1930.

8. *Dallas Morning News,* Oct. 9, 1924; Carey Shaw to CHS, Nov. 17, Dec. 11, 1928, F1308; J. H. McCracken to AFS, Nov. 20, 1928, NF; Ed Kennedy to JMK, Apr. 12, 1929, F1345; CHS to MJK, Apr. 25, 1929, F1354.

9. *Lubbock Avalanche,* Dec. 19, 1927; *Dallas Morning News,* Jan. 7, 1928; JMK to CHS, Dec. 28, 1927, F1308.

10. AFS to CHS, Dec. 19, 1928, NF; CHS to AFS, Dec. 19, 1928, NF; CHS to AFS, Dec. 26, 1929, NF; AFS to CHS, Jan. 12, 1929, NF; "Report on the Examination of Routes West of Floydada, Texas: Proposed Extension of the Quanah, Acme & Pacific Railway Company," Jan. 28, 1929, NF; CHS to JMK, Jan. 26, 1929, NF.

11. "Report on . . . Routes West of Floydada," passim.

12. Ibid.; F. G. Jonah to JMK, Feb. 2, 1929, NF; JMK to CHS, Feb. 11, 1929, NF; Dummy draft of application to ICC, Mar. 1929, NF.

13. "Report of the Committee from the El Paso Chapter, American Association of Engineers, on the Proposed El Paso South Plains Railroad" (1925), F1044; *El Paso Times,* Feb. 4, 1929; *Lubbock Avalanche-Journal,* Mar. 14, 1929; CHS to C. A. Lemp, Mar. 6, 1929, F1427.

14. CHS to JMK, June 14, 1929, F549; CHS to JMK, July 20, 1929, F1153.

15. CHS to JMK, Dec. 14, 1929, F1349; CHS to JMK, Mar. 10, 1930, F1354.

16. CHS to JMK, Mar. 10, 1930, F1354.

17. *Lubbock Avalanche-Journal,* Jan. 9, 1929; A. B. Davis to CHS, Feb. 1, 1929, F1354; GEH to CHS, Feb. 23, 1929, NF; Petitions, Submitted by the Morton, Texas, Chamber of Commerce, July 26, 1929, NF; *Cochran County News,* Aug. 22, Sept. 5, 1929.

18. CHS to AFS, Apr. 9, 1930; A. B. Davis to CHS, Mar. 19, 1930, both in F1354; WLR to CHS, Apr. 22, 1930, NF; CHS to JMK, Sept. 25, 1930, F1354.

19. H. P. Webb to CHS, Jan. 14, 1927, F1411; Maury Hopkins to CHS, July 27, 1927, NF; Albert G. Hinn to CHS, Jan. 22, 1929, NF; CHS to Charles Reinken, Jan. 26, 1929, NF; CHS to JMK, Feb. 4, 1929, NF.

20. Chamber of Commerce, Olton, Texas, *Olton: Mecca of the Plains?* (n.d. [1929?]); *Fort Worth Star-Telegram,* Apr. 21, 1930; WLR to CHS, Apr. 30, 1930, F549; WLR to CHS, Apr. 22, 1930, NF; CHS to JMK, Sept. 30, 1930.

21. CHS to JMK, Mar. 8, 1930, F1319; AFS to CHS, Mar. 30, 1930, NF; *Fort Worth Star-Telegram,* Mar. 2, 4, 6, 1930.

22. JMK to CHS, Feb. 11, 1929, NF; CHS to W. B. Storey, Feb. 13, 1929, NF; Storey to CHS, Feb. 15, 1929, NF; CHS to Storey, Feb. 19, 1929, F1328; CHS to JMK, Feb. 26, 1929, F1319; *Fort Worth Star-Telegram,* Feb. 23, 1930; E. J. Beard to CHS, Aug. 11, 1930, F1431.

23. JMK to CHS, Mar. 14, 1930, F1653-209; CHS to A. B. Davis May 27, 1930, F1354; JMK to J. R. Koontz, Sept. 24, 1930,

F1653-287; JMK to CHS, Dec. 4, 1931, F1653-209; *History of the Frisco,* pp. 22–23.

## CHAPTER 12

1. *Hardeman County, Agricultural and Industrial Edition,* p. 63; Deed Record 73, Hardeman County, Texas, pp. 558–64; Neal, p. 249.

2. G. B. Cromwell to L. M. Hogsett, Mar 19, 1928, F1340.

3. Orville Van Brunt to CHS, Aug. 2, 1928; CHS to Van Brunt, Aug. 4, 1928, both in F59.

4. George B. Cromwell to CHS, Aug. 17, 1928, F59.

5. CHS to F. E. Clarity, Aug. 22, 1928, F59.

6. F. E. Clarity to CHS, Aug. 25, 1928, F59.

7. George B. Cromwell to C. E. Spens, Sept. 5, 1928, F1340.

8. C. E. Spens to Orville Van Brunt, Oct. 29, 1928; Van Brunt to Spens, Nov. 12, 1928, both in F1340.

9. F. E. Clarity to CHS, Nov. 24, 1928; JMK to Hale Holden, Nov. 28, 1928; C. E. Spens to JMK, Nov. 30, 1928, all in F1340.

10. Orville Van Brunt to CHS, Jan. 9, Feb. 8, 1929; F. E. Clarity to E. E. Spens, Feb. 5, 1929; Clarity to CHS, Feb. 12, 1929; CHS to Clarity, Feb. 16, 1929, all in F1340.

11. AFS to CHS, Dec. 19, 1928; CHS to AFS, Dec. 22, 1928; CHS to JMK, Feb. 4, 1929, all in F1340.

12. CHS to Orville Van Brunt, Feb. 20, 1929, F1340; Petition, Finance Docket 7465, Feb. 20, 1929, F1340; *Wichita Falls Daily Times,* Feb. 26, 1929; Return to Questionnaire No. 1, Finance Docket 7464, Mar. 25, 1929; CHS to JMK, June 14, 1929, F1153.

13. *Dallas Morning News,* Mar. 29, 1929; ICC, Finance Dockets 7464 and 7465, Notice of Hearing, Apr. 16, 1929; Orville Van Brunt to CHS, Mar. 28, 1929, F1340; Petition to Intervene (FW&DC), Finance Dockets 7464 and 7465, Mar. 11, 1929, F1340; Statement of Charles H. Sommer, F1340.

14. ICC, Report Proposed by Thomas F. Sullivan, June 12, 1929; Orville Van Brunt to CHS, June 14, 1929, F1340.

15. C. E. Spens, "Memorandum," Apr. 19, 1929; C. E. Spens to JMK, Oct. 5, 1929; CHS to JMK, Oct. 7, 1929; JMK to Spens, Oct. 5, 1929, all in F1340.

16. ICC, Notice, Finance Docket 7464 et al., Aug. 27, 1929; *Fort Worth Record-Telegram,* Oct. 17, 1929; ICC, *Finance Reports,* 158:546–56.

17. CHS to F. E. Clarity, Nov. 6, Dec. 31, 1929; George B. Cromwell to C. E. Spens, Nov. 8, 1929; CHS to JMK, Nov. 26, Dec. 12, 1929; Clarity to CHS, Dec. 9, 1929; Cromwell to CHS, Dec. 23, 1929; JMK to CHS, Jan. 3, 1930; John A. Hulen to CHS, Jan. 5, 1930, all in F1340.

18. Orville Van Brunt to Frederick E. Williamson, Mar. 1, 1929, F1340; CHS to Van Brunt, July 3, 1929, F604; District Court of Hardeman County, Summons to Certain-teed Products Corporation, June 10, 1929, F1340; Orville Van Brunt to A. L. Reed, July 1, 1929, F1340; Orville Van Brunt to F. E. Williamson, Aug. 26, 1929, F1340.

19. ICC, *Finance Reports,* 158:699–704; *Quanah Tribune-Chief,* Feb. 4, 1930; CHS to JMK, Feb. 7, 1930, F1340; CHS to Orville Van Brunt, Mar. 12, 1931, F1480.

20. QA&P, Right-of-way and Track Maps, Quanah & Acme, Apr. 1931; Contract, QA&P with Lone Star Construction Company, F1408; AFE 167; O. E. Sweet to CHS, Mar. 5, 1931, F1340; AFS to CHS, Nov. 30, 1930, F1408.

21. Reed, pp. 522, 399; QA&P, Contract with Fort Worth & Denver City and Acme Tap Railroad, Jan. 1, 1931, and annual renewals through 1946.

## CHAPTER 13

1. Application of the Quanah, Acme & Pacific Railway, Return to Questionnaire, Finance Docket 4959 (1925), p. 11; WLR to AFS, Nov. 15, 1932, F401; United States, House of Representatives, Subcommittee of the Committee on Interstate and Foreign Commerce, Hearing on H.R. 5364, 74th Cong., p. 29.

2. AFS to CHS, July 16, 1927, NF; *Floyd County Hesperian,* Sept. 15, 29, 1927; AFS to CHS, Oct. 21, 1931, F313-5; *Floyd County Hesperian,* Mar. 8, 15, 1928; CHS to JMK, Mar. 3, 28, 1928, F1316.

3. CHS to J. R. Koontz, May 2, 1928; Koontz to CHS, May 26, 1928; AFS to CHS, Sept. 11, 1928; F. C. Freiburg to T. B. Gallagher, May 19, 1930; Gallagher to Freiburg, Aug. 14, 1929, all in F1347.

4. F. C. Freiburg to T. B. Gallagher, Feb. 17, 1931; J. R. Hayden to Freiburg, June 29, 1931; Freiburg to Hayden, Jan. 7, Apr. 16, 1932, all in F1582; Hayden to Freiburg, Apr. 27, 1932, F1507.

5. CHS to WLR, Jan. 2, 1931, F1286; J. R. Hayden to L. M. Hogsett, Nov. 17, 1932, F1582.

6. Trans-Continental Freight Bureau, Rate Advice No. Y-10070, Mar. 13, 1933; WLR to All Concerned, Mar. 25, 1933, F1853; Traffic Analysis, F1582.

7. WLR to All Concerned, Apr. 14, 1933, F1853; CHS to George B. McGinty, Apr. 20, 1933, F1582; CHS to W. B. Storey, Apr. 24, 1933, F450.

8. W. B. Storey to CHS, Apr. 26, 1933; J. R. Hayden to George B. McGinty, Apr. 28, 1933, both in F1582.

9. E. N. Adams to George B. McGinty, Apr. 26, 1933; G. E. Goodwin to McGinty, Apr. 25, 1933, both in F1582.

10. CHS to WLR, May 6, 1933, F1862; WLR to CHS, May 15, 1933, F1582; George B. McGinty to CHS, May 29, 1933, F1582; WLR to All Concerned, June 1, 1933, F1582.

11. CHS to Frank Kell, June 24, 1933; CHS to GEH, June 12, 1933; Bird M. Robinson to CHS, May 1, 1933; JMK to CHS, Oct. 6, 1933, all in F1582; WLR to Ben F. Grubbs, Nov. 27, 1933, F1862.

12. REQ to M. G. Roberts, July 13, 1933; CHS to JMK, June 4, 1934; WLR to REQ, June 16, 1934, REQ to CHS, June 26, 1934; ICC, Report to the Commission, Division 4, Docket 26070, Nov. 26, 1934, all in F1582; *Amarillo Daily News,* Nov. 10, 1934.

13. REQ to CHS, Dec. 14, 1934; W. L. White to CHS, Dec. 18, 1934; CHS to W. L. White, Dec. 21, 1934; ICC, Announcement, Docket 26070, Apr. 30, 1935, all in F1582.

14. REQ to CHS, Jan. 8, 1934; B. H. Stanage to CHS, Dec. 28, 1934, both in F1582.

15. ICC, Order, Docket 26070, Oct. 29, 1935, F1582.

16. CHS to C. A. Miller, Dec. 17, 1935, Apr. 23, 1936; REQ to CHS, Dec. 21, 1935, all in F1582.

17. CHS to WLR, Aug. 22, 1936, F1862; *Traffic World,* Aug. 29, 1936; ICC, Order, Docket 26070, Sept. 24, 1936, F1582; ICC, Examiner's Recommendation, Docket 26070, Mar. 30, 1937; CHS to REQ, Mar. 31, 1937, F1582; CHS to B. H. Stanage, Mar. 30, 1937, F1582.

18. ICC, *Finance Reports,* 226:201–24; *Railway Age* 104 (Mar. 5, 1938): 429; REQ to CHS, Mar. 2, 3, 1938, F1582.

19. CHS to GEH, Mar. 9, 1938; CHS to REQ, Mar. 3, 1938; CHS to B. H. Stanage, Mar. 3, 1938, all in F1582.

19. CHS to GEH, Mar. 9, 1938; CHS to REQ, Mar. 3, 1938; CHS to B. H. Stanage, Mar. 3, 1938, all in F1582.

20. WLR to CHS, Mar. 26, 1938; CHS to REQ, Mar. 29, May 29, 1938; CHS to Harry C. Barron, May 6, 18, 1938; CHS to

WLR, May 19, 1938, all in F1582; ICC, *Finance Reports,* 227:561–62; WLR to All Concerned, June 8, 1938, F1582.

21. CHS to WLR, June 8, 1938, F1862; *Railway Age* 108 (June 8, 1938): 1028; CHS to B. H. Stanage, June 8, 1938, F1582; WLR to A. M. Reinhardt, July 6, 1938, F1878-3; CHS to WLR, July 8, 1938, F1507; Paul P. Hastings to CHS, Feb. 27, 1939, F1507.

22. WLR to A. M. Reinhardt, Nov. 16, 23, Dec. 6, 1938; CHS to REQ, Mar. 14, Apr. 18, 1939; Paul R. Hastings to CHS, Mar. 8, 1939; CHS to J. J. Grogan, Mar. 18, 1939, all in F1507.

23. Paul R. Hastings to CHS, June 14, July 5, 1939; CHS to JMK, June 29, Sept 25, 1939; CHS to AFS, June 29, 1939; B. H. Stanage to CHS, Aug. 5, 1939, all in F1507.

24. WLR to CHS, Oct. 15, 1943, F1347; WLR to CHS, Sept. 19, 1946, Aug. 13, 1954, F1862; REQ to WLR, July 27, 1954, F1862.

25. C. R. Sherwood, interview with author, Mar. 26, 1976; CHS to WLR, Nov. 2, 1936, F1582.

## CHAPTER 14

1. Frank M. Dougherty to CHS, Apr. 5, 1928, NF. For a synopsis of Depression conditions in the area, see Rutherford's *One Corner of Heaven.*

2. Carl S. Guin to CHS, Sept. 20, 1928, NF; CHS to Guin, Sept. 22, 1928, F1314.

3. *Quanah Tribune-Chief,* Oct. 25, 1928; L. M. Hogsett, Memorandum, Aug. 30, 1930, NF; Hogsett to T. K. Hawkins, Aug. 30, 1930, F1314; CHS to AFS, Nov. 3, 1930, F1314; *Matador Tribune,* Oct. 30, 1930.

4. CHS to AFS, Apr. 9, 1930, F1354; F. M. Dougherty to CHS, July 7, 1930, F549; B. F. Hobson to CHS, Sept. 30, 1930, NF; L. M. Hogsett to All Agents, Sept. 18, 1930, F1314; AFS to CHS, Oct 14., 1930, NF; QA&P, Minute Book 3, p. 77; CHS to J. Sam Lewis, Dec. 31, 1930, F1354.

5. CHS to AFS, July 15, 1936, F99; RRCT, Special Authority 26, July 28, 1936, F1314.

6. CHS to J. R. Koontz, Feb. 11, 1931; AFS to T. K. Hawkins, Feb. 9, 1931; W. M. Baxter to CHS, Feb. 27, 1931; Z. D. Barber to WLR, Oct. 8, 1934; CHS to WLR, Oct. 23, 1934; CHS to AFS, Mar. 4, 1931, all in F1227. On Quanah and Hardeman County during the Depression see Winston M. Estes, *Another Part of the House.*

7. Robert Medlen to AFS, June 21, 1931, June 19, 1932, F68; QA&P, Minute Book 3, pp. 185, 199, 205, 219, 235, 249, 269, 281.

8. *Wichita Falls Daily Times,* Mar. 22, 1929; *Dallas Morning News,* Mar. 27, 1929; *Lubbock Avalanche,* Mar. 27, 1929.

9. *Quanah Tribune-Chief,* and *Quanah Times,* "Special Consolidated Issue for the Plainview Railway Hearing," July 19, 1925; *Fort Worth Record,* Aug. 16, 1925; *Paducah Post,* Nov. 25, 1926; *Floyd County Hesperian,* Aug. 6, 13, 1925; *A Message from the Panhandle and South Plains of Texas by Gamble Land Company* (Floydada, Texas, 1928); B. F. Hobson to CHS, Dec. 15, 1932, NF.

10. Statement of Charles H. Sommer, 1923, F984; *Fort Worth Record-Telegram,* Mar. 20, 1926.

11. *Dallas Morning News,* Dec. 1, 923; *Fort Worth Star-Telegram,* Dec. 1, 1923; Statement of Charles H. Sommer regarding the application of the Ardmore, Vernon & Lubbock Railway, 1927.

12. QA&P, Minute Book 3, pp. 163, 173; Railroad Employees Association of Houston to Fellow Railroad Employees, Jan. 5, 1935, NF; *Texas Highway Truck Accident and Tax Data 1833; Floyd County Hesperian,* Apr. 6, 1939; CHS to AFS, May 7, 1940, F949; AFS to CHS, May 1, 1940, NF; CHS to WLR, Aug. 8, 1939, F949.

13. L. M. Hogsett to T. K. Hawkins et al., Sept. 17, 1930, NF; M. E. Allen to CHS, May 16, 1933, F1582; "Rail-Truck Coordination, The Fitch System," n.d. [1939?], F949; CHS to WLR, July 26, 1939, F949.

14. *Paducah Post,* Nov. 1, 1940; CHS to E. A. Carlock, Nov. 16, 1940, NF; *Dallas Morning News,* Mar. 12, 1939; John P. Marrs to CHS, June 16, 1925, F1075.

15. Coordination Report of Terminals or Stations, Quanah, Texas, and Acme, Texas, 1934, F1598; CHS to JMK, Dec. 7, 1934, F1598; CHS to AFS, Sept. 19, 1933, F1597; SL to JMK, July 24, 1925, F1111; H. B. Lautz to AFS, Oct. 5, 1933, F1597; E. J. Engel to CHS, June 2, 1941, F1597.

16. CHS to GEH, Apr. 10, 1933, F949; GEH to CHS, Apr. 13, 1933, NF.

17. CHS to JMK, Apr. 25, 1925, F1107.

18. GEH to CHS, June 16, 1933, NF; CHS to GEH, Dec. 9, 1933, NF.

19. CHS to GEH, Dec. 9, 1933, NF; *Matador Tribune,* Jan. 11, 1934; CHS to WLR, Sept. 20, 1934, NF.

20. QA&P, Minute Book 3, pp. 189–91; CHS to GEH, Mar. 26, 1935, NF; GEH, memorandum, Mar. 29, 1935, NF.

21. CHS to GEH, May 17, 1935, NF; *Matador Tribune,* May 30, 1935.

22. *Matador Tribune,* June 13, 1935; W. T. Patton to AFS, June 26, 1935, NF; *Matador Tribune,* May 30, 1935; CHS to GEH, June 19, 1935, NF; GEH to CHS, June 15, 1935, NF; GEH to CHS, June 3, 1936, F313-6.

23. ICC, Notice, Finance Docket 10851, Oct. 9, 1935, F1652.

24. ICC, Application of the Quanah, Acme & Pacific Railway, Finance Docket 10851, Reporter's Minutes, Nov. 18–19, 1935, pp. 42–45, F1652 (hereafter, this document will be identified as RM).

25. RM, pp. 14, 16, 65; QA&P, Statement A; QA&P, Exhibit F, both in F1652.

26. RM, pp. 19, 67–80; QA&P, Statement IB; QA&P, Exhibits 21, 22, all in F1652.

27. RM, pp. 42, 195; Brief in Behalf of the Protestants, Feb. 27, 1936; Reply to and Contest of the Application, June 6, 1935, both in F1652.

28. ICC, Finance Docket 10851, Report Proposed by J. S. Prichard, Examiner, n.d. [Feb. 1936?], F1652; ICC, *Finance Reports,* 212:505–508. The official record misrepresented the $2,061.34 profit for 1928 as loss.

29. CHS to AFS, Apr. 21, 1936, F1652; WLR to All Concerned, "Abandonment Notice," Apr. 23, 1936, F1652; SL-SF, Embargo Notice 89, May 8, 1936, F313-6; AFS to W. T. Patton, May 7, 1936, F313-6-5; Benson Maxwell to Quanah & Floydada RPO, May 22, 1936, F313-6-3.

30. AFS to M. D. Braselton, May 28, 1936, F313-6-1; GEH to AFS, July 1, 1936, NF; AFS to Wayne H. Sager, Feb. 21, 1938, F313-6-2; QA&P, contract with J. W. McKissick, n.d., F1652; AFS to B. F. Wiley, June 24, 1936, F313-6-1; CHS to AFS, June 17, 1936, F313-6-2; AFS to CHS, July 17, 1936, F313; QA&P, Minute Book 3, p. 205.

31. Unidentified clipping from *Matador Tribune* [1926?], F1111; *Matador Tribune,* May 28, 1936.

32. *Matador Tribune,* May 28, 1936.

33. Unidentified clipping, F1652.

## CHAPTER 15

1. QA&P, Minute Book 1, pp. 2, 30; QA&P, Minute Book 2, pp. 141, 359, 373; QA&P, Annual Report to the ICC, 1928, p. 108; *St. Louis Globe-Democrat,* Mar. 7, 1926; QA&P, Application, Return to Questionnaire No. 1, Finance Docket 4959 (1925), p. 2; JMK to CHS, Oct. 31, 1933, F1582.

2. QA&P, Stock Certificate Book No. 1, Certificate 83; QA&P, Stock Ledger, pp. 29, 31, 33.

3. Data compiled from several sources, including the annual reports of the QA&P to the ICC.

4. Ibid.; Laura Lynn Wyman, "The Quanah, Acme & Pacific Railway," pp. 89–90.

5. Wyman, pp. 89–90; "Recap of Station Business Reports 1933," F304-14; "Statement Showing Number of Cars, Commodity—Total Freight," F1207; *Quanah Tribune-Chief,* Nov. 5, 1914; CHS to AFS, Aug. 11, 1924, F69; AFS to CHS, Sept. 2, 1924, F69.

6. Wyman, pp. 89–90; Robert Medlen to WLR, June 12, 13, July 18, 25, 1931, F68; *QA&P Employees' Magazine* 2 (Oct. 1936): 12.

7. D. J. Collins to WLR, Aug. 22, 1938; WLR to W. J. Weaver, Aug. 24, 1938, both in F185.

8. Bennett, p. 249; Williams, p. 95; Murdo MacKenzie, "The Matador Ranch," *Panhandle-Plains Historical Review* 21 (1948): 94–105; Pearce, pp. 145, 147; Bennett, p. 198; J. W. Finucane to AFS, Nov. 5, 1929, NF; W. A. Bishop to AFS, Dec. 4, 1929, NF.

9. Robert Cray to CHS, July 5, 1911, F16; *Floyd County Hesperian,* Oct. 4, 1928; AT&SF, Division Sheet No. 5 for Tariff No. 10476-D, Apr. 13, 1927; SL-SF, Division Basis No. 1158-B, Jan. 1, 1922.

10. M. M. Pomphrey to the author, Feb. 27, 1976; Robert Medlen to AFS, Nov. 16, 1929, F32.

11. M. M. Pomprhrey to the author, Feb. 27, 1976; QA&P, OS&D Report 433, Quanah, Texas, Sept. 14, 1934; QA&P, Live Stock Freight Waybill CS-74, Aug. 25, 1934.

12. Robert Medlen to W. H. Crawford, Mar. 22, 1937, F158; AFS to CHS, Sept. 30, 1932, F333-1; C. H. Harris to AFS, Oct. 27, 1932, NF; WLR to J. R. Meacham, Mar. 27, 1939, F121; W. H. Crawford to AFS, July 7, 1935, F26-2; WLR to AFS, Oct. 24, 1939, F121; *Paducah Post,* Apr. 30, 1936; *QA&P Employees' Magazine* 2 (Nov. 1936): 11, and (Dec. 1936): 19, and 5 (Mar.–Apr. 1939): 6.

13. E. F. Tillman to AFS, June 13, 1934, F121; WLR to CHS, Aug. 2, 1937, F1203-53; R. M. Swenson to WLR, Apr. 25, 1940, F121; WLR to J. G. Weaver, May 6, 1940, F121.

14. AFS to John C. Murphree, June 9, 1931, NF; CHS to AFS, Oct. 30, 1930, NF; AFS to CHS, Nov. 5, 1930, F116; J. R. Meacham to AFS, Nov. 5, 1930, NF; W. H. Crawford to AFS, July 7, 1935, F26-2; AFS to CHS, July 8, 1935, F333-1.

15. J. R. Meacham to GEH, Oct. 6, 1935, F333-8; John MacKenzie to CHS, July 22, 1937, NF; CHS to MacKenzie, July 3, 1937, NF.

16. GEH to CHS, Apr. 7, 1933, F333-1; J. A. Lovell to CHS, June 10, 1931, NF; John A. Hulen to CHS, May 7, 1931, F1526; CHS to Hulen, Apr. 13, 1933, F121; CHS to J. A. Lovell, June 13, 1933, F1526; Mary Wattey Clarke, *The Swenson Saga and the SMS Ranches,* p. 159; I. S. McConnell to QA&P, Feb. 24, 1931, F1203-110.

17. GEH to CHS, Apr. 7, 1933, F333-1; FS to CHS, Apr. 28, Aug. 11, 1933, all in F333-1.

18. John A. Hulen to CHS, Apr. 15, 1933, NF; WLR to J. A. Lovell, Oct. 26, 1933, F2009; AFS to CHS, Feb. 14, 1934, F333-1; WLR to All Agents and Others Concerned, Aug. 9, 1934, F2009-1203; E. F. Tillman to AFS, Dec. 14, 1933, F333-1; John D. Anderson to WLR, Mar. 8, 1937, NF; WLR to CHS, Sept. 30, 1937, Feb. 10, 1938, F957.

19. J. L. McCormack to AFS, Dec. 3, 14, 1929, F216; J. R. Meacham to AFS, Jan. 11, 1930, F216; W. A. Bishop to AFS, Jan. 2, 1930, F216; QA&P, OS&D Report 432, Quanah, Texas, Sept. 14, 1934.

20. QA&P, Station Log, Quanah, Texas, June 2, 1934, F26-2; W. H. Crawford to AFS, Oct. 19, 1935, F26-2; Crawford to AFS, Mar. 24, 1941, F26-4; Crawford to AFS, Apr. 26, 1939, F121; AFS to CHS, June 15, 1934, F333-1; Robert Medlen to AFS, Apr. 27, 1937, F158-1; Robert Medlen, interview with author, Jan. 16, 1976.

21. AFS to CHS, June 9, 1931, NF; WLR to AFS, Mar. 6, 1934, F1303-1203; AFS to Roy Williams, Oct. 13, 1938, F333-1; Williams to AFS, Oct. 14, 1938, F333-1; Williams to J. G. Weaver, Oct. 14, 1938, F1886-RW; AFS to All Agents, Apr. 27, 1939, F333-1; QA&P, Traffic Circular 128, July 31, 1939.

22. WLR to CHS, Mar. 8, 1933, F1138; AFS to WLR, Aug. 19, 1932, F320-2; WLR to AFS, Nov. 30, 1935, F1870–1612; AFS to CHS, June 6, 1929, F1359; Various items, F121–130; Various carriers' reports, F1132.

23. AFS, Bulletin N. 6, Aug. 4, 1930, F8-1; *QA&P Employees' Magazine* 2 (Oct. 1936): 11; AFS to CHS, Dec. 31, 1936, FRS-3-11; CHS to AFS, May 9, 1938, FRS-3-11; R. L. Johnson, interview with author, July 22, 1975.

24. S. S. Butler to J. H. Doggrell, Nov. 2, 1928, F1338; WLR to All Agents, Feb. 22, 1932, F1338; J. H. Doggrell to E. W. Miller, July 28, 1932, F1338; R. C. Canady to All Trainmen and Enginemen, Chickasha Subdivision, Dec. 24, 1933, F1338; W. H. Crawford to WLR, Dec. 28, 1933, F1338; WLR to CHS, Apr. 9, 1934, F2009-1; WLR to CHS, May 28, 1934, F1338.

25. WLR to Mr. Matador and Roaring Springs Business Man, May 31, 1932, NF; Robert Medlen, interview with author, Jan. 16, 1976; Floyd Hodo, interview with author, Jan. 26, 1976.

26. Various statistical tables, F1703; *Dallas Morning News,* Oct. 29, 1932.

27. T. K. Hawkins to F. I. Frink, Aug. 20, 1929, F51-4; Robert Cray to CHS, Jan. 20, 1916, F119-5; AFS to All Agents, Apr. 20, 1920, F728; T. K. Hawkins to Agent, Paducah, Texas, Sept. 27, Oct. 13, 1921, F728; Robert Cray to CHS, Sept. 22, 1916, F119-T; AFS to CHS, Sept. 22, 1928, F728; WLR to AFS, July 3, 1933, Oct. 24, 1935, F728; AFS to W. H. Crawford, Sept. 3, 1929, F51-4; WLR to J. W. Nourse, Oct. 29, 1935, F728. On circus trains, see Tom Parkinson and Charles Philip Fox, *The Circus Moves by Rail.*

28. *Official Guide of the Railways,* Apr. 1920, p. 537, and Oct. 1925, p. 637; SL-SF, Time Table, May 1924 and Nov. 1927; AFS to W. A. Nabors, Feb. 27, 1924, F989; AFEs 17 and 73.

29. *Paducah Post,* Aug. 30, 1923; H. H. Wilkins to the State Railroad Commission, Sept. 19, 1923; CHS to AFS, Sept. 6, 1923; AFS to Clarence E. Gilmore, Oct. 20, 1923; W. A. Nabors to AFS, Feb. 5, 1924, all in F989.

30. Cottle County Chamber of Commerce, Petition, Nov. 7, 1923, F989; RRCT, Special Notice, Nov. 13, 1923.

31. CHS to W. H. Wilkins, Nov. 12, 1923; CHS to J. P. Marrs, Dec. 19, 1923; AFS to W. A. Nabors, Feb. 13, 1924, all in F989.

32. Weekly and monthly statistical data, F1083; AFS to CHS, May 2, 1925, F51-8.

33. Walter Gerron, Traveling Inspector's Report to the RRCT, Feb. 8, 1924.

34. CHS to J. E. Hutchison, July 21, 1928, F76; CHS to AFS, Sept. 5, 1928, F76; J. W. Nourse to H. P. Clements, Sept. 12, 1928, F708; CHS to AFS, Sept. 24, 1928, F46; Nourse to A. V. Burr, Sept. 25, 1928, F708; AFS, Bulletin No. 9, Oct. 6, 1928; *Official Guide to the Railways,* Sept. 1928, p. 713.

35. CHS to AFS, Sept. 5, 1928, F76; CHS to AFS, Oct. 28, 1928, F50; J. B. Jenkins to CHS, Nov. 29, 1929, F1261; G. F. Stephens to CHS, Sept. 21, 1928, NF; CHS to AFS, Oct. 31, 1928, NF.

36. S. W. Gaines to AFS, Oct. 27, 1925, Sept. 21, 1928, F59-3; Robert Medlen, interview with author, Jan. 16, 1976.

37. QA&P, Contract with Wells Fargo & Company, July 1, 1916; Secretary's Contract No. 111; Various items, all in F89; QA&P, Local and Joint Tariff, Sept. 1, 1929; Robert Medlen to T. K. Hawkins, Oct. 25, 1929, F5.

38. Robert Medlen to AFS, Dec. 27, 1928, FP-53; Medlen to AFS, Feb. 6, 1929, F51-9; WLR to Ed. C. Abbott, Feb. 12, 1931, F1622; E. C. Slaughter to Medlen, Feb. 15, 1931, FP-53; Medlen to WLR, Sept. 16, 1929, FP-53; Medlen to J. G. Logsdon, Apr. 10, 1930, FP-53; *Railway Age* 89 (Dec. 27, 1930): 1383.

39. CHS to AFS, Dec. 13, 1929, F51-9; AFS to CHS, July 31, 1930, F52; Various data, F1702.

40. CHS to AFS, Mar. 24, June 16, 1931, F396-1; C. E. Harris to R. J. Cernak, May 9, 1955, F213-2; Various data, F245-2; J. B. Jenkins to CHS, June 20, 1931, NF; CHS to Jenkins, June 26, 1931, F396-1; *Official Guide of the Railways,* July 1931, p. 743; CHS to AFS, June 8, 1931, F461; CHS to T. K. Hawkins, June 27, 1931, F461.

41. Earl Jones to AFS, Oct. 4, 1938, F310-2; Robert Medlen to F. A. Bauchens, Mar. 6, 1931, F53-P; *QA&P Employees' Magazine* 12 (Jan. 1936): 11.

42. Various data, F1702.

43. CHS to AFS, Mar. 7, 24, 1933, Mar. 29, 1935, F918; CHS to AFS, Oct. 24, 1934, F46; *Paducah Post,* July 22, 1937; CHS to AFS, July 19, 1937, NF; AFS to Robert Medlen, May 27, 1939, NF.

44. CHS to AFS, Sept. 1, 1939, NF; AFS to All Concerned, Sept. 5, 1939, F396-1; CHS to J. M. Hood, Sept. 12, 1939, F396-1; AFS to W. H. Crawford, Dec. 9, 1939, NF; *Official Guide of the Railways,* Feb. 1940, p. 664.

45. C. J. Taylor to AFS, Dec. 7, 1939, F390-14; *Floyd County Hesperian,* Dec. 14, 1939; C. J. Taylor to AFS, Jan. 4, 8, 1940, F396-1.

46. Memo, Nov. 12, 1928, F51-9; *Fort Worth Star-Telegram,* Nov. 4, 1928; AFS to CHS, July 31, 1930, F51; AFS to CHS, Apr. 6, 1933, F396-1; C. T. Mason to AFS, Feb. 21, 1936, NF; Various data, F51; L. B. Clary to E. O. Daughtrey, Jan. 8, 1941, F396-4; QA&P Employee Time Tables No. 34, Dec. 10, 1939, and No. 36, July 1, 1940.

47. RRCT, Special Rate Order, May 4, 1932; Bennett, p. 193; RRCT, Special Rate Order No. 31, June 8, 1933; RRCT, Special Rate Order No. 32, June 19, 1933; RRCT, Special Tariff No. 45, May 13, 1936; J. R. Meacham to AFS, Jan. 1, 1939, F1622.

48. QA&P, Tariff Circular No. 1, Oct. 1, 1928; QA&P, Special Rate Order No. 2, Oct. 8, 1928; RRCT, Special Rate Order No. 21, Dec. 22, 1931, No. 22, Feb. 6, 1932, No. 26, Aug. 6, 1932; WLR to All Agents, Dec. 31, 1932, F303-4; RRCT, Special Rate Order No. 33, July 7, 1933; RRCT, Special Tariff No. 40, Nov. 17, 1933; RRCT, Special Rate Order No. 9, May 26, 1930; W. H. Crawford to AFS, Oct. 19, 1929, F51-4.

49. AFS to T. K. Hawkins et al., Apr. 20, 1929, F51-4; AFS to CHS, May 15, 1930, F51; FW&DC, Transportation Advice No. 975-R, Oct. 19, 1936; *QA&P Employees' Magazine* 2 (Nov. 1936): 10–11, 18–21, 24; AFS to CHS, Oct. 13, 1936, F396-6.

50. WLR to AFS, Oct. 3, 1934, F396-6; WLR to AFS, June 29, 1938, F1630; E. G. Baker to WLR, June 20, 1939, NF.

51. J. R. Whitworth to AFS, Nov. 23, 1933, F396-6; CHS to AFS, Oct. 29, 1930, F51; W. H. Crawford to AFS, Oct. 24, 1932, F396-6; WLR to AFS, Oct. 18, 1933, F396-6; CHS to AFS, Oct. 21, 1933, NF; RRCT, Special Rate Order No. 40, Nov. 3, 1933; AFS to CHS, Oct. 23, 1933, F396-6.

52. AFS to C&E Passenger Extra 25 West, Oct. 25, 1935, NF; AFS to Conductor Cadle, Oct. 25, 1935, NF; AFS to CHS, Nov. 1, 8, 1935, F396-6; CHS to F. F. Lester, Nov. 6, 1935, NF; CHS to AFS, Nov. 6, 1935, F396-6.

53. CHS to AFS, May 25, 1926, F6; QA&P, Statement of Foreign Private Cars Handled . . . 1923, 1924, 1925 (June 8, 1926), NF; *QA&P Employees' Magazine* 2 (Nov. 1936).

54. AFE 3; ICC, Engineering Report upon the Quanah, Acme & Pacific Railway, Apr. 14, 1922, Account 51 (revised, July 18, 1923); AFEs 5, 180, 183, 290; *QA&P Employees' Magazine* 2 (Jan. 1936): 10; AFEs 336, 358; AFS to CHS, Aug. 28, 1940, F1248; QA&P, Equipment Statistics, Dec. 31, 1941. On SL-SF's 2-10-0s, see Lloyd E. Stagner, *Steam Locomotives of the Frisco Lines.*

55. QA&P Employees' Magazine 4 (July 1938): 8; Elton B. Marsalis, interview with author, Jan. 13, 1976.

56. QA&P, Record of Equipment by Valuation Groups for Valuation Purposes, Account 53; ICC, Engineering Report upon the Quanah, Acme & Pacific Railway, Apr. 14, 1922, Account 57; QA&P, Equipment Owned as of December 31, 1922; Various data, F1123; VO3 1939; VO3 1940; AFS to D. W. Curnutt, Oct. 23, 1940, F187-12.

57. Various data from corporate files; *Moody's Manual of Investments* (title varies), for annual citations of the QA&P.

## CHAPTER 16

1. WLR to Al Fowle, Aug. 18, 1938, F1904; QA&P, Train Schedule, "Transcontinental Traffic via Floydada," Nov. 15, 1938, F2009; WLR to All Representatives, June 14, 1939, F2009.

2. J. R. Coulter to Various Personnel, Nov. 29, 1939, Mar. 23, 1940, F1734; CHS to WLR, Feb. 24, 1938, F397-5; CHS to J. R. Coulter, Jan. 26, 1939, F1734; Coulter to CHS, May 9, 1940, F1734; CHS to WLR, Aug. 1, 1940, F1667.

3. C. S. Edmonds to WLR Jan. 30, 1941, NF.

4. J. P. Blanton to Chief Operating Officer, May 18, 1942, F1851-2; CHS to WLR, May 22, 1942, F1851-2; Association of American Railroads, Circular No. T&T 329, May 27, 1942, NF. For a general survey of the American railroad industry during World War II, see Stover, pp. 180–91.

5. WLR to All Representatives, Jan. 30, 1942, F1734; QA&P, Traffic Circular SG-115, Nov. 28, 1941, F2009; CHS to J. R. Coulter, July 20, 1942, F1792.

6. AFS to CHS, Jan. 15, 1942, F397-4; CHS to WLR, Apr. 3, 1943, F378-1; CHS to WLR, Apr. 14, 1943, F1829; WLR to AFS, Mar. 29, 1943, F1851-2; WLR to AFS, Apr. 5, 1943, F378-1; CHS to AFS, Apr. 6, 1943, F1823; WLR to AFS, Apr. 9, 1943, F378-1; CHS to AFS, Apr. 14, 1943, F1829; WLR to CHS, Apr. 21, 1943, F378-1.

7. WLR to AFS, June 30, 1939, Oct. 30, 1941, both in F1630.

8. WLR to AFS, Dec. 14, 1941, Sept. 10, Oct. 11, 1943, Oct. 28, 1944, all in F1630.

9. E. G. Baker to A. M. Ball, Apr. 14, 1945; Raymond C. Stone to WLR, June 3, 1944, both in F1630.

10. Stagner, pp. 86–87; AFS to CHS, Oct. 31, 1942, F184-6; AFS to L. B. Clary, Sept. 16, 1942, NF; Clary to AFS, Sept. 12, 1942, NF.

11. Charles E. Harris to AFS, Aug. 22, 1942, F396-4; AFS to CHS, Mar. 1, 1943, NF.

12. WLR to R. C. Klostermeyer, Feb. 19, 1943, F11; WLR to CHS, Mar. 12, 1943, F89.

13. AFS to CHS, Jan. 27, 1945, F397-14.

14. AFS to AFS, Feb. 20, 1943, F89; AFS to CHS, Feb. 23, 1943, F89; WLR to CHS, Feb. 23, 1943, F401.

15. CHS to WLR, May 8, 1943, F89.

16. WLR to R. C. Klostermeyer, Feb. 24, 1943, F203; WLR to CHS, Jan. 26, 1945, F401; WLR to CHS, Jan. 12, 1945, F203; WLR to CHS, Dec. 4, 1944, F1734.

17. WLR to CHS, Apr. 14, 1942, F1792; CHS to J. R. Coulter, Jan. 27, 1943, F781; WLR to AFS, Oct. 31, 1944, F397-14; W. J. Irwin to WLR, Dec. 2, 1944, F1734.

18. REQ to CHS, Sept. 30, 1940, NF; WLR to AFS, Jan. 30, 1942, F401; CHS to Paul P. Hastings, Mar. 12, 1942, F1734; Hastings to CHS, Apr. 2, 1942, F1734; G. H. Minchin to AFS, June 3, 1942, F396-4; AFS to CHS, June 8, 1942, F396-4; CHS to AFS, Apr. 7, 1942, F1746.

19. AFS to CHS, Nov. 4, 1944, F397-14; WLR to CHS, Dec. 8, 1944, F2009; CHS to WLR, Mar. 30, 1945, F46.

20. Composite information from F91, 1667, and 1788.

21. E. H. Bunnell to Chief Accounting Officers, Sept. 30, Oct. 28, Nov. 15, 1940; J. M. Hood to All Members, Oct. 26, 1940, Mar. 6, 1941; C. A. Miller to All Members, May 7, 1942, all in 1786.

22. C. A. Miller to All Members, Oct. 3, 1940, F1786; JMK to J. R. Koontz, Sept. 30, 1940, F1786; CHS to L. E. Rhyne, Mar. 31, 1941, F1675; AFS to All Employees, Apr. 9, 1941, F1786; CHS to Rhyne, May 28, 1941, F1786.

23. GEH to CHS, Sept. 8, 1942, F1786; J. M. Hood to All Members, Sept. 14, 1942, F1786; CHS to L. E. Rhyne, Oct. 6, 1942, NF.

24. CHS to AFS, Apr. 26, Feb. 15, 1943; AFS to CHS, Mar. 12, May 5, 1943, all in F1830.

25. C. E. Harris to AFS, Feb. 17, 1944; Selective Service System, State Director Advice, Jan. 12, 1944, both in F1830.

26. *Dallas Morning News,* Mar. 4, 1945; AFS to CHS, Mar. 7, 9, June 18, 1945; CHS to AFS, June 27, 1945, all in F1830.

27. AFS to CHS, Feb. 20, 1943, NF; AFS to CHS, May 17, 1945, F331; CHS to WLR, May 17, 1945, F331; CHS to AFS, Feb. 13, 1945, F650.

28. J. W. Sampley to CHS, June 12, 1942; GEH to CHS, June 13, 1942; CHS to WLR, June 23, 1942, CHS to AFS, Nov. 25, 1942, all in F1830.

29. WLR to CHS, June 18, 1942, Mar. 27, 1943; WLR to Syl R. Fiorita, June 22, Oct. 17, 1942; CHS to WLR, Apr. 1, 1943; R. C. Klostermeyer to WLR, Apr. 10, 1943; T. A. Hicks to WLR, Nov. 3, 1943, all in F1830.

30. CHS to AFS, Jan. 20, 1932, F51; CHS to J. W. Sampley, Apr. 24, 1942, F51; CHS to AFS, Feb. 15, 1943, F650; CHS to AFS, Mar. 5, 1943, F51.

31. L. E. Rhyne to AFS, Oct. 26, 1942, F320-8-2; CHS to AFS, Oct. 27, 1942, F1675; AFS to L. E. Rhyne, Oct. 30, 1942, NF.

32. CHS to AFS, Jan. 27, Mar. 4, 1943, F1675; L. E. Rhyne to AFS, Nov. 2, 1942, F320-8-2; Rhyne to CHS, Feb. 12, 1943, NF; AFS to CHS, Feb. 23, Mar. 8, 1943, F320-8-2.

33. L. E. Rhyne to CHS, Sept. 8, 1943, F320-8-2; CHS to AFS, Sept. 10, 1943, F320-8-2; C. A. Miller to CHS, Sept. 28, 1943, F320-8-2; CHS to Miller, Oct. 9, 1943, F1675; Rhyne to F. E. Milliman, Oct. 5, 1943, F1675; Supplemental Agreement . . . , Feb. 18, 1944, F320-8-2.

34. AFS to CHS, Nov. 4, 1942; CHS to AFS, Oct. 31, 1942, both in F1675.

35. AFS to J. R. Ellis, May 26, 1945, F233-2; L. E. Rhyne to CHS, May 24, 1945, F388; CHS to AFS, May 29, 1945, F338; CHS to Rhyne, June 1, 1945, F388; CHS to C. A. Miller, June 2, 1945, F1675; Rhyne to CHS, June 9, 1945, F1675.

36. AFS to All Employees, Nov. 15, 1941; GEH to AFS, Nov. 18, 1941; AFS to Various Employees, May 21, 1942; D. C.

Riley to AFS, May 23, 1942; Guy Traylor to AFS, May 23, 1942; AFS to All Employees, May 29, 1942, all in F105-5.

37. AFS to All Employees, Aug. 22, 1942, F105-5; *Matador Tribune,* Sept. 23, 1943; *Floyd County Hesperian,* Nov. 17, 1944; QA&P, Analysis of Ledger Account, Dec. 31, 1945, F1816.

38. CHS to F. A. Thompson, Jan. 22, 1945, F835; AFS to H. G. Smith, Apr. 10, 1942, F287-1; John Pfeiffer to AFS, Sept. 7, 1942, F287-1; AFS to Wilmer Wilson, June 28, 1944, F287-1; AFS to Eunice Wilson, Aug. 8, 1945, F287-1.

39. CHS to J. R. Coulter, Jan. 27, 1943, F781; WLR to CHS, Dec. 5, 1944, F1734.

40. CHS to WLR, Dec. 21, 1944, F1734; CHS to F. A. Thompson, Jan. 20, 1945, F1667; WLR to CHS, Sept. 24, 1945, F1667; WLR to All Representatives, Nov. 3, 1945, F1734.

## CHAPTER 17

1. QA&P, Personnel Records, passim.

2. Personnel File 284-D-1; F. M. Gunter, interview with author, Oct. 24, 1975; Personnel File 284-S-3; B. H. Stone, interview with author, Jan. 26, 1976; Personnel File 284-S-1.

3. QA&P, Annual Report to the ICC, 1917, 1921.

4. QA&P, Fifth Re-Issue of Permanent Wage Schedule in Effect since February 1, 1910 (Aug. 1, 1917): CHS to AFS, Feb. 9, 1921, F341; AFS to H. L. Smith, Feb. 14, 1921, F31-2.

5. AFS to G. E. Pryor, Aug. 19, 1921, F31-4; AFS to Pryor, Oct. 4, 1921, F31-1; AFS to CHS, May 24, 1929, F31-4.

6. Robert Cray to CHS, May 5, 1914, F398; *Railway Age,* June 6, 1925, p. 1411; QA&P, Announcement of Employees' Insurance Plan, Mar. 27, 1925; CHS to All QA&P Employees, Jan. 9, 1928, NF; Various data, F585.

7. CHS to AFS, Dec. 22, 1924, F1043; AFS to CHS, Dec. 31, 1924, NF.

8. CHS to AFS, Dec. 20, 1926, Dec. 8, 1927, Dec. 8, 1928, Dec. 13, 27, 1929; Bill Cantrell to CHS, Dec. 24, 1929, all in F1043; *Railway Age,* Dec. 28, 1929.

9. QA&P, Annual Report to the ICC, 1930, 1939; CHS to AFS, Feb. 28, 1931, F51; CHS to WLR, Jan. 23, 1932, F51; AFS to All Employees, July 31, 1934, F318-6.

10. AFS to Carl Gallagher, Dec. 18, 1930, F336-2; George G. Sager to CHS, Dec. 30, 1930, F453; AFS to CHS, July 22, 1936, F120-5.

11. J. L. Clogdell to All Members of QA&P Employees Booster Club, June 13, 1935, F1634.

12. *QA&P Employee's Magazine* 1 (Dec. 1934); Orvis Weathers to CHS, Dec. 4, 1934; CHS to AFS, July 25, Dec. 21, 1935; O. M. Colston to CHS, Feb. 1, 1939, all in F1634.

13. CHS to J. W. Sampley, Nov. 10, 1937; CHS to C. E. Harris, Aug. 17, Nov. 16, 1938, all in F1634; Elton B. Marsalis, interview with author, Jan. 13, 1976.

14. AFS to W. D. Wilson, Mar. 19, 1938, F121-8; AFS to Ruby Lee Leary, Sept. 10, 1938, F121-4; AFS to Otto W. Selmon, Jan. 20, 1941, F121-4; J. R. Jernigan to C. E. Harris, June 16, 1938, F287-5; AFS to F. G. Hardwick, Sept. 22, 1939, F121-2; AFS to A. E. Stovall, Sept. 21, 1940, F121-3.

15. A. C. Drynan to AFS, Apr. 18, 1941, NF; CHS to AFS, Sept. 21, 1942, F1714; Personnel Files 284-B-61, 284-C-71, 284-C-62.

16. Personnel File 284-M-2; CHS to AFS, Apr. 21, 1936, F1652; Personnel File 284-B-5; CHS to AFS, Apr. 14, 1938, F585; Personnel File 284-20-6; CHS to W. H. Norman, July 2, 1945, F51.

17. Personnel Files 284-P-28 and 284-D-2; GEH to AFS, May 16, 1934, F284-B-13.

18. WLR to J. N. Lewis, Nov. 2, 1943, F127; CHS to WLR, Dec. 13, 1932, F1553; J. J. Stitt to AFS, Feb. 11, 1933, F1553; Floyd Snyder to CHS, Nov. 1, 1932, F1553.

19. J. M. Willson to AFS, May 19, 1932; GEH to AFS, Sept. 1, 1932; CHS to GEH, Feb. 16, 1933, all in F1553.

20. Personnel Files PR-79-L, 284-B-4, 284-M-79, and 284-A-2; AFS to Pink Collett, Sept. 13, 1929, F79-C; AFS to Gordon M. Jones, Aug. 3, 1938, F284-J-3.

21. Personnel Files 284-J-1, 284-B-3, 284-B-1, and 284-S-1; A. R. Turner to AFS, June 23, 1938, F284-S-1.

22. Personnel Files 284-B-76, 285-R-29, and 284-B-33.

23. GEH to AFS, June 10, 1930, F79-C; AFS to T. H. Steffens, Mar. 21, 1921, F79-1; Personnel File 284-M-11.

24. CHS to AFS, Aug. 9, 1944, F220; C. R. Flynn to E. H. Wilson, Sept. 7, 1944, F80; CHS to Wilson, Sept. 12, 1944, F80.

25. Elton B. Marsalis, interview with author, Jan. 13, 1976.

26. Floyd Hodo, interview with author, Jan. 26, 1976.

27. Robert Medlen, interview with author, Jan. 16, 1976; Personnel File 284-M-8; *Floyd County Hesperian,* July 14, 1960; QB to Robert Medlen, July 14, 1960, F284-M-8.

28. Elton B. Marsalis, interview with author, Jan. 13, 1976; F. M. Gunter, interview with author, Oct. 24, 1975; *QA&P Employees' Magazine* 1 (Apr.–May 1935): 12; Personnel File 284-W-1.

29. A. Shoemake to All Maintenance of Way Employees on the QA&P, July 7, 1937, F1675; Agreement Covering Rates of Pay, Rules, and Working Conditions between the QA&P Railway Company and Employees Thereon Represented by the Brotherhood of Maintenance of Way Employees, July 9, 1937, F1675; A. Shoemake to All Maintenance of Way Employees on the QA&P Railway, July 13, 1937, F1675; C. A. Miller to All Members, Dec. 9, 1942, F1675-1; CHS to Miller, Nov. 1, 1946, F1675; L. E. Rhyne to All Concerned, Oct. 22, 1946, F1675; CHS to E. E. Milliman, Nov. 19, 1946, F1675.

30. CHS to I. C. Huckaby, Jan. 18, 1935; George A. Cook to CHS, July 2, 1935; CHS to Cook, July 10, 1935; CHS to Fred Barr, July 10, 1935, all in F1129.

31. T. H. Steffens to CHS, May 14, 1943, F1659; QA&P, Agreement with the Brotherhood of Locomotive Firemen and Enginemen and the Brotherhood of Railroad Trainmen, June 1, 1936, F1659; CHS to Roy Bridge, June 3, 1936, F1659; CHS to W. O. Lucas, Jan. 15, 1938, F1662; Thomas E. Bickers to CHS, Oct. 13, 1943, F1662; C. A. Miller to CHS, Aug. 29, 1944, F1662; Robert F. Cole to CHS, Aug. 28, 1944, F1662; QA&P, Agreement with the Brotherhood of Locomotive Firemen and Enginemen and the Brotherhood of Railroad Trainmen, Sept. 1, 1944, F1662.

32. QA&P, Agreement with the Order of Railroad Telegraphers, Feb. 16, 1944; QA&P, Agreement with the International Brotherhood of Firemen, Oilers, Helpers, Roundhouse and Railway Shop Laborers, May 18, 1944; QA&P, Agreement with the International Association of Machinists, International Brotherhood of Boilermakers, Iron Ship Builders and Helpers of America, and the Brotherhood of Railway Carmen of America, May 18, 1944.

33. Mediation Proceedings before the National Mediation Board, Aug. 12, 1946, F1662; C. E. Harris to H. S. Morris, Dec. 31, 1951, F284-S-42; Elton B. Marsalis, interview with author, Jan. 25, 1976.

34. *Moody's Manual of Investments,* 1941, p. 1465; 1943, p. 1437; 1946, p. 1315; 1950, p. 4361; QA&P, Annual Report to the ICC, 1941, 1945, 1949.

## CHAPTER 18

1. On S. Burke Burnett, see C. L. Douglas, *Cattle Kings of Texas,* and Williams, *Big Ranch Country;* on Quanah Parker, see Clyde L. Jackson and Grace Jackson, *Quanah Parker, Last Chief of the Comanches: A Study in Southwestern Frontier History,* and Charles H. Sommer, *Quanah Parker: Last Chief of the Comanches,* p. 42; QA&P, Stock Certificate Book 1, passim; QA&P, Stock Ledger, passim.

2. CHS to Thomas P. Littlepage, Mar. 26, 1926, F1111.

3. *QA&P Employees' Magazine* 1 (Dec. 1934): 8; QA&P, Minute Book 3, p. 122; *Who's Who in Railroading in North America,* 10th ed. (1940), p. 598; QA&P, Minute Book 2, p. 367.

4. *QA&P Employees' Magazine* 1 (Dec. 1934): 8.

5. J. W. Sampley, interview with author, Mar. 18, 1976; CHS to GEH, June 20, 1935, NF; CHS to AFS, July 26, 1929, F1347; CHS to GEH, June 18, 1935, F333-11; GEH to CHS, Mar. 18, 1951, F1116; CHS to GEH, May 4, 1951, F1116; CHS to AFS, Oct. 16, 1926, F47; CHS to AFS, May 10, 1944, F106; CHS to Don Williams, Sept. 15, 1949, F50.

6. CHS to WLR, May 17, 1945, F331; CHS to AFS, Jan. 16, 1934, F1338.

7. CHS to QB, June 1, 1959, F213-2; CHS to F. M. Dougherty, June 8, 1935, NF.

8. *Railway Age* 131 (Dec. 17, 1951): 8; *All Aboard* 4 (Dec. 1951): 1–2; CHS to Fred W. Smith, Dec. 7, 1951, F50; *Quanah Tribune-Chief,* Jan. 19, 1961.

9. QA&P, Minute Book 3, p. 122; C. R. Sherwood, interview with author, Mar. 26, 1976.

10. QA&P, Minute Book 2, pp. 245, 247; *Who's Who in Railroading in North America,* 10th ed. (1940), p. 598; C. R. Sherwood, interview with author, Mar. 26, 1976; Floyd Hodo, interview with author, Jan. 26, 1976.

11. CHS to AFS, June 21, 1928, F31-5; *Who's Who in Railroading in North America,* 14th ed. (1959), p. 533; *Railway Age* 131 (Dec. 31, 1951): 57–58.

12. C. R. Sherwood, interview with author, Mar. 26, 1976; WLR to CHS, Nov. 2, 1946, F378-1; *Quanah Tribune-Chief,* Feb. 28, Mar. 7, 1957.

13. *Who's Who in Railroading in North America,* 15th ed. (1964), p. 25; *Railway Age* 131 (Dec. 31, 1951): 57–58.

14. R. T. Moore to QB, Feb. 2, 1956, F192-8; Mrs. Quin Baker to author, July 12, 1976.

15. QB to L. E. Rhyne, Jan. 26, 1946, F287-1; Elton B. Marsalis, interview with author, Jan. 13, 1976; Floyd Hodo, interview with author, Jan. 26, 1976; C. R. Sherwood, interview with author, Mar. 26, 1976; Robert Medlen to QB, July 1, 1960, F284-M-8; L. A. Elliott, interview with author, June 3, 1976.

16. WLR to CHS, Oct. 7, 1938, F1885-CA&S.

17. W. A. Mackay to WLR, June 1, 1931, NF; WLR to All Concerned, July 22, 1932, F127; W. H. Andrews to WLR, May 10, 1930, NF; Various materials, F137; H. H. Meyer to WLR, Sept. 23, 1930, NF.

18. WLR to George L. Johnston, Aug. 19, 1935, F122; QA&P, Schedule of Pay at May 31, 1939; QA&P, Total Compensation and Expenses Paid Off-Line Agencies, 1940, F1412; ibid., 1948, F1412; Various data, F311-136; Various data, F1303-13-SNR; *Official Guide of the Railways,* Oct. 1960, p. 602.

19. WLR to QB, June 22, 1950, NF; WLR to All Concerned, Dec. 27, 1947, June 14, July 5, Sept. 19, 1949, F1412.

20. AFS to CHS, Sept. 4, 1934, F378-1; WLR to All Agents, Mar. 30, 1945, F378-1; WLR to All Agents, Feb. 26, 1946, F222-1; Robert Medlen to AFS, May 4, 1939, NF.

21. C. B. Sudborough to CHS, Apr. 24, 1944; D. V. Fraser to CHS, July 15, 1946, both in F1667; E. L. Luckett to author, Oct. 18, 1976; WLR to T. P. Troy, Sept. 19, 1939, F2100-1203; R. M. Harpel to WLR, Feb. 3, 1953, NF.

22. WLR to All Representatives, Sept. 23, 1949, F1884; WLR to J. E. Payne, Feb. 7, 1949, F1884; E. G. Baker to WLR, Sept. 2, 1953, NF; WLR to Baker, Sept. 4, 1953, NF; T. H. Banister to WLR, Sept. 21, 1953, NF.

23. Various data, F1886-129, 1886-123.

24. QA&P, Advertising Contract Nos. 3, 5, 6, 7, Secretary's files 97, 107, 108, 109; *Quanah Tribune-Chief,* Dec. 23, 1948; *Floyd County Hesperian,* July 15, 1965; *Texas Booster* 2 (Dec. 1937): 2; *Sheriff's Association Magazine,* n.d., F7871; WLR to AFS, Mar. 20, 1941, F103; Various data, F50.

25. CHS to C. J. Stephenson, Mar. 6, 1951, F50; CHS to AFS, June 12, 1941, F120-1; AFS to CHS, June 7, 1939, F184-1; WLR to CHS, Oct. 6, 1949, F50.

26. AFS to CHS, June 6, 1941, F153-14; Purchase Order 12214, Oct. 9, 1951.

27. I. L. Kerr to CHS, Aug. 21, 1950, F50; Various data, F50.

28. Various circulars, F1904; WLR to All Representatives, Feb. 6, 1946, F1904.

29. J. W. Barriger to CHS, July 30, 1951, NF; WLR to T. H. Banister, Apr. 24, 1951, F103-10; W. I. Hall to WLR, Sept. 24, 1946, NF; R. A. Potter to WLR, Oct. 3, 1946, NF; G. Mueller to WLR, Apr. 20, 1951, NF; CHS to C. J. Stephenson, Mar. 6, 1951, F50.

30. R. C. Russell to WLR, Jan. 19, 1942, NF; Frank D. Grout to QB, Jan. 28, 1946, NF; D. E. Fuller to WLR, Apr. 26, 1951, NF; Les Fischer to WLR, Aug. 16, 1951, NF; W. B. Hinchman to WLR, Jan. 20, 1942, NF; G. H. Alfriend to WLR, Jan. 22, 1942, NF; C. R. Sherwood, interview with author, Mar. 26, 1976; L. B. Williams to CHS, Dec. 23, 1947, F1487.

31. *Dallas Morning News,* Oct. 25, 1910; *Tulsa Tribune,* July 22, 1949; *St. Louis Post-Dispatch,* May 24, 1954; *Detroit Sunday Times,* June 5, 1955; *Cincinnati Enquirer,* May 31, 1960; *Daily Commercial News and Shipping Guide,* May 31, 1960; *Waco Tribune-Herald,* Oct. 7, 1962; *Chicago Daily Tribune,* Nov. 24, 1950; WLR to All Representatives, Apr. 10, 1950, F1904.

32. W. V. Anderson to CHS, Jan. 27, 1948, F50; CHS to QB, July 6, 1948, F50; WLR to CHS, Aug. 13, 1948, F103-5; *Trains Magazine,* Apr. 1961, pp. 35–39; WLR to CHS, Sept. 24, 1951, F1886; WLR to John S. Gallagher, Sept. 27, 1951, F1886; *Railway Age,* Sept. 1, 1952, pp. 92–95.

## CHAPTER 19

1. *Quanah Tribune-Chief,* July 3, 1913; AFS to C. E. Gilmore, Oct. 22, 1926, F275-1; *QA&P Employees' Magazine* 1 (June 1935): 30, and 2 (Oct. 1936): 21; AFS to CHS, June 5, 8, 1943, F99; QB to CHS, Sept. 14, 1946, May 14, 1949, F99.

2. *QA&P Employees' Magazine* 2 (Apr.–May 1935): 24; M. E. Black to AFS, Jan. 15, 1938, NF.

3. AFS to Frank Wiley, Apr. 20, 1938, NF; *QA&P Employees' Magazine* 4 (May 1938): 10–11; Elton B. Marsalis, interview with author, Mar. 4, 1976.

4. AFS to SL, June 1, 1918, F91; AFS to CHS, Nov. 22, 1920, F91; M. E. Black to AFS, Mar. 8, 1939, F197-2; Robert Medlen to AFS, Oct. 28, 1930, F197-16; CHS to E. H. Bunnell, Mar. 8, 1933, F91; QB to CHS, Apr. 25, 1949, F91.

5. AFS to Department of the Interior, Mar. 13, 1930, F39; Elton B. Marsalis, interview with author, Jan. 13, 1976.

6. QB to Kenneth F. Burgess, Jan. 13, 1948, F302; AFS to

CHS, Dec. 30, 1943, F29; QB to CHS, July 15, 1948, Mar. 25, 1949, F47; Bennett, p. 109.

7. Various data, F311-3; AFS to CHS, Mar. 10, 1937, F100-7; *Wichita Falls Record News,* Mar. 10, 1937; *Paducah Post,* Dec. 23, 1954.

8. AFS to CHS, Apr. 9, 1930, F38-17; *Lubbock Avalanche-Journal,* Dec. 17, 1959; J. W. White to AFS, Apr. 14, 1944, F381-1.

9. WEG (initials only) to QB, Jan. 31, 1949, F99; Elton B. Marsalis, interview with author, Jan. 25, 1976; AFS to CHS, Mar. 9, 1920, NF.

10. QB to CHS, June 20, 1949, F47; W. H. Crawford to AFS, Apr. 1, 1927, F188-1.

11. O. J. Day to AFS, Jan. 7, 1932, NF; Harry H. Campbell, *The Early History of Motley County,* pp. 55–56; AFS to CHS, July 30, 1931, May 7, 1934, F80; AFS to E. T. Butler, Aug. 17, 1934, F80; W. T. Patton to AFS, Dec. 30, 1938, F308-11; W. L. Hovey to AFS, Jan. 27, 1938, F308-1; MEB (initials only) to AFS, Dec. 17, 1937, F80; GEH to J. D. Bell, July 28, 1931, F80.

12. *Fort Worth Star-Telegram,* Sept. 25, 1931; T. K. Hawkins to CHS, Sept. 22, 1931, F1545; CHS to JMK, Sept. 28, 1931; CHS to Wichita State Bank & Trust, Dec. 4, 1931; CHS to American Surety Company, Feb. 9, 1932, all in F1545; *Quanah Tribune-Chief,* Mar. 29, 1932; GEH to CHS, Oct. 28, 1936, F1545; Estes, pp. 94–107.

13. CHS to R. B. Jenkins, Feb. 21, 1911; Jenkins to CHS, Feb. 25, 1911; Robert Cray to CHS, Sept. 30, 1913; John P. Marrs to T. K. Hawkins, June 17, 1924; GEH to CHS, Sept. 30, Nov. 4, 1926; CHS to AFS, Aug. 1, 1928, all in F338; Robert Cray to DED, Aug. 15, 1912, F321; Cray to CHS, Mar. 1, 1915, F338; QB to GEH, May 9, 1946, F152-60; Various data, F338.

14. GEH to AFS, Dec. 18, 1930, F333-2; AFS to John P. Marrs, Sept. 13, 1927, NF; CHS to GEH, July 20, 1928, F338; AFS to CHS, July 25, 1938, NF.

15. GEH to AFS, Feb. 17, 1931, F333-3; B. F. Wiley to AFS, Mar. 26, 1931, F333-2; Wiley to GEH, Nov. 3, 1934, NF.


CHAPTER 20

1. QA&P, Minute Book 8, pp. 3–4, 14–15.

2. Various materials, F1702.

3. WLR to CHS, Aug. 14, 1942, NF.

4. AFS to CHS, Aug. 18, 1942; Robert Medlen to QB, July 29, 1946; Oscar Hall to AFS, Nov. 27, 1943, all in F396-1.

5. AFS, Bulletin 21, Feb. 10, 1943; CHS to AFS, Feb. 19, 1943, F396-1; Data from F1702.

6. WLR to CHS, Aug. 14, 1942, NF.

7. QA&P, "Statement Showing Amount of Ticket Sales Local and Interline Combined at Quanah, Texas, by Months for the Years 1922 to November 1948, Inclusive," NF; Cumulative data, F29-2.

8. T. E. Shoemake to QB, May 28, 1948, F396-1; WLR to QB, June 3, 1948, F918.

9. WLR to QB, July 12, 1948, F1629; QB to R. C. Canady, June 8, 1948; QB, Memo to file, July 6, 1948, both in F396-1; *Paducah Post,* Aug. 5, 1948; T. E. Shoemake to QB, Juy 22, 1948; Railway Mail Service, Order No. 1199, July 29, 1948; O. W. Watson to George Mahon, July 1, 1948; Mahon to Watson, July 3, 1948, all in F396-1.

10. CHS to QB, Apr. 18, May 17, June 22, 1949, Feb. 6, 1950; QB to CHS, Apr. 21, 1949, Jan. 23, 1950; QB to T. E. Shoemake, Sept. 21, 1949, all in F396-1; *Floyd County Hesperian,* Sept. 29, Oct. 13, 1949; RRCT, Docket 1070-RO, Hearing Held in the County Court House at Paducah, Texas, Nov. 3, 1949 (tran-

script), F396-1; *Wichita Falls Record Times,* Nov. 4, 1949; *Floyd County Hesperian,* Nov. 3, 1949.

11. *Fort Worth Star-Telegram,* Feb. 19, 22, 1950; QB to CHS, Feb. 18, 1950, F396-1; *Matador Tribune,* Feb. 23, Mar. 2, 1950; *Floyd County Hesperian,* Feb. 23, 1950; QA&P, Passenger Traffic—"Plainsman," Feb. 18, 1950.

12. CHS to Hon. Marvin Jones, Dec. 8, 1927, F1083; CHS to QB, Feb. 25, 1952, F396-1.

13. Tabular data, F299-2; *Quanah Tribune-Chief,* May 5, 1955; C. E. Harris to QB, May 11, 1955; John E. McCullough to Messrs. Allen, Gambill & Gambill, Attorneys, May 10, 1955; QB, Memo for file, June 15, 1955; John E. McCullough to Clark Hungerford, July 1, 1955, all in F396-4; *Quanah Tribune-Chief,* July 7, 1955.

14. Statistics, from F76 and 1248; C. J. McCready, interview with author, Jan. 26, 1976; Elton B. Marsalis, interview with author, Jan. 13, 1976; AFEs 421, 428, 459; CHS to AFS, July 28, 1943, F79; CHS to AFS, May 26, 1944, F222; CHS to QB, Jan. 23, 1946, F76.

15. QB to CHS, Oct. 5, 1949, July 13, 1950; W. F. Lewis to QB, Feb. 24, 1950; L. B. Clary to QB, Feb. 23, 1950, all in F184-5; QB to CHS, May 9, 1950, F1025; QB to CHS, Aug. 1, 1950, F184-5; CHS to QB, Aug. 25, 1950, F397-14.

16. QB to CHS, Feb. 27, May 21, 1951, F184-5; QB to G. H. Jury, Mar. 2, 1951, F184-6; QB to CHS, Apr. 23, 1951, F1025; QB to CHS, June 11, 1951, F76; CHS to QB, June 7, 1951, F184-5; Martin M. Pomphrey to author, Feb. 27, 1976; QB to CHS, July 16, 1951, F425-18; QB to G. H. Jury, Aug. 2, 1951, F76; *All Aboard* 5 (Mar. 1952): 1, 3.

17. CHS to Arthur M. Cox, Jr., Dec. 26, 1951, F49.

18. Ross Simpson to CHS, Dec. 14, 1946, NF; QB to H. B. Linley, Jan. 26, 1950, F313-2; CHS to QB, July 14, 1950, F549; CHS to QB, June 13, 1950, F99; CHS to C. C. Kratky, Aug. 27, 1946; CHS to F. A. Thompson, Dec. 30, 1949, F549.

19. AFS to CHS, Oct. 4, 1940, F313-7; CHS to QB, Feb. 14, 16, 1951, F256; R. Wright Armstrong to CHS, Sept. 27, 1950, NF; J. M. Crook to CHS, Apr. 19, 1951, NF; *Lubbock Avalanche-Journal,* May 31, June 3, 1951; A. B. Davis to CHS, June 2, 1951, NF; *Floyd County Hesperian,* July 7, 1951.

20. CHS to QB, Apr. 18, 1951; CHS to WLR, Oct. 12, 1951; WLR to CHS, May 3, 1951; REQ to WLR, Dec. 20, 1951, all in F102.

21. CHS to Clark Hungerford, Jan. 23, 1952, NF; CHS to QB, Apr. 28, 1952, F249-2; CHS to J. M. Crook, Aug. 19, 1952, F313-2; QB, Memo, Oct. 17, 1952, NF.

22. WLR to CHS, Nov. 26, 1951, NF; CHS to QB, Oct. 23, 1952, NF; T. H. Banister to WLR, Sept. 23, 1953, NF; WLR to Banister, Oct. 23, 1953, F313-2; CHS to WLR, Nov. 6, 1953, F313-2.

23. E. L. Anderson to M. Stone, Apr. 26, 1954, NF; E. P. Ripley to SL, Oct. 14, 1912, NF; QB to J. W. Sampley, Apr. 23, 1958; CHS to QB, Oct. 15, 1954, both in F313-2.

24. Data from *Moody's Manual of Investments,* 1930–52.


CHAPTER 21

1. QB to Frank H. Myers, June 10, 1963, F120-17.

2. United States Bureau of the Census, Maps GE-50, No. 37; WLR to W. M. Hughes, Mar. 2, 1949, F949.

3. CHS to WLR, Oct. 3, 1949, F1703; QA&P, Secretary's Contracts 1069 and 1032.

4. CHS to JMK, June 30, 1937, F1667; *Paducah Post,* July 3, 1947; *Matador Tribune,* July 17, 1947; E. L. Luckett to author, Oct. 8, 1976; QA&P, Daily Report Wheat Movement, July 31,

1951; QB to C. T. Williams, June 27, 1961, NF; Roger D. Poage to QB, Sept. 19, 1960, NF; QB to M. G. Monaghan, June 27, 1961, NF.

5. CHS to WLR, July 23, 1942, F467; Jack C. Wilson to QB, May 22, 1961, F162-1; Eugene B. Smith to CHS, Mar. 19, 1951, F467.

6. *Floyd County Hesperian,* Sept. 30, 1948; QB to CHS and WLR, Oct. 23, 1948, F161-7; WLR to CHS, Dec. 8, 1948, F194; QA&P, Secretary's Contracts 920 and 990; RPC, 1966.

7. F. M. Gunter, interview with author, Oct. 24, 1975; QB to CHS, Oct. 7, 1947; QB to CHS, Oct. 14, 1947, Dec. 20, 1948, May 31, 1949; QB to J. D. Mitchell, Dec. 14, 1948, all in FRS-5-1; WLR to RRCT, Oct. 29, 1953, Application No. 69, NF; *Official Railway Equipment Register* 74 (Oct. 1958): 415.

8. QB to AMB(?), Aug. 17, 1946, F331-1; WLR to E. B. Nattemer, Jan. 19, 1948, F121; AFS to CHS, Oct. 22, 1943, F333-1.

9. Robert Medlen to WLR, Nov. 9, 1946; O. Weathers to AFS, Aug. 8, 1944; Medlen to QB, Oct. 23, 1951, Oct. 3, 1946, all in F333-1; WLR to Frank O'Kane, Apr. 15, 1947, F1303-18; QB to J. L. Corbitt, Apr. 29, 1946, F331-1; Robert Medlen, interview with author, Jan. 16, 1976; F. M. Gunter, interview with author, Feb. 5, 1976; CHS to JMK, June 30, 1937, F1667; WLR to CHS, Aug. 21, 1933, F333-1.

10. M. M. Pomphrey to author, Feb. 27, 1976; WLR to QB, June 21, 22, 1955; QB to WLR, Oct. 21, 1957, all in 9-9-2; Robert Medlen to QB, Nov. 26, 1957, F333-1; WLR to RRCT, Feb. 11, 1958, F902-80; QB to Dick Carpenter, Mar. 27, 1964, F333-1; J. R. Detiviler to L. A. Thomas, Mar. 29, 1966, F7176-A; M. M. Pomphrey to author, Feb. 27, 1976.

11. CHS to Clark Hungerford, Mar. 13, 1947, Feb. 3, 1948, Feb. 9, 1950, Feb. 16, 1951, F1153.

12. J. W. Sampley to CHS, Nov. 3, 1947, F378-1; WLR to QB, Aug. 13, 1953, F186-11.

13. WLR to J. J. Grogan, July 21, 1947; W. P. Bartel to WLR, Nov. 10, 1938, both in F1809; WLR to CHS, Sept. 26, 1947, F1746; WLR to W. M. Hugle, Feb. 3, 1949; WLR to CHS, Oct. 28, 1949, both in F1809; CHS to QB, Feb. 24, 1950, all in F1809; WLR to Gerald E. Duffy, Oct. 16, 1950, F2009; WLR to CHS, June 16, 1954; WLR to All Concerned, Jan. 5, 1954, both in F184-5.

14. L. A. Elliott, interview with author, June 3, 1976.

15. QA&P, RPCs, 1952-73; QA&P, Secretary's file 945, 1127; QB to B. H. Crosland, May 22, 1961, F213-2; Robin Morris, interview with author, July 18, 1975.

16. QB to J. C. Wilson, June 15, 1948, F378-1; C. R. Sherwood, interview with author, Mar. 26, 1976; S. M. Blashuk to F. A. Hill, Aug. 10, 1959, F1885-CNR; A. C. Leake to C. R. Sherwood, Mar. 24, 1959, F1885-M&StL.

17. WLR to J. E. Payne, June 15, 1949, F1884; CHS to Buxton & Skinner, May 29, 1950, F50; WLR to All Representatives, Apr. 28, 1950, F2009; QA&P, Time Table No. 57, Sept. 27, 1959, p. 3; QA&P, Time Table No. 59, Sept. 1, 1963, p. 3; SL-SF, Time Table No. 1, Oct. 17, 1971, p. 15.

18. QB to Guy Traylor, Sept. 30, 1960, Mar. 5, 1962, F172-1; H. O. Wagner to QB, Oct. 29, 1952, F397-14; A. A. Francis to A. L. Pursley, May 13, 1958, F903-77.

19. QA&P, "Potash from Carlsbad, N.M., to Southeastern Destinations," NF; WLR to All Concerned, June 20, 1955, F145-16; QA&P, Secretary's file 916, 847; WLR to All Representatives, June 16, 1950, F1303-30; QB to A. L. Lane, Jan. 27, 1959, F221-4.

20. WLR to Allan A. Lister, Jan. 3, 1957, F1885-TRRA.

21. Don L. Hofsommer, *The Southern Pacific, 1901–1985,* p. 274; *Railway Age* 182 (Dec. 14, 1981): 3; *Texas Railways* 20 (Summer 1979): 7; SL-SF, "Annual Meeting of Stockholders," May 10,

1960, pp. 3–6; SL-SF, "Your Traffic Newsletter," Jan. 1960, p. 1; ibid., June–July 1960, p. 1; SL-SF, *Annual Report,* 1957, pp. 5, 20; *Time,* Oct. 24, 1960, p. 96.

22. *Floyd County Hesperian,* July 30, Oct. 1, 1959; F. M. Gunter, interview with author, Oct. 24, 1975; QA&P, Secretary's files 1077, 1083; SL-SF, *Annual Report,* 1960, pp. 5, 7; QA&P, RPCs, 1959–70; QA&P, Minute Book 3, p. 227.

23. F. M. Gunter, interview with author, June 20, 1980; QA&P, Time Table No. 59, Sept. 1, 1963, p. 3; SL-SF, Time Table No. 1, Oct. 17, 1971, p. 15.

24. F. M. Gunter, interview with author, June 20, 1980; Glenn E. Martin, interview with author, Oct. 18, 1978; QA&P, Time Table No. 59, Sept. 1, 1963, p. 3; SL-SF, Time Table No. 1, Oct. 17, 1971, p. 15.

25. F. M. Gunter, interview with author, Jan. 6, 1976; QB to P. J. Schmitz, Dec. 14, 1962, F172-7.

26. Robert Medlen to AFS, Oct. 20, 1942, F308-13; QA&P, Claims 11916, 11636, 11987, 11973, 12026, 11229, 11239, and 11903.

27. C. F. Harris to QB, Mar. 14, 1961, F100-4; *Matador Tribune,* Mar. 9, 1961; QA&P, Situation Report, Mar. 9, 1961; George Adams to QB, Mar. 11, 1961; QB to Fred Willing, Mar. 14, 1961, both in F100-4.

28. Data from *Moody's Manual of Investments* (title varies) for the years 1951–72.

29. Ibid.

## CHAPTER 22

1. QA&P, Train Register, Floydada, Texas, Aug. 1, 1973.

2. *Modern Railroads* 16 (Nov. 1961): 43–122; CHS to WLR, Nov. 1, 1949; WLR to CHS, Nov. 22, 1949, both in F50; SL-SF, *Annual Report,* 1971, p. 13.

3. *Railway Age* 157 (Sept. 28, 1964): 72; Mrs. Quin Baker to author, July 12, 1976; *Quanah Tribune-Chief,* Apr. 15, 1965, Sept. 8, 1966; Leo A. Elliott, interview with author, June 3, 1976; QA&P, Minute Book 3, p. 232.

4. *Railway Age* 151 (Feb. 20, 1961): 44, and 159 (Apr. 27, 1964): 16; L. A. Elliott to Foreign Line, Dec. 31, 1964, NF; Charlene Crisp, interview with author, Apr. 30, 1980.

5. AT&SF, *Annual Report,* 1973, p. 8; SL-SF, *Annual Report,* 1973, p. 2.

6. J. R. Coulter to R. C. Culter, Mar. 22, 1939, F1884; WLR to John N. Lewis, Oct. 19, 1939, F1792; J. R. Coulter to R. E. Buchanan et al., Nov. 29, 1939, F1884; T. H. Banister to WLR, June 15, 1949, F1884; WLR to CHS, June 22, 1949; CHS, Memorandum, Aug. 26, 1941, both in F1792; SL-SF, Southwestern Division Time Table No. 46, Sept. 18, 1964, p. 20; SL-SF, Southwestern Division Time Table No. 47, May 28, 1967, p. 19.

7. *Floyd County Hesperian,* Mar. 22, Apr. 5, 1973.

8. QA&P, Train Register, Floydada, Texas, Aug. 30–31, 1973; QA&P, Train Register, Quanah, Texas, Aug. 31, 1973; T. M. Galloway to M. M. Pomphrey, Sept. 14, 1973, NF; F. A. Tipple to Pomphrey, Sept. 10, 1973, NF; *Modern Railroads,* Dec. 1974, p. 71.

9. *Floyd County Hesperian,* Aug. 9, 1973; QA&P, Train Register, Floydada, Texas, Sept. 4, 1973.

10. SL-SF, *Annual Report,* 1973, p. 2; *Lubbock Avalanche-Journal,* Sept. 10, 1973; QA&P, Minutes of Special Meeting [of the board of directors], Quanah, Nov. 30, Dec. 3, 1973; *Lubbock Avalanche-Journal,* Dec. 6, 1973; *Amarillo Daily News,* Dec. 7, 1973; *Railway Age* 174 (Dec. 31, 1973): 8, CHS to H. C. Clark, May 7, 1927, NF; Robert W. Downing, interview with author,

Feb. 2, 1987; *Santa Fe Railway News* 2 (Oct. 1987): 8; *Lubbock Avalanche-Journal*, Jan. 13, 1975; SL-SF *Annual Report, 1974,* p. 12; QA&P, Train Register, Floydada, Texas, Dec. 31, 1974, Jan. 1, 1975.

11. QA&P, Train Register, Floydada, Texas, Jan. 20–26, 1974; FW&D, File Q-11148 (1/1974), containing Federal Railroad Administration Form T reports; SL-SF, Time Table No. 1, Oct. 17, 1971, p. 15.

12. Floyd Hodo, interview with author, Jan. 26, 1976; QA&P, Train Register, Floydada, Texas, Sept. 1, 1973–Feb. 15, 1975; Charlene Crisp to author, July 11, 1977.

13. *Moody's Manual,* 1975, p. 357.

14. QA&P, Minute Book 3, pp. 298–305; *Floyd County Hesperian,* Apr. 13, 1975; CHS to Bob McDonald, Aug. 12, 1954, F1862; *Quanah Tribune-Chief,* July 29, 1976.

15. *Quanah Tribune-Chief,* Nov. 11, 1976; *Wichita Falls Record-News,* Nov. 11, 1976; *Paducah Post,* Nov. 11, 18, 1976.

16. ICC, Initial Decision, No. AB-109, June 2, 1977; *Quanah Tribune-Chief,* June 9, July 14, 1977; *Floyd County Hesperian,* June 5, 12, 1977; *Wichita Falls Times,* July 10, 1977; *Wichita Falls Record-News,* Oct. 13, 1977; *Plainview Daily Herald,* Oct. 16, 1977; ICC, Decision and Order, No. AB-109, June 12, 1977.

17. *Altus Times-Democrat,* Feb. 12–18, 1978.

18. *Matador Tribune,* Sept. 1, 1977; *Plainview Daily Herald,* Dec. 9, 1979, Nov. 5, 1981; Richard C. Grayson to Richard I. Chais, Mar. 18, 1976, NF; *Quanah Tribune-Chief,* Oct. 25, 1979, Apr. 8, 1982.

19. *Moody's Manual,* 1976, p. 194; 1977, p. 482; 1978, p. 460; *Plainview Daily Herald,* Dec. 31, 1977, Jan. 12, 1978; *Quanah Tribune-Chief,* Feb. 16, Apr. 11, 1978; ICC, Application of the [QA&P] . . . to Abandon . . . No. AB-109 Sub-No. 1F, Mar. 10, 1978.

20. Mickey Nunlay to Ray Farabee, Apr. 16, 1979; Michael G. Klaus to Ed Kasparik, Apr. 25, 1979; Kasparik to Klaus, May 22, 1979; Klaus to Homer Long, May 24, 1979; Farabee to Attorney General's Office, June 11, 1979, all NF; *Paducah Post,* Feb. 19, 1980; *Plainview Daily Herald,* Aug. 22, 1984; *Houston Post,* Sept. 16, 1984.

21. SL-SF, *Annual Report,* 1976, p. 2; 1979, p. 5; *Wall Street Journal,* Apr. 18, May 15, Nov. 24, 1980; J. H. Hertog and W. F. Thompson to All Frisco Employees, two teletype bulletins, Nov. 21, 1980; Public Relations Department to All Frisco Employees, teletype bulletin, Nov. 25, 1980.

22. ICC, Application of the [QA&P] . . . to Abandon . . . No. AB-109 Sub-No. 1F, May 22, 1980; J. R. Fitzgerald to W. F. Thompson, Aug. 30, 1979; Donald E. Ransom to Lon Davis, Feb. 7, 1980; Ransom to Garland Cates, Feb. 20, 1980; Ransom to Rufus Gibbs, Feb. 7, 1980, all NF; *Paducah Post,* Nov. 27, 1980; ICC, Certificate and Decision, No. AB-109 Sub-No. 1, decided Jan. 21, 1981.

23. *Floyd County Hesperian,* Apr. 2, 1981.

24. QA&P, Report on Train 3311, May 5, 1981; QA&P, Report on Train 3310, May 5, 1981; W. C. Clawson, interview with author, May 5, 1981.

25. *Burlington Northern News,* Aug.–Sept. 1981, p. 4.

# *Bibliography*

Documentary support for this study derives primarily from rich primary sources of the Quanah, Acme & Pacific Railway that were housed by the company at Quanah, Texas. The QA&P has disappeared since this research was conducted, but some records survive at the Panhandle-Plains Museum in Canyon, Texas, others at the Llano Estacado Museum in Plainview, Texas, and some are held by the author. The most complete record is on microfilm at the Southwest Collection, Texas Tech University, Lubbock.

## BOOKS AND THESES

Allhands, J. L. *Railroads to the Rio*. Salado, Tex.: Anson Jones Press, 1960.

Bain, William E. *Frisco Folk: Stories of Steam Days on the Frisco*. Denver: Sage Books, 1961.

Bennett, Carmen Taylor. *Our Roots Grow Deep: A History of Cottle County*. Floydada, Tex.: Blanco Offset Printing, 1970.

Bryant, Keith L., Jr. *History of the Atchison, Topeka & Santa Fe Railway*. New York: Macmillan, 1974.

Campbell, Harry H. *The Early History of Motley County*. San Antonio: Naylor, 1958.

Clark, Ira G. *Then Came the Railroads: The Century from Steam to Diesel in the Southwest*. Norman: University of Oklahoma Press, 1958.

Clarke, Mary Whattey. *The Swenson Saga and the SMS Ranches*. Austin: Jenkins, 1976.

Douglas, C. L. *Cattle Kings of Texas*. Fort Worth: Branch-Smith, 1968.

Estes, Winston M. *Another Part of the House*. Philadelphia: J. B. Lippincott, 1970.

Gracy, David B., III. *Littlefield Lands: Colonization on the Texas Plains, 1912–1920*. Austin: University of Texas Press, 1968.

Graves, Lawrence. *A History of Lubbock*. Lubbock: West Texas Museum Association, 1962.

Grodinsky, Julius. *Railroad Consolidation: Its Economic and Controlling Principles*. New York: D. Appleton, 1930.

Hamner, Laura V. *Short Grass and Longhorns*. Norman: University of Oklahoma Press, 1943.

*Hardeman County, Agricultural and Industrial Edition*. Quanah, Tex.: N.p., 1928.

Harper, Carl. "Movement toward Railroad Building on the South Plains of Texas, 1907–1914." M.A. thesis, Texas Tech College, 1935.

Hayes, William Edward. *Iron Road to Empire: The History of 100 Years of the Progress and Achievements of the Rock Island Lines*. New York: Simmons-Boardman, 1953.

*History of the Frisco*. Compiled by the Public Relations Department of the St. Louis–San Francisco Railway, n.d. [1959?].

Hofsommer, Donovan L. *Katy Northwest: The Story of a Branch Line Railroad*. Boulder, Colo.: Pruett, 1976.

———. *The Southern Pacific, 1901–1985*. College Station: Texas A&M University Press, 1986.

Jackson, Clyde L., and Grace Jackson. *Quanah Parker, Last Chief of the Comanches: A Study in Southwestern Frontier History*. New York: Exposition Press, 1963.

Johnson, Vance. *Heaven's Tableland: The Dust Bowl Story*. New York: Farrar, Straus, 1947.

Lemly, James Hutton. *The Gulf, Mobile & Ohio: A Railroad That Had to Expand or Expire*. Indiana University School of Business Study No. 36. Homewood, Ill.: Richard D. Irwin, 1953.

Lewis, Edward A. *American Shortline Railway Guide*. Morrisville, Vt.: Baggage Car, 1978.

Lowe, Ida Marie Williams. "The Role of the Railroads in the Settlement of the Texas Panhandle." M.A. thesis, West Texas State University, 1962.

Marre, Louis A., and John Baskin Harper. *Frisco Diesel Power*. Glendale, Calif.: Interurbans Press, 1984.

Marshall, James. *Santa Fe: The Railroad That Built an Empire*. New York: Random House, 1945.

Martin, Albro. *Enterprise Denied: Origins of the Decline of American Railroads, 1897–1917*. New York: Columbia University Press, 1971.

Meador, Doublas. *Trail Dust*. Quanah, Tex.: Nortex

Publishing, 1970.

Miller, Sidney L. *Tomorrow in West Texas: Economic Opportunities along the Texas & Pacific Railway.* Lubbock: Texas Tech Press, 1956.

Morgan, Jonnie R. *The History of Wichita Falls.* Wichita Falls, Tex.: Nortex Offset Press, 1971.

Neal, Bill. *The Last Frontier: The Story of Hardeman County.* Quanah, Tex.: Quanah Tribune-Chief, 1966.

Overton, Richard C. *Gulf-to-Rockies: The Heritage of the Fort Worth and Denver—Colorado and Southern Railways, 1861–1898.* Austin: University of Texas Press, 1953.

Paddock, B. B., ed. *History of Texas.* 4 vols. Chicago: Lewis, 1922.

Parkinson, Tom, and Charles Philip Fox. *The Circus Moves by Rail.* Boulder, Colo.: Pruett, 1978.

Payne, H. L. *Three Railroads to Mineral Wells.* Privately published by the author, 1975.

Pearce, W. M. *The Matador Land and Cattle Company.* Norman: University of Oklahoma Press, 1964.

*Poor's Manual of the Railroads of the United States.* 1895–1924.

Rathjen, Frederick W. *The Texas Panhandle Frontier.* Austin: University of Texas Press, 1973.

Reed, St. Clair Griffin. *A History of the Texas Railroads and of Transportation Conditions under Spain and Mexico and the Republic and the State.* Houston: St. Clair, 1941.

Rister, Carl Coke. *The Southwestern Frontier.* Cleveland: Arthur H. Clarke, 1928.

Rutherford, Blanche Scott. *One Corner of Heaven.* San Antonio: Naylor, 1964.

Saunders, Richard. *The Railroad Mergers and the Coming of Conrail.* Westport, Conn.: Greenwood Press, 1978.

Scarborough, Dorothy. *The Wind.* Rpt. Austin: University of Texas Press, 1979.

Sommer, Charles H. *History of the Quanah, Acme & Pacific Railway.* Quanah, Tex.: QA&P Railway, various issues, 1932–51.

———. *Quanah Parker: Last Chief of the Comanches.* Quanah, Tex.: Privately published by QA&P, 1945.

Spence, Vernon Gladden. *Colonel Morgan Jones: Grand Old Man of Texas Railroading.* Norman: University of Oklahoma Press, 1971.

Stagner, Lloyd E. *Steam Locomotives of the Frisco Line.* Boulder, Colo.: Pruett, 1976.

Stover, John F. *American Railroads.* Chicago: University of Chicago Press, 1961.

———. *The Life and Decline of the American Railroad.* New York: Oxford University Press, 1970.

*Texas Almanac, 1961–1962.* Dallas: A. H. Belo Corp., 1961.

*Texas Highway Truck Accident and Tax Data 1933.* Houston: Railway and Express Employees Association of Texas, 1934.

Wagner, F. Hol, Jr. *The Colorado Road: History, Motive Power, and Equipment of the Colorado & Southern and Fort Worth & Denver Railways.* Denver: Intermountain Chapter, National Railway Historical Society, 1970.

Waters, L. L. *Steel Trails to Santa Fe.* Lawrence: University of Kansas Press, 1950.

Webb, Walter Prescott. *The Great Plains.* New York: Grosset & Dunlap, 1931.

*Who's Who in Railroading in North America.* Title varies, 1940–80.

Williams, J. R. *The Big Ranch Country.* Wichita Falls, Tex.: Terry Brothers Printing, 1954.

Wilson, James. *Agricultural Resources of the Texas Panhandle.* Denver: Privately published by the author, 1888.

Wyman, Laura Lynn. "The Quanah, Acme & Pacific Railway." M.A. thesis, Midwestern University, 1967.

## PERIODICALS, JOURNALS, AND PAMPHLETS

*Burlington Northern News.* August–September 1981.

Chamber of Commerce, Levelland, Tex. *Facts and Figures Concerning Levelland and Hockley County.* 1928.

Chamber of Commerce, Lovington, N.Mex.: *The Last of the Cheap Good Lands.* 1928.

Chamber of Commerce, Lubbock, Tex. *Rainfall Record for Thirty-five Year Period.* 1929.

Chamber of Commerce, Olton, Tex. *Olton: Mecca of the Plains.* 1929.

Chamber of Commerce, Quanah, Tex. Brochure. 1909.

Chamber of Commerce of the United States. *The Railroad Strikes.* July 10, 1922.

Chicago Great Western Historical and Technical Society. *Newsletter No. 21.* 1979.

de Shazo, Maj. Gen. T. E. Speech given on the occasion of the reburial ceremony for Chief Quanah Parker and Cynthia Ann, August 9, 1957, at Fort Sill, Oklahoma.

Elliot, Margaret. "History of D. B. Gardner's Pitchfork Ranch of Texas." *Panhandle-Plains Historical Review* 18 (1945): 12–79.

George, Preston, and Sylvan R. Wood. "The Railroads of Oklahoma." *Bulletin No. 60,* Railway &

Locomotive Historical Society. 1948.

Gracy, David B. "A Preliminary Survey of Land Colonization in the Panhandle-Plains of Texas." *Museum Journal* 11 (1969): 52–79.

Hofsommer, Don L. "The Acme, Red River & Northern: An Early Texas Short Line Railroad." *Red River Valley Historical Review* 5 (Fall 1980): 17–26.

———. "Town Building on a Texas Short Line: The Quanah, Acme & Pacific Railway, 1909–1920." *Arizona and the West* 21 (Winter 1979): 355–68.

Kelso, H. L. "A Mighty Freight-Hauler: The Decapod." *Railroad Magazine* 73 (April 1961): 23–28.

MacKenzie, Murdo. "The Matador Ranch." *Panhandle-Plains Historical Review* 21 (1948): 94–105.

Manley, Curtis S. "Early Background and Break-up of the Matador Ranch." *West Texas Historical Association Yearbook* 37 (1961): 57–69.

*Modern Railroads.* 1961, 1974.

*Moody's Manual of Investments and Security Ratings* (Railroads, Transportation, etc.). Title varies. 1895–1981.

*Official Guide of the Railways.* 1895–1981.

*Official Railway Equipment Register* 74 (October 1958).

*Poor's Manual of the Railroads of the United States.* 1895–1924.

Potts, Charles S. "Railroad Transportation in Texas." *Bulletin of the University of Texas, Number 119, Humanities Series 7.* 1909.

*Railway Age.* 1917–81.

*Rock Island Magazine.* May 1929. CRI&P.

*Santa Fe Railway News* 2 (October 1978): 8.

Sims, Donald. "Quanah Means Quick." *Trains* 21 (February 1961): 35–38.

*Texas Railways.* 1979.

*Traffic World.* 1936.

*Trains Magazine.* April 1961.

### GOVERNMENT SOURCES

General Land Office of Texas. Abstract of Land Titles. Vols. 7 and 8.

Interstate Commerce Commission. Certificate and Decision, No. AB-109 Sub-no. 1. January 26, 1981.

———. Decision and Order, No. AB-109. June 12, 1977.

———. Engineering Report upon the Quanah, Acme & Pacific Railway. April 14, 1922.

———. *Finance Reports,* 111:137–46.

———. *Finance Reports,* 117:233–80.

———. *Finance Reports,* 124:302–303.

———. *Finance Reports,* 158:95–704.

———. *Finance Reports,* 159:522–89.

———. *Finance Reports,* 212:505–508.

———. *Finance Reports,* 226:201–24.

———. *Finance Reports,* 227:561–62.

———. *Valuation Reports,* 41:818.

———. *Valuation Reports,* 110:212–19.

———. *Valuation Reports,* 134:738–39.

Railroad Commission of Texas. Circular No. 3046, General Order, Recognizing the Quanah, Acme & Pacific Railway Company. March 17, 1909.

United States. Bureau of the Census. Maps GE-50, No. 37.

———. House of Representatives, Subcommittee of the Committee on Interstate and Foreign Commerce, Hearing on H.R. 5364, 74th Cong. (1936).

### QA&P SOURCES

The author had full access to the complete files of all departments of the railroad, including but not restricted to those listed here.

Agreement with the Brotherhood of Locomotive Firemen and Enginemen and the Brotherhood of Railroad Trainmen, June 1, 1936.

Agreement with the International Association of Machinists, International Brotherhoods of Iron Ship Builders and Helpers of America, and the Brotherhood of Railway Carmen of America, May 18, 1944.

Agreement with the International Brotherhood of Firemen, Oilers, Helpers, Roundhouse and Railway Shop Laborers, May 18, 1944.

Agreement with the Order of Railroad Telegraphers, February 16, 1944.

Annual Report to the Interstate Commerce Commission, 1914–79.

Annual Reports to the Railroad Commission of Texas.

Authority for Expenditures, 1909–79.

Employee Time Tables No. 34–59, 1939–63.

*Employees' Magazine,* 1934–38.

Minute Books, vols. 1–3.

Record of Property Changes, 1909–80.

Right-of-Way and Track Maps.

Secretary's Files (contracts).

Stock Certificate Books 1–2.

Train Registers, Quanah and Floydada, 1973–81.

VO3 Reports.

PUBLICATIONS AND MATERIALS
FROM OTHER COMPANIES

Acme, Red River & Northern. Minute Book.
Atchison, Topeka & Santa Fe Railway. *Annual Report.* 1973.
————. *Excerpts from the President's Annual Reports to the Stockholders with Special Reference to the Construction History of System Lines,* 1873–1916. Known internally as *Santa Fe Splinters.* 34 vols. AT&SF, n.d.
Motley County Railway. Annual Report to the Interstate Commerce Commission 1925.
————. Articles of Incorporation.
————. Minute Book.
————. VO3 Reports. 1924–25.
St. Louis–San Francisco Railway. *All Aboard.* 1951–52.
————. *Annual Reports.* 1957–79.
————. Southwestern Division Time Tables 43–48. 1961–69.
————. System Time Table No. 1. October 1, 1971.
————. Western Division Time Table No. 3. January 1, 1975.

NEWSPAPERS

*Altus* (Oklahoma) *Times-Democrat.* 1978.
*Amarillo Daily News.* 1927–34, 1973.
*Childress* (Texas) *Daily Index.* 1929.
*Dallas Morning News.* 1923–31.
*El Paso Times.* 1929.
*Floyd County* (Floydada, Texas) *Hesperian.* 1915–81.
*Floyd County* (Floydada, Texas) *Times.* 1891.
*Fort Worth Record.* 1925.
*Fort Worth Record-Telegram.* 1929.
*Fort Worth Star-Telegram.* 1923–51.
*Hale County* (Plainview, Texas) *Herald.* 1911.
*Lovington* (New Mexico) *Leader.* 1928.
*Lubbock Avalanche.* 1908–28.
*Lubbock Avalanche-Journal.* 1929–81.
*Matador* (Texas) *Tribune.* 1934–77.
*Motley County* (Matador, Texas) *News.* 1925.
*Paducah* (Texas) *Post.* 1923–80.
*Plainview* (Texas) *Daily Herald.* 1977–84.
*Plainview* (Texas) *Evening Herald.* 1928.
*Plainview* (Texas) *News.* 1920–28.
*Quanah* (Texas) *Times.* 1925.
*Quanah* (Texas) *Tribune-Chief.* 1903–82.
*St. Louis Globe-Democrat.* 1926.
*St. Louis Post-Dispatch.* 1926.
*Texas Booster.* 1937.
*Texas Commercial News.* 1924.
*Texas* (Floydada, Texas) *Kicker.* 1890.
*Vernon* (Texas) *Record.* 1930.
*Wall Street Journal.* 1925–1980.
*Wichita Falls Daily Times.* 1929–77.
*Wichita Falls Record-News.* 1924–77.

INTERVIEWS WITH THE AUTHOR

Clawson, W. C. Former QA&P conductor. May 5, 1981.
Crisp, Charlene. Former QA&P treasurer, auditor, and assistant secretary. April 30, 1980.
Downing, Robert W. Former vice-chairman of the Burlington Northern. February 2, 1987.
Elliott, Leo A. Former QA&P vice-president. June 3, 1976.
Gunter, Francis M. Former QA&P station agent. October 24, 1975, January 6, February 5, 1976, June 20, 1980.
Hodo, Floyd. Former QA&P conductor. January 26, 1976.
Johnson, R. L. Former QA&P station agent. July 22, 1975.
McCready, C. J. Former QA&P mechanical officer. January 26, 1976.
Marsalis, Elton B. Former QA&P locomotive engineer. January 13, 25, March 4, 1976.
Martin, Glenn E. Former SL-SF sales representative. October 18, 1978.
Medlen, Robert. Former station agent for the Motley County Railway and the QA&P. January 16, 1976.
Morris, Robin. Former QA&P roadmaster. July 18, 1975.
Sampley, J. W. Former QA&P treasurer. March 18, 1976.
Sherwood, C. R. Former QA&P traffic manager. March 26, 1976.
Stone, B. H. Former QA&P locomotive engineer. January 26, 1976.

# Index

*The Quanah Route* was composed into type on a Linotron 202 digital phototypesetter in ten point Galliard with two points of spacing between the lines. Galliard was also selected for display. The book was composed by G&S Typesetters, Inc., printed offset by Thomson-Shore, Inc., and bound by John H. Dekker and Sons, Inc. The paper on which this book is printed carries acid-free characteristics for an effective life of at least three hundred years.

TEXAS A&M UNIVERSITY PRESS
COLLEGE STATION